THE COLLECTED
WORKS OF
JEREMY BENTHAM

General Editor
F. Rosen

CONSTITUTIONAL LAW

The four essays collected in this volume, 'Economy as applied to Office', 'Identification of Interests', 'Supreme Operative' and 'Constitutional Code Rationale', dating from the spring and summer of 1822, are based exclusively on manuscripts, many of which have never been previously published. Bentham here develops the general principles of constitutional law and government which underpin the detailed administrative provisions set out in *Constitutional Code*. Original and penetrating discussions of such topics as sovereignty, constitutional rule, democratic and monarchical government, public finance, the aptitude and powers of officials, corruption, the influence of public opinion and the delusive effect of religion and titles of honour, affirm Bentham's status as a political theorist of the first rank.

The Collected Works of Jeremy Bentham

The new critical edition of the works and correspondence of Jeremy Bentham (1748–1832) is being prepared and published under the supervision of the Bentham Committee of University College London. In spite of his importance as jurist, philosopher, and social scientist, and leader of the Utilitarian reformers, the only previous edition of his works was a poorly edited and incomplete one brought out within a decade or so of his death. Eight volumes of the new *Collected Works*, five of correspondence, and three of writings on jurisprudence, appeared between 1968 and 1981, published by the Athlone Press. Further volumes in the series since then are published by Oxford University Press. The overall plan and principles of the edition are set out in the General Preface to *The Correspondence of Jeremy Bentham* vol. 1, which was the first volume of the *Collected Works* to be published.

Volumes published by Oxford University Press

Constitutional Code
Volume 1
Edited by F. Rosen and J. H. Burns 1983

Deontology, together with A Table of the Springs of Action and Article on Utilitarianism
Edited by Amnon Goldworth 1983

Chrestomathia
Edited by M. J. Smith and W. H. Burston 1983

Correspondence, volume 6: January 1798 to December 1801
Edited by J. R. Dinwiddy 1984

Correspondence, volume 7: January 1802 to December 1808
Edited by J. R. Dinwiddy 1988

Correspondence, volume 8: January 1809 to December 1816
Edited by Stephen Conway 1988

FIRST PRINCIPLES PREPARATORY TO CONSTITUTIONAL CODE

edited by

PHILIP SCHOFIELD

CLARENDON PRESS · OXFORD

1989

Oxford University Press, Walton Street, Oxford OX2 6DP
Oxford New York Toronto
Delhi Bombay Calcutta Madras Karachi
Petaling Jaya Singapore Hong Kong Tokyo
Nairobi Dar es Salaam Cape Town
Melbourne Auckland
and associated companies in
Berlin Ibadan

Oxford is a trade mark of Oxford University Press

Published in the United States
by Oxford University Press, New York

British Library Cataloguing in Publication Data
Bentham, Jeremy, 1748–1832
First principles preparatory to
constitutional code.—(The Collected works
of Jeremy Bentham).
1. Constitutional law—Codes—Proposals.
Early works
I. Title II. Schofield, Philip
342.2′02632
ISBN 0-19-822747-7

Library of Congress Cataloging in Publication Data
First principles preparatory to constitutional code/edited by Philip Schofield.
1. Constitutional law. I. Schofield, Philip.
K3240.4.F536 1989 342′.001—dc 19 [342.2001] 88-17998
ISBN 0-19-822747-7

Typeset by Joshua Associates Ltd, Oxford
Printed in Great Britain
at the Alden Press, Oxford

PREFACE

The Bentham Committee wishes to thank the Economic and Social Research Council whose generous grant allowing for the appointment of an editor and half-time Research Assistant has made possible the preparation of the present volume. The Committee is also indebted to the Pilgrim Trust, which has kindly provided a publication subsidy, and to the British Academy, the Leverhulme Trust and University College London for their continuing support.

The editor wishes to thank the following repositories for permission to quote from manuscripts in their possession: University College London Library; the National Library of Scotland; and the Bibliothèque Publique et Universitaire, Geneva.

I am especially indebted to Dr F. Rosen, the General Editor and Director of the Bentham Project, who has read the whole of the text, offered invaluable criticisms and suggested many improvements, and to Ms Claire Creffield and Ms Marilyn Morris, who in their capacity as Research Assistants have helped in the transcription of manuscripts, the gathering of information for purposes of annotation and the preparation of the text on computer disk. I am particularly grateful to Dr Stephen Conway, Correspondence Editor, for his advice and assistance on a whole range of points too numerous to detail. Thanks are also due to Professor J. H. Burns for reading and commenting on the Editorial Introduction; Mr T. Venning for making preliminary transcriptions of some of the manuscripts; Dr Cyprian Blamires for helping with the annotation; Ms Catherine Atkinson for helping with the annotation and reading the proofs; Ms Jane Haville for reading the proofs and preparing the name index; and Mrs Rosamine Hayeem for typing the subject index and providing general secretarial assistance.

I gratefully acknowledge the help received in the elucidation of certain references in the text from the following scholars: Dr Roger Bartlett, Dr Carlos Rodriguez Braun, Mr A. D. E. Lewis, Dr J. L. Miller and Master D. R. Thompson CB, QC.

T.P.S.

CONTENTS

SYMBOLS AND ABBREVIATIONS

Symbols

| | Space left in manuscript.
[to]   Word(s) editorially supplied.
<. . .>   Word(s) torn away.
<so>   Conjectural restoration of mutilated word.
[?]   Reading doubtful.
[. . . ?]   Word(s) proved illegible.

Abbreviations

Apart from standard abbreviations the following should be noted:

Bowring	*The Works of Jeremy Bentham*, published under the superintendence of . . . John Bowring, 11 vols., Edinburgh, 1843.
UC	Bentham papers in the Library of University College London. Roman numerals refer to boxes in which the papers are placed, arabic to the leaves within each box.
BL Add. MS	British Library Additional Manuscript.
CW	This edition of *The Collected Works of Jeremy Bentham*.
MS alt.	Alternative manuscript reading, usually interlinear or marginal.
MS del.	Word(s) deleted in manuscript.
MS orig.	Original manuscript reading.

EDITORIAL INTRODUCTION

The four essays included in this volume, 'Economy as applied to Office', 'Identification of Interests', 'Supreme Operative' and 'Constitutional Code Rationale', written between April and August 1822, deal with similar themes and are closely inter-related. Indeed, 'Identification of Interests' was initially intended by Bentham to form a chapter in 'Economy as applied to Office', while 'Supreme Operative' seems to have been conceived as part of 'Constitutional Code Rationale'. Bentham himself never published any of these essays, nor have any of them appeared subsequently in their original form. Since Bentham never finally revised the texts and failed to deal with some of the topics he proposed to consider, each may be regarded as incomplete to a greater or lesser degree. Nevertheless, each is coherent and contains large portions of text that is continuous.

HISTORY OF THE ESSAYS

These essays represent Bentham's first attempts to draft material for *Constitutional Code*.[1] His aim was apparently to compose a fairly general essay expounding the principles on which the code would be based, leaving the exposition of the detailed provisions to the main body of the work. Bentham published the first of the three projected volumes of *Constitutional Code* in 1830, the only part of the work to appear during his lifetime. He noted in the Preface that though sufficient material had been written to form an 'Introductory Dissertation', it had not yet been satisfactorily organized and therefore the first volume had been published without it. This dissertation was to have for 'its *subject-matter* the various forms of which the supreme authority in a state is susceptible' and for 'its *object*, by bringing to view the advantages and disadvantages of each, to exhibit their respective degrees of eligibility'.[2] It is possible that the manuscripts written in the late spring and summer of 1822 formed part of the material which he had in mind.

In the event, Bentham never did publish an introductory essay to

[1] For the development of this work, Bentham's major endeavour in the final decade of his life, see the Editorial Introduction in *Constitutional Code*, vol. I, ed. F. Rosen and J.H. Burns, Oxford, 1983 (*CW*), pp. xi-xlv.

[2] Ibid., p. 3.

Constitutional Code. This duty was left to Richard Doane[1] who edited *Constitutional Code* for the Bowring edition of *The Works of Jeremy Bentham* published in 1843.[2] Departing from Bentham's conception of a three volume work, Doane divided *Constitutional Code* into two Books. Book I represented the promised 'Introductory Dissertation': it was assembled predominantly from the mass of papers dealing with more general themes which Bentham had written for the code, but had not incorporated into the main body of the text. Book II represented *Constitutional Code* proper: it comprized volume I as published by Bentham (that is the first nine chapters), and the second and third projected volumes based on manuscripts which had been provisionally organized by Bentham (apart from Ch. X, Defensive Force, which followed the version privately printed in 1830).[3] The relationship of Book I to the essays included in the present volume is not straightforward, and is perhaps best explained by examining the way in which Doane set about editing *Constitutional Code*.

Edwin Chadwick,[4] and not Doane, had in fact been initially appointed editor of *Constitutional Code*. As early as August 1838, however, Bowring had expressed his concern that Chadwick's workload would not allow him to complete the task.[5] Repeated enquiries about progress from Bowring were followed by assurances from Chadwick, but in January 1840 Bowring finally had the manuscripts taken from him and transferred to Doane.[6] The new editor began to work on the code in February 1840, but found to his dismay that Chadwick and Arthur Moore, who had been assisting him, had scarcely made a start on the work, while the manuscripts for what was to become Book I remained 'exactly in the state (most confused and incomplete) in which the author left them'.[7] He referred to the difficulties with which this material had presented him when reporting on the state of the volume just over five months later:

[1] Doane (1805–48) had entered Bentham's service in 1819 to be trained as his amanuensis, and had remained with him until 1831; he had entered the Inner Temple in 1824 and been called to the bar in 1830. He practised in the London Sessions in the Old Bailey and was a member of the North Circuit.

[2] See Bowring, ix. *passim*. Sir John Bowring (1792–1872), first editor of the *Westminster Review*, radical MP and diplomat, was Bentham's literary executor.

[3] See Doane's note in Bowring, ix. pp. iii-iv.

[4] Chadwick (1800–90), the sanitary reformer and Secretary of the Poor Law Commission 1834–46, had been intimate with Bentham since 1829.

[5] Bowring to John Hill Burton, 22 August 1838, John Hill Burton Papers, National Library of Scotland MS 9404, fo.6. Burton (1809–81), author and historian of Scotland, was helping Bowring to supervise the production of the *Works*.

[6] Bowring to Burton, 22 January 1840, ibid., fo.40.

[7] Doane to Chadwick, 14 February 1840, UC clv. 95; Doane to Burton, 24 February 1840, NLS MS 9404, fo.319.

> as I have to copy out the *whole* of the original M.S. my progress has been very much retarded. I have finished nearly 400 pages of the original which makes somewhat more than 200 pages of large letter paper in my handwriting: this however is not finally revised, as every day I find passages, which have to be inserted under titles, that had been apparently concluded. There are about 500 pages more of the original, belonging to what I intend to make an introductory volume, to that which is already in print. The M.S. belonging to the continuation of the second printed vol. will not take so long, as the matter is already arranged under its proper heads; whereas the matter which I have been engaged upon, was all in the greatest uproar.[1]

Bowring again became apprehensive about the progress of *Constitutional Code*, and reported his fears to Burton,[2] who seems to have pressed Doane for a completion date. Doane replied in November 1840 that he envisaged completing the work in February or March 1841,[3] and true to his word sent the copy to the Edinburgh publisher, William Tait, on 13 March.[4] It seems that work on *Constitutional Code* was finally completed by January 1842, the proofs by then having been checked and corrected.[5]

For the Bowring edition, Doane added an introductory note in which he described the problems he had faced and the means he had adopted to try to overcome them. He explained that it had been Bentham's wish for an 'Introductory Dissertation' to be prefixed to the main part of the work, but on examining the relevant material he had found it 'to comprise a much more extensive range' than a discussion of 'the various forms of government, and their respective degrees of eligibility' which Bentham had suggested it should contain. He had therefore decided to devote a distinct Book to it.

> The MSS. of this part of the work were very voluminous, having been written at various times between the years 1818 and 1830: the greater portion of them were in a very confused and unfinished condition, and none of them had ever been revised.[6]

[1] Doane to Burton, 1 August 1840, NLS MS 9404, fos.320–1.

[2] Bowring to Burton, 19 October 1840, ibid., fos.60–1; Bowring to Burton, 13 November 1840, ibid., fo.64.

[3] Doane to Burton, 14 November 1840, ibid., fo.324.

[4] Doane to Burton, 15 March 1841, ibid., fos.327–8.

[5] Doane to Burton, 17 January 1842, ibid., fo.336.

[6] Cf. Doane to Burton, 15 March 1841, ibid., fos.327–8: 'You can have no conception of the confusion, in which the papers are, from which I have formed Book I. The same subjects are treated of, over and over again, from the year 1815 down to 1830. The plan I adopted was, to compare one with another, and take out a bit here and a bit there;—and so, though to a much more limited extent, with respect to Book II. My task, has in a great degree, been what I may call *literary dovetailing*.'

In organizing this material his guiding principle had been,

> to incorporate into one chapter all that related to the same subject-matter; to place those chapters first, which were of most general application, and to make those follow, which discussed more particularly the leading provisions of the Code itself, and constituted as it were, a general Rationale to the whole work.
>
> The introductory chapters on Law in general, and the various branches of law, were apparently designed by Mr Bentham to give to the reader of the Constitutional Code, a clear and comprehensive idea of a complete body of law, or as he called it, the *Pannomion*.[1]

In fact the general material on law and its branches was taken from a short essay written in the spring of 1821 entitled 'First Lines of a Proposed Code of Law for every nation compleat and rationalized',[2] which does not properly belong to *Constitutional Code*. Apart from this essay, the bulk of the material incorporated by Doane into Book I was written in 1822 and 1823.

Doane's object, extrapolating from Bentham's declared wishes, seems to have been to present an outline of the major principles of political philosophy and constitutional law which underlay the detailed provisions in the main body of *Constitutional Code*. Having studied the relevant manuscripts, and ascertained the major themes considered by Bentham, he compiled chapters under these various heads by bringing together material from different drafts. He paid little regard to the fact that these different drafts were written at different times for different essays. There is no doubt that Doane's handling of the material was skilful and sympathetic, but his editorial methods have resulted in the material being taken out of its proper context. Doane himself recognized that his arrangement of the material was not altogether satisfactory: 'In several instances it will appear that the same ground has been travelled over more than once.' He went on to explain that this was 'necessary, in order to render the argument in each instance complete: for it will be observed that many of the Chapters constitute in themselves distinct and independent Essays'.[3] But as well as being repetitive, significant portions of text have been omitted, an inevitable consequence given the constraints of time and space within which Doane had to work. There are also more detailed problems with Doane's text. Words and phrases are often altered, either because of mistranscription or misunderstanding: other

[1] Bowring, ix. p. iv.

[2] Bowring, ix. 8–41; the MSS for this essay are at UC xxxvi. 1–74, xxxvii. 4–70 and clx. 148–236.

[3] Bowring, ix. p. iv.

passages are expurgated, and alternative readings chosen, without any obvious regard to consistency. Punctuation has been liberally added, and while this may help to clarify the sense of a passage, it may also distort it.

Whereas Doane's object was to compose one work by conflating a whole range and variety of materials, the object here is to present a portion of these materials in the form Bentham intended for them at the time of their composition, and to reproduce his text as accurately as possible. This has involved a comprehensive survey of the original manuscripts and the use of Bentham's contemporaneous plans and tables of contents. The four essays presented here, as noted above, have emerged from manuscripts written under the heading of 'Constitutional Code' in the late spring and summer of 1822. On a wrapper found amongst this material, Bentham commented: '1822. May to August. First Principles preparatory to Constitutl. Code.'[1] Since this is apparently Bentham's contemporary description of the material, and accurately reflects its content, it has been taken for the title of the present volume.

Economy as applied to Office

'Economy as applied to Office' had its genesis in a score of manuscript sheets written intermittently in February and March 1822 under the heading 'Thoughts on Official Economy'.[2] By the end of March the title had evolved to 'Thoughts on Economy as applied to Office'.[3] These sheets barely go beyond a few introductory remarks and general statements on the curtailment of government expense. Bentham seems to have considered dedicating the work to his friend, the politician Joseph Hume (1777–1855), who was prominent for his attacks on financial waste and abuse in government.[4] The irregular nature of Bentham's attempts to compose material for 'Official Economy' is perhaps explained by his preoccupation at this time with

[1] Wrapper preceding UC clx. 84.

[2] UC clx. 37–46, cii. 439v, cxii. 219 (17–18 February 1822) and clx. 54 (17 March 1822) carry this heading. UC clx. 52–3 (9 March 1822), originally headed 'Codification Offer', have been emended to 'Thoughts on Official Economy'. Variants are as follows: UC cxlix. 205 (18 February 1822), headed 'Constitutional Law—Official Establishment', carries the marginal sub-heading 'Official Economy', which at some later date has been crossed out and 'Economy as applied to Office' inserted; UC clx. 51 (28 February 1822) is headed 'Thoughts on the Official Establishment'.

[3] This title is used at UC clx. 55 (26 March 1822) and (with the addition of 'or Constitut. Code') at UC xxxvi. 101 (14 April 1822).

[4] See the note at the top of UC clx. 37.

the publication of *Codification Proposal*[1] and of *Letters to Count Toreno*,[2] and the continued drafting of 'Rid Yourselves of Ultramaria'.[3] He was prompted to begin working in earnest, and almost exclusively, on 'Economy as applied to Office' when towards the end of April he received an acceptance of his offer to draw up a code of law from the Portuguese Cortes.[4] The connection of 'Economy as applied to Office' with the projected code is confirmed by the fact that many of the earlier manuscripts for the essay are headed 'Constitutional Code or Economy'.[5] From the middle of May, however, all but a few sheets are headed 'Economy', which perhaps suggests that Bentham had begun to view the essay as a work which, though closely related to what would be the substantive part of a constitutional code, would stand independently of it. By the time he wrote to Étienne Dumont on 26 May 1822, in which he described the scope and extent of 'Economy as applied to Office', he had clearly come to conceive of the work as a wide-ranging introductory essay to his projected constitutional code:

To *stop the creation* of useless, needless, overpaid, and mischievous Offices—that, being much easier than to *annihilate* them when created, by way of a forerunner and in part of my *Constitutional Code*, being that one of the three which for divers reasons had been designed to come *last* (since I dispatched Count Toreno, Codification Proposal and the more essential parts of "Rid yourselves of Ultramaria", sent in manuscript to Madrid, Lisbon, and Rio de Janeiro) I have been occupied with a work intituled "*Economy as applied to Office*." *Motto* and memento, "*Aptitude maximized, Expence minimized*". In this, both being understood in the largest sense, *every* thing is contained. The advance already made is considerable. *Securities* for *moral* aptitude: 1. identification of functionaries' particular interest with *universal interest*, thence with *duty*. 2. Minimization of *power*. 3. Minimization of public money, at their disposal. 4. Application of *apt counter force*: *apt*, the force of popular or moral sanction, applied by public opinion tribunal; *unapt*, force of the *religious* sanction as applied by Government. . . . By minimization of money employed in dotation of office not only is *expence* minimized but appropriate official *aptitude, moral, intellectual and active*, in all served.[6]

[1] *Codification Proposal addressed . . . to All Nations Professing Liberal Opinions*, London, 1822 (Bowring, iv. 535–94).

[2] *Letters to Count Toreno, on the Proposed Penal Code, delivered in by the Legislation Committee of the Spanish Cortes, April 25th, 1821*, London, 1822 (Bowring, viii. 487–554).

[3] See especially UC clxvii and clxxii.

[4] Bentham's letter offering to draw up penal, civil and constitutional codes, sent on 7 November 1821, was presented on 26 November to the Portuguese Cortes, which resolved to accept his offer. Bentham received their reply, informing him of their decision, on 22 April 1822 (see Bowring, iv. 575–6 and Journal of John Flowerdew Colls, 1821–5, BL Add. MS 33,563, fo. 100).

[5] Bentham often abbreviated 'Constitutional Code' to 'Constitut. Code' or 'Constit.', and 'Economy as applied to Office' to 'Economy as to Office', 'Economy etc.', or 'Economy'.

[6] Bentham to Dumont, 26 May 1822, Dumont MSS, Bibliothèque Publique et Universitaire,

He had incorporated the theme of official economy into a much broader analysis dealing with the securing of good government by the complementary means of maximizing aptitude and minimizing expense.

Bentham began to concentrate on 'Economy as applied to Office' from 25 April,[1] and continued with it until 27 June.[2] Though the latest material written under the heading of 'Economy as applied to Office' is dated 27 June, a sequence of eight manuscript sheets on factitious dignity dated 28 June, and carrying the main heading 'Constitutional Code', has been incorporated into the present text.[3] There survive from this period a total of 299 manuscript sheets of text which relate to 'Economy as applied to Office', all in the collection in the Library at University College London,[4] bar four sheets which are in the Bentham Papers held at the British Library.[5] Additionally there are forty-four marginal summary sheets in the hand of Bentham's secretary, John Flowerdew Colls.[6] These correspond with the marginal summaries on 149 sheets of text, while there are a further forty-three sheets of marginalized text, mainly for the chapter on the public opinion tribunal,[7] but for which the marginal summary sheets either were never copied or have not survived. The remaining text sheets have not been marginalized. There are also several sheets

Geneva, 33/V, fos.24–7. Pierre Étienne Louis Dumont (1759–1829), Bentham's Genevan editor and translator, had produced several recensions of Bentham's work.

[1] UC cxiii. 112 is dated 22 April, but the text was almost certainly written on 29 or 30 April.

[2] Bentham seems to have slipped UC xliv. 23 (12 July 1822) into Ch. 14 as a footnote (see pp. 107–8n below) at some later date. The only other material which has survived from this period is 'Junctiana Proposal', written between 20 and 25 June, containing Bentham's proposal for the cutting of a canal across Nicaragua in order to link the Pacific and Atlantic Oceans. A MS copy of this essay is at UC cvi. 264–97 (first published in Bowring, ii. 561–71).

[3] See 'Economy as applied to Office', Ch. 7, pp. 48–52 below. The inclusion here of these sheets (UC clx. 240–7) seems appropriate on the following grounds: firstly, they carry the marginal sub-heading 'Securities for I Moral Aptitude', which is also carried by other manuscripts written on the theme of moral aptitude for 'Economy as applied to Office'; and secondly, Bentham does not appear to have written any other material specifically for this chapter.

[4] UC xxxiv. 88–9; xxxviii. 34; xlii. 615; xliv. 6–7, 14–28; cviii. 150–2; cxiii. 1–137, 156–9; cxiv. 1–31; clx. 36, 56–74, 76–116, 240–7, 409–21, 456–73. This list includes those MSS written for the chapter on 'Identification of Interests', but reproduced here as a separate essay. For a description of the state of the MSS, and an explanation of the terms used in relation to them, see pp. xxxv–xxxvii below.

[5] BL Add. MS 33,549 fo.175 (9 May 1822) contains several fragmentary notes on judges; Add. MS 33,551 fos.304–6 (19 May 1822) is a fragment discussing visions and dreams, and headed 'Introduction to the Conversation parts', but appears to have been abandoned. The relationship of these MSS to the main body of the essay is unclear.

[6] UC xxxviii. 21, 33, 35–54, 59–60, 157–8, 174–6, 206, 281; clviii. 339–51. Colls (1801–78) was Bentham's amanuensis from 1816 until 1829, author of *Utilitarianism Unmasked*, London, 1844, and Rector of Laindon, Hertfordshire, 1853–78.

[7] See Ch. 9, pp. 56–76 below.

which contain notes on various relevant themes and on ideas for possible development.[1]

There is no satisfactory overall plan of the work, though the most wide-ranging and ambitious is one of 9 May 1822.[2] At this time Bentham envisaged four parts: the first, 'Aptitude maximized'; the second, 'Expence minimized'; the third, 'Things as they are in England: aptitude minimized, expence maximized'; and the fourth, 'Things as they ought to be and are in the Anglo-American United States'. The bulk of the surviving material is concerned with the first part, the maximization of aptitude in government functionaries. Apart from the fragments written in February and March, there are only a few sheets dealing with 'expence minimized', or 'frugality',[3] and these do not form a coherent or continuous sequence. There are several series of fragments headed or concerned with 'England',[4] but again these seem to be provisional drafts which Bentham failed to develop into a coherent account. No material at all was written under the heading of 'Anglo-American United States'. Bentham was unsure how to present these final two parts, as he noted on the plan of 9 May: 'Quere whether to put these parts separate or engraft them onto Parts I and II.' He did draw on English and American experience to illustrate various points in the material on 'aptitude maximized', but did not make any thorough and systematic consideration of the respective governments. Perhaps most consistent with the surviving material is a further plan, or rather table of contents, dated 25 May 1822, dealing with the theme of aptitude maximized, and carrying the marginal sub-heading 'Securities enumerated'.[5] Though this table contains a list of chapter headings, subsequently emended, it does not discuss the specific organization of the material within each chapter.[6] Nevertheless, according with the bulk of the completed material, and following the order implied by internal evidence, it represents the basis on which the essay has been constructed.[7]

[1] UC xxxiv. 9 (26 April 1822); xxxiv. 31 (20 May 1822); xxxviii. 3 (13–14 May 1822); xxxviii. 5 (26 May 1822).

[2] UC xxxviii. 11.

[3] UC cxiv. 2–3 (30 April 1822); clx. 68–74 (8–9 May 1822); clx. 98 (18 May 1822).

[4] UC clx. 93–5 (8 May 1822); clx. 96 (9 May 1822); clx. 99 (16 May 1822); clx. 101 (27 May 1822); clx. 107–9 (28 May 1822); clx. 110–14 (10 June 1822); clx. 115–16 (11 June 1822).

[5] UC cxiii. 34–6.

[6] There are several sheets which do contain more detailed plans of fairly small portions of text: UC xxxviii. 6 (26 May 1822); xxxviii. 7 (9 June 1822); and clviii. 339 (14 June 1822). In the absence of such plans, clues to the internal ordering of individual chapters and sections are provided by the dating and pagination of sheets of text and the numbering of marginal summary paragraphs.

[7] For the decision to exclude the chapter on 'Identification of Interests' from the text of 'Economy as applied to Office' see pp. xxvi–xxviii below.

Two related difficulties arising from the absence of a definitive table of contents are firstly, the choice of chapter and section titles, and secondly, their enumeration. The chapter and section titles have been taken from a variety of sources. The text sheets themselves, where appropriate, usually carry a chapter or section title, with an abbreviated title at the head of the marginal summaries. This abbreviated title is often used at the head of the columns on the marginal summary sheets. Other headings are found on the plans and the tables of contents, while wrappers enfolding the various sequences of manuscript sometimes carry quite detailed headings. Variations often occur between the headings given in the text and those on the corresponding marginal summary sheets, on the plans, and on the wrappers. The title chosen for each chapter or section has of course been that which seems most accurately to reflect the content of the text, and in practice this has meant that where possible it has been taken from the text sheet itself. Some section headings, however, have been taken from the marginal summary headings on the text sheets, some from the marginal summary sheets themselves, some from plans where these are more detailed (for instance the plan at UC clviii. 339 has yielded headings for Ch. 2, §§2, 4, 6 and 8), and some from the wrappers. It should be noted that titles exist for projected chapters for which no material appears to have been written, or at least for which no manuscript has survived. For instance, there is no text for the third security for moral aptitude, minimizing factitious remuneration, though the topic is discussed in the context of a security for active aptitude.[1] Again, according to the table of contents at UC cxiii. 36, for the Appendix on false securities, in addition to the three chapters on exclusions from constitutive power (Ch.13), division of the supreme operative power into two or more bodies (Ch.14), and disposition of the supreme power according to fantastic theories (Ch.15), Bentham intended to compose a fourth chapter entitled 'Application of the power of the Religious Sanction, under the management of the supreme operative power, in the character of a security for appropriate moral aptitude, or in that of a counterforce to legal power in the hands of the possessors of supreme operative power and their subordinates', but no manuscript on this topic appears to have been written.

The enumeration of chapters and sections has in effect been supplied editorially. Bentham sometimes numbered the sections and chapters, but at other times left a blank space for the numbering to be filled in. Furthermore, Bentham often presented differing numbering

[1] See Ch. 6, p. 47 below, and Ch. 11, §2, pp. 89–94 below.

schemes for the same sequence of material: the text sheets, for instance, and the relevant plan might contain a different series of section headings, and consequently a divergent series of section numbers. In order to obviate these inconsistencies, the enumeration of chapters and titles has simply followed the order of the work as presented: it has not been thought necessary to indicate Bentham's original, and obviously provisional, enumeration. Bentham did however consistently divide the writings on aptitude into three parts—Part I for moral aptitude, Part II for intellectual aptitude, and Part III for active aptitude—and this division has been maintained. These Parts bear no relation to the four Parts of the work as envisaged on the plan of 9 May 1822.[1]

Bentham experimented with several different sorts of layout for the text. Many of the manuscripts are written in the form of continuous prose, but considerable portions are in the form of a catechism ('Question' often being abbreviated to 'Q', and 'Answer' to 'A'). Two other methods of presentation deserve mention. Firstly, a category heading is followed by a portion of text. In Ch. 8, Bentham used a sequence of four categories—position, exposition, rationale and English practice—which resembles the form finally taken by *Constitutional Code*, albeit with the five categories of enactive, expositive, ratiocinative, instructional and exemplificational. A further variation on this theme is found in §§3 and 4 of Ch. 10, where Bentham presented the material in the form of a position and rationale.[2] Secondly, a few sheets contain series of aphorisms which summarize some of the arguments developed in the main body of the text. Some of these sheets are included in the Supplement to the work.[3]

It should be noted that the sequence in which the material was written bears little relation to its logical order. Moreover, Bentham drafted many sections more than once: for example he made three attempts to write the expository matter (25–8 April, 10–11 May and 17–19 June) and three attempts to write the chapter on securities for intellectual aptitude (29–30 April, 5–6 May and 9–10 June). The other material was drafted as follows: moral responsibility on the part of rulers and the public opinion tribunal (27–9 April, 3–5 and 8 May); minimizing factitious remuneration (30 April, 5 May); expense minimized (8–9 May); England (8–9 and 27–8 May and 10–11 June); exclusions from constitutive power (12–13 May); expository

[1] See p. xxii above.

[2] See also superseded material at UC cxiii. 1–4 (25 April 1822) and xliv. 6 (26 April 1822) which follows an enactive and expositive scheme.

[3] See pp. 117–22 below.

matter for minimizing power (14 and 16 May and 26 June); minimizing money (15 and 17–18 May); active aptitude (16 May); minimizing power (18–20 May); division of the legislature into two or more chambers (21 May); identification of interests (24–9 May); maximizing legal responsibility (10–11 June); and expository matter for the securities for moral aptitude (12–16 June).

'Economy as applied to Office' has never been previously published as a work in its own right, nor has very much of the material intended for it appeared in print elsewhere. Doane used eighteen manuscript sheets or parts of sheets in Book I, Ch. VIII, Public Opinion Tribunal,[1] and one sheet contrasting 'Good Government' with 'English Government' in Ch. IX, Good Rule and Bad Rule,[2] of his version of *Constitutional Code*, and one sheet in Book II, Ch. XII, Judiciary Collectively, § 32, Securities for appropriate aptitude.[3] Another fifteen sheets were published by C.W. Everett in 1926, making up the first section of his version of 'Anti-Senatica'.[4] In 1830 Bentham had collected together a series of manuscripts, had them copied and sent to President Andrew Jackson of the United States of America, with the hope that Jackson might give his approval to their content. With such encouragement, Bentham promised to revise them for publication.[5] Their common theme was the mischievousness of a second legislative chamber, but being compiled from fragments written independently over a period of two and a half years in the early 1820s, and with no attempt made to link them into a coherent whole, the result was, as Bentham himself appreciated, unsatisfactory. Bentham never regarded it as a completed work, but rather an outline of arguments which might be marshalled against the existence of a second chamber, and form the basis of an essay on the subject. Indeed, Doane seems to have been responsible for preparing the manuscripts, and it is the rough copy made under Doane's supervision, rather than

[1] UC clx. 406, 409 are at Bowring, ix. 41; clx. 473, 472 at ix. 41–2; clx. 461–4 at ix. 42–3; clx. 416–18 at ix. 43–4; clx. 410–12 at ix. 44–5; and clx. 414–15, 406, 456–7 at ix. 45.

[2] UC clx. 114 is at Bowring, ix. 59–60.

[3] UC xlii. 615 is at Bowring, ix. 536–7.

[4] 'Anti-Senatica. An attack on the U.S. Senate, sent by Jeremy Bentham to Andrew Jackson, President of the United States', ed. C.W. Everett, in *Smith College Studies in History*, xi (1926), 207–67. The original MSS, all in Bentham's hand apart from the final six sheets, and corresponding to the version published by Everett, are at UC xliv. 14–77 (Doane has made interlineations, deletions and emendations on these MSS, presumably to aid their copying); a rough copy is at UC xliv. 78–137 (some of this is in Doane's hand, other sheets bear his corrections); and part of a fair second copy is at UC xliv. 138–62. The original MSS have been paginated in sequence from UC xliv. 17 (p.4) to UC xliv. 77 (p.65), a pagination which Everett has reproduced. The MSS taken from 'Economy as applied to Office' are at UC xliv. 14–28, and compose pp. 1–15 in Everett's version.

[5] Bentham to Jackson, 14 June 1830, Nicholas P. Trist Papers, Library of Congress.

the Bentham original, that Everett appears to have taken for his text.[1]

Though Bentham does not appear to have given any serious consideration to publishing 'Economy as applied to Office', he did not completely discard the material but came back to look over it when drafting later versions of *Constitutional Code*. The marginal summary sheets for Ch. 1, Expository matter, at UC xxxviii. 174–6, carry the comment, 'Consult. 1823 June 30', while the final sheet of this sequence carries the additional remark, '☛ 14 Apr. 1823. Superseded by Constitut. Code Ch. 1'. A further marginal summary sheet (UC xxxviii. 157), which contains the marginal summaries for part of Ch. 1, §7, carries the comment: 'Reinspected 30 June 1823'. On a note pinned to UC cxiii. 25, dated 21 February 1827, he instructed his amanuensis:

> Memm. Transcribe from this packet the titles of Sections on one Table, and the Questions on the papers that follow them, on another on the same or a different Sheet according to the quantity.
>
> The matter is probably superseded by tit. Securities in Const. Code.

As the relevant transcription has not been traced, it is unclear what titles and questions Bentham had in mind (UC cxiii. 25 heads the sequence which forms Ch. 3). A further comment of the same date appears on UC cxiii. 39: 'Per Consti. Code, Power maximized so wi[ll] Securities against abuse be so too.'

Identification of Interests

The material presented here as a separate essay was initially intended by Bentham to form a single chapter in 'Economy as applied to Office'. On the table of contents for 'Economy as applied to Office',[2] 'Identification of individual with universal interest in the situation of

[1] This however has resulted in a slight inaccuracy in the organization of Everett's version. The material from the first three manuscript pages in the 'Anti-Senatica' sequence is missing from the rough copy; the first surviving page is a copy of UC xliv. 17 (p.4). Everett has therefore reproduced UC xliv. 14–16 as pp. 1–3. Yet it seems clear that for these first three pages Bentham employed UC cviii. 150–2, which appear to be a later draft of the material at UC xliv. 14–16. One may presume that since the three introductory pages are missing from the rough copy, Everett assumed that the three pages of Bentham's manuscript which now precede those which had been copied must have formed the first three pages of the essay. There are two points which suggest that Everett was mistaken: in the first place, UC cviii. 150–2 have been paginated as pp. 1–3 in the 'Anti-Senatica' sequence, whereas UC xliv. 14–16 carry no such pagination; second, the partial fair copy of 'Anti-Senatica' (UC xliv. 138–62) begins with UC cviii. 150–2, but does not include UC xliv. 14–16 at all.

[2] UC cxiii. 34 (25 May 1822).

possessors of the supreme Constitutive power' is listed as the first of the securities for moral aptitude. This accords with the description of the organization of the essay given by Bentham to Dumont in his letter of 26 May 1822.[1] However the table of contents was subsequently altered by Bentham indicating a decision to exclude this chapter. He crossed through the title and renumbered the following three securities in the list, namely minimizing power, minimizing money and minimizing factitious remuneration, as securities one to three. He added exclusion of factitious dignity as a new fourth security, and retained the final two securities, maximizing legal and moral responsibility, as securities five and six. This new scheme matches precisely with the list of securities drawn up on 17 June for Ch. 3, § 2, of 'Economy as applied to Office'.[2] At some stage between 26 May and 17 June Bentham changed his mind on the organization of the text relating to the securities for moral aptitude, deciding to exclude the material written for 'Identification of Interests' from the main body of the work.

There is no direct evidence which explains why Bentham made this decision, but certain conjectures are possible. In 'Economy as applied to Office' Bentham approached the questions raised in 'Identification of Interests' in the material written for the chapter on minimization of power.[3] Perhaps he felt that the inclusion of both discussions would have been repetitive. Moreover, in 'Identification of Interests' Bentham presents two different sets of interests which require identification: in the first place, the interests of rulers with those of subjects; and in the second, the interests of the possessors of constitutive power with the universal interest. This is reflected in the different versions of the title for the chapter: for instance, in the former case, 'Identification of rulers' with subjects' interest';[4] and in the latter, 'Identification of individual with universal interest in the breasts of functionaries: and in particular in the possessors of the Supreme Constitutive power'.[5] In fact, the text discusses the identification of both these sets of interests.[6] Bentham's main concern in 'Economy as applied to Office', however, was with the superordinate functionaries, hence the identification of rulers' with subjects' interests. This was the aspect most thoroughly considered in the material on minimization of power, and Bentham may have felt

[1] See p. xx above.
[2] See pp. 27–9 below.
[3] See 'Economy as applied to Office', Ch. 4, § 1, pp. 30–5 below.
[4] Sheet wrapping UC cxiii. 89–105.
[5] UC cxiii. 67 (as used for the title of § 1). See also the title on the table of contents at UC cxiii. 34 as given above.
[6] See § 7, pp. 132–5 below.

that this, rather than the discussion in the material he had written for 'Identification of Interests', was more appropriate to the structure of the work. Nevertheless the chapter retains its coherence and is felt to be of sufficient interest to be incorporated here as a separate essay.

There are in all thirty-five manuscript sheets of text written on this subject between 24 and 29 May 1822,[1] and six marginal summary sheets corresponding to twenty-four of these text sheets.[2] The main title is Bentham's usual abbreviated heading for this material, as found for instance in the marginal sub-headings of the text sheets. A plan at UC xxxviii. 6 (26 May 1822) divides the material into sections using the numbers of the marginal summary paragraphs to indicate the relevant material. This however relates only to §§1–5 and 7, the material corresponding to the marginal summary paragraphs included on the marginal summary sheets at UC clviii. 345–6. The remainder of the material (apart from unmarginalized sheets UC clx. 102–6) seems to have been written after this plan was drawn up. The titles of §§2–5 and 7 are taken from this plan; the remaining titles are taken from the relevant text sheets, except for the title of §1, which is a conflation of the heading on the text sheet and that on the plan, and the title of §8, which is taken from the corresponding marginal summary sheet (UC clviii. 347). The order of the text follows roughly the chronological order in which the sheets were written.

Supreme Operative

Once Bentham had abandoned 'Economy as applied to Office', he began to work on manuscripts under the general heading of 'Constitutional Code Rationale', and amongst the mass of writings which date from late June, July and August 1822 is a series of manuscripts under the sub-heading 'Supreme Operative'. Together with an earlier group of manuscripts, composed for *Codification Proposal* but eventually discarded from that work, they form the present essay. This first group of manuscripts, taken from the *Codification Proposal* material, was written between December 1821 and February 1822,[3]

[1] UC xxxiv. 88–9; cxiii. 55–61, 67–71, 74–80, 102–6, 117–23; cxiv. 13–14. A further sheet (UC cxiv. 15) was written on 7 June, though its relationship to the remainder of the material is unclear. Six more sheets, UC cxiii. 65–6 (12 May 1822) and clx. 81–4 (13 May 1822), were written under the marginal sub-heading of 'Identification of Interests', but these were used by Bentham in Ch. 13 of 'Economy as applied to Office'. UC cxiii. 64 (12 May 1822) also carried the marginal sub-heading 'Identification of Interests': for this sheet see p. 27n below. The marginal summary sheet for UC cxiii. 64–6, sub-headed 'Identification of Interests', is at UC clviii. 351.

[2] UC xxxviii. 281; clviii. 345–7, 349–50.

[3] UC lxxxiv. 1–191; xxxvi. 113v, 163v.

with the exception of five sheets written in late August 1821.[1] Most of these sheets carry the headings '§5. Draughtsman single' or '§5. Admission Universal'. In the published version of *Codification Proposal*, the former became §5 of Part I, characterized by the maxim, 'Receive draughts from all hands', while the latter became §7, 'Hands, not more than one'. At some stage Bentham considered arranging this additional material into an appendix, but at the beginning of February 1822 seems to have decided to exclude it altogether.[2] When Bentham came to draw up the plan for 'Supreme Operative',[3] he excluded large portions of this material, presumably because he felt it inappropriate in the context of the new essay.[4] In *Codification Proposal*, Bentham had considered the question of aptitude in relation to rulers and the production of a code of laws. He had argued that invitations for the drafting of a code of laws should be 'open', that is accepted from anyone who cared to submit a proposed draft, and had gone on to suggest that present legislators were by their situation, their liability to be corrupted by the influence of sinister interests, not suited to the task. For the purposes of 'Supreme Operative', Bentham was on the whole careful to use only the more general and abstract discussions of inaptitude in rulers, laying aside sections and paragraphs which bore direct relation to the drafting of a code of laws. Certain references do remain which can only be understood in relation to *Codification Proposal*, and are redundant to 'Supreme Operative'. These therefore have been excluded from the text in the present edition.

The second group of manuscripts, most of which date from the end of June and beginning of July 1822, was written specifically for 'Supreme Operative'.[5] This was one of several topics developed by Bentham in a series of essays composed during these months under the general heading of 'Constitutional Code Rationale'. It appears from this heading that Bentham had originally intended these essays to form one work, but he quickly seems to have decided to let 'Supreme Operative' stand by itself. This is evidenced by Bentham's construction of a separate detailed plan on 22 July 1822,[6] the drawing up of which effectively marked the cessation of his writing on the theme of

[1] UC xxiv. 455v, 420v, 448v, 466v, 449v.

[2] See Bentham's comment on the sheet preceding UC lxxxiv. 73: 'Constitutional Code—discarded from Codification Offer 3 Feby. 1822.'

[3] See below.

[4] The MSS incorporated into the plan are as follows: UC lxxxiv. 16–22, 28–35, 74–6, 78–83, 91–105, 107–24, 144–51, 153–8, 168–76, 178–81.

[5] These MSS are at UC xxxvi. 102–75, xxxvii. 71–6. The bulk of them were written between 28 June and 4 July 1822.

[6] See UC xxxiv. 11. A fair copy, dated 6 August 1822, is at UC xxxiv. 15.

'Supreme Operative'. Two sheets were written on 22 July itself:[1] as it seems reasonable to assume that these owed their provenance to Bentham's review of the essay, and as they are a summary of general principles developed in it, they have been incorporated into the text as the final section of the work (§ 23). After this there survive only a further five sheets dated intermittently between 24 July and 14 August 1822.[2]

Bentham's plan of 22 July 1822, which brings together these two groups of manuscripts, divides the essay into twenty-two sections whose titles form the section titles in the present edition of the text, except where otherwise indicated in an editorial footnote.[3] It has been assumed that these titles supersede the headings which Bentham had applied to the text sheets in the course of drafting them.[4] Bentham organized the material in the following manner. Taking the relevant marginal summary sheets, he numbered the marginal summary paragraphs in sequence from 1 to 372.[5] Paragraph numbers 1–143 indicate material written in June and July 1822, while the remaining paragraph numbers indicate the material discarded from *Codification Proposal*.[6] On the plan, the section title is followed by the marginal summary paragraph numbers which Bentham intended to be considered for inclusion in that particular section.[7] The relevant text has been located by collating the marginal summary paragraphs on the marginal summary sheets with the original marginal summary paragraphs on the text sheets.[8]

It should be emphasized that the plan does not represent a final organization of the text, but is rather an amalgam of materials which Bentham considered appropriate for each section. Consequently,

[1] UC xxxvi. 169–70.

[2] UC xxxvi. 171–5.

[3] On the plan, Bentham numbered the sections 1–4, 4*, 5–8, 8*, 9–14, 14*, 15–19, but here they have been renumbered 1–22 respectively.

[4] An exception is the additional § 23, where the title is taken from the marginal sub-headings on the text sheets. For the sub-section titles used in §§ 14, 16 and 19 see p. xxxiii below.

[5] There is no marginal paragraph 246.

[6] Marginal summary sheets UC xxxviii. 123–39 contain marginal summary paragraphs 1–143; xxxviii. 108–12 contain 144–92; xxxviii. 13–20 contain 193–267; and xxxviii. 113–22 contain 268–372. Some of these sheets (UC xxxviii. 19–20, 113–16 and 118–19) contain draft plans for their respective marginal summary paragraphs. The text corresponding to marginal summary paragraphs 369–72 has not been traced.

[7] Not all the marginal summary paragraphs enumerated in the 'Supreme Operative' sequence find their way onto the plan: those excluded, with corresponding text sheets, are as follows: marginal summary paragraph 1 (UC xxxvi. 102); 193, 195–205 (UC lxxxiv. 117–24); 221–43 (UC lxxxiv. 101–5); 244–5 (UC lxxxiv. 93, 96); 295 (UC lxxxiv. 176); 314–15 (UC lxxxiv. 115–16); 346 (UC lxxxiv. 158); 356 (UC lxxxiv. 76).

[8] For Bentham's normal working practice, and the relationship between the text, marginal summaries and marginal summary sheets, see pp. xxxv–xxxvii below.

many of the sections have several different sequences of text marked for inclusion in them, while many sequences of text are marked for inclusion in more than one section. Some series of text do not appear very relevant to the title of the section, while some appear relevant to other section titles. To have followed rigidly Bentham's plan would have been to present a text replete with repetition and irrelevancy. It seems rather that Bentham, where he indicated more than one series of material for inclusion in a particular section, intended that one should be preferred to another. Editorial discretion has therefore been exercised, sometimes in choosing one portion of text and excluding another, and sometimes in moving portions of text into a section where its content appears more relevant.[1] In general, material written specifically for 'Supreme Operative' has been preferred to that discarded from *Codification Proposal*, and where material has been relocated, it is usually put back into the original sequence from which Bentham had isolated it.[2] Special mention should be made of §§ 14, 16 and 19, each of which incorporates two different series of text. In each case, neither sequence clearly supersedes the other, and so both have been retained. In order to clarify the organization of the text, sub-section titles have here been inserted.[3] For the relationship between Bentham's plan and the manuscripts used in the present edition, reference should be made to the Table of Manuscripts.[4] The only significant sequence of text written for 'Supreme Operative' but not included on Bentham's plan has been reproduced in a Supplement to the essay.[5] The first sheet of this material was marginalized, but no marginal summary sheet appears to have been copied.

[1] Marginal summary paragraphs, with their relevant text sheets, included on the 'Supreme Operative' plan, but excluded from the present edition, are as follows: § 1, marginal summary paragraphs 321–5 (UC lxxxiv. 153), 347–55 (UC lxxxiv. 74–6), 366–8 (UC xxxvi. 113v, 163v), 369–71 (the corresponding text has not been traced); § 2, 329 (UC lxxxiv. 155); § 3, 154–5 (UC xxiv. 455v, 420v), 194 (UC lxxxiv. 118); § 5, 194 (UC lxxxiv. 118), 206–10 (UC lxxxiv. 98), 321–5 (UC lxxxiv. 153); § 9, 371 (see § 1 above); § 10, 57–68 (UC xxxvi. 126–7); § 11, 167–8 (UC lxxxiv. 20); § 13, 308–13 (UC lxxxiv. 109–10, 114), 372 (this paragraph was added by Bentham to the marginal summary sheet at UC xxxviii. 122, and it is possible that no corresponding text was ever written); § 14, 173–4 (UC lxxxiv. 22–3); § 17, 303 (UC lxxxiv. 150: this paragraph is directly concerned with *Codification Proposal*, and is redundant in the context of 'Supreme Operative'—Bentham seems to have marked it for exclusion on the marginal summary sheet at UC xxxviii. 115), 372 (see § 13 above); § 20, 275–6 (UC lxxxiv. 169–70), 329–30 (UC lxxxiv. 155).

[2] For instance, marginal summary paragraphs 331–5 (UC lxxxiv. 155–6) have been removed from § 19, and marginal summary paragraph 340 (UC lxxxiv. 156) from § 16, and placed in § 18 with marginal summary paragraphs 336–9 (UC lxxxiv. 156).

[3] The sub-section titles for §§ 14 and 16 are taken from the relevant text sheets; for § 19, from the draft plan on the marginal summary sheet at UC xxxviii. 19 and from the main plan at xxxiv. 11.

[4] See pp. xxxix–xli below.

[5] See pp. 223–6 below.

A considerable number of the 'Supreme Operative' manuscripts from June and July 1822 were published by Doane in Book I of his version of *Constitutional Code*. A total of fifty-seven sheets found their way into Ch. XVII, Supreme Operative,[1] while three sheets were included in Ch. IX, Good Rule and Bad Rule,[2] five in Ch. XV, Supreme Constitutive,[3] and two in Ch. XVI, Supreme Legislative.[4] Doane however did not follow Bentham's plan for the arrangement of his chapter on 'Supreme Operative', ignoring the earlier material discarded from *Codification Proposal*, while inserting additional materials from elsewhere.

Constitutional Code Rationale

Following 'Economy as applied to Office', Bentham's second major attempt in the summer of 1822 to draft an introductory essay to his projected *Constitutional Code* is contained in a group of manuscripts written under the heading of 'Constitutional Code Rationale'. Apart from internal evidence, the only clue to the organization of this work is a single surviving plan, dated 30 July and 3 August 1822, and headed 'Constitutional Code—Heads proposed'.[5] The arrangement of the work proposed in the plan does not correspond exactly to the topics considered in the surviving manuscripts. When Bentham drafted the plan, he intended to include chapters on the following themes: 'First principles', 'Rule in general', 'Good Rule', 'Misrule', 'Corruption', 'Expence of good rule and misrule', 'Appropriate aptitude and corresponding inaptitude on the part of rulers', and 'Securities against Misrule'. In the event he composed material under the following short headings: 'First Principles', 'Interest Junction', 'Rule—Good and Bad', 'Securities', 'Securities—Counterforces', 'Securities—Factitious Honor' and 'Established Religion None'. Therefore no manuscripts were written for the chapters on 'Expence' and 'Aptitude'. For the chapter on 'Corruption', Bentham may at some stage have intended using a group of manuscripts which he had written in June, July and August 1820 under the heading of 'Emancipation Spanish'.[6] These he organized at the beginning of

[1] UC xxxvi. 128–9 are at Bowring, ix. 127; xxxvi. 102–18 at ix. 128–33; xxxvi. 120, 165, 121–6 at ix. 134–6; xxxvi. 130–1, 133, 132, 134–43 at ix. 136–40; xxxvi. 144–7 at ix. 140–1; xxxvi. 150–1 at ix. 142; xxxvi. 171–2 at ix. 143–4; and xxxvi. 156–63 at ix. 144–5.

[2] UC xxxvi. 166–8 are at Bowring, ix. 59.

[3] UC xxxvii. 72–6 are at Bowring, ix. 100–1.

[4] UC xxxvi. 164, 127 are at Bowring, ix. 114.

[5] UC xxxiv. 12.

[6] See UC clxiv. 94–269.

August 1822, adding new titles and marking them for use in *Constitutional Code*.[1] He did not, however, make any determined effort to integrate them into 'Constitutional Code Rationale'.[2] Moreover, Bentham wrote only a portion of the material he had at one time envisaged for the chapter on 'Securities'. On 22 July 1822, he drew up the following list of 'securities for good government':

1. Minimizing the quantity of power in the hands of functionaries.
2. Minimizing the quantity of the matter of wealth in the disposal of functionaries.
3. Minimizing the quantity of the matter of wealth employed as pay of functionaries.
4. Applying legal counterforces to the power of functionaries.
5. Applying moral counterforces to the power of functionaries.
6. Exclusion of factitious honor, or say factitious dignity.
7. Exclusion of all other factitious instruments of delusive influence.[3]

The 'Rationale' material contains full discussions of points 4 and 5 (see Ch. 5) and point 6 (see Ch. 6).[4] Bentham may of course have intended to use the material written for 'Economy as applied to Office' to fill up the first two points, but there is no direct evidence to support this surmise. On the contrary, only a few days after drawing up this list he appears to have abandoned the idea of a comprehensive treatment of securities, and decided to reduce the scope of his discussion. In his analysis of securities (Ch. 4), composed at the end of July, he referred explicitly to the material on counterforces and factitious honour, but gave no hint that he intended to discuss any further securities. The topics of minimizing power, money and pay are therefore not considered in 'Constitutional Code Rationale'.

The titles of the chapters and sections throughout the work are taken from the relevant text sheets. The internal organization of the chapters has in general followed the order clearly marked out by Bentham in his page numbers and marginal summaries. The chapter on 'Rule' was perhaps less clearly organized, but the order roughly follows the chronological sequence in which the various sections of manuscript were written. The first two sections of Ch. 5, Counter-

[1] See the plan at UC xxxiv. 14 (5, 7 August 1822).

[2] They have not been included in the present volume, but will be published in a further volume in the *Collected Works*. The topic of corruption is in fact considered in Ch. 3, §5, pp. 252–61 below.

[3] UC clx. 434. Apart from the seventh security, and a change in the order, this list accords with the treatment of the subject in 'Economy as applied to Office'.

[4] A fragment at UC clx. 435–7 deals with point 7 in the context of a security for good government: the topic is however considered in Ch. 3, §6, pp. 261–7 below.

forces, follow a sequence of fifty-four marginal summary paragraphs.[1] This is to ignore a plan for this material which Bentham drew up on 21 July 1822 and which he headed 'Public Opinion Tribunal Ordo Novus'.[2] This plan, arranged in a similar manner to the plan for 'Supreme Operative', refers to a total of 127 marginal summary paragraphs.[3] The additional paragraph numbers (beyond those corresponding to the material written for 'Rationale') may possibly refer to the material on the public opinion tribunal written for 'Economy as applied to Office', but as no relevant marginal summary sheets have survived, this cannot be confirmed. Bentham therefore may have considered conflating these two sequences of manuscript. However, any attempt to reconstruct such a chapter according to this plan would be problematical because of the absence of these marginal summary sheets. The material has been left in the essays for which it was originally intended: hence the separate discussions of the public opinion tribunal in 'Economy as applied to Office' and 'Constitutional Code Rationale'.

As noted above, the earliest material which Bentham headed 'Rationale' was that composed mainly at the end of June and beginning of July 1822 for 'Supreme Operative'.[4] Through the remainder of July and August he concentrated on the material which is presented here as, and belongs properly to, 'Constitutional Code Rationale'. Most of the manuscripts for factitious honour were written between 4 and 12 July, though several more sheets date from 18 and 20–1 July. He began to work on counterforces on 8 July, and bar one sheet dated 29 July, completed it by 25 July. Meanwhile several shorter sequences of manuscript were written: 'Established Religion None' on 7 July, a few introductory sheets and the fragment on delusive influence on 21–2 July, the first draft of 'First Principles' on 26–7 July, and the 'Securities' material on 26 and 28–9 July. He then devoted little time to 'Rationale' until composing the second draft of 'First Principles' on 12–13 and 16 August, and 'Interest Junction' on 15–17 August. The material on 'Rule' followed on 17–18 and 21–3 August, and finally 'Incorporeal Instruments' between 19 and 31 August. There are in total 237 sheets of text,[5] and forty-four marginal summary

[1] See the marginal summary sheets at UC xxxviii. 22–7. Marginal summary paragraph numbers 55–60 are at UC xxxviii. 28, and correspond to text sheets UC clx. 366–7, but since these appear to be superseded by UC clx. 359–63, they have not been incorporated into the present text.

[2] UC xxxiv. 6.

[3] In addition there are references to marginal summary paragraphs on the 'Supreme Operative' plan, presumably inserted at a later date.

[4] See pp. xxix–xxx above.

[5] UC xxiv. 433v; xxxiv. 93–102; xxxvi. 78–100, 180–203; xxxvii. 77–87; cvi. 313–26;

sheets,[1] which correspond to the marginal summaries on 160 of the text sheets. There are fifteen sheets of text which have been marginalized but for which the marginal summary sheets do not survive or were never copied. A total of 141 sheets or parts of sheets of text written for 'Rationale' were incorporated by Doane into Book I of the Bowring edition of *Constitutional Code*.[2] As with 'Economy as applied to Office' and 'Supreme Operative', the material was re-organized by Doane to suit his conception of the introductory material, and bears little relation to the scheme of the work which Bentham seems to have had in mind at the time of its composition.

In September 1822, Bentham, having come into contact with Hassuna D'Ghies, the ambassador from Tripoli, turned to drafting 'Securities against Misrule, adapted to a Mahommedan State, and prepared with particular reference to Tripoli in Barbary'.[3] It was the stimulus afforded by events in Greece that once again encouraged Bentham to return to his labours on *Constitutional Code* in the spring of 1823.

TEXT

The Manuscripts

Almost the whole of the text material incorporated into this volume is in Bentham's own hand, written on single sheets of foolscap ruled with a wide margin and with a double line at the top for the date and the heading. Many of the text sheets contain numerous additions (usually interlinear, but sometimes marginal), deletions and emendations. Bentham's habit at this time seems to have been to date the

cxiii. 138–55; clx. 237, 248–65, 273–311, 339–68, 374–82, 406–8, 422–55, 425v. There are two sheets numbered UC xxxvi. 186.

[1] UC xxxviii. 22–32, 68–76, 81–96, 159–60, 162; xcvii. 192; clviii. 335–8. No text appears to have survived for UC xcvii. 192, which contains sixteen marginal summary paragraphs on the topic of factitious dignity.

[2] UC xxxvi. 78–9 is at Bowring ix. 1; xxxvi. 96–9 at ix. 3–5; xxxvi. 81, 100, 90–1, 83 at ix. 5; xxxvi. 92–5, 86–9 at ix. 5–7; xxxvi. 80–3 at ix. 7–8; xxxvi. 184–8, 190, 189 at ix. 47–8; clx. 434 at ix. 49; clx. 422–8 at ix. 49–51; clx. 339–57 at ix. 51–5; clx. 359–62 at ix. 55–6; clx. 376–8 at ix. 56–7; clx. 366–7 at ix. 57–8; clx. 429–32 at ix. 58–9; xxxvi. 198–202 at ix. 64–5; clx. 448 at ix. 77; clx. 436 at ix. 77; xxxvi. 180–1, 183, 182 at ix. 77–8; clx. 248, 250, 240, 250, 248, 250–2 at ix. 78–9; clx. 289–99 at ix. 79–82; clx. 248–9 at ix. 82–3; clx. 306 at ix. 83; clx. 262–3 at ix. 84–5; clx. 260–1 at ix. 85; clx. 274–83 at ix. 85–7; clx. 300–1 at ix. 87; clx. 253–5 at ix. 87–8; clx. 301 at ix. 88; clx. 285–6 at ix. 88–9; clx. 288 at ix. 89; clx. 264–5 at ix. 89–90; clx. 256–9 at ix. 90–1; clx. 307–11 at ix. 91–2; xxxvii. 77–83 at ix. 92–4; and xxxvii. 85, 87, 86 at ix. 94–5.

[3] First published in Bowring, viii. 555–600.

sheets and to write a sequence of several sheets of text, to read it over and make corrections, and then to write summaries of the content in the margin. The marginal summaries were written in the form of short paragraphs and numbered consecutively. These marginal summary paragraphs were then copied out onto separate sheets (marginal summary sheets) by an amanuensis—in the case of the manuscripts used here, by John Colls. The marginal summary sheets also contain occasional additions and emendations in Bentham's hand. The marginal summary sheets are written on single sheets of foolscap ruled into four columns with a double line at the top for the date and the heading. Bentham did not add marginal summaries to all the text sheets which he wrote, while marginal summary sheets corresponding to some of the marginal summaries on the text sheets were either never made or have not survived. It should be noted that the marginal summary paragraphs were not intended for publication, unlike the marginal headings incorporated in some of the earlier works,[1] but rather seem to have been used by Bentham for purposes of reference. Additionally a few sheets containing 'Rudiments', or general statements or positions, and others containing plans, are written on double sheets of foolscap, each sheet again being ruled into four columns.

Many of the manuscripts are found in paper wrappers on which Bentham has inscribed a descriptive heading. These headings are sometimes detailed and specific, where the number of manuscripts is small and they comprise one continuous sequence, and at other times more general, where the number of manuscripts is larger and the content more wide-ranging. These wrappers were presumably used by Bentham as a rough contents index, allowing him to find and organize his material more easily. However, some of the wrappers have been misplaced, and are therefore not always a reliable guide to the content of the material they enfold.

A few general points should be made with regard to the organization of the texts. The manuscripts are in some confusion, which is apparently the state in which Bentham himself left them.[2] Surviving plans have assisted in establishing the overall structure of the texts, though these are usually inadequate and considerable reliance has had to be placed on internal evidence. The internal organization of each chapter or section has been ascertained by paying regard, where applicable, to the dating and pagination of sheets of text, the numbering of marginal summary paragraphs and of course the sense. Difficulties arise from the existence in some cases of several drafts for

[1] See for instance *An Introduction to the Principles of Morals and Legislation*, ed. J.H. Burns and H.L.A. Hart, London, 1970 (*CW*).

[2] See p. xvi above.

the same chapter or section, not to mention other isolated and abandoned fragments on the same theme. Usually the later draft has been preferred as representing Bentham's more mature consideration of the subject-matter in question. The location and date of any alternative draft has been indicated, where appropriate, in an editorial footnote, as has any other related manuscript which has been excluded from the text.[1] For the manuscripts used in this edition, reference should be made to the Table of Manuscripts below.

Table of Manuscripts

Economy as applied to Office

Chapter	*Section*	*MSS (UC)*	*Date (1822)*
1	1	cxiv. 8	17 June
	2	cxiv. 9	17 June
	3	cxiv. 9–11	17 June
	4	cxiii. 9–11	17 June
	5	cxiv. 12	17 June
	6	cxiii. 12–17	17–19 June
2	1	cxiii. 81–3	16 May
	2	cxiv. 4–5, 24	12 June
	3	cxiv. 24	12 June
	4	cxiv. 25–6	12 June
	5	cxiv. 6–7	13 June
	6	cxiv. 16–18	12 June
	7	cxiv. 19	16 June
	8	cxiv. 19–21	16 June
	9	cxiv. 22–3	16 June
3	1	cxiii. 25	19 June
	2	cxiii. 26–8	17, 26 June
4	1	cxiii. 39–41	16 May
		cxiii. 89–95	19–20 May

[1] With the exception of 'Supreme Operative', where material indicated on Bentham's plan but excluded from the present edition is given at p. xxxin above.

Chapter	*Section*	*MSS (UC)*	*Date (1822)*
	2	cxiii. 97–8	18 May
	3	cxiii. 99, 103, 102, 104–5	18 May
5		cxiii. 44, 47, 46, 45, 47–51 clx. 56–7	15, 17–18 May 28 April
6		————	
7		clx. 240–7	28 June
8		cxiii. 30–4	10–11 June
9	1	cxiii. 84–8	27 April
	2	clx. 461–6, xlii. 615, clx. 467 clx. 469 clx. 468 clx. 470, 471, 473	28–9 April 4 May 29 April 3–4 May
	3	clx. 416–18 clx. 419	4 May 8 June
	4	clx. 409 clx. 456–7	9 May 5 May
	5	clx. 458–60, 420–1	5 May
	6	clx. 410–15	8 May
10	1	cxiii. 106–7	9 June
	2	cxiii. 108–9	9 June
	3	cxiii. 110	10 June
	4	cxiii. 111 cxiii. 126 cxiii. 112–13[1]	10 June 5 May 30 April
	5	cxiii. 127–8	5 May
	6	cxiii. 134–5, 132–3	6 May
11	1	cxiii. 156–9	16 May
	2	clx. 58–60, 63 clx. 66–7, 61–2 cxiii. 137	30 April 5 May 30 April
12		clx. 100	24 May
13		cxiii. 65–6 clx. 81–4	12 May 13 May

[1] UC cxiii. 112 is mis-dated 22 April.

Chapter	*Section*	*MSS (UC)*	*Date (1822)*
14		clx. 76–80, xliv. 19–22	21 May
		xliv. 23	12 July
		xliv. 24–8	21 May
15		xliv. 14–15	25 May
		cviii. 150–2	30 May

Supplement to Economy as applied to Office

cxiii. 52–4	10 May
clx. 92	15 June
clx. 89–90	17–18 June
clx. 91	18 June
cxiii. 29	22 May

Identification of Interests

Section	*MSS (UC)*	*Date (1822)*
1	cxiii. 67–8	24 May
2	cxiii. 68	24 May
3	cxiii. 69	24 May
4	cxiii. 70	24 May
5	cxiii. 70–1	24–5 May
6	clx. 102–6	24 May
7	cxiii. 55–7	25 May
8	cxiii. 58–61	26–7 May
9	cxiii. 74–80	27, 29 May
10	cxiii. 117–19	28 May
11	cxiii. 120–3	28 May

Supreme Operative

Section	*MSS (UC)*	*Date*	*Marginal summary paragraph nos. as per plan*
1	lxxxiv. 107–8	20 January 1822	316–20
2	lxxxiv. 154	6 February 1822	326–8

Section	*MSS (UC)*	*Date*	*Marginal summary paragraph nos. as per plan*
3	lxxxiv. 16–20	5 December 1821	144–53, 164–6
4	xxxvi. 130–1, 133, 132, 134–6	29 June 1822	69–94
5	xxxvi. 102–8	28, 30 June, 1 July 1822	2–16
6	xxiv. 420v, 448v, 466v, 449v	24–6 August 1821	156–63
7	xxxvi. 109–19	28–30 June 1822	17–43
8	xxxvi. 137–41	13, 15 July 1822	95–108
9	lxxxiv. 78–83	25–6, 28 December 1821	357–65
10	xxxvi. 120–5	2, 4 July 1822	44–56
11	lxxxiv. 157–8	6 February 1822	341–6
12	xxxvi. 129	28 June 1822	124
13	xxxvi. 142–3	28 June 1822	109–12
14	lxxxiv. 21	5 December 1821	169–72
	lxxxiv. 28–30	7–8 December 1821	174*–82
15	lxxxiv. 168–9	14 February 1822	268–74
16	lxxxiv. 99–101	14–15 January 1822	211–20
	lxxxiv. 31–5	7–10 December 1821	183–92
17	lxxxiv. 170–5[1]	14, 16 February 1822	277–94
	lxxxiv. 147–52[2]	6–7 February 1822	296–302, 304–7
18	lxxxiv. 155–6	6 February 1822	331–40
19	lxxxiv. 178–9	15 February 1822	259–62
	lxxxiv. 144–6	5 February 1822	247–58

[1] UC lxxxiv. 176, which appears to have contained the text corresponding to marginal summary paragraph 294, is missing from the Bentham papers.

[2] Though not marginalized, and so not included on the 'Supreme Operative' plan, UC lxxxiv. 152 was clearly intended to follow UC lxxxiv. 147–51, and has therefore been incorporated into the text.

Section	*MSS (UC)*	*Date*	*Marginal summary paragraph nos. as per plan*
	lxxxiv. 180–1	5, 15 February 1822	263–7
20	xxxvii. 71–6	4 July 1822	113–18
21	xxxvi. 128	n.d.	119–23
22	xxxvi. 156–63	1 July 1822	125–43
23	xxxvi. 169–70[1]	22 July 1822	

Supplement to Supreme Operative

	xxxvi. 144–9	16, 19 July 1822

Constitutional Code Rationale

Chapter	*Section*	*MSS (UC)*	*Date (1822)*
1	1	xxxvi. 96–100	12–13 August
	2	xxxvi. 90–5, 86–9	12–13, 16 August
2		xxxiv. 93–102	15–17 August
3	1	cxiii. 151–3	21 August
	2	cxiii. 154–5	21 August
	3	cxiii. 146–9	22–3 August
	4	xxxvi. 184–8[2]	22, 24 August
		clx. 451	25 August
	5	xxxvi. 198–203	30–1 August
		xxxvi. 195–7	27 August
		cvi. 323–6	29 August
	6	cvi. 313–22[3]	29 August
	7	xxxvi. 180–1, 183, 182[4]	9 August
4	1	clx. 438–47	26 July
	2	clx. 422–32	28–9 July

[1] For the inclusion of this material see p. xxx above.
[2] There are two sheets numbered UC xxxvi. 186.
[3] UC cvi. 322 is mis-dated 19 August.
[4] UC xxxvi. 182–3 were originally dated 19 May 1821.

Chapter	*Section*	*MSS (UC)*	*Date (1822)*
5	1	clx. 339–45	11–13 July
	2	clx. 346–58	12, 14–15, 18 July
	3	clx. 359–63	25, 29 July
6	1	clx. 250–2	4, 8 July
	2	clx. 253–5	9 July
		clx. 249	n.d.
	3	clx. 260–1	9 July
	4	clx. 262–3	9 July
	5	clx. 256–9	4 July
	6	clx. 274–6	5, 7 July
		clx. 284	20 July
		clx. 276	7 July
		clx. 277	18 July
		clx. 285–7	8 July
		clx. 288	18 July
		clx. 278	12 July
		clx. 279	18 July
		clx. 280	6 July
		clx. 281–3	20 July
		clx. 300–1	8 July
	7	clx. 296–8, 306	6 July
	8	clx. 307–10	6 July
7		xxxvii. 77–87	7 July

Presentation of the Text

It has been editorial policy to reflect as far as possible the manuscript sources on which the texts in this volume are exclusively based, but without the sacrifice thereby of clarity and sense. Bentham's spelling and capitalization have in most instances been retained, though editorial discretion has been exercised with regard to his punctuation, inconsistent and sparse as it often is. Punctuation marks have been adjusted and supplied where clearly indicated by the sense or required for the sake of clarity, but not in cases where this might involve a dubious interpretation of the meaning. The words and phrases underlined by Bentham for emphasis have been rendered in italics, as have all foreign words and phrases, some of which Bentham underlined and some of which he did not. In general, standard abbreviations have been retained, though some abbreviated words have been expanded into their full form (thus 'do.' is rendered as 'ditto'). It should however be emphasized that Bentham's syntax is often very complicated and involved, and in certain passages the sense is not immediately apparent. In these cases, no attempt has been made to give any explanation of the sense, since this could give rise to the opposite danger of over-simplification and miss some nuance in the argument. Nevertheless, where there does appear to be some genuine confusion, an explanatory editorial footnote is added.

The manuscripts contain many deletions, additions and emendations, representing Bentham's later corrections to the text. The final alternative reading is usually given in the text, unless indicated otherwise by an editorial footnote. Original readings have usually not been indicated. Where there is no text corresponding to some part of the marginal summary, the marginal summary is reproduced in an editorial footnote. Unless otherwise indicated, these passages are taken from the original in Bentham's hand on the text sheet, and not from the copy on the marginal sheet. Square brackets in the text are reserved for editorially inserted words: if these replace a word or phrase in the manuscript, Bentham's original is given in an editorial footnote, but where these are simple additions, there is no corresponding footnote. Round brackets are those supplied by Bentham. Perpendicular strokes indicate a gap or blank space in the manuscript.

Bentham had a habit of numbering with the figure '1' the first paragraph in a section, or the first point, or indeed the only point, he wished to make in a particular passage, but then failing where appropriate to continue the enumeration. This enumeration has been suppressed. In those cases where the enumeration is continued, it has of course been retained.

A specific problem with 'Supreme Operative' arises from the inclusion in this essay of manuscripts originally written for *Codification Proposal*. There are references in the text of these manuscripts to matters which are particular to *Codification Proposal* and seem redundant in the context of 'Supreme Operative': they have therefore been excluded.

Bentham's own footnotes are indicated by suprascript letters and editorial footnotes by suprascript numerals, with a separate sequence for each page of the text.

ECONOMY AS APPLIED TO OFFICE

CHAPTER 1. EXPOSITORY MATTER[1]

§ 1. *Law—its branches*

Taken in the aggregate, the whole body of the law may be considered as divided into two main branches: the immediately operative and the remotely operative branch. The immediately operative branch is composed of the branches commonly called Penal and Civil taken together: the remotely operative branch is the branch commonly called the Constitutional branch.

The Constitutional branch is that which establishes the denominations, powers and duties of the several servants[a] of thc Community, and determines the operations or other events or states of things by which they respectively begin and cease to be so.

In the body of the law taken in the aggregate is comprized the expression of so much of the will of the person or persons in whose hands, at the time in question, the powers of government are exercised as is committed to writing with the intent of its receiving obedience at the hands of the several persons and classes of persons therein designated: the will of all persons formerly in the several Official situations in question being considered as continuing to be the will of the several persons by whom, at the time being, those several situations are occupied: except in so far as the contrary has been declared.

§ 2. *End of Good Government*

The greatest happiness of the greatest number is the only right and proper end of government: of all, in so far as the happiness of all can be encreased without lessening the happiness of any: of the greatest number, in so far as the happiness of some can not be encreased unless by defalcation made from the happiness of others.

The net amount of happiness thus produced will be directly as the sum of happiness, or say good, produced, and inversely the sum of unhappiness, or say evil, produced by the same means.

[a] Synonyms: 1. Agents: 2. Functionaries: 3. Trustees, in so far as power is regarded as necessary to the performance of the service.

[1] An earlier draft of this chapter is at UC cxiii. 1–5 (25, 27 April 1822). Related fragments are at UC cxiv. 1 (25 April 1822), xliv. 6 (26 April 1822) and cxiii. 6–8 (10–11 May 1822).

§3. *Immediate means of Good Government: Aptitude maximized, Expence minimized*

All government is in the very essence of it an evil: for government can not be carried on but in proportion as obligation is created; and taken by itself all obligation is an evil. To exercise the powers of government is accordingly to do evil: to exercise the powers of government in pursuance of the only right and proper end of government, is to do evil, to the end and with the intent that in the greatest possible quantity good may come.

The goodness of the government will be as the aptitude of the portions of law enacted by it and the operations performed by it: their aptitude with relation to that same end.

External circumstances the same, the aptitude of these same portions of law will be as the appropriate, or say relative, aptitude of the persons bearing part respectively in the enactment of them: the aptitude of the operations will be as the aptitude of the operators.

Taken by itself and abstraction made [of] all pleasure and profit produced by it, on this occasion as on others, all expence is evil, all expence, in whatsoever shape.

Hence for remembrance and standards of reference, we have these aphorisms.

1. Sole justifiable end of laws, greatest happiness of greatest number.

2. Immediate direct means or immediately subordinate end, aptitude maximized on the part of functionaries of all sorts employed about and under the law, appropriate aptitude maximized, maximization of appropriate aptitude.

3. Collateral means and immediately subordinate end, expence minimized, minimization of expence.

I. Aptitude.

Appropriate aptitude is aptitude with relation to the end. In the case of a functionary of Government, appropriate aptitude is appropriate official aptitude.

Of appropriate official aptitude with relation to the end of government and laws, three branches or elements require to be distinguished, namely, 1. appropriate moral aptitude: 2. appropriate intellectual aptitude: 3. appropriate active aptitude.

Appropriate intellectual aptitude again requires to be distinguished into: 1. appropriate knowledge: 2. appropriate judgment.

For maximizing appropriate official aptitude in these its several branches, the arrangements and other means employed by the Constitutional branch of law may be termed Securities for these several branches of appropriate official aptitude: these securities for it, are so many efficient causes of it: they[1] respectively so many concurrent causes: the aptitude produced by them, their common effect.

II. Expence.

Under the head or appellation of the expence of Government, the word expence being taken in its largest sense, may be comprized the evil in all shapes produced while endeavouring or not endeavouring to produce the good, the production of which is the only proper end or object of government.

Taxation is productive of evil: taxation is imposition of expence.

Punition is productive of evil: the suffering produced by punishment is expence.

Remuneration is productive of evil, in so far as the instruments of remuneration are produced by imposition of expence.

Creation of factitious dignity is creation of evil: by it, respect is given to the new dignitary at the expence of every body else.

Obligation in every shape is evil: whether it be obligation on the sensitive faculty, as in the case of punishment, or obligation on the active faculty, as in the case of coercion, i.e. imposition of constraint and restraint.

In so far as any person knowingly concurring in the production of it is in whole or in part receiver to his own use of any profit derived by means of it, all superfluous expence is depredation, the matter of superfluous expence is the matter of depredation.

Depredation is either simple or aggravated.

Simple depredation has place in so far as by reason of the loss imposed on the public, [the depredator] receives a profit not less than the loss.

Aggravated depredation is where to produce profit to a certain amount to himself, the depredator is concerned in producing loss to a greater amount to the public.

For the purpose of punishment and other means of prevention, the loss to the public is the object to be considered. Considered apart from the loss, the profit to the depredator is not an evil: it is on the contrary a good.

[1] i.e. the securities.

§4. *Of the different powers of Government*

Considered in respect of the nature of its functions, all power in a Government is either *operative* or *constitutive*.

Operative power is that in the exercise of which the business [is] done: *Constitutive power* is that by the exercise of which it is determined who the person or persons are by whom the operative power shall be exercised. Constitutive is therefore such with relation to the operative.

Considering its rank in the scale of subordination, all power is either supreme or subordinate.

Supreme Operative power is either Supreme Legislative or Supreme Executive.

By Supreme Legislative power understand the power of imposing upon persons of all classes, obligations of all sorts, for purposes of all sorts, and with reference to things of all sorts: obligations such as are not capable of being annulled or varied by any other power in the State.

By Supreme Executive power understand the power of giving, by means of acts having for their subjects individual persons and things or aggregates of individual persons or things—of giving in detail execution and effect to ordinances issued by the Legislative authority.

Although with reference to all other persons this power may be stiled as being supreme, yet, with reference to the Supreme Legislative power, it is essentially subordinate.[1]

Supreme Executive power is either Administrative or Judicial.

To the Administrative power it belongs to apply such general rules and ordinances as have the sanction of the Supreme Legislative power to particular persons and things for the several purposes designated by the same and according to directions given by the same: and in particular to make disposal of all such things specially placed at its disposal for the service of the State, as also of all such personal services as by special appointment are rendered exigible for the use of the state.

The Administrative Department is the Department by which the Administrative power is exercised.

To the Administrative Department belong the following Sub-Departments:[2]

[1] Bentham noted at this point: 'Why subordinate?' The relationship between the supreme legislative power and the supreme executive power is discussed at Ch. 4, §1, pp. 30–5 below.

[2] Bentham left the text blank, but supplied the following list in the marginal summary. Cf. *Constitutional Code*, vol. I, ed. F. Rosen and J.H. Burns, Oxford, 1983 (*CW*), Ch. IX, §2, Art. 1, pp. 171–2.

I. Universally necessary.

1. Interior Affairs.
2. Land force.
3. Foreign Affairs.
4. Finance.

II. Contingently necessary.

5. Naval force.
6. Distant dependencies.

To the Judicial Department it belongs also to apply to individual persons and things, as also to aggregates of persons and things, such rules and ordinances as have the sanction of the Supreme Legislative power: but this only in the case of a contest between two or more parties in respect to the point of right, reference being had to such sanction as above: application being made by some party in the character of plaintiff praying that something be done by another party, by whom, in case of evitation manifested or apprehended, it is alledged on the part of the plaintiff, but for the interposition of the judicial power, something that ought to be done will not be done.

The exercise given to the Supreme Legislative power may be distinguished into ordinary and extraordinary.[1]

The extraordinary exercise of the Supreme Legislative power is that which would have place if, on the ground of alledged insubordination on the part of any possessor of the Supreme Executive power or Subordinate Administrative power or any possessor of Supreme or Subordinate Judicial power, measures were deemed necessary to be taken for the dislocation of the alledged delinquents and, in case of need, for their punishment, as also for the location of other individuals in the place of those so dislocated.

§5. *Of integrality and fractionality as applied to official power*[2]

There are two modes in which such fractionization may have place: one may be stiled the *simple* mode, the other the compound, or say the complex or composite or complicated, mode.[a]

[a] To the Anatomist, the appellation *compound fracture* will here be apt to present itself.

---

[1] According to the marginal summary, 'ordinary' legislative power is exercised 'on persons at large'.

[2] Bentham did not define integrality and fractionality in the text, but did so in the marginal summary: 'Modes of holding power: 1. integral; 2. fractional; integral where the power is all in one hand; fractional where in divers, not acting but in conjunction.'

The *simple* mode is where it is only among one set of functionaries acting together in a body that the power is divided: so that to give validity to an act of the supreme operative power, nothing more is required than the concurrence of a majority of that same body. This mode stands exemplified in the case of the Portugueze Government: and among the Anglo-American United States, in a state of greater simplicity, in the State of Vermont.[1]

The compound, complex, composite or complicated mode is where at different times, to acquire its binding force, an act of the constituted authority must have received the consent of parties more than one. Examples:

1. Two bodies, as in the Anglo-American States, all but one.[2]
2. A single person and a body: as in the case of the Spanish Constitution.[3]
3. A single person and two bodies: as in the case of England.[4]
4. A single person and two bodies, as in the case of France: the exclusive initiative being in the single person.[5]
5. A single person and three or four bodies: as in the case of Sweden.[6]

§6. *Different modes of subordination in the case of official power*[7]

In so far as between two functionaries a relation has place in such sort that the one of them has an adequate inducement to submitt his will to that of the other, and cause his line of conduct to be conformable to such other will as if it were his own, subordination has place between their respective powers: he whose will is conformed to may be termed the *superior*, or say *superordinate*, *functionary*; the other, by whom

[1] The Portuguese Constitution of 1821 vested the legislative power in a Cortes formed of a single chamber, but subject to the suspensive veto of the Crown. The Vermont Constitution of 1793 vested the legislative power in a single chamber, the House of Representatives, but again subject to a suspensive veto in the Governor and Council.

[2] With the exception of Vermont, the remaining twenty-three states each had a bicameral legislature.

[3] Under the Constitution of 1812, overturned by Ferdinand VII (1784–1833), King of Spain from 1808, in 1814, but restored by the revolution of 1820, the legislative power was vested in the Monarch and the Cortes.

[4] The Monarch, House of Lords and House of Commons.

[5] The *Constitutional Charter* of 1814 vested the legislative power in the Monarch, who alone could initiate laws, the Chamber of Peers and the Chamber of Deputies.

[6] With regard to the legislative arrangements in Sweden, Bentham noted in the marginal summary: 'Enquire'. In fact, the Monarch ruled in conjunction with the *Riksdag*, which was composed of four houses representing the four estates of clergy, nobles, burgesses and peasants.

[7] A related fragment is at UC cxiii. 62 (30 May 1822).

his own will is thus rendered conformable to that of the other, the *subordinate*.

For the causing such subordination to have place, the following are the different modes or states of things which the nature of the case affords:

1. The subordinate liable to be removed out of his official situation by the will of the superordinate. Say, Subordination by dislocability.

2. The subordinate liable to be avowedly subjected to legal punishment by the superordinate. Say, Subordination by declared punibility. The subordinate legally punishable.

3. The subordinate liable to be vexed by the superordinate in any other way than by declared punishment. Say, Subordination by undeclared punibility: or say, by inevitable vexation. In this way it is that subordination by dislocability involves in it subordination by undeclared punibility. The subordinate practically, or say virtually, punishable.

By punishment undeclared, so far as it has place and is applicable, a much more effectual and compleat subjection, and thence subordination, it is evident, is produced or producible than by punishment not inflictible unless declared. By punishment declared, understand evil not capable of being produced without the formality of prosecution. But by the odium of prosecution, the delay, the expence, the vexation, ever on the [part] of the prosecution, added to the uncertainty of success, a counterforce is produced by which to every eye, even where judicial procedure is in the highest state of aptitude, the disposition to prosecute will be in a great degree diminished, and thence the apparent probability of the suffering, and its restrictive efficacy, be proportionably diminished.

By neither of these modes of subordination—namely subordination by dislocability and subordination by punibility, understand by being punishable in a legal and formal way only—is the subordination rendered compleatly effective without the other. The utmost degree of subjection and [subordination][1] producible by dislocability depends on the value of the situation in the eyes of the functionary: if it has no value at all, or none but what may be outweighed by the profit which he promises to himself from any such acts as it will be in his power to exercise before his dislocation can have place, the subordination he is in will be but nominal only, not effective and entire.

Again by punibility alone without dislocability, neither will the subordination be compleatly effective. The deficiency is already

[1] MS 'superordination'.

indicated. It has for its cause the uncertainty of success in the case of prosecution, coupled with the certainty of odium, delay, expence and vexation on the part of the prosecution: the odium not always considerable, the burthen of expence capable of being taken off by compensation: but the uncertainty, delay and vexation still remaining unremovable and incapable of being compensated.

Of the three, the most surely efficient cause of subjection, thence of subordination, is subordination by undeclared punibility: i.e. vexability. If the vexation capable of being inflicted on the subordinate, without material suffering or danger of suffering on the part of the superordinate, is in the subordinate's eyes greater than the value of the situation is to him, in this case added to the virtual punibility is virtual dislocability: for rather than endure the vexation any longer he will dislocate himself—he will resign the place.

Dislocation is capable of being ordained and effected in either of two modes: the one direct; the other indirect. It is direct where, to the continuance of the functionary in the office, no precise duration is assigned: but he is rendered dislocable by some superordinate, whether at the will of such superordinate or not but on conviction of delinquency in some determinate shape in the way of judicial procedure: in such case, in default of such conviction, his continuance in the situation is coæval with his life.

The indirect mode has place where, a determinate duration being assigned to the continuance of each individual functionary in such his situation, at the end of the term a fresh election is appointed to be made. In this indirect mode the subordination is much more effective than by dislocation in the direct mode. If it be in the direct mode that the functionary is dislocated, the act of dislocation involves in it a judgment of condemnation pronounced—a declaration of positive inaptitude, a declaration that he is absolutely unapt with relation to the office. If it be only in the indirect mode, as above described, no such judgment of condemnation is pronounced by any person: the opinion involved in the election of another person amounts to nothing more than this—namely that among the whole number of persons capable of being elected and not unwilling to serve, there is one person more apt than he—than the individual who fails to be reelected.

In this supposed case however is involved the supposition that it is by election that the fresh location is performed: by election—the act of a multitude: for supposing the fresh location the act of no more than a single individual, or some small number of individuals, in this case the non-reelection will be apt to be considered as involving in it a tacit declaration of positive unaptitude.

Relation being had to the occasion on which it has place, Subordination is either *General* or *Special*.

It is General in so far as it extends over the whole of the Subordinate's Official time, the whole of the time during which he continues in the Office: Special in so far as its application is confined to this or that individual measure or set of measures.

The Superordinate authority may be an individual sole in office, or a simple body, or a composite body howsoever compounded of bodies one or more, and individuals one or more.

The Subordinate authority may in like manner be an individual sole in office, or a simple body, or a composite body composed of bodies one or more and individuals one or more.

A mode of subordination may be made to have place by difference in the degrees of power and influence between the two parties in relation to and over a common subject. Neither is by dislocability or by punibility, avowed or unavowed, in subordination to the other. But one and the same person is in a state of subordination with relation to them both: and this in such sort that in case of disagreement between the two, the conduct of the common subject is more likely to be determined by the will of the one of them than by that of the other. In this state of things, the one of them may be said to be subordinate to the other by inferiority of power in relation to a common subject.

So, in regard to a thing: the same sort of relation may have place where the common subject belongs not to the class of *persons*, but to that of things. Instead of conduct as in the former case, say *condition* in this case.[1]

In the case where the power of an Office is fractionalized in the compound mode, a sort of subordination may be made to have place as between one element and another of the compound aggregate: viz. by means of the different degrees of power and influence capable of being possessed by them respectively, with relation to the ultimate result of their conjunct action: in respect of their respective degrees of influence on the existence of any measure for the carrying of which into effect a conjunct act on their part is necessary.

In this state of things, the one of them may be said to be subordinate to the other by means of inferiority of influence with reference to the existence and character of an act done in the exercise of the official power in which they share.[2]

The judicial is the function in the exercise of which these

[1] Bentham noted at this point, '☛ Quere, Examples', but none appear to have been written.

[2] In the marginal summary, Bentham listed the following powers which a functionary might possess in relation to official acts: '1. Exclusive initiative. 2. Power of invalidation by non-consent. 3. Power of inhibition, viz. by dissent. 4. Power of cessation. 5. Power of suspension.'

diversifications are more naturally and frequently exemplified than in the exercise of the legislative.

Judicial power [is]: 1. ordinary: 2. inquisitorial.

In the ordinary case, the power is narrowed by the need of concurrence on the part of some person in the situation of plaintiff: in the case where it is inquisitorial, this limitation has no place—the Judge of his own accord commences the inquiry, or say the cause or suit, by an act purely his own and not at the solicitation of any other person. In the ordinary case, the procedure being criminal is in German law stiled accusatorial.[1]

The power in this case is rendered narrower and narrower as the description of the persons capable of giving commencement to the process is narrower and narrower.

So, in the case where a Jury is called in: the power of the Judge receives a further restriction by the necessity of the intervention of a Jury, and its previous concurrence to any judgment of condemnation which the Judge would be inclined to pronounce.

[1] This appears to be an allusion to procedure under Romano-canonical Law, which was practised in the Imperial courts of Germany.

PART I.
SECURITIES FOR MORAL APTITUDE

CHAPTER 2. APPROPRIATE MORAL APTITUDE. EXPOSITORY MATTER

§ 1. *Moral aptitude, what*

Considered with relation to the business here in question, moral aptitude is a negative quality: it is constituted by the absence, in so far as possible, of a certain propensity universal in human nature. This propensity in the breast of each individual is the propensity to sacrifice all other interests to that which at each moment appears to him to be his own preponderant interest: to obtain happiness for himself to whatsoever amount by so doing, he abstracts or withholds it from all other individuals.

Meantime no propensity, no desire, or at any rate no endeavour, can have place in any considerable force without some admixture of correspondent hope. Man will not expend his endeavour to obtain that of the attainment of which, in his view of it, no probability has place.[1] Thus it is that while the endeavour by manifest impossibility or improbability of success is absolutely prevented altogether, desire is kept down and weakened: the propensity exists but in the character of a lambent flame by which no combustion is ever produced.

This then is what is possible to be done, done by a form of government such as the desire of rendering the exercise of it conducive to the greatest happiness of the greatest number is capable of discovering and recommending for adoption. On the part of an individual, in whose instance [there existed] any expectation of being able to render the form of government conducive in the highest degree to his own greatest happiness at the expence of all other happinesses, no such desire could reasonably be looked for: no: at the hands of no other individual than one in whose eye, his situation considered, no such expectation could ever have had place.

In this case is the author of the present pages. On his part, to propose for adoption whatsoever is in each country most conducive to the greatest happiness of the greatest number requires no self-sacrifice.

[1] In the text, Bentham added at this point, '(Illustration)', but none appears to have been written.

To invest the ruler or rulers in chief in the political state in question with appropriate moral aptitude, and that in the highest degree, is therefore nothing more than this: namely to place them in such a situation as that while they have no prospect of being able to encrease each of them his own happiness by diminishing the happiness of the greatest number, they have each of them a prospect of giving encrease to his own happiness by giving encrease to the happiness of the greatest number—of encreasing the respect bestowed upon himself and the services of all sorts which his fellow countrymen and others are ready upon occasion to render to him, by means of and in return for the services in all shapes which he is continually occupied in rendering to them.[1]

Meantime, though self-regard, the desire in man to feel himself happy, is in every situation the predominant desire and propensity in human nature, neither is social regard, sympathetic regard, the desire to see others happy, less extensively inherent in it. To conceive either of the one as being in all breasts other than generally predominant, or the other as being from any breast altogether absent—are two opposite conceptions both of them erroneous, both of them, if consistently acted upon, pregnant with pernicious consequences. He who is not within himself conscious of the existence of any sympathetic regard in his own breast for the happiness of others is thereby destitute of one source of happiness, and that a very fruitful one. His situation may be compared with that of the individual in whom the sense of smell is wanting, or that desire on which the species depends for its continuance. Supposing the man in question destitute himself of all sympathetic regard, nothing is more natural than that he should deem the belief of the existence of it in others a misconception, and on the part of others the assertion of its existence an imposture. If in himself this affection be so weak as that for want of the habit of looking into his own mind he has never been conscious of it, his disposition to disbelieve the existence of it in others will be the same as in the case just mentioned.

With private life the present work has no immediate concern—only with public. If, taking life in the aggregate, both these opinions are erroneous, in public life at any rate that error which asserts the

[1] There is no text corresponding to the following marginal summary, which belongs here: 'Sources or elements of self-happiness thus obtainable by legislative draughtsmen and rulers: 1. Pleasure of sympathy: pleasure of seeing happy those whose agents they are. 2. Pleasure of power: pleasure of seeing great effects produced by the exercise of a man's inward powers. 3. Pleasure of reputation—pleasure from the thought of the respect and affection, thence the incalculable good offices and corresponding services, receivable upon occasion [from] the witnesses to the exercise thus given to such power.'

existence of the predominance of social regard in the breast of any public man in any such degree as shall engage him willingly to give up, for the sake of any quantity of happiness in all other breasts put together, any the smallest particle of his own happiness is in its practical consequences by far the most pernicious, productive of evil in the greatest quantity. In the framing of laws, suspicion can not possibly be carried to too high a pitch. No man ought to be presumed actually guilty to the purpose of judicial punishment: every man ought to be presumed disposed to be guilty and endeavouring to be guilty to the purpose of legislative enactment: every man, and most of all he who, having it most in his power to be guilty, and most assured of being guilty with impunity, has the strongest propensity to be guilty, and at the same time is most vehement in his assurance that in his breast no such propensity has place. In a state of society in which men, while they are suffering under depredation and under oppression in its other various shapes, have it in their power by any means to rid themselves of it, all the miseries they feel are the result of over-confidence: of a confidence which in the instance of every individual in which it is reposed—has in every such individual without exception at all times been sure to be misplaced. The most impudent quacks in medicine are modest in comparison of the quacks in politics. For not to speak of corruption, the quacks in medicine have not in their hands any such instruments of delusion as have the quacks in politics—the quack whose station is on a stage which is called a portable stage is sincerity itself in comparison of him whose [station][1] is on a seat called a throne. In that station, vice by the unchangeable nature of man is raised to the highest pitch, to a higher than that in which it can be found in any other station. Yet in that station, Vice stands forth and says, 'my name is Virtue': and from all stations with which it is surrounded that same unchangeable cause has secured a full chorus of indefatigable echoes vociferating in uninterrupted harmony.

By moral aptitude is therefore here meant but practical innoxiousness; and such innoxiousness not having any other cause than impotence, in the station of each functionary to establish this impotence, leaving to him at the same time the necessary power—to render him unable to do wrong, yet sufficiently able to do right, is the great difficulty, and ought to be the constant object and endeavour of whatsoever labour is employed in the field of legislation.

[1] MS 'seat'.

§ 2. *General Security: Removal of opposition of functionary's private interest to the universal interest—i.e. his share in ditto. Natural opposition shewn in Monarch's case. Consequent sinister sacrifice*

On the part of a ruling or other public functionary, appropriate moral aptitude has place in so far as, on every occasion on which his function is or ought to be exercised, the end to the accomplishment of which his endeavours are directed is the promotion of the universal interest, whatsoever may be the effect with regard to his own personal or any other particular interest.

In this state of things, supposing it realized, aptitude in the shape here in question is at its maximum.

Abstraction made of what may be done by laws and institutions to exclude or lessen it, the particular interest of the ruling class is in a state of natural and diametrical opposition to that of the whole people considered in the correspondent character of subjects.

Take for example the case of a single ruler—in one word a Monarch.

The greatest felicity of the greatest number of the people requires that the external instruments of felicity, whatsoever they may be, be shared by the whole number in a proportion as near to equality as is consistent with universal security, and with that abundance at each moment of time which is itself necessary in the character of a security for the permanency of universal subsistence.

On the other hand, the greatest felicity of the Monarch requires, or at least, what in practice comes to the same thing, is by him understood to require, that the aggregate mass of the several external instruments of felicity be in the largest possible proportion at his absolute disposal.

Thus then as between the Monarch on the one hand and the whole number of the members of the community in question on the other, a diametrical opposition of interests has place.

But, setting aside what change may have been made by social habits and political institutions, exactly such is the state of interests between every member of every community on the one part and every other member of the same community on the other.

The difference is—the Monarch has actually at his disposal, with a power more or less approaching to absolute, the aggregate mass of those same instruments: the power of employing them in the character of instruments of his own personal gratification and enjoyment: the individual, not.

The identification of rulers' interest with people's interest has place in so far as that same opposition is removed. A state of diametrical opposition being the natural state, except in so far as it may happen for it to be removed by social habits alone, only by means of laws and institutions can it be removed, and identity as between the one and the other of these same interests substituted to it.[1]

To bring to view the means which the nature of the case affords for the removal of that same opposition—for the substitution of this same identification—will be the business of the remainder of this part of the work.

In so far as, in the instance of the functionary in question, this identification fails to have place, the consequence is—on his part, in so far as depends on his endeavours, the sacrifice of the universal interest to his personal or other particular interest: say, for shortness, *the sinister sacrifice*.

§3. *Political corruption, what*

In the case of a functionary, corruption—political corruption, according to the common acceptation of the word, is understood to have place as often as by any act of his the sinister sacrifice has, with [his] consent and knowledge, and in pursuance of his endeavours, been effected.

In the case of this corruption, the evil produced by the sinister sacrifice made in consequence will be more or less permanent and irremovable, and thereby, the magnitude of the sacrifice being given, more or less great, according to the sort of relation borne to it by the state of the government, and the body of the laws and institutions framed by it. If the case be such that the sacrifice in question is repugnant to the object of the government and as such taken for an object of punishment and prohibition by the laws, evil has its seat in the mind of the individual, and by apt execution given to a particular amendment made in the appropriate part of the law, may be removed, and without any need of change in any respect in the form of the government. On the contrary, if so the case be that instead of being in a state of repugnancy, it is in a state of conformity to the object of the government, and is accordingly either positively established or left unprohibited or unpunishable by the body of the laws, especially if resistance be all along made by the government to any such endeavours as come to be made for the removal of it, the evil has its seat in the form of the government itself, nor can it in the nature of the

[1] A related fragment on this theme is at UC cxiv. 31 (15 June 1822).

case be removed, but by a change made in the form of government: namely by a substitution of the one form which has for its object the greatest happiness of the greatest number to the form of government which has for its object this same sinister sacrifice.

§4. *Sinister sacrifice exemplified. Difference, English State Chief and U.S. ditto*

Take an example. Scene lies (say) in England. Excise man's lawful pay, say £100 a year. In consideration of a present (*a bribe* in this case the language is) received [from] a manufacturer, [from][1] whose hands it is his business to cause the produce of his proportion of a tax upon the manufactory to be received on the account of the Government, the Exciseman has connived at a fraudulent operation or state of things by which the manufacturer has gained £100, the Government, which in this case is as much as to say the whole community, suffered a loss to that same amount. Bribe-giver or Corrupter, the manufacturer: bribe-taker, functionary corrupted, the Exciseman.

So much for the Exciseman, the functionary in the lowest stage of the department in question, in the lowest level in the scale of subordination.

Ascend now to the highest level. Take in hand the Monarch. Pay of the Chief of the State in the case of the Anglo-American United States, £5,000 a year. Whether there be in it or be not any thing of superfluity, [it] is at any rate sufficient. On no occasion has any demand for any addition been ever made: on no occasion has any public indication been given of preponderant evil in any individual shape as having been produced for want of an addition to such or such amount alledged to have been requisite. Pay of the Monarch, say £1,000,000 a year.[2] Intelligible and justifiable demand for any more than the abovementioned £5,000 a year, none ever brought to view or ever capable of being brought to view. Source of this pay, money exacted from the whole nation, unwilling contributors. Here to those same contributors, so much loss: and in a greater or less degree by all those who are capable of feeling it, the whole of the loss felt. This feeling being so much correspondent evil, it rests on all such as are disposed

[1] MS 'at'.

[2] The salary of the first President had been fixed at $25,000 per annum by an Act of Congress of 1789, and had been made permanent by an Act of 1793. This sum was the equivalent of about £5,000. The Civil List of England and Ireland in 1821 had amounted to over £1m. It provided, however, not only for the expenses of the Court but also for those of the civil government departments and legal offices.

and regard themselves as competent to the task of producing justification for this excess, to produce it.

No such justification being produced or producible, here then is amount [of] sinister sacrifice, sinister sacrifice annually and perpetually received, £995,000: amount [of] corruptive benefit extorted, so much. Party Corrupted and Corrupters, the Monarch and the several members of whom the two other branches of the supreme operative body—the supreme Legislature called the Parliament—composed. Act taken for the subject of a prohibition and efficient cause of punishment to the agent, none: punishable crime, none. Seat of the evil, the form of government itself: remedy, none but by substitution of a different form to that form: by the substitution of a form of government having for its object the greatest happiness of the greatest number to a form having for its view the greatest happiness of that one.

In proportion as the extent to which as above this sinister sacrifice with the correspondent corruption has place, in that same proportion is appropriate moral aptitude on the part of the supremely ruling functionaries taken in the aggregate diminished.

But as the investigation proceeds in taking in hand the several securities which the nature of the case affords for appropriate moral aptitude on the part of these same functionaries, it will in regard to each of these same several securities be respectively seen[1] either that it has no place at all, that no employment at all is given to it, or that the employment given to it is so inconsiderable, that in respect of appropriate moral aptitude in the aggregate, in so far as dependent on the use made of [it],[2] the general result may without material error stand expressed in these words—namely *appropriate moral aptitude minimized*.

§5. *Matter of corruption, what*

By the matter of corruption understand that, whatsoever it be, by the operation of which, on the mind of the individual in question, the corruptive effect—the sinister sacrifice—is produced. It is composed

[1] Bentham was referring specifically to the English government, as the marginal summary makes clear: 'Seen below, in regard to each of the several securities for [appropriate moral] aptitude, employment given to them under English Government either none or a minimum: thence on the whole, *Anglicé* appropriate moral aptitude minimized.' Bentham did not give this topic any detailed treatment beyond that in the fragments intended for 'Part III. England': see the Editorial Introduction, p. xxii above.

[2] MS 'them'.

of the aggregate of the external instruments of felicity, in so far as they are respectively at the disposal of the persons exercising in the nation in question the powers of government.

Into the composition of this matter may occasionally enter every object of human desire: enter, that is to say either immediately of itself, or unimmediately, through the intervention of some other by means of which it is procurable or receivable.

The objects of desire capable of thus operating require to be distinguished by being divided into two classes.

One is composed of those which must of necessity be at the disposal of government: these are, 1. power and 2. money: the other, of those which as will be seen need not nor ought to be at the disposal of government, but with one exception[a] will be found to have place to an extent more or less considerable, in the Official Establishment under all as yet existing governments. These are factitious dignity, *ease*, in the present case *undue ease*, and *vengeance*, in the present case *privileged vengeance*.

By privileged vengeance, understand the application of official power to the purpose of affording, for the benefit [of] the functionary or his associates, a gratification for the appetite of vengeance; by what cause so ever excited: a gratification such as is not within the reach of a member of the community at large.[1]

By *undue ease*, understand ease at the expence of official duty.[2]

§6. *Corruptive effect, how produced.* Anglicé, *Barrow-woman*

The manner in which it[3] is productive of the corruptive effect, namely the sinister sacrifice, is this: in the event of his performing, or according to his situation contributing to the mischievous effect—to the performance of the sinister sacrifice, the functionary in question receives or looks to receive the correspondent sinister profit: in the opposite event, not; of this profit, the contemplation constitutes the inducement, the temptation, the tempting and seductive motive, by the force of which his conduct is in this case determined, and the sinister act produced.

[a] Perhaps here and there among small Republics might be found a few others.[4]

---

[1] In the text, Bentham added at this point, 'See | |', but failed to provide any reference. For a discussion of vengeance see 'Constitutional Code Rationale', Ch. 3, §3, pp. 247–9 below.

[2] In the text, Bentham added at this point, 'See | |', but failed to provide any reference. For a discussion of ease see 'Constitutional Code Rationale', Ch. 3, §3, pp. 247–9 below.

[3] i.e. the matter of corruption.

[4] The exception Bentham had in mind was presumably the government of the United States of America.

To produce this corruptive effect in the mind and conduct of the thus corrupted functionary, it is not on any occasion necessary that any intercourse, either in the way of discourse or even in the way of purposed deportment, should have place between him and any individual by the contemplation of whose eventually expected agency the corruptive effect—the sinister sacrifice—is produced. All that is necessary is—in the two situations, namely that of the corrupting functionary and that of the functionary corrupted, that of the corrupter and that of the corruptee, two habitually corresponding lines of conduct: the one contributing to the sinister sacrifice in question in the way in question, the other placing within his reach the portion of the matter of corruption in the shape in question—in a word the sinister profit, upon which thereupon the corruptee lays his hand, and converts it into his own use.

Of this process, to be at once correct and, upon attentive inspection, clear, thus abstract must be any description given in words, but nothing can be more frequent, perfectly practical and familiar, than the exemplifications given of it. For the performance of it, on the part of the individual corrupted no extraordinary degree of intellectual aptitude—nor so much as the most ordinary human intelligence—is necessary: the degree of intellectual aptitude universally possessed by all domestic animals of an inferior degree is quite sufficient. In any one of the Streets of London, taking observation of the appointed time, behold the sort of commercial intercourse that has place between three parties—the cat's-meat barrow-woman, the householder and the cats. The hour arrived, the interesting vehicle makes its appearance, the householders and the cats repair to their respective doors: at each door, as the vehicle arrives along side of it, the householder sallies forth, pays the purchase money for the ration, and places it within the reach of the four-legged domestic functionary.[1] At a certain time of the day, or upon the hearing of a certain sound, the sound of the barrow, or upon the sight of that vehicle, its directrix and its contents, the watchful functionary, on making his[2] appearance at the door, has been in the habit of receiving his ration: no speech affording the assurance that, in the event of his making his

[1] Bentham deleted the following passage from the text at this point: 'On the mind of this useful functionary, whose office is no sinecure, true it is that no such sinister conduct the idea of which is involved in the import of the word corruption can with truth and justice be said to have place. But the purpose for which this example is produced is the shewing that to produce the requisite association betwixt conduct in a certain shape on the one side [and] conduct in a different but correspondent shape on the other, no verbal explanation, no verbal discourse, such as that the proof of which has been required for a man's conviction of the species of offence called bribery, is necessary.'

[2] MS alt. 'her'.

appearance on the spot, the ration will be placed within his reach has, unless by accident, ever been addressed to him, either by his employer or by his purveyor. Yet of his part of the contract, the performance has not been the less punctual, or the less effectual.[1]

Far be it from this pen to seek to degrade the ever vigilant and faithful functionary to a level with any such unfaithful ones.[2] All that is meant is—to afford proof and illustration of two positions: 1. that for the saddling a nation with the load of 800 millions of debt,[a] no higher degree of intellectual aptitude is necessary than that which is in the possession of every such quadruped: 2. that by contributing his share to the production of the correspondent mass of evil, neither King nor Lord, nor Honorable Gentleman, has as yet subjected himself to any greater danger of legal punishment, or of punishment in any shape, unless the exasperation of an injured nation may one day produce the effect of punishment, than the innoxious and useful quadruped subjects himself to by such his regular and altogether uncensurable attendance.

§7. *Parties concerned in the corruptive process*[3]

In the idea of political corruption is necessarily included the idea of two parties as being concerned in the corruptive process—a party

[a] For alledged amounts of Debt, interest, and standing army, absolute and comparative, see Foot's speech at Maidstone, as per Morng. Chron., 12 June 1822.[4]

---

[1] There is no text corresponding to the following marginal summary, which belongs here: 'Thus in Honorable House [i.e. the House of Commons]: Minister, barrow-woman; lucrative Office, Cat's-meat; Honorable Gentleman, Cat. Honorable Gentleman speaks or votes, nomination to the Office for Gentleman or his friend drops into his pocket. Speak or vote on that side never, Office received never. As to intercourse: for the conveyance of Office appointed into voting functionary's pocket, intercourse by words or other general instruments of discourse is no more necessary between the one and the [other] than between Barrow-woman and cat.'

[2] MS del. 'to a level with an English King or Member of the House of which the characteristic appellation is Honorable'.

[3] Earlier drafts of this and the following section are at UC cxiv. 27–8 (13 June 1822), cxiv. 29 (16 June 1822) and cxiv. 30 (16 June 1822).

[4] The *Morning Chronicle* of 12 June 1822 reported a 'Meeting of the Freeholders of the County of Kent' held at Maidstone on the previous day 'to consider of a Petition to Parliament on the Distressed State of the Country, and the Defective Representation of the People'. Though a Mr. Foote (probably Robert Foote, an unsuccessful candidate at the Canterbury parliamentary election of 1820) proposed the petition, the figures referred to by Bentham were given by a Mr. Rider (probably Thomas Rider, MP for Kent 1831–2 and West Kent 1832–5). Rider stated that in 1792 the revenue of the country had been £19m., and the armed forces had consisted of 86,000 men with a maintenance charge of £2.3m., while at that moment these figures had increased to £71m., 243,000 men and £8.9m. respectively. The comparative amounts of national debt were not mentioned, though according to the *Finance Accounts for year ended 5 January 1822*, the total stood at over £802m.

whose situation disposes him to be a corrupter, say a corrupter, and a party whose situation exposes him to be corrupted, say a party corrupted or corruptee: an *agent* in the process of corruption, and a *patient*. The corrupter is the party who, being intent on the keeping up for his own benefit the sinister sacrifice, applies his endeavours to the party corruptible for the purpose of securing his cooperation.

Functionaries considered as exposed to corruption may be in the first place distinguished into functionaries whose place is in the highest rank in the scale of subordination, and functionaries whose place is in any inferior rank. In respect of the importance of its effects, in comparison of corruption on the part of functionaries of the highest rank, the utmost evil producible by functionaries in any subordinate rank is so inconsiderable that for the present it may be put out of consideration and put aside.

§8. *Corruption in rulers, peculiar to Representative Government*

Two parties being supposed necessary, corruption in the highest rank supposes and requires for its existence a division of the power of government in that rank: in one place a corrupter, in another place a corruptee.

In an absolute Monarchy, called also a pure one, in the highest rank either corruption has no place, or the same individual, the Monarch, is *corrupter* and *corruptee*. No person besides himself being in that same highest rank, he performs the sinister sacrifice with his own hands and without need of co-operators, in any other capacity than that of blind instruments.

The case in which alone it has place is that in which by delegates of theirs in the character of their representatives, having the right as representatives of the people a share in the supreme operative power, they[1] in this way exercise, with relation to that mass of supreme operative power, the correspondent constitutive power. These possessors of supreme operative power may be either sole possessors of it or sharers in it in conjunction with some other functionary or functionaries. In the case of an ordinary mixt Monarchy, supposing that in so far as in the mixture Democracy is included, a functionary with whom they share it is the Monarch.

In no form of government,[2] to this bad purpose any more than to any good one, can profit in any shape be conveyed for a continuance

[1] i.e. the people.

[2] Bentham commented at this point, 'Note making a salvo in the case of a small Democracy', but none appears to have been written.

into individual hands otherwise than through the intervention of a Supreme Executive, doing or professing to do the will of the Supreme Legislative. When in the highest sphere of government, for the purpose of the sinister sacrifice, the game of corruption is carried on, it is by the hands of the Chief of the Executive Department. In a Monarchy, he is the Monarch, the Chief of the State to whom this subordinate Office also belongs in addition to whatsoever share it happens to him to possess in the supreme operative, commonly stiled the legislative. In a representative democracy, he is also the Chief of the State, by whatsoever appellative distinguished, such as President, Supreme Director, Protector or any other.

In either of these cases there exists a functionary by who[m], to this purpose without his being recognized, not the less effectually is exercised a function which may be termed that of Corrupter General. For in his hands, as will be seen from the very necessity of the case, must be the disposal of a multitude of offices: in a greater or less degree these offices can not but be in the eyes of the members of the community, in an indefinite multitude, objects of general desire. Here then we have a functionary operating, whether he will or no, in the character of Corrupter General: and on the other part, persons in indefinite number, functionaries of all sorts included, occupying the situation of persons exposed to corruption, exposed to the being his *corruptees*.

In this state of things the Corrupter General sees before him two different sets of eventual corruptees: 1. the members of the Representative body, constituting part and parcel of the supreme operative power; 2. the members of the supreme constitutive body—those members of the community in whose hands is the supreme constitutive power with reference to those same representatives who acknowledge them.

It is by the representatives alone, in contradiction to their constituents, that the particular arrangements are continued or set on foot by which, through the medium of the Executive department, the sinister sacrifice is carried on: by constituents as such no part can be taken in it. But on the will and agency of these same constituents will, in a greater or less degree, depend the composition of the body of these representatives and to this, as to other purposes, the conduct of the several members. To their situation it belongs to provide that which is at once chief matter of corruption and matter of sinister sacrifice: to the Executive Chief to make application and distribution of it, among the members of the Representative body, and his and their connections.

Here then we have Corrupter General, one; the Chief of the State:

in a mixt Monarchy, the Monarch, in a Representative Democracy, the President: eventual Corruptees, two sets: corruptible on their own account, the Representatives of the People: corruptible for the purpose of extending the corruption to the Representatives of the people, the people themselves in different constitutive bodies, the people themselves in their character of constituents with reference to these same sharers in the supreme operative power—their Representatives.

§9. *Manner in which corruption operates. Antiseptics, the Securities for appropriate moral aptitude*

In this state of things, the process of corruption as between the Chief Executive of the State in his situation of Corrupter General, and the Representatives of the people in their situation of eventual Corruptees, carries itself on of itself, without any the smallest need of perceptible operation in either of those two situations. In the gift of the Corrupter General the Offices in question—objects of general desire—are, and by the Representatives of the people, seen to be: that in their own hands, or if that be prevented by law—in the hands of other persons whose condition [is] more or less intimately connected with theirs, they being men, it is of course their wish to see these same Offices lodged to the greatest amount, in respect of number and value together, possible. The Corrupter General being a man, to know that he is so is to know that it can not but be his wish that these good things, which being at his disposal are in the above indirect way capable of being disposed of to his own profit and in some instances even to as great profit as if they were his, should in respect of number and value be accumulated to the greatest amount possible: moreover, throughout every other part of his authority, by noting the exercise actually made of it on all past occasions, they learn without much exposure to error the exercise which it would be most agreable to him to give to it in future—in a word, what without any the least need of explanation on the part of either party is sufficiently known to each, that the probability of his seeing that to have place which would be most agreable to himself is as is the degree in which he contributes to the causing that to have place which would be most agreable to the other. But the thing which to men in neither situation, so long as men are men, can fail to be generally agreable, is to see, in so far as benefit in any shape results to himself from the performance of it, the performance of the sinister sacrifice.

Thus it is that exposure to corruption is of the very essence of the representative system. It is of the very essence of a Representative Democracy. It is of the very essence of a mixt Monarchy having in its mixture any other body, and in particular a body of Representatives of the people. To found, to establish, any such mixt Monarchy is therefore to establish Corruption—to establish it, and even by law: to establish any such Representative Democracy is to establish Corruption, to establish it even by law: in this respect, between a Representative Democracy and a mixt Monarchy with a Representative body in it there is no difference.

Between the two Governments, not then in that point lies the difference: it lies in this: namely, that in a Representative Democracy arrangements are capable [of being] made, and accordingly have actually been made, by which the tendency to corruption has been prevented from being, at least to any degree worth considering, carried into effect: and the sinister sacrifice, to any considerable [degree], prevented from taking place: whereas in a mixt Monarchy, by no arrangements can that tendency be prevented from being carried into effect: by no arrangements can that tendency be prevented from being continually on the encrease: by no arrangements can the effect itself be prevented from being continually on the encrease: on the encrease, untill either all difference in effect between the mixt Monarchy and an absolute one be obliterated, or in consequence of the suffering produced by the degree to which the sinister sacrifice has been carried, the people be to such a degree exasperated as to rise and abolish the mixt Monarchy, now become in effect a pure one, and set up another in the stead of it.

CHAPTER 3. APPROPRIATE MORAL APTITUDE ON THE PART OF FUNCTIONARIES. EFFICIENT CAUSES OF IT—SECURITIES, OR MEANS OF SECURITY, FOR ITS EXISTENCE[1]

§ 1. *Need of such Securities—the opposite inaptitude natural and universal*

The possessors of the power in question—these men whosoever they are, are men: in them therefore can not but be found whatsoever propensities are common to human nature.

In the breast of every sensitive being, the general predominance of self-preference is prevalent universally: for proof take the existence of the species: look, and you will see, that upon such predominance the species is absolutely dependent for its existence.[2]

By *self-preference*, understand the pursuit of a man's own interest at the expence of all other interests put together: by *his own interest*, understand that which at the moment of action, presents itself to a man as being his interest:[3] at the expence of all other interests, and, as far as appears necessary, to the sacrifice of all such other interests. In the situation of a public functionary, he being, in respect of whatsoever power he has, a trustee for the public, such sacrifice may for shortness be termed the sinister sacrifice. Note that in any such situation, natural as it is, its being so does not render it the less pernicious: all the skill and all the exertion that the nature of the case admitts of for the diminution and if possible for the compleat prevention of it, can never be excessive.

§ 2. *Appropriate Securities which the nature of the case admitts of—their mutual relations*

The problem here is—how to effect and secure the prevention of the sinister sacrifice by reducing the natural opposition of the interests of operative functionaries to those of the other Members of the

[1] Fragments discussing a similar theme are at UC cxiii. 63–4 (12 May 1822) and cxiii. 72–3 (20 May 1822).

[2] In the margin, Bentham commented at this point: 'Note in proof of this, put on another page'. For such a discussion see 'Constitutional Code Rationale', Ch. 1, § 2, pp. 233–4 below.

[3] In the margin, Bentham commented at this point, 'Note in illustration, on another page', but none appears to have been written.

community, including the possessors of the constitutive power, constituents of these same operative function[aries].[1]

For the solution of this problem, note in the first place that to produce this effect in the situation of the supremely operative functionaries is of course to produce this same effect in the respective situations of all their several subordinates.

The situation of those whose place is highest in the scale of subordination is therefore the only one which on this occasion and for this purpose requires to be spoken of.

The means or arrangements applicable to this purpose may in the first place [be] divided and distinguished into direct and indirect. By the direct means, understand those means which bear in a direct manner upon the force in question, tending in so many various ways to lessen the amount of it. These are those means the design and tendency of which is to produce the following effects: 1. Minimization of the aggregate mass of power lodged in the hands of the functionaries in question—say, Minimization of power. 2. In particular, minimization of the quantity of public money placed or left at their disposal—say, minimization of government money. 3. More particularly still, minimization of the quantity of government money applied to the purpose of being employed in the character of pay for the purpose of obtaining service at men's hands in the situation of public functionaries—say, Minimization of official pay. 4. Exclusion of factitious dignity: namely as being a sort of substitute to official pay but essentially unapt for any such purpose, and as well as in every point of view pernicious, pregnant with unmixt evil in various shapes. Say, Exclusion of factitious Dignity.

By the indirect means, understand those by which a counterforce—the force of another class—is employed to the same purpose: brought into action in the view of its opposing itself to the power of the trustees in question in the event of their engaging on any occasion in the sinister sacrifice, and thereby acting in breach of such their trust. These are: 1. Maximization of their legal responsibility, in so far as the nature of the case, that is to say the height of their situation and the magnitude of their power, admitts of: say, Maximization of their legal responsibility. 2. Maximizing moral responsibility on their part: responsible to men in general, and to their Constituents in particular, in the character of Members of the Public Opinion Tribunal, having for its function the application of the force of the popular or moral sanction. Say, Maximization of their moral responsibility.

[1] In the marginal summary, Bentham posed the question in a different manner: 'Problem—the sinister sacrifice being the universal object of all operatives, how prevent it? General answer—render the people at large their constituents.'

In addition to the power of these possessors of the supreme Operative power, there being no other power in the state but that of the possessors of the supreme Constitutive power, their Constituents, this last it is evident is the only counterforce which the nature of the case admitts of. In the one instance the counterforce is applied to the purpose of eventual punishment in a determinate shape: in the other case to no other use, to no other purpose, than that of disrepute, loss of more or less of that respect, the abstraction of which is the result of each man's free agency, and a process of which, though incapable of being brought to view in any determinate shape, the effect is not to the sufferer the less sensible. In what way these several effects are producible will be seen in its place.

By the mention here made of the popular or moral sanction, the idea of its generally supposed Colleague, the religious sanction, can scarce fail to be called up into the minds of readers. It belongs not however to this place. So far from being a counterforce operating in protection of the universal interest, and accordingly in obstruction of the sinister sacrifice, the making of which is the natural and necessary object of endeavour to all public functionaries, what is called *religion*, and thence the force of the religious sanction, has in all governments by which it has been employed, been employed with more or less energy and success, as a force in aid—a main instrument—of the sinister sacrifice. And of all existing governments, there is but one in which in aid of government employment has not been given to it.[1]

[1] In the text, Bentham commented at this point: 'See further on.' He did not in fact go on to discuss the topic of the religious sanction in 'Economy as applied to Office', but did so in 'Constitutional Code Rationale', Ch. 7, pp. 325–31 below. The exception referred to by Bentham was the government of the United States of America, the First Amendment to the Constitution passed in 1791 declaring that 'Congress shall make no law respecting an establishment of religion'.

CHAPTER 4. FIRST SECURITY FOR THE EXISTENCE OF APPROPRIATE MORAL APTITUDE IN THE BREAST OF A PUBLIC FUNCTIONARY IN THE HIGHEST AND OTHER GRADES—REDUCING TO ITS LOWEST DIMENSIONS THE QUANTITY OF POWER IN HIS HANDS. SAY, MINIMIZATION OF POWER: VIZ. IN ALL GRADES, BUT MORE ESPECIALLY THE HIGHEST[1]

§ 1. *Power minimized in highest grades by dislocability, punibility*

Power in a certain quantity and in certain shapes is of the essence of the situation: it is the instrument and the only instrument which he who is placed in that situation has to work with. The points therefore to be ascertained are—in what shapes in each class and rank of Offices it is capable of being reduced or kept low or withholden altogether, without prejudice to the end in view—in what shapes, and in each shape by what course, and by what means.

Power, in the sense that belongs to the present subject—power is the power of disposing of certain things and certain services of certain persons with a view to a certain end: under things, money being included: the object and problem is so to order matters that in each situation having power to make application of the things and human services in question to the benefit of the whole community or a certain portion of it according to the department to which the office of the functionary belongs, he should at the same time not have power to dispose of it to his own benefit exclusively or to the benefit of particular individuals connected with him by this or that special line of interest or sympathy.

Let us now see in what shapes power must be conceded, and in that situation which occupies the highest grade maximized, and in what other shapes without prejudice to the end in view it may be, and therefore ought to be, withholden altogether or minimized.

One power presents itself at first view—one power which can not consistently with the only right and proper end experience diminution. This is the power of the people at large in their quality of possessors of the supreme constitutive power: of the constitutive power with reference to the possessors of the supreme operative power. It is the interest of all that in this shape the power of all be as great as possible.

[1] Other drafts of this chapter are at UC cxiii. 38 (24 May 1822), cxiii. 42–3 (18 June 1822) and cxiii. 19–24, 18 (26–7 June 1822). A related fragment is at UC cxiii. 37 (14 May 1822).

Next below this level stands that of the possessors of the supreme operative power.

In this case, an obvious mode and obviously apt mode is subordination: locating the functionaries of this class in a station inferior in the scale of subordination to that of the possessors of the correspondent constitutive power as above.

By the possessors of the correspondent constitutive power, these are by the supposition located. By these same hands—or they could not in any way be subject to them—it is necessary that they should be liable to be dislocated. For without the power of dislocation, the subjection, the subordination, would be but nominal: to be a trustee for the people and to be an unfaithful one would be one and the same thing.

Supposing them not in the same hand, the power of dislocation would towards the supposed end be of the two the most efficient. A servant whom, whatsoever be his behaviour towards you, it has been out of your power to dismiss is by that very thing made your master: your master in reality, your servant only in name. So you have but the power of dismissing him, a servant chosen though it be by an adversary will be less annoying to you than in the other case a servant chosen by yourself may be.

Q. The possessor or possessors of the supreme operative power being thus dislocable as well as located by the people in their quality of possessors of the supreme [constitutive][1] power, at what times shall the dislocation be made capable of being effected? at any time or only at stated times? and on the supposition of the supreme operative power being fractionized, the members each at a different time or all at the same time?

A. At stated times: provided they be short ones.

Reason 1. If the dislocation were capable of being performed at any time, two opposite inconveniences might be capable of being the result: on the part of constituents, constant supineness, indifference, negligence: and thence on the part of representatives, virtual independence in relation to these same constituents: or on the part of constituents, uninterrupted vigilance. But if all were at all times occupied in watching with uninterrupted and unabated vigilance over the conduct of these their agents, none would have time sufficient for the watching each of them over his own affairs, amongst other things for providing the means of subsistence for the joint use of themselves and these their agents.[2]

Reason the 2. Moreover, if the dislocation were equally capable of

[1] MS 'constituted'.

[2] In the marginal summary, Bentham commented: 'Addend. Effective power engrossed by the constantly vigilant few.'

being made at all times, there would be no one time at which the attention of all would be drawn to this same subject, as is the case where stated times are appointed for the joint consideration of all whether it shall have place.

Reason the 3d. If stated times were not appointed, every proposition brought forward by a member of the constitutive body for the dislocation of a member of the operative body would be regarded as an act of hostility, and as such excite resentment in the breasts of his friends, in a word of all persons thinking well of him, whereas when for the consideration of this subject a stated time is appointed by law without regard had to any individual more than another, no resentment is excited in any breast, there being in no breast any efficient cause for it.

The Members sharing in the supreme operative body should as such be in a certain way subordinate to the functionaries sharing in the supreme constitutive power: namely by subjection to punitive power—the punishment to be administered not by the constitutive functionaries themselves, but by functionaries located by them for that purpose: namely by the members of the next supremely operative body, located as they will be of course by their respective bodies of constituents.

Q. Subordination [by] subjection to dislocative power, would it not suffice in this case without the addition of subordination by subjection to power of punition? and if not, why not?

A. No. On the supposition of his being free from all apprehension of punishment in any other shape, [there is] not a Member in whose instance his being induced by the matter of corruptive influence to concurr in measures productive of the sinister sacrifice to an indefinite extent would in any degree be either extraordinary [or] unprecedented. Members, say 300: time during which the office is occupied by him, one year: salary allowed to each for his attendance during that time, £300: bribe sufficient to engage each one out of a majority, he risking thereby the loss of his situation for the remainder of the year, to concurr in a breach of trust profitable to the giver of the bribe, say £500: majority sufficient to secure the consummation of the breach of trust, say 200: £500 multiplied by 200 makes £100,000.

The corrupter might be either the agent of a foreign power, or the Chief Executive functionary of the state in question. In this last case it would be given in the shape of lucrative Offices.

To accomplish the purpose as effectually as if the bribes were given to the Members themselves, they might be given to their respective relatives, dependents, and other known connections. For any one act of this sort taken by itself, punishment could not in any instance be employed with advantage. But, by the majority of a body of this sort during its year's continuance in Office, supposing a course of conduct to a certain degree adverse to the universal interest pursued, and in the same course of time Offices in a certain number and value conferred, on this supposition a general scrutiny might be made, and from the mischievousness of the proceeding, coupled with the notorious or discoverable connections of the authors, sufficient ground for punishment might peradventure be extracted.[1]

As a security for moral aptitude on the part of all operative functionaries other than those by whom the supreme operative power is exercised, it is necessary that the functionary or functionaries by whom the supreme Executive power is exercised be in all the modes of subordination subordinate to those by whom the Office of legislative functionary in the highest grade is filled. Say, the Executive functionary or functionaries of the highest grade are in all modes of subordination subordinate to the legislative, viz.

1. by subjection to power of dislocation:
2. by subjection to power of punishment judicially exercised:
3. by subjection to power of prevention applied to his acts:
4. by subjection to power of sistition[2] applied to his acts:
5. by subjection to power of cessation applied to his instruments: to written instruments by the issuing of which his power is exercised.

Reasons in the case of the Executive functionary, supposing but one functionary in that office.

But for this subordination, the Executive functionary would have a negative upon all acts of the Legislative body in so far as their receiving execution and effect depended upon his concurrence and cooperation. Every act by which the universal interest were endeavoured to be promoted at the expence of any particular and sinister interest might be, and of course would be, stopt.

By means of the Offices at his disposal, he would have it in his power to corrupt the Members of the supreme legislative to an indefinite and ever-encreasing number, as below, and thus in partnership with them transform the government into a Monarchico-Aristocratical Despotism.

The possessor of the supreme Executive power should be

[1] Bentham noted at this point: 'Reference to the case of Spain, Anno 1822.' Bentham perhaps had in mind two separate proposals which had been defeated in the Cortes: the first of 13 February 1822 would have prevented deputies from accepting any office, pension or honour for a period of two years after each session, the second of 12 March 1822 any office of royal provision for a period of one year.

[2] Bentham defined sistition as 'execution-staying' in *Constitutional Code*, I (*CW*), Ch. IX, §24, Art. 5, p. 418.

subordinate to the possessors of the supreme operative power, and this not only by subjection to dislocative power, but by subjection to punitive power at their hands.

Q. Subordination by subjection to dislocative power would it not suffice without the addition of subjection to punitive power in this case? and if not, why not?

A. No. If he were free from apprehension of punishment in any other shape, if the value of the bribe received or expected by him for the breach of trust exceeded in his eyes the net value of his office—power, salary, patronage and all other perquisites put together—an inducement adequate to the production of such breach of trust might without difficulty present itself. For example, President's salary, say £5,000 a year: years of continuance in office, 4: total value at the utmost, not so much as £20,000, patronage excluded. Impunity suppose certain, £50,000 or less might without any extravagant supposition suffice to produce the breach of trust.

Scarcely is there that imaginable evil that it might not be in his power to bring down upon the state.

For the encrease of his own particular share of power, he might, in confederacy with a set of dependents and other adherents provided by him for that purpose, [engage][1] in the subversion of the Constitution and the transforming it from a representative democracy, a democracy acting by delegation, into an absolute Monarchy.

By means of the matter of corruption administered to him, he might be engaged by a foreign enemy purposely to diminish in all manner of ways the defensive power in the hands of his own state, or to plunge it into war without necessity or justification.[a] In no misdeed of this sort is there any thing at all extraordinary or unprecedented: any thing but what should at all times be regarded as probable and provided against.

The Members of the supreme operative[2] body are dislocable at any time by the Supreme Executive functionary: their immediate successors being thereupon located as if the dislocation had been effected not by human will but by time.

[a] George 3 the war with Spain commenced for Droits of Admiralty.[3]

[1] MS 'employing'. The emendation is supported by the marginal summary.

[2] MS alt. 'ordinative'.

[3] Bentham believed that a British monarch, in this case George III (1738–1820), King of Great Britain and Ireland from 1760, had an incentive to instigate war because of the way in which Prize Law was administered. Hostilities between Britain and Spain commenced in October 1804 with the capture of a Spanish treasure fleet by British frigates, but war was not formally declared until January 1805. In the meantime a large number of Spanish vessels were taken and later condemned by the Prize Courts as droits of the Crown (not droits of Admiralty), the proceeds being paid directly to the Crown. For a fuller explanation of the question of droits see pp. 257–8n below.

But for this, they might substitute to the form of government in question an aristocratical government permanent in their own persons and hereditary in the persons of their natural descendants.

True it is, that supposing the Chief Executive functionary in a league with them, he could not reasonably be expected to be very prompt or inclined to give this exercise to his power. In this case, the only means of redress would be in petitions, petitions such as the Citizens at large, whether in their quality of simple inhabitants, or in that of Constituents, sharers in the supreme Constitutive power, would naturally be disposed to pour in, and thus hold out to his view a contest tending to a revolution, in the progress of which he might become a sufferer to an indefinite amount.

Q. In this sort of mutual subjection as between the two authorities, the possessor of the Supreme Executive power and the possessors of the Supreme Operative power, is there not a certain inconsistency and mutual incompatibility?—the possessor of the Supreme Executive power being liable to be dislocated by the possessors of the Supreme Operative power as also punished by them, and the possessors of the Supreme Operative power at the same time liable to be dislocated by the possessor of the Supreme Executive power?

A. No. In both cases one and the same effect would be produced—an appeal ultimately made to the people at large in their character of possessors of the supreme Constitutive power. By them, if in their opinion, by the dislocation made of the supreme Executive functionary by the supreme Operative function[aries], the universal interest had to a certain amount suffered or been in danger of suffering detriment—by them, namely by the hands of a new set of Representatives located by them in that view, the supposed unfaithful authors of the dislocation would have to be punished. So by them again, if in their opinion, by the dislocation made of the supreme Operative functionaries by the supreme Executive ditto, the universal interest had to a certain amount suffered or been in danger of suffering—by them, by the ministry of their ensuing set of Representatives, the supposed unfaithful author of the dislocation would have to be punished. The people at large are, as their interest and happiness requires, the principals on whose will the ultimate result depends: the other authorities being in this as in other cases but their instruments. Without any thing like inconsistency or incongruity, by the same master, his servants may, in any numbers, on any number of occasions, be occupied in the doing of his will each of them on the rest, and maintaining such authority as he has over them.[1]

[1] At the end of this section, Bentham made the following note (see UC cxiii. 96, 20 May 1822): 'To Supreme Executive, location and dislocation of: 1. Finance Director—out of tried

§ 2. *Second mode of diminution or reduction or substraction as applied [to] power in the highest grade in the office of supreme operative functionary, dividing the power into shares, or fractional parts, allotted to different individuals or bodies or individuals and bodies*[1]

Q. Of such fractionization, what is the necessity or use?

If power, in this shape and magnitude, were the whole of it in the hands of a single individual, the counterforce applied to it by the constitutive power lodged in the hands of all the members of the community would be plainly insufficient. Possessor of absolute power for and during one whole year, it would not be difficult for a man to be so again the next: whatever had been the cause of his being so just before the first year, the same cause would with encreased force be in operation for the next: it would again be still easier the next to that, and so on till the chances against his ceasing to be so would be next to nothing.

Stronger and stronger every year would be the *vis inertiae* operating in support of it.

In the case of this grade, in addition to this primary reason comes another. If the supreme operative power were in an undivided, an unfractionalized state (and the community numerous enough to defend itself against the neighbouring ones), the constitutive power being at the same time shared—as above by all who for their well-being were dependent upon the exercise given to the supreme operative power thus created and conferred by the aggregate number of them, the smallness of the force and value of each share, added to the labour, expence and consumption of time necessary to the exercise of it by the whole multitude at the same time and place, would be apt to exclude them in a large proportion from the exercise of it: the power would be nominally and apparently in all, really and effectively only in a small portion of them, namely those who were nearest to the place of election, those who were most remote being thus deprived of this their security and placed in this respect under the uncontrolled dominion of the rest.

Thus in addition to annuality of election, we have the supreme operative office shared among a multitude of individuals, each individual receiving his share from the hands of a separate set of constituents; a member of the supreme operative assembly thus

Candidates. 2. Land-Force Director General and Local—out of tried Candidates. 3. Sea-Force Director—out of tried Candidates. 4. Foreign Relations Functionaries—out of Candidates bidding for the Pay. 5. Justice Director—subject to Appeal to Legislature.'

[1] The first mode is presumably subjection by dislocability and punibility, dealt with in § 1 above.

formed being allotted to each one of a number of districts into which for this purpose the whole territory has been divided: one member, placed in that assembly by a correspondent division of the members of the whole community in character of sharers in the supreme constitutive power—in one word, *constituents*.

§3. *Third mode of diminution or reduction considered as applicable to operative power in this grade, limitation in respect of extent as applied to the field of operation, analogous to limitation of extent as applied to the field of judicature in the subordinate grades*

To this head belongs the distinction between the Constitutional branch of government on the one part, and the penal and civil together on the other part: the Constitutional branch with one set of functionaries to exercise it, and the penal and civil together with another set of functionaries to exercise them. Supposing two or more such sets of supremely operating functionaries, whatsoever portion is given to each is so much taken from the other.

Of reduction as applied in this instance, the usefulness—relation being had to the greatest happiness of the greatest number—is not quite so clear as it is in the use made of it in those other instances and in those which will follow.[1]

Of the geographical, the material field of power, the division is easy, and capable of being cleared of ambiguity in every shape. Not equally so, the division of the ideal field—the logical: especially when it is considered that in extent it must be all-comprehensive.[2]

[1] Bentham did not discuss any further modes of diminution of power.

[2] A passage consisting of two sheets of MS (UC cxiii. 100–1) has been excluded from the text at this point. Neither the sense of the passage nor its relationship to the argument in the rest of the section is altogether clear. Since it was evidently intended by Bentham to form part of this sequence and has not been superseded, it is reproduced here: 'To the usefulness of this mode of reduction applies at the outset this question. Whichsoever of the two branches be the most important, to the purpose of locating the operative functionaries invested with this branch you provide the most apt set of constitutive functionaries that the nature of government affords: for the other branch to what end then look out for a different set of constitutive functionaries? being a different set they will not be in so high a degree apt: for two different ones both apt in exactly the same degree, the nature of the case does not admitt of.

'To this objection, the answer which the nature of the case admitts of is this. Of the two branches, the constitutional is by far the most important: why? because upon the texture given to the constitutional branch it depends, who and by whom located shall at all times be the individuals by whom the supreme operative power shall be exercised. The supreme operative power is indeed the only power of the two the exercise of which, whether in respect of good or evil, is felt: the only one from the exercise of which evil and good immediately flow: flow as immediate offspring from parent, as effects from their proximate causes. Still however it is the constitutional branch that is the most important of the two as being that on which the other depends for all its qualities and all its effects, as an effect upon its proximate cause. Having given to one body the penal and civil branch alone, to another body the constitutional branch

The evils liable in this case to be produced may be reduced under three heads.

1. For the possession of one of the two branches of supreme power, a set of functionaries placed by a set of constitutive functionaries not so apt as the aptest that might have been chosen (namely the other set) for this purpose.

2. The clashing of authorities liable to be produced by the necessity of demarcation in a case where clear demarcation free from all obscurity and ambiguity is so difficult to be made: clashing of authorities, thence on one side or on both, persuasion or suspicion of usurpation and injustice: the two sets of functionaries in a state of contest with each other, and the other members of the community, their respective constituents, thus divided likewise into parties.

3. Complication—more than necessary complication—on the part of the whole body of laws taken together: complication thence untransparency: want of transparency, thence lurking places for sinister design and consequent endeavour for and accomplishment [of] sacrifice of universal to particular interest.

So many real or supposed evils as above, so many heads of objection.

But to these objections, answer is not altogether wanting.

As to the inferiority of aptitude as between one set of constituents and another, the utmost evil capable of resulting, or at least likely to result, from it may be rather ideal than real: possible without being actual or probable: so nearly equal in point of appropriate aptitude might the two sets be constituted.

Thus in the Anglo-American United States. States by this time four and twenty:[1] in all of them, sets of constituents and operatives more or less different. Yet in no one of all these instances the state of government with reference to the greatest happiness of the greatest

alone, let the one that has the penal and civil branch begin to operate, it may indeed produce preponderant good to a vast extent: it may produce preponderant evil to a vast extent: still however if in addition to this body there be another in which is vested a mass of constitutional power such as to enable them to destroy or amend the organization of the penal and civil branch of supremely operative power, here is a remedy which otherwise would not have place.

'When the stated time for election returned, true it is that, if, in the effects produced by the functionaries in question, evil in the judgment of their respective sets of constituents preponderated, the supposed unapt set of operators might by non-reelection be dislocated, and others regarded as more apt substituted. Still however there would not in this case have place a set of supremely operative functionaries to whom the supremely important branch in question—the constitutional, had been a special and exclusive object of study and care: for want of such special study and care, to the unapt set of functionaries by whom the mass of preponderant evil in question had been done, or by whom more evil than necessary, or not so much good as might have been done, had been done, might succeed a second set of functionaries more unapt than the first.'

[1] Missouri was the twenty-fourth state to be admitted to the Union on 10 August 1821.

number (the slave part of the population always excepted) in any remarkably or clearly evidenced degree better or worse than another: the good conduct of the operative functionaries in those which have the most apt set of constituents serving as an example to, and check upon misconduct on the part of, the others.

As to lines of demarcation, note that as in every, in that confederacy of United States, such lines are unavoidable—a circumstance by which, in the case of that sort of compounded government compared with an uncompounded one, no inconsiderable disadvantage is produced. But forasmuch as in the case in question such lines of demarcation are unavoidable, thence it is that the minds of men in general are universally and necessarily and constantly turned to them: and from this habit of close attention, penetration and clearness of conception and expression [are][1] rendered general, and mental power kept on foot adequate to the mastery of the difficulty.

But the most satisfactory answer of all is—that here, whatsoever clashing of opinions there may be, there is little or no clashing of interests: and thence, whatsoever may be the determination of the majority is by the minority submitted to without heartburning or repugnance.

In this particular thus does this case of logical demarcation stand so happily distinguished from the like case as applied in almost all governments to judicatories. In this constitutional case there is nothing more than a difference of opinion: all interests that are in existence[?] being the same and the only question, the only source and mode of division and dissention, being a difference of opinion concerning the construction, the interpretation that is most apt with reference to this or that phrase that has been employed. But in the case of judicature, jurisdiction being distinguished from jurisdiction by logical, or say metaphysical, lines of demarcation, the difference between one judicatory and another judicatory is produced by a clashing of interests—by a competition and contest of which the objects are power and money. In the one case, mutual sincerity, mutual candour and mutual forbearance may be expected: in the other case, whatsoever may have been expected, no such virtuous affection has ever been demonstrated—by nothing but impotence has acquiescence been ever produced. At the hands of the professors of sincerity, on what ground can sincerity be ever looked for? Look for sincerity in a lawyer? look for love of justice in a lawyer? Look for moderation in concupiscence? Look in a bulrush for a knot.[2]

[1] MS 'is'.

[2] An allusion to Plautus, *Menaechmi*, II. i. 22, 'In scirpo nodum quaeris', i.e. 'You are looking for a knot in a bulrush'.

CHAPTER 5. SECOND SECURITY FOR MORAL APTITUDE ON THE PART OF THE OPERATIVE FUNCTIONARIES OF THE HIGHEST GRADE—MONEY AT THEIR DISPOSAL MINIMIZED

On this occasion two points will fall to be considered: 1. the necessity of such minimization; 2. the most apt means of effecting it.

1. First then as to the necessity.

The Office of Chief Executive functionary there must be, and in a single hand must the power be located.

In this Office must be lodged the power of locating the functionaries of subordinate grades: as also to a great extent that of dislocating them.

To these Offices, to an extent more or less considerable, the annexation of the matter of reward in a pecuniary shape will be necessary: otherwise without compulsion they can not be filled. Offices[1] to which no power is attached may be filled by compulsion: and to a vast extent are customarily so filled: witness privates in both branches of military service—service by land and service by sea. Not so Offices clothed with power: for, supposing the functionary unwilling to exact them, none of the services which it belongs to the Office to exact would be exacted: men would desert, remain inactive, or be erroneously and mischievously enactive: of the things subject to the power, [some][2] would remain unemployed, and thus yielding no useful service, others but be unserviceably or mischievously employed, or deteriorate, or perish.

Pay therefore can not be altogether withdrawn from Office. Of Offices, to a large extent the location can not be in any other hand than that of a Chief Executive functionary, whose Office is itself in a state of subordination to the situation of the body in which as above the greatest happiness of the greatest number requires that the supreme operative power be located.

To prevent the Chief Executive functionary from locating in these endowed Offices individuals whose receipt of the money or money's worth will, with reference to the interests and wishes [of] the several Members of the supreme legislative body, have the same effect as if the money were given to themselves is not in the nature of the case

[1] MS alt. 'Functions'.
[2] MS 'all'.

possible. For in the first place, whatsoever may be the advantage to the legislative functionary from the receipt of the money by another person, in no case can the receipt of it be proved if any discretion be employed in the passing it from hand to hand: in the next place, neither on any such occasion could one man be punished for the act how mischievous so ever of another man without manifest injustice. The law can not say, no man with whom any Member of the supreme operative body has any connection in the way of pecuniary interest or sympathy shall be located in the Office in question whatsoever it may be: no law can say, no Member of that body shall receive gratification or feel grateful from the seeing [a kindness done to][1] a person who is dear to him or a person from whose opulence his own will or may peradventure receive encrease: no law can say, no Member of the supreme legislative body shall be disposed to do the will of the giver of good-gifts[2] in consequence of the Chief functionary having done or being expected to do *his* will.

These things considered, to propose any such thing as a law inhibiting a Member of the legislative body from the acceptance of any such endowed Office, and this too under any such notion as that of its preventing him from doing the will of the giver of these good gifts to the detriment of the whole community, is either imbecillity or hypocrisy and imposture. It is imbecillity if, by the proposer of the law in question, the utter inefficiency of it to its professed end is not observed: imposture and hypocrisy if it is observed: imposture because a desire is expressed which in fact is not entertained: hypocrisy because the desire, if really entertained and pursued and the gratification of it endeavoured at, would be a publickly beneficial and laudable one. So far from contributing to prevent the supreme legislative functionaries from sacrificing the universal interest to their own personal and sinister interests in partnership with that of the Chief Executive functionary, so far from preventing or contributing to prevent the sinister sacrifice, the tendency of any such law would be to give facility and encrease to it. How? even by producing on the part of the community at large the persuasion that by this means the formation and carrying on of the sinister partnership stands prevented, and thereby preventing men from looking out for any arrangements which should, in reality as well as profession, be preventive of it.

[1] The insertion is suggested by the marginal summary, where Bentham commented that a 'law, by punishment or invalidation, inhi[bi]ting A from being gratified by a kindness done to B' was not enactable.

[2] i.e. the Chief Executive functionary.

Qui facit per alium facit per se. Qui recipit per alium recipit per se. Qui recipit patitur. Qui recipit bonum, bene patitur. ευπαθει.[1]

But in contact with the sharers in the supreme Operative power to place a functionary with money and money's worth at his disposal, that is to say placing within reach of the Legislative functionary good gifts at the disposal of the Chief Executive functionary, is to plant in the Constitution the seeds of corruptive influence: which influence, unless the most anxious precautions be taken, will sooner or later, as surely as flesh is made putrid by summer heat, prevail and render the Chief Executive functionary, be he who he may, and the majority of the possessors of the supreme Operative power, accomplices with one another in the betraying of their trust.

The seeds of corruption being thus sown by necessity, all that remains to be done for the prevention or obstruction of the sinister sacrifice, is to nip in the bud or branch[?] the putrid fungus, and as far as possible prevent its growth, preventing its acquiring any such an extent as to operate the destruction of the political edifice.

It is the interest of the locator in chief that as well the number of the Offices at his disposal, as the quantum of emolument in every shape attached to each, be maximized. But this maximization depends upon the sharers in the supreme legislative power. By the person of relatives of one sort or other, it is not possible to prevent them from receiving at the hands of the Chief Executive functionary these masses of emolument. But unless the most efficient preventives be employed, of which further on, it is impossible to prevent a compact, express or virtual, from being entered into between this giver of good gifts, and these creators of the same: a compact in virtue of which [they] collectively join in the imposition of the necessary burthens, and by his hand, receive individually their shares in the correspondent mass of benefit.

A compact, it has been said, either express or virtual. An express one is possible: but a virtual compact is all that is necessary [and is][2] indeed well-adapted to the purpose. This sort of compact is actually and of necessity established as above by the Constitution itself. To neither of the parties can any words which any language can afford make it more thoroughly known than their respective situations, and the species which they see each other belonging to, make known to each what are the objects of desire to the other. Seeing that the Chief Executive functionary is a man, to what member of the supreme

[1] 'What a man does by the agency of another is his own act. What a man receives through another person, he receives for himself. Whoever receives, experiences. Whoever receives a good, experiences pleasure. He enjoys himself.'

[2] MS 'or'.

legislative body can it be unknown or matter of doubt that it is his desire—his never-failing desire—to see the Offices which are at his disposal as numerous and as richly endowed as possible? To what Chief Executive functionary can it be matter of doubt whether to each member of the supreme legislative body it is an object of desire to see his relations of all sorts as richly endowed with the same good things as possible?

Now then in the case of the member of the supreme legislature, what course of action is it that is most conducive to the fulfilment of those wishes? By what course of conduct other than the rendering his operations on every occasion as effectually subservient and contributory to the so well-known desires of that giver of good gifts as possible?

But this inducement which any one of these functionaries has for thus doing whatsoever depends upon him for affording a gratification to these same known desires, the same has every other: and thus it is that for the favour of that arbiter of destiny they become all of them competitors: every one beholds a rival in every other. An auction—a perpetual auction—has place: in the Assembly, the biddings are made by votes and speeches and motions in favour of whatsoever measures have contributed or have a tendency to contribute towards the augmentation of that mass which, while in the character of benefit it enriches and exhilarates the ruling few, acts in the character of a burthen and presses affliction into the bosom of the subject many.

Otherwise than by speaking of matter, it is not possible to speak of mind: as corruption in the physical sense is to matter, so is corruption in the psychological sense to mind: a more apt mode of designation—of archetypation—was never found in any case. To employ it is not rhetoric: it is the work of the purest and most indispensable logic.

In this case as in others, as it is with matter, so it is with mind. As it is in two out of the three physical kingdoms,[1] so is it in the political one. To sow seed is to prepare corruption: to put together male and female is to breed corruption. But in the two living,[2] say growing, kingdoms, corruption has its antidotes—its antiseptics: and e'en so has it in the one political: in both it has its preventives and its retardatives: nor in either is it destitute of its acceleratives.

Every member of a representative body, if he be of the human species, has a propensity to sacrifice to his own individual interests all other interests, and thereby on the occasion of the exercise given to such his function in that quality, to betray his trust. But in a

[1] The allusion is to the animal and vegetable kingdoms, the third being the mineral.

[2] MS orig. is preferred here to MS alt. 'material', since there are three material kingdoms, but only two living ones.

Constitution which has for its object the prevention of this sacrifice, arrangements there may be and actually are, by which this propensity, this disposition, may be and is with not much less than compleat efficiency counteracted.

A man who in such a body should rise up and say, 'I have never propensity thus to become corrupt—any desire thus to obtain power [and] money for myself or friends', has as much title to credence, and no more, as if he were to say, 'I never have any desire to eat'.

In the way of legislation or of judicature, to seek to punish any one man for saying of any other that he at all times has this desire, of being in this sense corrupter or corrupted, is as consistent with justice and honesty, with the greatest happiness of the greatest number, as it would be to seek to punish him for saying of another, that man has every day of his life a desire to eat.

Unless these precautions are taken or a reform intervenes, the conversion of the form of Government, whatsoever it may be, into an absolute despotism is as certain and infallible as the conversion of a joint of meat into a putrid mass if kept in an equal quantity of water in a summer temperature.

As in the case of the physical corruption, every day gives additional promptitude to the approaching dissolution, so in the case of the political corruption does every fresh mass of money or power lodged by the supreme [legislative][1] functionaries in the hands of the supreme executive. Call it arithmetical, call it geometrical, the progression is incessant.[2] At the outset of his career, suppose him with no more than one endowed office at his disposal. By the expectation of that one office what may happen is, that by the industry of some man of influence in the Assembly and the negligence of the rest he may obtain another. But whatsoever facility he had in that first instance is now doubled: it will be as easy again to him to get a third as it was to get the second: it will be still easier to obtain a fourth: and so on till the subjugation of the legislative to the supreme executive, or rather of the people to both, is as uncontrolled, and misrule as consummate, as in England.

Under the notion of extirpating or lessening corruption in the form in question, suppose now a man instituting a prosecution for an act of this sort or proposing a new law professing to give encrease to the magnitude or probability of infliction as applied to the provision already made for punishment. Of this zeal of his, what is the object?

[1] MS 'executive'.

[2] An allusion to T.R. Malthus, *An Essay on the Principle of Population*, London, 1798, p. 14: 'Population, when unchecked, increases in a geometrical ratio. Subsistence increases only in an arithmetical ratio.'

to put an end to the practice? No: but to give additional permanence to it. Why? By promoting a persuasion that on the part of the body of which he is a member, there exists really a desire to put a stop, or so much as to put a limit, to the sort of corruption in question: a desire which in the breasts of any thing like a majority of the persons so situated, never has had place, nor ever could have.

Besides contributing as it does to minimization of the aggregate of expence, which is the direct and only obvious use of minimization as applied to money extracted as in the case in question from unwilling contributors, it will be seen operating as a security for every branch of appropriate aptitude: for intellectual aptitude in both its subramifications and for appropriate active aptitude.

[2. The most apt means of effecting minimization of money.][1]

Q. In what manner may the principle of minimization and the other safeguards be applied with the greatest advantage to the case of money?

A. By observation of the following rules, viz.

1. Except as excepted, suffer no man to make for himself profit in any shape from public money deposited in his hands or at his disposal.

2. In the instance of each functionary having charge of public money, minimize the quantity of money at [his] disposal.

3. Not suffering to be lodged in the hands of any money-keeping functionary, money in any quantity exceeding the sum in relation to which he has obtained fide-jussors, bound by agreement on their part to the eventual payment thereof into the hands of government in the event of his failure to pay it when called upon in due course.

4. If there be in or can be brought into existence any Banking Company of sufficient pecuniary trustworthiness who are willing to receive public money upon the ordinary terms essential to Banking Companies, keep as much as may be in their hands, ordering matters at the same time by law in such sort that in case of failure the public shall have the preference as against all private creditors.

By this means, instead of paying functionaries of its own for the keeping of the public money in their charge, the government may so order matters as to receive a compensation for money so deposited by it.

By some governments the concurrence of functionaries more than one has been rendered necessary to the issue of each sum out of a public treasury: and to render this concurrence necessary, physical

[1] Bentham did not go on to discuss this second topic in the main sequence of MSS (UC cxiii. 44–51). The remainder of the chapter is taken from a fragment at UC clx. 56–7.

means have been employed: such as the rendering the opening of locks more than one necessary to the extraction of it, locks to the opening of which so many keys of different forms are necessary, and allotting to that same number of persons the custody of the keys. In Russia such has accordingly been the practice as appears by an Ordinance of the Empress Catherine creative of an Official Establishment for the several Provinces of the Empire: three is in that instance the number of the keys.[1] The inconvenience here is that in this case there must be this number of functionaries unremittingly occupied, and on account of the constancy of their attendance and the magnitude of the trust, highly paid.

The keeping of money by the government of a country in treasuries of its own is but a makeshift employed by necessity where no sufficiently trustworthy Banking Companies for the keeping of it can be found.

[1] Bentham perhaps had in mind the reorganization of the provincial governments undertaken in November 1775 by Catherine II (1729–96), Empress of Russia from 1762. The new measures were published in *Règlements de Sa Majesté Impériale Catherine II, pour L'Administration des Gouvernements de l'Empire des Russies*, Liege, 1777, a work with which Bentham was familiar (see *Of Laws in General*, ed. H.L.A. Hart, London, 1970 (*CW*), p. 151n). However the provision to which Bentham refers was not contained here, but in the Craft Statute of the Charter to the Towns of 1785 (clause 123, paragraph 23) which provided that, 'In the craft board chamber there shall be a cupboard and a table with a drawer, closed by a lock with three keys, in which shall be kept [a copy of] the Craft Statute, the craft symbol, the board's seal, the craft treasury, and the accounts of income and expenditure. One key [shall be held] by the board elder, the other keys one each by the elder's deputies.' See *Rossiiskoe zakonodatel'stvo x–xx vekov v deviati tomakh*, vol. V, ed. E. I. Indova, Moscow, 1987, pp. 99–100.

CHAPTER 6. MINIMIZING FACTITIOUS REMUNERATION: THE QUANTITY OF MONEY AND MONEY'S WORTH APPLIED IN REMUNERATION OF THE SERVICES OF PUBLIC FUNCTIONARIES, POSSESSORS OF THE SUPREME OPERATIVE POWER AND THEIR SUBORDINATES[1]

[1] No MSS exist for this chapter, but the topic was discussed by Bentham in the context of a security for active aptitude (see Ch. 11, §2, pp. 89–94 below).

CHAPTER 7. SECURITY THE [FOURTH].[1] EXCLUSION OF FACTITIOUS DIGNITY[2]

Dignity is the name given to a quality in the human character. The idea annext to it seems to be not altogether a very determinate one—that quality in man which is such that by the opinion of its existence *respect* is produced on the part of others as towards him in whom it is regarded as existing. Say for shortness, Dignity is the efficient cause of respect.

The dignity may be stiled natural in so far as the respect, of the token of which the possessor is the object, has for its efficient cause the opinion entertained by him who pays it in relation to the conduct and thence the frame of mind of him who is the object of it.

The dignity is factitious in so far as it has for its efficient cause the act of another person: a person other than he in whom the quality is considered as having its existence.

Of this factitious sort, the distinctive character is this: namely that by it respect may be caused to be shewn to men in unlimited number to no one of whom, in so far as depends upon his conduct and frame of mind, respect would be paid; to whom, but for the operation by which this dignity is conferred, no respect at all would ever be paid by any one.

The exclusion of the species of manufacture here in question, and thereby of every article manufactured by it, whatsoever may be the shape given to the article, has here been mentioned as a necessary article in the list of the arrangements and institutions which have for their object the lessening the aggregate mass of operative power in the hands of governors without prejudice to the right and proper end of government. The conception on which the proposed exclusion is grounded is that the existence of a power of this sort is productive [of] so much unmixed evil, unalloyed by good in any quantity or in any shape.

For the purpose of bringing to view the quality and quantity of the evil, two divisions derived from so many different sources require to be made.

Division the 1. Factitious dignity is either personal or successional: personal in so far as it is confined to a single individual: successional

[1] MS blank.

[2] For the text used in this chapter see the Editorial Introduction, p. xxi above. An unfinished fragment on this topic, apparently intended for the projected part of the essay dealing with 'Expence minimized', is at UC clx. 72–4 (8–9 May 1822).

in so far as it has been made to appertain to a set of men standing in succession to each other. Successional factitious dignity is again distinguishable into classical (or say Official) and genealogical: genealogical, in so far as the successor stands related to his predecessor in the way of genealogical relationship; classical, or say Official, where he stands no otherwise related to him than by occupying the same political situation—say the same Office.

Division the 2. The act by which the benefit has been conferred has been either grounded or ungrounded.

Grounded it may be termed in so far as in performing the act by which it is conferred, he by whom it has been conferred is supposed to have had in view service in some shape either rendered or likely to be rendered to some individual person or persons: if to some persons, to some determinate but particular assemblage of individuals or to the indeterminate aggregate composed of the public at large.

In whatsoever shape this benefit has been conferred, and whatsoever may have been the ground, if any, on which it has been conferred, it can not by the power in question be conferred on any one individual but at the expence of some other, or rather of all others. As it is with money, so is it with respect. More respect can not be paid to and enjoyed by one man, but less respect is paid to another or others: every act by which factitious dignity is thus conferred on a man, a quantity of respect secured to him over and above whatsoever he would otherwise have received and enjoyed, has therefore in this particular the effect of a tax: the gain to one party is attended with loss to another party, and the defalcation made by the operation from the aggregate of felicity is more than equivalent [to] the addition made to it.

Scarcely any where else than in a Monarchy has a manufactory of this sort been established: and in a Monarchy it has never been customary either to declare or to ask for the reason of any thing that is done.

An article of this sort is never manufactured but that in the breasts of two persons at least pleasure in a certain shape has been produced: the person by whom it has been produced, and the person on whom it has been conferred.

In this, whether *groundless* or not groundless, it may at any rate with indisputable propriety be said to be *ungrounded*.

In so far as for the conferring of this benefit any ground or justificative cause is vouchsafed to be assigned, it is the attaching reward to meritorious service: of which phrase again it is the design to cause it to be believed that it is to the community at large that the service in question has been rendered, that the quantity of happiness in the community has thereby been rendered greater than it would have been otherwise: or if this be not the certain effect, it was at any rate at the time when the operation was performed, a probable effect, of the act.

But that which never has been disputed, nor seems likely to be in any direct way disputed, is—that in each individual instance, of the reward conferred the quantity ought to bear a correct proportion to the quality of the service, that is the quantity of felicity actually or probably produced by the service.

Moreover, that at any rate, the reward ought to be in proportion between service and service: in so much that as between two services, the one pregnant [with] more good than the other, the reward given for that which is productive of least good ought not to be so great as the reward given for that which is productive of the greatest quantity of good: much less still greater.

If there were a shape in which the collation of reward did not involve in it the imposition of a tax, in that shape the matter of reward might be given blindfold and in short ought so to be: it should be given not to this or that individual only, or this or that aggregate of individuals, but to all mankind without reserve. For where is the individual who, being endowed with an ordinary store of benevolence, would not on every occasion be made more happy if by the same operation no other were made less happy?

But there scarcely exists that shape or that occasion on which the matter of reward can be known to be conferred by the act of government without its involving in its composition the evil of a tax: certainly if there be any such shape, factitious dignity is not that shape.

On every occasion and in every shape, service useful to the public ought to be procured: procured and at the same time at the least expence possible: of the good thus produced, the least quantity of evil possible ought to be made the accompaniment.

To service of a nature useful to the public, in a certain shape and in a certain quantity, a mass of the matter of reward stands naturally attached: this naturally attached mass of reward is natural dignity: by the knowledge possessed by the public that by the individual in question service in effect or in tendency useful to the community in question has been rendered, respect on the part of the community as towards the individual in question is in a natural way produced.

Of this natural reward an inherent property is the being in exact proportion to the supposed magnitude of the supposed service.

Take two individuals, Primus and Secundus: by both of them, let service useful in effect or tendency to the community at large have been rendered: but by Primus service more useful than that rendered by Secundus, the reward which in the shape of respect is bestowed upon Primus will be greater than the reward bestowed upon Secundus. If the good regarded as having been done by Primus is twice as great as the good regarded as having [been] done by Secundus, the quantity of respect bestowed upon Primus will be twice as great as the quantity of respect bestowed upon Secundus, unless obtainable at a less expence.

Those by whom in this case the reward is bestowed are exposed to the being deceived.[1] But just so in every imaginable case is one liable to be deceived. But by the greatest happiness principle a remedy to the danger of deception is in this case afforded: a remedy which the Monarchical principle never yet did afford nor could ever admitt to be afforded.[2]

1. Note that in the case here in question, the reward is extraordinary reward rendered in consideration of extraordinary service. This will be either service rendered by an individual at large, by an individual who was not by any official situation laid under the obligation of rendering the service, or service rendered by a public functionary over and above all such service as in virtue of his office he stood bound to render.

2. Note likewise that the question here is—not between reward in other shapes and reward in the shape of dignity; but only between reward in the shape of natural dignity, and reward in the shape of factitious dignity.

Cases there are in which the nature of the service is such that to constitute an adequate inducement in relation to it, an inducement of sufficient strength to cause the service to be rendered, dignity can not in any shape be sufficient: reward in a more substantial and universally acceptable shape, viz. in the shape of money—is necessary. Take for example extraordinary service rendered at the hazard of life, limb and health, in the line of military service. Accordingly in the wisest and most frugal of all governments as yet in existence—the government of the United States, for the procurement of such service, reward in this shape is not grudged. For the widow and orphan of him who is killed in the performance of such service, a pension is profited. So likewise for him by whom, in the performance of service in that

[1] In the marginal summary, Bentham listed the following 'Subjects of deception': '1. Existence of the supposed service. 2. Magnitude of ditto. 3. Need of reward for producing it. 4. Quantity of reward needed.'

[2] Bentham was presumably referring to the idea of giving publicity to meritorious acts, a theme he developed in 'Constitutional Code Rationale', Ch. 6, §5, pp. 306–9 below.

shape, a limb has been lost or other irreparable bodily damage sustained.[1]

3. Note likewise that when Factitious Dignity is spoken of as a species of reward marked for exclusion, by it is meant Factitious Dignity considered in the shape and manner in which it is ordinarily conferred in Monarchies—i.e. without the collection and publication of evidence probative of the existence and indicative of the nature and shape of the service, in remuneration of which it is desired that it should be understood to have been conferred.

4. Note. That which on this occasion is not meant to be dis-recommended but recommended is—the taking, by government appointment made in the way of legislation, a factitious course for the causing to be known the existence, shape, and quantity of the service that has been rendered: together with the sacrifice made by him on the occasion of his rendering it: i.e. the evil to himself sustained or risked by the rendering it: in a word, to place upon its proper *ground* the reward attached in this shape to the service.

[1] A general pension law making provision for disabled officers, soldiers and sailors was first enacted by Congress in 1792. Provision was made for widows and orphans of servicemen by Acts of 1812 and 1816.

CHAPTER 8. FIFTH SECURITY FOR APPROPRIATE MORAL APTITUDE ON THE PART OF RULING FUNCTIONARIES—LEGAL RESPONSIBILITY

Position. The greatest happiness of the greatest number requires that every possessor of supreme Operative power in whatsoever shape without exception[a] be compleatly responsible[b] in a legal sense to the people in their quality of possessors of the supreme Constitutive power.

Exposition.

[a] *Without exception* in favour of any one such functionary: in particular in favour of the Chief of the State, say the Supreme Director.

[b] *Compleatly Responsible.* Namely by all the several appropriate modes of subordination applicable to that same situation.

These are as follows:

1. by Dislocability.
2. by Punibility.[1]

Rationale.

Without exception, why?

If any one such functionary there were, his power would, though in an indirect way, be compleatly despotic. In his hands would be the power of inflicting injury in every imaginable shape on every member of the community without exception. The power of inflicting such injury in every shape would comprize power punitory in every shape applicable to every purpose: also by the power of extorting thereby the tangible matter of reward in every shape, power remuneratory in unlimited quantity and in every shape.

[Given][2] such irresponsibility on the part of the Supreme Director, by no responsibility on the part of other functionaries or individuals in the character of instruments supposed to be necessary to the exercise of such his power could the effect or any thing like the effect be produced. For by consideration of such responsibility on this or that occasion, suppose this or that functionary prevented from the giving execution to this or that sinister design, what matters it? he turns aside from this individual and betakes himself to another: the consequence is, so long as whatsoever be the number necessary to the exercise in question, the assistance of that number can be

[1] In the text, after both 'Dislocability' and 'Punibility', Bentham added, 'See | |', but failed to provide any reference. Both topics are discussed in Ch. 1, §7, pp. 8–12 above.

[2] MS 'Of'.

procured—procured whether among members of the community in question or foreigners, his will remains as to the matter in question unconstrained, and the evil which it is his desire to produce is produced accordingly.

English Practice.

In the English Government, the Monarch, mixt as is the Monarchy, is altogether exempt from legal responsibility in every shape. Do whatever evil he will, he can neither be punished nor so much as dislocated. What is the consequence? that the doing of political evil in all manner of shapes, evil and nothing but evil, is in that Monarchy as in every other, the uninterrupted occupation of the Monarch's political life.

The King can do no wrong.[1] By this phrase it is that his exemption from all legal responsibility, the compleat licence for the operating of evil in every imaginable shape, is expressed.

Out of this real security, pregnant as it has been seen to be with absolute and irresistible power, by a forced construction, a sort of lawyers' will—an abuse of words—has been deduced his alledged impotence. Be the thing what it may that it is his desire to do, if it be wrong, power adequate to the production of the effect is not in his hands.

In fact however nothing can be more compleatly false.

To any great extent it may be said it is not in this man's power—for it is not in any man's power to do wrong—without instruments: and all but he being legally responsible, if the thing whatever it be which it is his desire to do have any thing wrong in it, no such instruments will he find. Of the supreme functionary no written act is valid without some appropriate counter-signature. Were this even true it would as above amount to nothing. But neither is it true. For to him belongs the command of the whole army. With this instrument therefore in his hand, what need of any such thing as a counter-signature—what act is there that can not be done by him?[2]

[1] According to William Blackstone, *Commentaries on the Laws of England*, 4 vols., Oxford, 1765–9, i. 238–9, this 'antient and fundamental maxim is not to be understood, as if everything transacted by the government was of course just and lawful, but means only two things. First, that whatever is exceptionable in the conduct of public affairs is not to be imputed to the king, nor is he answerable for it personally to his people: for this doctrine would totally destroy that constitutional independence of the crown, which is necessary for the balance of power, in our free and active, and therefore compounded, constitution. And, secondly, it means that the prerogative of the crown extends not to do any injury: it is created for the benefit of the people, and therefore cannot be exerted to their prejudice.' Bentham himself discussed this principle more fully in *A Comment on the Commentaries and A Fragment on Government*, ed. J.H. Burns and H.L.A. Hart, London, 1977 (*CW*), pp. 185–9, 304–7.

[2] The Crown was invested with the prerogative right to the sole command of the armed forces of the kingdom, except where that authority was regulated and controlled by the Mutiny Act and

Then as to the alledged responsibility of all other individuals—the highest functionaries under this one not excepted—neither in this is there any truth.

1. First as to the Members of the two coordinate bodies—the two Houses of Parliament.

So long as they act in a body, not so much as the pretence of responsibility has place in either instance.

2. As to functionaries acting individually. If in their situation any such thing as effective responsibility is asserted, it is but a pretence.[1]

In regard to the power of the King, one fundamental principle [is] that whatever wrong the King does, is converted into right by his doing it. Of this theoretical axiom, one practical consequence is that the King has in his power the life of every individual who is his subject. Different courses might be mentioned by which an object so convenient might be accomplished. One is—where a man is deemed sufficiently troublesome—give it in command to any man to put the troublesome man to death in any way: the deed done, a pardon is given to the doer, and every thing is as it should be done. To a certain extent, an antique but not altogether antiquated form of proceeding was found to stand in the way of so convenient a prerogative—it was called an Appeal of or for Murder. If, when to please the King, a man had been murdered, a person bearing this or that particular relationship happened to be left alive, the relative by a form of proceeding so denominated might prosecute the murderer, in which case supposing him convicted, a pardon from the King would not have the effect of saving him. How far from being any thing like adequate the restraint was that was endeavoured to be opposed to high-seated depravity is sufficiently obvious. Still however it was some check: and that the life of an English subject should have even this precarious protection against a Monarch's vengeance was no longer endurable. By the King's Attorney General a Bill for the removal of it was brought in and by both Houses, after a few words to save appearance, passed of course.[2] The way was thus cleared for as many imitations of the Manchester Massacre[3] as may from time to time be found convenient.

other statute laws. However the constitutional principle that all orders given by the Crown required the counter-signature of a responsible minister applied to the army as well as to the civil government.

[1] In the marginal summary, Bentham explained that the King could exempt anyone he pleased from legal punishment by means of a pardon.

[2] The appeal of murder was abolished in 1819 by 59 Geo. III, c.46. The Bill was introduced into the House of Commons on 9 February 1819 by Sir Samuel Shepherd (1760–1840), Attorney General 1817–19.

[3] An allusion to events in St. Peter's Field, Manchester, on 16 August 1819, when troops were used to disperse a reform meeting and eleven people were said to have been killed and hundreds injured.

CHAPTER 9. MAXIMIZING MORAL RESPONSIBILITY—I.E. SUBJECTION TO REPROACH AT THE HANDS OF THE PUBLIC OPINION TRIBUNAL, BY WHICH THE POWER OF THE MORAL OR POPULAR SANCTION IS APPLIED AS A COUNTERFORCE TO THE LEGAL POWER OF THE STATE

§1. *Public Opinion Tribunal—its subserviency to greatest happiness*[1]

Question. By what means may appropriate *moral* aptitude be secured? What are the means applicable to the purpose of securing appropriate moral aptitude? What are the efficient causes of appropriate moral aptitude?

A.1. Abstaining from attaching to the office more power than is necessary to the apt execution of the functions appertaining to it. Principle, minimization as to power.

A.2. In so far as the nature of the case permitts, making application of counterforces.

Q. What are the forces applicable in the character of counterforces to official power?

A. 1. The force of the popular or moral sanction as applied by the tribunal of public opinion: 2. the force of particular interests in so far as the nature of the case causes it, or admitts of its being caused, to operate in alliance with the universal interest.[2]

Q. Of the force of the popular or moral sanction, what is the efficient cause?

A. Publicity—the means of divulgation, as applicable to the appropriate subject matters of divulgation.

Q. What are the subject matters by the divulgation of which the force of the popular or moral sanction is applied as a counterforce to official power and in favour of and to the protection of the universal interest?

A. 1. The decision pronounced by the tribunal of public opinion in the case in question: 2. the grounds on which that decision has been formed.

Q. The decision pronounced by the tribunal of public opinion in each case or in any case, how can it be ascertained? what can be the efficient cause of its formation?

[1] The MSS used in this section were originally intended to follow the first draft of 'Expository matter' (UC cxiii. 1–5: see Ch. 1, p. 3n above), hence the general nature of the introductory remarks in the first five paragraphs.

[2] Bentham did not develop this second point in 'Economy as applied to Office'.

A. To the decision pronounced by the tribunal of public [opinion], the nature of the case admitts not of any efficient cause of ascertainment: the members of this tribunal being among the inhabitants not only of the territory of the political state in question, but of every other territory on the earth's surface, all such as to the power add the will of taking cognizance of the subject in question whatever it be. Therefore in the nature of the case not being capable of being ascertained, it can only be presumed.

Q. What are the subjects of inference to which the presumption in this case applies?

A. 1. The purport of the decision: 2. the rectitude of it.

Q. In the case of the purport of the decision, what are the efficient causes or grounds of the presumption?

A. The circumstances expressive of the nature of the case. From the view taken by him of those circumstances, each individual in his character of member of the tribunal of public opinion will form his conclusion respecting the decision likely to be pronounced by the several other members: not omitting to take into account the appropriate aptitude or inaptitude of each, the aptitude and inaptitude being considered with reference to their several appropriate efficient causes.

Q. What are the evidences in favour of the rectitude of the decision of the tribunal of public opinion in the case in question?

A. In the nature of [the] case, that is to say consistently with the nature of man, rectitude can not be positive: it can be no other than comparative: in other words, of rectitude there can not be a certainty: nothing more than a greater or less degree of probability: taking for the subjects of comparison any such other decisions as the nature of the case can be supposed to admitt of.

Q. What are those decisions?

A. The tribunal of public opinion having for its members the majority of all such individuals as take cognizance of the individual case in question, the decision capable of being in a state of contrast with and opposition to the decision of such majority can not be any otherwise than the decision of the smaller number.[1]

Q. The character in which, as a security for appropriate moral aptitude on the part of a public functionary, the decisions of the tribunal of public opinion have been mentioned being that of a *counterforce* to the force attached to the Office in question, the

[1] Bentham seems to have confused two ideas in this paragraph. On the one hand, the public opinion tribunal was composed of all the individuals who took notice of the question, while on the other hand, the decision to be regarded as that of the tribunal was that expressed by the majority of those individuals.

decisions of the tribunal must be supposed to be the decisions expressive of the volitional and intellectual faculty of an aggregate body in which neither the functionary in question nor any of those of whom it is held for certain that they will act in conjunction with him are comprized: that is to say, the several other members of the aggregate body in which the aggregate mass of the operative power in the state is lodged. To speak of the decisions of the tribunal of public opinion as possessing a greater chance for rectitude than the decisions correspondent to and approbative of the operations of the public functionary is to say in other words that in the breast of every public functionary as such there is a constant tendency to relative inaptitude in that branch of it which stands opposed to appropriate moral aptitude. Of this tendency, if it has place, what are the efficient causes?

Answer. The facilities which the power in question affords to the functionary in question for giving effective prevalence to his particular and sinister interest to the detriment and *pro tanto* to the sacrifice of the right and proper interest, the interest of the greatest happiness of the greatest number. Of these means, the efficiency is in the direct ratio of the magnitude of the power: and as to the general preponderance of personal interest over regard for public interest, it is of the essence of the human species as well as of every other class of sensitive beings, and the existence of it an inseparable condition of the existence of the species.

Q. The decision of the tribunal of public opinion being thus a decision which in the nature of the case can not possibly be pronounced, in such sort that any mass of discourse uttered as a decision emaning from this source can not be any thing other than a fiction, does the nature of the case afford on any individual occasion any decision, any really pronounced and thus ascertainable decision, which to the purpose in question can consistently with reason and utility be accepted as a substitute for it, and as such be acted upon?

A. Yes: such is the decision pronounced by the functionary body which in the judicial department is termed a Jury: it being assumed that this body is on each occasion constituted in a manner conducive to the generally declared purpose: namely ensuring rectitude of judgment and operation on the part of the entire Judicatory, whatever it may be.

N.B. considered in this point of view, a Jury may be stiled a section of the tribunal of public opinion.

Q. In what manner, in its character of a section of the tribunal of public opinion, may a Jury be constituted in such sort as to be in the greatest degree contributory to the purpose in question?

A. By making the allocation of its members the result of chance, applied to the aggregate number of those who are regarded as susceptible of appropriate aptitude with reference to the purpose.

Note that if on this occasion the power of location be in the hands of any public functionary, the exercise of any such power may with propriety be regarded as equivalent to the power of determining the operations of the functionary in question[1] by means of corruptive influence. But there exists not that individual in the state, in regard to whom there can be any adequate assurance of his not being in a state of subjection to corruptive influence in the hands of the public functionary whosoever he may be. Therefore the determination of the individuals of whom the Jury is composed should not in any case depend upon the will of any individual whatsoever, but be the result of the operation of chance. By chance should a Jury be determined, not by choice. To the legislature it belongs on each occasion or class of occasions to determine out of what class Jurymen shall be taken: to the power of chance it belongs to determine on each individual occasion of what individuals the functionary body called a Jury shall be composed.[2]

[1] MS orig. 'Juryman'.

[2] In the marginal summary, Bentham commented at this point: '☛ Add here the distinction between Jury with an obligatory verdict and ditto with an unobligatory ditto: Jury of *volition* and ditto of opinion only.' Bentham discussed this matter at UC clx. 472 (20 May 1822): 'Public Opinion Tribunal—its modes of operating, and correspondent degrees of force.

'1. Mode 1. The mode which has place in the case of a Jury commonly so called: a Jury the decision of which is called a *verdict*, and, like that of a Judge so called in cases where the power of the Judge is exercised by him alone without need of associates, is productive of an obligatory effect: i.e. determines the fate of the cause. Say, Public Opinion Tribunal adopted into, and a constituent part of, a Legal Tribunal: Public Opinion Tribunal delivering its verdicts, and these verdicts obligatory in law, unless in each instance declaredly and after argument heard set aside by the Judge.

'2. Mode 2. The mode which would have place on the supposition that the verdict of a Jury, though pronounced—pronounced in the same manner as in the former case—would not be productive of any such obligatory effect: would not be obligatory upon the Judge: but would leave him at liberty either to give effect to it, or to give effect to a decision of his framing, howsoever different from it or even directly repugnant to it. Say, Public Opinion Tribunal delivering verdicts but these verdicts not obligatory.

'3. Mode 3. The mode which would have place on the supposition that, in the character of a Section of the Public Opinion Tribunal, a set of men of a certain description and in not less than a certain number stood engaged to be present during this or that part or during the whole progression of a cause or suit: but without either obligation or power, or at any rate without obligation, to deliver any conjunct portion of discourse in the character of a verdict. Say, a silent Jury.

'In the second mode the effect produced on the mind of the Judge by the counterforce thus applied would be produced by what they were by him *known* to think: in the third case, by what they were supposed by him to think.'

§ 2. *Means of bringing the force of the popular or moral sanction to bear with greatest advantage upon the conduct of public functionaries in the several departments*

In every apartment in which a public functionary sits to do business, keep in view of the public a Table in Placard form containing Admonitory Rules and Notices having for their object the prevention of the moral failings to which by his situation the functionary is most exposed. To these Admonitory Rules and Notices, the distinction between universally applying and particularly applying will be found applicable.

I. Notices.

1. Name of the edifice, over every door that opens into or is visible from a public high-way.
2. In each edifice, over each door of each Chamber, the name of the Chamber.
3. In each Chamber, over the seat occupied by each functionary, the name of the Office, and the proper name of the functionary who sits in it.
4. In each Chamber, over the door, designation of the hour at which the functionary ought to take his seat and of the hour at which he is at liberty to desist from the exercise of his Office.[1]

II. Admonitory Rules.

1. Admonitory Rules of general applicability expressive of the Duties of the functionary.
2. Admonitory Rules of general applicability expressive of the Duties of persons attending at the Office as having business therein.
3. Admonitory Rules of general applicability expressive of the Powers given to the functionaries in question for preventing interruption of the business of the Office and annoyance of them in the exercise of their functions.

1. Rules of general applicability expressive of the Duties of the functionary.

[a.][2] Duty of urbanity: abstinence from the insolence of office.

[1] In the marginal summary, Bentham added: '5. So, an Almanack marking the Months, Weeks and Days of his attendance in each year.'

[2] MS '1' has been altered in order to clarify the hierarchy of rules presented here. Bentham's intention was not to formulate a comprehensive list of rules, but rather to put forward a few specimens for the sake of example. Hence the duty of urbanity would be the first in a series of general rules expressive of the duties of the functionary, which together formed one of the three classes of admonitory rules.

1. Let the functionary consider that it becomes him not, in quality of his Office, to assume any superiority over any person having business therein—that, in his quality of public functionary, his situation with reference to every such person is rather that of a servant than that of a master, he being remunerated at the public expence for the rendering of such services, such as appertain to the nature of his Office.

2. If, in his dealings with any suitor to the Office, any expression which by such suitor is regarded as an expression of contumely, ill-humour or impotence or contempt, be uttered by the functionary, the suitor may, if he pleases, upon the spot committ the same [to] paper, and require of the functionary under his signature to averr or deny the having employed it.[1]

The functionary is not the master of any person having business to do at his Office. The relation of a public functionary is not that of a Master, but that of a Servant: with relation to the people, yes, with relation to individuals having business to do at his Office, yes or not, according to the nature of the Office.

[3.] Of the powers given to the public functionary, the sole object is—the enabling him to fulfill his duties: to render to the public the services for the rendering of which the Office has been instituted. The institution of it has not among its objects the affording gratification to the vanity, much less to the pride, of the functionary at the expence of the feelings of those who have business to do at his Office.

Of these admonitory rules, the use is to apply the force of the popular or moral sanction in cases where, by reason of the over-weening power of the functionary, or the impossibility or difficulty of obtaining in case of transgression adequate evidence, the force of the political sanction is not efficiently applicable.

A solemn engagement in which either the rules themselves or the substance of them is repeated should be pronounced by the functionary in the face of the public upon his entrance into Office: it might, if worth while, be repeated periodically: for example in case of a new Constitution, on the anniversary of the celebration of the Constitution.

The end here aimed at being the greatest happiness of the greatest number, the form of the proposed instrument is such as is conducive to that end. A sort of instrument having the same professed object has been in customary use in governments having for their real object the greatest happiness of the ruling few at the expence of the subject

[1] In the marginal summary, Bentham added: 'on his refusal, memorandum made of such refusal: this a ground of accusation before a Judicatory.'

many. The Oath of Office is the name by which this instrument is commonly designated. In governments in general the design of it has been twofold: 1. to secure on the part of the functionary a conduct beneficial to the universal interest but so far and so far only as the universal interest is not at variance with the particular interest of the rulers: 2. to produce on the part of the people at large [the belief][1] that the intention of the functionary really is to render his official conduct in every particular without exception conformable to his declared duty, and in this way subservient to the universal interest. Here then are two purposes: a really intended purpose, and a falsely and deceptiously intended purpose. To the really intended purpose, a formulary in any considerable degree well-adapted will hardly be to be found any where. To the falsely pretended purpose, under favour of the established prejudice, every instrument which has ever been employed for this purpose is tolerably well or effectually adapted.

The design of the instrument as here proposed is—that by it the force of the popular or moral sanction should, to the purposes in question, be really brought to bear upon the conduct of the functionary in such sort as to produce or contribute to the production of observance of the rules in question. The design of the sort of instrument customarily employed is—that the force of the popular or moral sanction should in the eyes of the people be thought to be brought to bear upon the conduct of the functionary in question in such sort as to produce the observance in question, but that it should not do so in reality except with exceptions to an extent more or less considerable. To the former purpose it is not efficiently adapted. No: to the latter purpose it has hitherto in every instance been with great felicity adapted. For binding his subordinates to observance, the supreme ruler has had no need of any such comparatively feeble and precariously efficient ties: if in his eyes the functionary should have been deficient in respect of obsequiousness to the will of his august superior, the superior can at any time rid himself of the incumbrance.

For an efficient instrument of this sort, on the part of the people only, in respect of their interest, is it that any real need has place.

For aiding the conception of what is meant by the here proposed admonitory rules, subjoined is a set of rules of this description adapted to the situation of Judge, of a member of the Judicial Department. With some little additions and omissions they have for

[1] The addition is suggested by the marginal summary: '2. Causing people to believe that the object is to secure subservience to their interest.'

their basis the form of an instrument proposed in the character of an Oath of Office applying to the Judicial Office: which is [in] the "Draught of a Code for the organization of the Judicial Establishment of France", the acceptance of which was moved for in the first National Assembly of France by the Duc de le Rochefoucault of that day, but declined at the instance of the Abbé Sieyes.[1]

For an object of comparison, subjoined is also the Oath of a Chief Justice of England, reprinted from a Book intituled "The Book of Oaths", London, Anno 16 | |.[2]

[1] For the oath of office see 'Draught of a Code for the organization of the Judicial Establishment', Title III, §4, pp. 9–10 (Bowring, iv. 292–3), in *Draught of a New Plan for the organisation of the Judicial Establishment in France*, printed March 1790 (Bowring, iv. 285–406). According to Bentham, Louis Alexandre, Duc de La Rochefoucauld d'Enville (1743–92), had moved in the French National Assembly in 1790 that a translation should be made of *Draught of a New Plan for the organisation of the Judicial Establishment* for the use of the Constitutional Committee then drawing up proposals for a new judicial system, but that Emmanuel Joseph, Comte Sieyès (1748–1830) had succeeded in having the motion voted down (see Bentham to William Plumer Jr., *circa* December 1818, William Plumer Jr. MSS, New Hampshire State Library). Though it seems that no formal motion was made in the National Assembly, it is possible that Sieyès used his influence in some more indirect way to prevent any consideration of Bentham's plan.

[2] See 'The Oath of a Judge', sworn by the Lord Chief Justices and Puisne Judges, in *The Book of Oaths, and The severall forms thereof, both Antient and Modern. Faithfully Collected out of sundry Authentike Books and Records, not heretofore extant, compiled in one Volume*, London, 1649, pp. 216–19: 'Yee shall sweare, That well and truly yee shall serve our Soveraigne Lord, the King and his People in the Office of Justice; And that yee shall counsell, our Soveraigne Lord the King in his needes; And that yee shall not give any connsaile, or assent to any thing the which might turne to hurt or dis-her[i]ting of the King by any way or colour, and that ye shall not know any hurt or dis-heriting of the King; but that ye shall make it to him known by you or by some other person, And that yee shall doe equall Law and Execution of Right, to all the Kings Subjects Rich and Poore, without having regard to any person; And that ye shall not take by you, or by any other privily, ne appart any gift, or reward of Gold or of Silver, nor of any other thing, the which might turne you to profit, But if it be meat or drinke, and that of little value, of any man, that shall have any Plea or Processe hanging before you, as long as before your selfe two Pleas and Processes shall be hanging nor after for that cause; And that ye shall take no fees, as long as ye be Justice, nor Roab of any person, great or small in any case, But of the King himselfe; And that yee shall not give any counsaile or advice to any person, great or small in any case, where the King is party; And in case that any persons in what estate that they be of, come before you in Sessions with force and Armes, or otherwise, against the Peace, or against the forme of the Statute hereof made, for to disturbe the Execution of the Common Law, or for to Mennasse the people, that may not doe the Law; That yee shall doe, Arrest their Bodies, and put them in prison; and in case they be such as yee may not Arrest, that ye shall certifie the King of their names, and of their misdoing hastily, to that end that ye may thereof Ordaine remedy; And that ye shall not maintaine by your selfe, nor by none other privily nor openly, any Plea, or Quarrell, hanging in the Kings Cour[t]s, or else where in the Country; And that ye shall not delay any person of Common Right, for the Letters of the King, or of any other person, nor for any other cause; And in case that any Letters come to you contrary to the Law, that ye shall nothing doe for such Letters, but ye thereof shall certifie the King; And yee shall proceede to doe the Law, the same Letters notwithstanding; and that ye shall do, and procure the profit of the King and his Crowne, in all things where ye them reasonable may doe; And in case that ye be found in default hereafter, in any of the points aforesaid, ye shall be at the Kings will, of Bodies, Lands, and of honour, to doe thereof that that shall please the King.'

Benefits and virtues meant to be promoted.

1. Impartiality.
2. Publicity in general.
3. Secrecy, in appointed cases.
4. Unsolicitableness.
5. Incorruptibility in a passive way.
6. Incorruptibility in an active way.
7. Abstinence from abuse of power in Elections: viz. by usurpation of patronage.
8. Constancy of attendance.
9. Promptitude of dispatch.
10. Closeness and continuity of attention, even to the smallest causes.
11. Minimization of expence.
12. Non-partiality towards Advocates. Indulgence and assistance towards suitors.
13. Punctuality of obedience towards the legislative law.
14. Certification of its imperfections whenever observed.

Evils and vices meant to be excluded.

1. Partiality through sympathy or antipathy.
2. Concealment where adverse to Justice.
3. Divulgation, where adverse to Justice.
4. Inchoate partiality by admitting private solicitation.
5. Yielding to corruptive applications.
6. Solicitation of corruptive agreements.
7. Abuse of power by usurpation of patronage.
8. Violation of duty by non-attendance.
9. Dilatoriness by indolence, negligence or design.
10. Inattention—particularly to small causes, thence Precipitation.
11. Creation or permission of needless expence to suitors: so, vexation.
12. Partiality towards hireling Advocates: contempt towards and non-assistance of Suitors and their gratuitous Assistants.
13. Disobedience as towards the law: viz. by misinterpretation or arbitrary decision.
14. Insolence, pride and contemptuousness as to Suitors and visitors in general.
15. Harshness towards delinquents and persons accused of delinquency.
16. Assumption of superior virtue on the ground of superior power.

In like manner, in the theatre [of] every Political or other Debating Assembly let two Tables of Rules be kept suspended in an universally conspicuous situation—viz.

1. A Tactical Table, exhibiting the rules required to be observed at the time of the discussion by the Members and other persons present.

If the Chamber is so circumstanced that the contents of one Table will not be visible to all the persons present, a Table or Tables must be added till the number requisite for that purpose be compleated. Let one Table at least be within reach of the chair of the President, in such sort that by a wand kept within his reach, as often as in his judgment any one of these rules is contravened, he may by direction given to his wand be able, without danger of being misunderstood, to give indication of the rule so regarded as contravened.[1]

2. A Table of Fallacies, indicative of the principal deceptitious arguments by which proposed measures and arguments conducive to the only right and proper end of government are in use to be encountered by men whose sinister interests or prejudices are adverse to that end. The quality of irrelevancy—irrelevancy with reference to the subject matter in debate whatsoever it be—is a quality of which, though not all, the greater part of their number would be found possessed. Of the nature of these fallacious argument[s] a sufficient indication may in some instances require to be given by their two denominations—the one classical, the other generical: in other instances, a short exposition or exemplification may be requisite. By a little practice, any man of ordinary judgment in the situation of President will, as often as any one of the Fallacies mentioned in the Table is employed, be able to give indication of it as above.

In a corrupt Assembly, a debate is a mass composed of one-tenth of silver drowned in nine-tenths of an alloy composed of lead and arsenic. To this compound, a Book of Fallacies aptly constructed would be an appropriate test. Applied to it, the arsenic would fly off in fumes: the lead would sink: the lucid bullion would be left pure.[2]

In two different ways, both these Tables will have their use.

In so far as deviation from the line of rectitude would, if committed, be accompanied by a consciousness of its own existence, by a self-condemning consciousness, the use of them is to prevent it by eventual indication given of it to the persons present in their quality of members of a section of the tribunal of public opinion: in so far as for want of being aware of such its deviation a man would otherwise be liable to fall into transgression in any shape, by supplying him in time with the appropriate information. In the former way, the proposed institution is subservient to the moral branch of appropriate aptitude: in the other, to the intellectual branch, namely to that which consists of knowledge and that which consists of judgment.

[1] Cf. *Tactique des assemblées législatives*, ed. Étienne Dumont, 2nd edn., 2 vols., Paris, 1822, i. 245–7 (Bowring, ii. 320).

[2] Bentham did not prepare a Table of Fallacies either for *The Book of Fallacies*, London, 1824 (Bowring, ii. 375–487), or for *Constitutional Code*: see *Constitutional Code*, I (*CW*), p. 146n.

Under the head of the Judicial department, and therein under the head of the Judicial Establishment, mention will come to be made of two cases in which the institution of a Jury is capable of being employed with advantage. One—the only one as yet any where in use, that in which, when the verdict of the Jury has been delivered, an obligatory effect, except where taken away by an appropriate act of the Official Judge, is given to it: the verdict is in this case expressive not of opinion only, but of volition likewise: the other, that in which no such obligatory effect would be given to it: the verdict would in such case be expressive of opinion merely and not of volition: not of volition, because a will in relation to which a man is previously assured would not, if expressed, be productive of any effect will not in the natural and ordinary course of things be expressed. Supposing the verdict unobligatory, as above, the only effect it can have is that of operating as a sort of decision of a section of the tribunal of public opinion—a section of which the Jurymen are members. As for the uses of a Jury of which the power is thus limited, if power it can be called, they may already in some measure perhaps be anticipated: they will be developed in their proper place.[1]

Q. Rules thus strict and minute, will they not be in a high degree offensive to almost every functionary to whose situation it can happen to them to be applied?

A. Doubtless to almost every individual to whom it happens to occupy or to have any expectation of occupying any such situation. His aversion will be in the exact proportion of the strength of his propensity to practice the several misdeeds against which the expedients in question are proposed to be employed in the character of preventive remedies.

Q. What sort of arguments will the recalcitrant functionary be likely to employ in the course of his endeavours to prevent these or any other such efficaciously preventive remedies to official malpractice from being employed?

A. He will look over that Table of Fallacies which, in a degree of amplitude more or less approaching to compleatness, every public functionary who has a propensity to transgression in any shape (and every public functionary has a propensity more or less strong to transgression in most shapes) has in store in the recesses of his mind. With a confidence proportioned as he is cravenous, [if] they will be useful with reference to that purpose he will pronounce them mischievous: if efficacious, inefficacious: if important, trifling: if

[1] In *Constitutional Code*, Bentham replaced the traditional jury with his conception of the quasi-jury. This could exercise a wide variety of functions but did not pronounce an obligatory verdict (see Bowring, ix. 554–68).

productive [of] good effects, theoretical, visionary, and absurd. If any such hope be entertained by him as that by pronouncing words such as honour, dignity, high reputation, he can engage men to ascribe to him any of the praise, esteem and title to respect, the idea of which stands associated with those words, he will declare that checks such as these are derogatory to his honour—to his dignity, that if fit, in any case they are fit only in the case of children, not for men grown, much less for men as elevated as he is in the scales of public worth, private worth, public reputation and age.

Q. Is it right that men, men of all ages—should be thus treated as if they were children?

A. Yes: if it adds any thing to the probability of obtaining in their situation the maximum of appropriate aptitude. Rules of this sort are applied to the situation of children—why? ever because it is the sincere wish that for guidance and instruction such instruments should be employed as afford the greatest probability of their proving effectual with relation to the end in view: in that view these instruments are in that case employed: and in that case the utility and efficiency of them is attested by universal experience and acknowledgement. If the instruments thus efficacious in the unmature stages of life have failed to be employed in the maturer ones it is—not because they are inapposite, inefficacious or pernicious, but because if applied to public functionaries they would be efficacious, and with a view to the public interest indeed beneficial, but to the functionaries in question burthensome: namely by laying restraints on them—restraints the effect of which as far as they were efficacious would be to prevent their making sacrifice of the public interest to their own private interest in all manner of shapes, and in particular those which correspond to love of money, love of power and love of ease.

There are two distinguishable forms in which influence more or less effective may be given to the will and understanding of the great body of the people: in the one form[1] their opinion—that is the opinion of such of them whose opinions can be brought to bear upon the subject in question—is accompanied with a will cloathed with power—political power is added to the corresponding will: in the other form whatsoever effect is given to what passes in their minds, it is by their opinion alone that the effect is produced—by the declaration made of it by themselves, or by the opinion entertained by the conjecture made by the functionaries in question as to what that opinion is. In the one case, if any declaration of their opinion is made, *obligatory* effects are made to follow it: in the other case, no such effects are made to

[1] MS del. 'in the one form' is preferred to MS 'in both forms'.

follow it. Of the case in which its sentiments receive an obligatory effect, the function of a Jury is an example. A Jury in so far as it is what it professes to be, in so far as the institution is productive of any of that good which it is spoken of as intended to produce, is a sort of Committee of the whole body of the people—a *section* of that vast *polypus*. In the case of Trial by Jury as at present established, the opinion it pronounces is termed a verdict: to it is given an obligatory effect: over the body composed of these impermanent functionaries is placed a permanent functionary or body of permanent functionaries by which the verdict is left in possession of its obligatory power or deprived of it as they please—but if no express measure is taken for the depriving it of its power, effect is given to it of course.

§3. *Public Opinion Tribunal—its sections, Democratical and Aristocratical*

The Tribunal of Public Opinion may be considered as composed of two Sections: the Democratical and the Aristocratical. On every occasion, the conduct of every human being will be determined by his own interest:[a] his own interest meaning according to his own conception of it, to the conception correct or incorrect entertained in relation to it by himself at the moment of action. On every occasion the opinion *acted upon* by each individual in his character of member of the Public Opinion Tribunal will therefore be determined by his own interest: therefore so will that of the Tribunal considered as a whole be determined by the interest of the majority of those who act as Members.

The interest of the Democratical Section is that of the majority of the Members of which the whole Tribunal taken in the aggregate is composed: it is consequently the interest of the subject many: the opinion on which it *acts* will be that which is in the highest degree contributory to the greatest happiness of the greatest number, in so far as the conception entertained by the several Members in relation to their respective interests is correct: in the highest degree contributory to the greatest happiness of the greatest number, and therefore in the highest degree accordant with the universal interest.

The interest of the Aristocratical Section of the Public Opinion Tribunal is that of the Members or the Majority of the Members of that portion of the entire number of the Members of the political

[a] His own interest taken in its most extensive sense, that in which it is coextensive with the whole aggregate of pains and pleasures.

Community which is composed of the ruling and otherwise influential few: of the highest ranks of functionaries in the state, with the addition of such other classes whose particular interests are in a league with theirs. The opinion, on which, as in their several other characters so in their character of Members of the Public Opinion Tribunal, the Members belonging to this Section of that all-comprehensive Tribunal act will therefore be in each instance determined by the interest common to the Members of this Section. But in a great, not to say the greatest, part of the field of morals including that of legislation the interest common to the Members of this narrow Section is in direct opposition to the interest of the more comprehensive Section.

The section of the subject many is composed chiefly of the productive classes.[a] The section of the ruling and otherwise influential few is composed principally of the non-productive classes.

Corresponding to the diversity in regard to interest will be the several opinions pronounced and acted upon by these two Sections. By the Democratical Section, *disrepute* will be attached to all such actions as in the conception of its members are pernicious to the universal interest: and that in a degree of force proportioned to the degree of such injuriousness: good repute, to all such actions as in that same conception are in an eminent degree salutary to the universal interest, contributory to the greatest happiness of the greatest number.

Determined by these respectively opposite interests will be disposal made of such expressions of disapprobation and approbation as it is respectively in their power to make with regard to human conduct in every part of the field of law and morals.[1]

By the Democratical Section, disapprobation will be manifested to every modification of human action in so far as it is regarded as being detrimental to the aggregate interest of its members, which is as much as to say in so far as to the universal interest: to every modification of human conduct, whether comprized among the subjects of legal obligation, or not so included: whether subjected to the power of the political, including [the] legal sanction, or left to the dominion of the popular or moral sanction alone.

[a] Under the import of the word *productive*, taken in the original sense, that of the word distribution is comprized; *production* brought forward: also productive.

[1] There is no text corresponding to the following marginal summary, which belongs here: 'By [Members] of Aristocratical [Section], disapprobation attached to all actions regarded by them as eminently detrimental to ruling few's happiness: approbation to all ditto regarded as ditto contributory to ditto.'

By disapprobation understand in both cases, that which is *expressed*: not, except in so far as it agrees with that which is expressed, that which is inwardly entertained. That, and that alone, which is of practical importance is that which is declared and acted upon. Now this it is that in the instance of each section is determined by that which in the eyes of the several members of the respective sections is their interest. But in a great, not to say the greater, part of the whole field of legislation, the interest of the aristocratical section taken in the aggregate is in a state of diametrical opposition to the interest of the democratical section taken in the aggregate, and thereby to the universal interest. It is so in every part in which a competition between the two interests has place.

§4. *Members of the Public Opinion Tribunal—Full and Committee*

The Public Opinion Tribunal may be conceived as sitting and acting in full Assembly, or through the medium of a Committee: a specially and actually appointed Committee.

In the character of a full Assembly, whatsoever is said of it may contain more or less of truth, but must unavoidably be mixt with more or less of fiction. The best course therefore will be to consider it as acting by a Committee—in this case all fiction may be excluded. That which is real being thus explained, the explanation may afterwards be applied with advantage to the mixture of the real and the fictitious.[1]

If in a *Committee of the Public [Opinion Tribunal]*, the presence of a Member of the Aristocratical Section of it can, with reference to the interest of the public taken in the aggregate, be of use, it can only be with a view to appropriate intellectual aptitude, knowledge and judgment taken together. In respect of moral aptitude, it can scarcely happen but that in comparison of an average Member of the Democratical Section he will be inferior: his situation exposing him to those temptations from particular and sinister interest to which the Member of the Democratical as such is not exposed. But of whatever knowledge and judgment is possessed by a man, communication may as easily be given without a vote as with a vote possessed by that same individual. If then there be any preponderant demand for the assistance of a person of that class with a view to accession of appropriate knowledge and judgment, a single individual of that class may be regarded as sufficient whatsoever be the number of the

[1] The discussion appears to have been broken off at this point. The remainder of the section is taken from a different sequence of MSS (UC clx. 456–7) which discusses the composition of a committee of the public opinion tribunal.

remainder: in which case his having or not having a vote in common with them will hardly be worth contending for.

As practice and experience under the Constitution in question encrease, any deficiency which at the outset may have place in regard to these requisites in [the] instance of the Democratical Members will be receiving continual supplies: the demand, if any such there were, for any such aristocratical assistance will therefore in the same proportion decrease.

In comparison of the aggregate number of the Members of the Democratical Section of the Public Opinion Tribunal, that of those of the Aristocratical will be small. Here then is another reason why the number of the Aristocratical Members on each such Committee should be small: for the larger it were, the greater would be the number of those on whom the burthen of such attendance, in proportion as the attendance were felt as burthensome, would be incumbent.

By these two considerations, the principles proper for the determination of the members in the case of a Committee other than that which is formed by a common Jury differ from those which apply with propriety to the case in which in trial by Jury, if one of the parties be a foreigner, one half of the Jury is at his instance to be composed of foreigners.[1]

§5. *Tribunal's two Sections—Interests opposite*

In regard to the matter of wealth, it is the common interest of the productive classes that [of] the matter of wealth in all its several forms, the enjoyment derived from the use and consumption of it be in the largest proportion possible reaped by those by whose labour that same protean matter has been produced: and that consequently [by those by whom no part of it has been produced,] it be enjoyed in the smallest proportion possible, or what is best of all that it should not be enjoyed in any proportion at all:[2] and by this community of interest is produced a community of sympathy.

It is an interest common to the non-productive classes that the enjoyment derived by themselves from the use and consumption of

[1] At Common Law, an alien was entitled to be tried by a jury of which half the members were aliens: this was known as the jury *de medietate linguae* (of a moiety of tongue). Moreover certain borough courts, where one of the litigants in commercial cases was a foreign merchant, allowed a jury composed half of natives and half of foreigners.

[2] MS 'and that consequently it be enjoyed in the smallest proportion possible, or what is best of all that by those by whom no part of it has been produced it should not be enjoyed in any proportion at all'. The syntax has been altered in order to clarify the meaning.

the quantity of the matter of wealth brought into existence by the labour of the productive classes be enjoyment reaped in as large a proportion as possible: and consequently the enjoyment derived from that same source by those by whose labour it has been produced be reaped in as small a quantity as possible, or what would be best of all not reaped in any quantity.

In regard to obligations, those obligations in all their several shapes, by the creation of which rights are created and the enjoyment of them secured, and therewith such portion of felicity as man by his nature is qualified for the enjoyment of put within his reach, it is the interest of the subject many that they be fulfilled in as large a proportion as possible. Not but that in regard to each such obligation, in proportion as he feels it burthensome to himself, each man would be desirous and disposed to shake it off from himself if not restrained by a preponderant force under almost any government that can have existence. But forasmuch as in the general fulfilment of the aggregate of the obligations he always has more or less enjoyment to hope for, and from the general non-fulfilment of them nothing at all—and so, whatsoever be the proportion in question, more to hope from the fulfilment of it than from the non-fulfilment of it, at the same time in the class to which he belongs he can not find for the claiming of any preference for himself in this particular any pretence which other men of that same section or of the other sections would be disposed to be in any degree influenced by, thus it is that in this class the interest and desire of each are in pretty uniform accordance with the interest and desire of all.

In regard to oppression in its several other shapes, and that of depredation in particular, it is in like manner the interest of every member of the subject many that it should not at any time or place be committed by any person in any of its shapes: and accordingly in consequence of which, suppose a law by which all such misconduct were rendered as above impossible put to the vote, there could be no doubt but that his vote would be of course in favour of it.[a] It is therefore his interest that in the Official Establishment of the country[?] to which he belongs there should not be to any extent any useless Offices and Pensions, needless Offices and Pensions, overpay of useful and needful Offices and Pensions: and if for the abolishing of all such instruments of unpunishable depredation in the lump, a law

[a] Unless by the excitation [of] some extraordinarily violent appetite, accompanied with an apparent chance of its finding in his instance a gratification by his means, he were for the moment so blinded to the aggregate interest of his whole life, as to sacrifice it to the interest of the moment in respect of the affording a gratification to such his appetite.

capable of producing that effect were proposed, a vote given by him in relation to it would without doubt be given in favour of it: and so in case of a law affording, in so far as depended upon the state of the law, protection in equal degree to rich and poor: to men possessed of a share in the aggregate mass of power and to men not possessing any such share: in the case of such a law in preference to a law which, while it afforded to the rich full protection against the poor, put into the hands of the rich arms with which they were enabled to committ oppression and depredation at the expence of the poor at pleasure.

Not so in the case of a member of the ruling and otherwise influential [few] in any fully established political state as yet known, the Anglo-American United States excepted. It is his interest as such, that the quantity of depredation and oppression in other shapes exercisible by men of his class should be at its maximum: just as in the case of a purchaser of a ticket in a lottery, it is his interest that, the price of a ticket being given, the value of the aggregate number of the prizes be in as great a ratio to it as possible. On the other hand as a member of the whole community at large, and as such under the unavoidable obligation of bearing in some proportion or other a part more or less considerable of the aggregate burthen attached to the support of it, it is his interest that that same quantity be as small as possible. In a manner more or less careful and exact, he will therefore form a calculation for determining which of two values is the greatest, the value of his probable loss by being subject to the depredation and oppression or the value of his probable profit by the share he hopes for in the benefit of it.[1]

In regard to money in the disposal of rulers, it is the interest of a Member of the Aristocratical Section of the Public Opinion Tribunal as such that the quantity of it placed within the reach of the Section to which he belongs be as great as possible: it is therefore his interest to give his support to all things the tendency of which is to give augmentation to that quantity—to all laws, institutions, customs, opinions, prejudices, desires, hopes, fears, in so far as the tendency of them is to give existence to that effect.

§6. *Tribunal's two Sections—Aristocratical erroneous*

Offences against the person of individuals, offences against the property of individuals, offences against the reputation of individuals,

[1] In the marginal summary, Bentham commented at this point: 'Addend. English Aristocrat's calculation, now that taxation has reached its maximum, and Radicalism rises.'

offences against the condition in life, including the power, of individuals—under these denominations may be included all modifications of conduct detrimental to the happiness of individuals individually considered. It is the interest of a Member of the Democratical [Section] as such, that no such misdeeds as come under any of these denominations should have place in any instance.

With respect to the aggregate of these same misdeeds, it is the interest of a member of the Aristocratical Section as such that no offence of any one of these descriptions should have place to the detriment of the happiness of the particular Section to which he appertains. But, in so far as the effect of any such misdeed is to operate to his own benefit, though it be to the detriment of the more numerous class to which he does not belong—to his own individual benefit to any amount how great so ever—it is in his view of the matter, generally speaking, his interest that to the extent of that case those misdeeds in all their several shapes and denominations should be as abundant as possible, that in regard to all other individuals in general, and in regard to all individuals whose place in the public opinion tribunal is in the Democratical Section of it, it should at all times be in his power to inflict on them evil in all these several shapes in so far as by the infliction of it gratification to himself in some shape shall thereby be produced. It is his interest to have it in his power to beat, maim or otherwise maltreat, for example, the person of every other man whose lot it has been to fall under his displeasure: to cover him with reproach cast upon him on the supposition of his having committed misdeeds which in truth he has not committed: to dispart him of any part or of the whole of his means of subsistence: to deprive him of the power of giving direction [to] the conduct of his children during the time of their immaturity: by fraud or force to violate the person of his wife, his daughters or sisters in any number: all this without danger of suffering on his own part, on the ground of any of these misdeeds, at the hands of law or otherwise—on the contrary, to possess the assurance of seeing the force of the law employed in securing him against suffering in any shape on the account of his having committed them—in a word, to have by law a right to committ them respectively.

A right of this sort—this right of doing wrong—is, in so far as it is enjoyed by the members of a small class at the charge of the aggregate of the members of the community, in the laws of all nations termed a privilege: in so far as it is possessed by a single individual, it is in the language of English law termed a prerogative.

It is in a higher degree a man's interest to be the sole possessor [of] a privilege of this sort or any other: and the value of such privilege decreases with the number of those with whom he shares it. At the same time, it ceases not to have to him a value with reference to his interest so long as there exists in the whole community one individual who does not share in it.

It is the interest of every Member of the Aristocratical Section as such that there should exist a class of Citizens, provided he be one of them, in whose power it should be to enjoy benefits in all imaginable shapes at the expence of the greatest number: in a word to produce suffering in all manner of shapes [and] to enjoy impunity for misdeeds to as great an extent as possible.

If by any efficient cause one set of men, the Members of the Aristocratical Section, receive the power of producing on the part of the Members of the Democratical Section suffering in all manner of shapes for the gratification of their own appetites, while the Members of the Democratical Section as such stand debarred from doing the like to the injury of the Members of the Aristocratical, a natural consequence is that the judgment, or at any rate the language, the judgment really entertained as well as the judgment declared, on this subject should on the part of the Members of the Democratical Section be unfavorable and condemnatory with relation to this state of things, and so far to a Government in which any such state of things is kept in existence.

But for the correspondent and opposite reason a consequence equally natural is that of the Members of the Aristocratical Section as such, the judgment pronounced on this same state of things should be favorable and commendatory.

For the giving expression to this judgment, a formulary has accordingly been invented. Litigation is a bad thing, such a state of things is productive of good: the good that consists in the prevention or diminution of litigation.

If by litigation be meant and understood, applying to use beneficial to all the members of the community without distinction the power of the Judicial Establishment, this is not true. But if by litigation be meant and understood, applying to an use beneficial to a small portion of the whole number of the members of that same community, this is true.

If there be that government under which the protection of the law is afforded to a small portion, say one-tenth, of the whole number, [and][1] denied to the rest, say nine-tenths, thereby placing all those who have not the faculty [of] the purchasing of that protection at the mercy of those who possess that faculty, it is the interest of the

[1] MS 'it should be'.

one-tenth that such government be preserved and supported: but it is the interest of the nine-tenths that it be subverted if there be any other government in which the faculty of obtaining the protection of the law is extended to any greater number.

What is the conclusion of all this? that in so far as it differs from the judgment pronounced by the Democratical Section, the judgment pronounced by the Aristocratical Section will be erroneous—erroneous to the prejudice of the greatest happiness of the greatest number.

From this it follows again that in every factitious and instituted assemblage of functionaries, instituted for the purpose of serving as a representation of the Public Opinion Tribunal, all individuals of whom it appears that [they appertain][1] to the Aristocratical Section ought to be either excluded altogether or, if admitted, not admitted but in a number extremely small: admitted not in the quality of voters whose votes shall have an obligative effect, but only in the quality of instructors and advisers whose votes shall not be possessed of an obligative effect. Why? Because be the community what it may, the aggregate interest of all the members of it is never so opposite to the interest of the smaller number as the aggregate interest of the smaller number may be and generally is to the aggregate interest of the greater number.

A Jury is a Section of the Public Opinion Tribunal called in on certain occasions of judicature to serve as a counterforce to the operation of particular and sinister interest in the situation of permanent Judge.

In [the] practice of English law there are two sorts of Petty Juries, Common and Special. The Common Jury is a Committee of the Democratical Section: the Special Jury, of the Aristocratical. The Common Jury is a safeguard against oppression: the Special Jury an instrument of oppression[2]--an instrument fabricated by the Corruption System, and in comparison of the other Jury, a recently fabricated instrument.[3]

The judgment of the Democratical Section has many errors in it: it has some that are common to it and the Aristocratical Section: it has some which are peculiar to itself. But in proportion as it becomes more and more mature, it becomes more and more conformable to the universal interest: whereas the judgment of the Aristocratical Section as it becomes more and more mature, becomes more and more adverse and prejudicial to the universal interest.

[1] MS 'he appertains'.

[2] In the marginal summary, Bentham commented at this point: 'Addend. So, Grand Jury.'

[3] Courts of Common Law were authorized in 1730 by 3 Geo. II, c.25 (made perpetual by 6 Geo. II, c.37) to order special juries to be struck at the request of the prosecutor or defendant in a trial for misdemeanour, or at that of either party in a civil action.

PART II. SECURITIES FOR INTELLECTUAL APTITUDE

CHAPTER 10. SECURITIES FOR APPROPRIATE INTELLECTUAL APTITUDE: VIZ. APPROPRIATE KNOWLEDGE AND APPROPRIATE JUDGMENT[1]

§ 1. *Axiom and Exposition. Sole adequate mode of ascertaining adequate aptitude, Examination*[2]

1. The greatest happiness of the greatest number requires, that in each office that individual be located in whose instance the maximum of appropriate aptitude taken in all its branches has place.[a] Concerning moral aptitude, see above. Comes in the next place appropriate intellectual aptitude: its two branches, appropriate knowledge and appropriate judgment.[b]

2. For accomplishing this object, the only suitable course of operation admitts of but one description, and that with small exception the same for all Offices in all departments: this one course is universally designated by one and the same word, *examination*: reference being had to the characteristic nature of the business of the Office in each case—say *appropriate examination*.[c]

3. Examination into the aptitude of the individual in question with reference to the business of the Office supposes the existence of some person or persons by whom the operation is to be performed. Call them the Examining functionary or functionaries: or for shortness, the Examiner or Examiners. Any person who, in the character or situation of a Candidate for the Office, is regarded as being willing that his aptitude with reference to the Office shall be taken into consideration and enquired into, call him an Examinee.

[a] Axiom, Political.
[b] Exposition, Division.
[c] Exposition, Definition.

---

[1] Bentham made three attempts to draft this chapter, UC cxiii. 114, 116, 130–1, 112–13, 129 (29–30 April 1822), cxiii. 115, 124–8, 134–5, 132–3 (5–6 May 1822), and cxiii. 106–11 (9–10 June 1822) respectively, none of which is complete. The ordering of these MSS has followed as closely as possible the plan at UC xxxviii. 7, using material where appropriate from each draft, and in cases of duplication giving preference to the later draft.

[2] This section is based on UC cxiii. 106–7 (9 June 1822), which is preferred to the earlier drafts at UC cxiii. 114, 116 (29–30 April 1822) and UC cxiii. 115, 124–5 (5 May 1822).

4. To examine into the aptitude of the individual in question with reference to the business of the Office in question in respect of knowledge, or say the scientific branch of intellectual aptitude, or in one word appropriate knowledge, supposes the correspondence of certain subjects of knowledge coming within the field of duty in question. In so far as an Examiner examines into [the] aptitude of an Examinee in this respect, he takes the requisite method or course for ascertaining and knowing whether, with reference to the subject matter in question, he is in possession of the requisite knowledge.

5. For the obtaining of this information by the Examiner at the hands of the Examinee, the nature of the case admitts but of one course or species of operation, and that is the causing it to be known to the Examinant that it is his will or desire that the Examinant shall, with reference [to] the several subjects in question, make declaration of that which as it seems to him he knows. For the expression of any such desire, the most direct and obvious and customary form of words is termed *a question*—the act of giving expression to such desire, the putting of a question: or in one word, *interrogation*.

For the exposition of whatsoever other modes there are of aiming at the accomplishment of this same end, the most simple and clearest course is that of making reference to this one.

Any form of words by which, reference being made to a question put by an Examiner, compliance with such his will is by an Examinee manifested or refused or endeavoured to be evaded is termed an *answer*, or say a *response*.[1]

Reference being had to supposed Candidates, or say Examinees, more than one, appropriate aptitude is either absolute or comparative. Of absolute appropriate aptitude, the existence or non-existence is capable of being ascertained by examination made of that one: of comparative aptitude, the existence or non-existence is not capable of being ascertained with reference to any number of candidates otherwise than by examination made of these same Candidates: examination performed upon all of them, on one and the same plan.

Of the maximum of appropriate aptitude on the part of any one, the existence is not capable of being ascertained otherwise than by the examination of all such persons as either in their own opinion, or in the opinion of any other persons whose opinions are taken into the account, are each of them in possession of absolute aptitude.

[1] There is no text corresponding to the following marginal summary, which belongs here: 'Reference had to Office, every Examinee is a *Candidate*.'

§2. *Neglect of this sole adequate security, nearly universal—why*[1]

On the mention of this mode of making provision for the maximum of appropriate aptitude with reference to political Offices in general, two propositions there are which can scarcely fail to press themselves upon the attention of the reader whosoever he be.

One is—that for ascertaining of the points in question on adequate grounds, this is the only mode which the nature of the case admitts of.

The other is—that scarcely with reference to any political Office has this most obviously apt, and most obviously sole apt, course been taken in any government as yet in existence.

This omission then—to what cause is it to be ascribed? in this may be seen another question that can not fail to press itself upon every mind of the wishes of which the accomplishment of this great object—maximization of official aptitude—forms an object.

The answer is—that, except in so far as the case of one government presents an exception, to no government as yet in existence has the accomplishment of this object been an object of desire.[2] Ask again the *reason*, say the efficient or *rational cause*—the answer is—because, with the above exception, in no government has the greatest happiness of the greatest number been ever the end in view or object aimed at: in no government has any end in view or object been directly aimed at other than the particular and thence sinister interest of the rulers: of those persons in whose hands the powers of government are lodged.

Of this position, this one fact—this almost universal omission of the most obviously necessary means—might of itself, for any practical purpose, serve for a sufficiently conclusive proof. In private life, scarcely by any the most careless Master, when a Servant is to be hired, is this operation altogether neglected: although in political life it is so uniformly neglected. Whence the difference? Whence? unless it be because by the individual it is felt to be his interest that his servants be endowed with appropriate aptitude, whereas in political life, by the chief functionaries it is felt to be their interest that in a large proportion the functionaries under them be not endowed with appropriate aptitude. Of this difference the cause, though not unobvious, will in express terms be stated a little further on.[3]

[1] This section is based on UC cxiii. 108–9 (9 June 1822), which is preferred to the earlier draft at UC cxiii. 130–1 (30 April 1822).

[2] Bentham's point seems to be that only the government in question, presumably that of the United States of America, had the maximization of official aptitude for an object. In the United States, however, examination for entrance to the civil service was not introduced until 1853.

[3] Bentham did not go on to discuss this question in the context of securities for intellectual

In relation to the possession of the endowment in question, the only direct evidence which the nature of the case admitts of is that which it is the nature of the process above-mentioned to bring into existence: of such direct evidence, such examination is the only source.

Instead of this direct evidence, the course taken is to ground practice on mere circumstantial, or say presumptive, evidence: and for the presumption in question, there are either no grounds at all, or at best ones such as are, as well in themselves, so in comparison of that direct one, obviously inadequate.[1]

§ 3. *Examination should be comparative: number of Examinees, a maximum*

Position. The greatest happiness of the greatest number requires that on the occasion of the examination of a Candidate for any public Office, the number of the Examinees be a maximum.

Rationale.

The mode of examination being (suppose) the same in the instance of each, the greater the number of Candidates, the greater the probability of the maximum of appropriate aptitude on the part of some one of them.

§ 4. *The Examination should be public: degree of publicity, a maximum*

Position. The greatest happiness of the greatest number requires that on the occasion of the examination of a Candidate for any Public

aptitude, but for a general discussion of the sinister interest of chief functionaries see Ch. 2, pp. 13–26 above.

[1] In the text, Bentham noted at this point: 'See further on.' He did not go on to discuss this particular topic, though in an earlier draft of this chapter at UC cxiii. 131 (30 April 1822), he had described, in relation to a government containing a representative body, the course pursued by the chief functionary in the choice of his subordinates: 'Each Assembly is a School in the exercises of which manifestation is made [of] the talents possessed by the respective Scholars. In so far as appropriate aptitude on the part of his subordinates is regarded by him as necessary or conducive to his purposes, whatever they be, he looks to that Assembly as to the most instructive if not the only School in which such manifestation has been or can be made. Between the place of exercise for Adults called a Representative Assembly, and the place of exercise for Non-Adults called a *School*, the only difference is, that that information which in the Schools is obtained with certainty—obtained in execution of a prearranged plan—obtained to an all-comprehensive extent—is in the place called an Assembly no otherwise obtained than to an inadequate extent, in a casual, and thence imperfect, manner, without the help of the requisite instruments of extraction.'

Office, the degree of publicity of the examination shall in all apt ways be maximized.

Rationale.

That the force of the Tribunal of Public Opinion may be made to bear upon the whole process with the maximum of its force, operating thus as a counterforce to the power of the Examiner or Examiners whosoever they may be.[1]

Q. What is the most apt mode of making application of the process stiled Examination?

A. Individual parties to this process there are not necessarily more than two: namely a party examined and a party by whom he is examined. This mode being manifestly of all imaginable modes the most simple is on that account the most apt, unless some point or points of aptitude be brought to view in which it is deficient, and in respect of which it may be rendered apt or less unapt by additional arrangements.

Q. What are those several points of comparative inaptitude?

A. On the part of the Examiner, facility given to partiality in favour of the Candidate at its maximum: facility for partiality, that is to say facility for deficiency in respect of moral aptitude.

Q. For imperfection in this form, what is the most apt remedy?

A. Instead of secrecy in the extreme, publicity in the extreme: facility given to the presence of the people at large in their character of members of the public opinion tribunal, to the people at large in the greatest number in which they choose to be present, and can be present without producing mutual annoyance to each other to such a degree as to be productive of preponderant evil in this or that shape.

Q. Of examination in this mode, is it in any case to be found?

A. Yes:—English Ecclesiastical law. Antecedently to his admission into orders called holy orders, every Candidate undergoes examination at the hands of one of several Priests serving in the character of Chaplain to a Bishop, to a Bishop chosen by the Candidate himself: no person being ever present but the individual so examining, and the individual so examined.[2]

Q. This publicity of examination, would it not have for its effect the

[1] Thus far, the chapter has followed the third draft of 9–10 June 1822, which Bentham appears to have abandoned at this point. Henceforward, the chapter is based on the first and second drafts of 29–30 April and 5–6 May 1822 respectively (see p. 77n above).

[2] Under English Ecclesiastical Law, the archdeacon was responsible for the examination of candidates presented to a bishop for ordination. It was his duty to ensure that they were 'apt and meet, for their learning and godly conversation, to exercise their Ministry duly, to the honour of God, and the edifying of his Church'. (See Richard Burn, *Ecclesiastical Law*, 2nd edn., 4 vols., London, 1767, iii. 32–3.)

excluding from the competition many individuals who by an extraordinary degree of sensitiveness in relation to public opinion might thus be excluded from the chance of taking in the scale of Office that station to which their aptitude in other respects would entitle them?

A. In regard to some, this would naturally be the case: but the force of this reason does not appear to make any near approach to the condition of a preponderant one.

The public would not by this exclusion be deprived of such other service as the persons labouring under infirmity in this shape may be enabled to render: nor they of whatever benefit may be derived by individuals from the rendering of such service: the course of the pen would still be open to them.

Of those who, in the first instance, might suppose themselves incapable of enduring this test, and who, by the faculty of obtaining the benefits in question without subjecting themselves to it, are withheld from subjecting themselves to it, will, when they find the necessity of subjecting themselves to it, make up their minds to the doing so, prepare themselves accordingly, and in virtue of such preparation enable themselves to endure it, and in the result endure it with success.

Thus it is in the case of the Advocate's profession. Few are the individuals who for a very considerable time after their entrance into the profession are not in a very acute degree sufferers from this cause. But such suffering has never been alledged as a reason why all judicial proceedings in general should be carried on in secret, in the closet of the Judge. Those whose nervous system enables them to speak in public, become Pleading Advocates: the others become Chamber Advocates.

By the incapacity of enduring such probation, a person is not rendered the more apt in respect of any of the other points of aptitude. By the capacity of enduring it, he is not rendered the less apt. The competition is between the interest of the community in so far as depends on the aptitude of its several functionaries, and the interests of the comparatively few individuals who to an incurable degree labour under this infirmity: nor by the exclusion are they debarred from the faculty of rendering service to the public in all shapes, but only from the faculty of rendering it in the particular shapes in question: in which shapes they are in this respect, by the very supposition, comparatively or absolutely, ill-qualified for the rendering it.

A man who is to a certain degree deaf stands by that infirmity excluded from the faculty of taking part in a public debate, of pleading *vivâ voce* in answer to arguments urged in the same manner on the other side. But this incapacity was never alledged as a reason, much less as an adequate and conclusive reason, for the carrying on judicial proceedings in secret, and by writing only, and not in public, and by oral discourse.

§5. *Examiners, who and how many*[1]

Q. The plan of Examination, is it not in respect of the aggregate of appropriate aptitude capable of receiving any addition except as above?

A. Yes: in respect of probability of appropriate moral aptitude. Notwithstanding all checks that it is in the nature of publicity as above to apply to partiality or carelessness on the part of the Examiners, it may still remain in a high degree imperfect. To render it compleatly apt, one thing is still wanting: and that is to give to each of the Candidates, to which may perhaps be added in some cases to each of the other persons present, the faculty of taking a part in the examination of the several Candidates. Each Candidate will in the highest degree be partial in disfavour of every other: and by this partiality he will stand engaged to look out for every question by which any deficiency on the part of the several other Candidates, his rivals and competitors, may be brought to light. Each Candidate will in like manner be in the highest possible degree partial in his own favour: but by this partiality, this deficiency in respect of appropriate moral aptitude in the person [of the Candidate], no deficiency absolute or comparative that may happen to have place in his instance will be prevented from being brought to light. Thus out of a deficiency in respect of moral aptitude on the part of each Candidate taken by himself, an extraordinary supply of intellectual aptitude on the part of every one of them will be the result.

Q. Can any other point of aptitude be mentioned in relation to which this mode of examination is deficient?

A. Not necessarily deficient and in all cases. But suppose such the variety of subjects that for the eliciting of the information requested to produce an adequate evidence of the aggregate of appropriate aptitude, acquirements of such sort are required that the aggregate of them is not [as] likely to be possessed by any one such man as can be found, as they are to be possessed by a number of men, each possessed of appropriate knowledge and judgment in some one line in a higher degree than any one of them is in all the lines in question

[1] This section is based on UC cxiii. 127–8 (5 May 1822), which is preferred to the earlier draft at UC cxiii. 129 (30 April 1822).

taken together. Here then arises[?] a demand for a distinct Examiner whose knowledge and judgment and active talent affords a fairer promise of being applied with advantage to that one of the several lines than to that and the others taken in the aggregate.

Thereupon comes the Rule. For each line of art and science, a separate Examiner.

Q. Would there be any use in the confining the operations of each such Examiner to that line which may be termed his own line?

A. None at all. But the contrary. For as to the evidence of a superiority of aptitude in comparison of all other persons in relation to this or that line, it can be nothing but a somewhat vague and indeterminate presumption, and that applying no otherwise than to the whole of the matter belonging to that line taken in the aggregate, not to each separate point belonging to it. Examiner A knows more as to line A than Examiner B does: but as to this or that point in line A, Examiner B happens at the instant in question to know more than Examiner A does: and so *vice versâ*.

§6. *Examination system public and comparative preferable to didactic ditto*

Q. Would not official scientific aptitude be more effectually promoted by Foundations of Schools and Lecturers for the instruction of youth in the several branches of science and art regarded as appertaining to the several Offices?

A. No: nor any thing near so well. In the establishment of a system of Examination, there is nothing that precludes the application of those other institutions in the character of means to the end in question. Both therefore may have place. But, in so far as an option requires to be made, compared with a Government establishment for the conveyance of instruction, a Government establishment upon the above plan, having for its immediate object the ascertaining by what individuals, and in what degree, instruction in the branches of art and science has actually been attained, will be found in a high degree preferable.

To prevent misconception, fixt denominations must be attached to the two different systems which on this occasion come to be compared. Calling the one the Public Examination System, let the name of the other be the Didactic System—that according to which, what instruction is received, is received from the lectures given or exercises set by a Master or a set of Masters, operating in private.

Note that the question is—not which of them shall have place: but which of them shall have place in preference, according to rules prescribed by Government and conducted by functionaries, the placing of whom is ordained by Government.

In the instance of any individual considered in the character of a learner, the Examination system can not have place, but in proportion as the Didactic system has previously had place: unless the means of learning had previously been placed within his reach, in vain would it be [to] enquire of any person whether he has learnt that which it is desired he shall have learnt. But a thing of which there can be no doubt is this—namely that, in a country rich enough to afford the matter of a Didactic system at the expence of Government, if a comfortable subsistence be offered to a certain number of persons by whom public proofs by Public Examination have been given of a certain degree of proficiency in certain branches of art and science, the provision requisite in the Didactic shape for the acquisition of the proficiency in question will have been made by individuals: made by individuals each of them defraying it in expectation of the emolument expected from it [to][1] himself: the burthen being shared by the individuals thus expecting to receive the benefit: and this without throwing any burthen, any part of it, on any of those by whom no part of the benefit is either expected or received.

On this occasion as on so many others, the interests of *appropriate aptitude* and the interests of *frugality* will be seen going hand in hand: the cheapest plan it will be seen is not only the cheapest but in every other respect the best.

By lectures and exercises, information may in some way or other have been presented to non-adults and adults in any multitude, and still no useful knowledge have been attained by any one of them. Such is the case of the Didactic system. Of the Public Examination system, no man will venture to say any thing like it. Under the Didactic system, there may have been a thousand learners, and not one of them in such sort assured of having learnt that which has been taught as to venture to subject himself to a Public Examination in the subjects in question, whatsoever were the reward provided for preeminence. Proficiency being the fact, the Public Examination system establishes, in the face of the public, the existence of the fact: all that without the aid of [the] Public Examination system can be done by the Didactic system carried on in private, is to afford a probability more or less considerable of the existence of that same fact: and in general so small is that probability, that the ratio of 1 to 10, or the ratio of 1 to 20, may be the representation of it.

[1] MS 'by'. The sense of the passage seems to require the emendation.

Q. So far as Government is concerned, what are the objects really pursued in those institutions which have for their ostensible and professed objects the promotion of useful learning?

A. Four, namely 1. waste and corruption: for these objects, though separable in idea being inseparable in fact, constitute in effect but one: 2. instillation of mischievous error: 3. exclusion of useful truth: 4. extirpation of useful morality, by planting a mischievous fabrication under the name of *religion* in the place of it.

Q. Waste, how is it promoted by these means?

A. Because of the benefits professed to be conferred on the people, none are actually conferred by the expenditure thus applied: so that the correspondent burthen—the burthen of the taxes laid and levied for furnishing the expenditure—remains uncompensated.

Q. Corruption—how is it promoted?

A. Correspondent to the money thus expended is a quantity of patronage: patronage exercised by the appointment of the individuals by whom, in different shapes, the mass of benefit belonging to the case shall be received, namely the instruction such as it is; and the money given to those by whom it is or is supposed to be communicated.

Q. Mischievous error, how is it thus instilled and propagated?

A. That what is instilled and propagated is error is thus demonstrated. Matters are so ordered, that unless the person will so comport himself that he shall be thought to hold certain prescribed opinions on the subject of religion, he has no chance for coming in for any share in the benefit.[1]

[1] This section appears to have been abandoned at this point, there being no discussion of the third and fourth topics.

PART III.
SECURITIES FOR ACTIVE APTITUDE

CHAPTER 11. SECURITIES FOR APPROPRIATE ACTIVE APTITUDE ON THE PART OF PUBLIC FUNCTIONARIES

§ 1. *Attendance unintermitted in the field of duty—its importance in relation to appropriate active aptitude—means of securing it*

In relation to appropriate active aptitude, securities are not difficult to find. Nor in the lowest grades is there any difficulty in finding effectual ones. But it is in the lowest grades that the importance of it is least: in the highest grades it is that the importance of it is greatest: and it is in these that to find it having place in any proportion approaching to perfection, and not to ideal perfection alone but in that degree of perfection in which it is actually established in the lowest grades, is most difficult.

Necessary to activity in whatsoever shape, in whatsoever line of service, is *attendance*: existence in that individual spot, if such a spot there be, in which alone the service can be rendered.

The periodical day of rest excepted or not excepted, on no one day throughout the year in the highest grades should [the omission of] appropriate attendance be permitted. In the lowest grades, it is not permitted. But if in any it ought to be permitted, it is in the lowest that it ought to be permitted rather than in the highest. Why? for this plain reason: that it is in the highest that its importance is greatest—the omission of it capable of being most mischievous.

If an office were thus loaded with duty—if a gentleman were thus sunk down with common Soldiers, common Writing Clerks and School-boys, no Gentleman would accept of it. Whatsoever else be meant by the said Gentleman, thus much being meant, that he preferred violation of duty to fulfilment of duty, if no Gentleman would accept of it, so much the better for the service.

Of all classes of society, the best-informed, best-instructed and most surely meritorious are the medical classes: their occupation from first to last consists in the uninterrupted endeavour to afford relief to the sufferings of their fellow men. Among all those men, by whom is the obligation of attendance—attendance the most unremitted—ever regarded as a hardship: by whom is it regarded as derogating from the character of gentleman, if gentleman must be the word? By no one. And why not? For this plain cause and reason, because in this closest contact with the burthen comes the benefit.

In no instance should sickness be regarded as a cause of exemption. The functionary being paid for his time and in proportion to his time, on each day no attendance, no pay, should be the inexorable rule. If no attendance, then no pay, such the rule for every day.

Why? For exactly the same [reason][1] in this case as in the case of *half-pay*, and pensions of retreat. If really unable to attend, the man is not fit for the service. Why pay for serving, or suffer to remain in the service, men who are not fit for it?

By no other means is the prevention of fraud [possible].[2]

In the case of that labour which each man bestows for his own benefit, for his own benefit in any profit-seeking occupation, in so far as a man ceases attendance in the business, by him and no one else are borne whatsoever sufferings his failure has for its effects. In the case where the purpose to which his labour is applied is the service of the public at large, why should a man be upon any better footing in this case than in the other? Who that has any regard for the service of the public could concurr in any arrangement by which, where it is to the whole community that the service is due, men are suffered and encouraged to leave it undone?

On such or such a day there is no business to do—very well: then on that day no business will be done. The functionary is at his post and where is the harm of his being so? of his being so on that day any more than any other? Nay: there is not so much harm: for being there in readiness to perform service to the public should any demand for such service present itself, he may take that time for doing his private business—for reading and answering letters and the like. In a word, he may do what the supremely ruling operative functionaries of the Anglo-American United States are in the habit of doing.[3]

On such or such a day so it happens no business requiring to be done on that day has happened to present itself. Good. But what is that day on which it can be matter of certainty that no business requiring to be transacted without delay—no business from the non-

[1] MS 'rule'.

[2] MS 'impossible'.

[3] The Constitution of the United States authorized Congress 'to compel the attendance of absent members, in such manner, and under such penalties as each House may provide' (Art. I, §5). Members of Congress were not allowed to absent themselves without leave of their respective Houses, and were liable to be taken into custody for so doing and made to pay the expenses consequent upon their arrest. (See 'Rules for conducting business in the Senate of the United States', no. 8, and 'Standing Rules and Orders for Conducting Business in the House of Representatives of the United States', nos.47, 50–2.)

performance of which on that very day, mischief beyond all calculation may ensue—will not present itself? In this or that portion of the territory, famine is raging—by apt arrangements taken by the supreme operative authority it might be stopped. The subject many by thousands shall they perish, and for no better reason than that while they are perishing, the ruling few may enjoy uninterrupted pleasure?

When a man must be in the indispensable local field of his duty, he may as well do his duty as not do it: and do it well as do it ill and negligently: if he is not there, well or ill, it is not possible for him to do it.[a]

§2. *Minimizing factitious remuneration—in what way a security for appropriate active aptitude*[1]

Q. What are the means capable of being applied with advantage to the purpose of securing on the part of public functionaries in general the existence of appropriate active aptitude?

A. The magnitude of the price which the individual is content to pay for the faculty of rendering service to the public in the shape in question. In the scale of this price there are three distinguishable degrees. 1. Serving for small pay: [2.] serving without receiving money in the quality of pay, but at the same time without giving money for the office: [3.][2] paying money for the office.

The higher the price an individual is willing to pay for the Office, the Office being of the number of those to which duties are attached, the greater is the pleasure he proves himself to enjoy or to anticipate from the performance of the operations belonging to it. But *caeteris paribus*,

[a] Anno 1791 in the tract on the subject of the Judicial Establishment, these principles were applied to the Judicial Establishment: in Anno 1817 in the 'Introduction' to the *Parliamentary Reform Catechism* they were employed to the case of the English House of Commons: to the case of that section of the supreme operative power in the English Empire.[3]

---

[1] The ordering of this section is conjectural, since no plan survives and the MSS are unmarginalized and lack any consecutive enumeration. Related fragments are at UC clx. 64 (30 April 1822) and clx. 65 (2 May 1822).

[2] MS '2'.

[3] See 'Draught of a Code for the organization of the Judicial Establishment', Ch. V, Title III, §3, pp. 6–7 and Ch. V, Observations, §8, pp. 53–5 (Bowring, iv. 356 and 378), in *Draught of a New Plan for the organisation of the Judicial Establishment in France*, printed 1790 (and not 1791); *Plan of Parliamentary Reform, in the form of a Catechism, with reasons for each article: with an Introduction, shewing the necessity of radical, and the inadequacy of moderate, reform*, London, 1817, pp. 199–250 (Bowring, iii. 495–511).

be the operations what [they][1] may, the greater the pleasure a man takes in the performance of them, the greater is the skill which is likely to be possessed by him and manifested in his performance of them.

Q. What securities does the nature of the case afford for the ascertaining what is the highest price which any individual will give for the Office in question?

A. Public competition: this is a means and the only one. Note that in this case, as in those others, room is afforded for the distinction between obligatory and unobligatory.[2] With reference to him who acts in the situation of patron, it may have the one effect or the other. He may be bound to place the highest bidder, or after hearing who is the highest bidder, it may be left free to him to give the Office to a lower bidder, or to an individual by whom no bidding has been made. In the instance of each, which of all these courses is the most beneficial will depend upon the nature of the Office and perhaps some other circumstances.

Q. An arrangement of this sort, is it not an unprecedented[a] one?

A. No matter whether it be or no, if conducive to the production of good in the shape in question, and not productive of preponderant evil in any shape.

Objection. An arrangement of this sort, would it not have among its effects that of producing in the mind of the functionary a notion that, having bought the office, he would be entitled to make the most of it? warranted in his own conscience and in the eye of the world, in the eye of the tribunal of public opinion, in the endeavour to make the most of it for his own private advantage?

A. Whether it would or would not be productive of any such effect is not worth enquiring. What is certain is that howsoever the matter stands in respect of power—power given by him—power received by him—endeavour to make the most of it for such his private advantage will not be wanting. By nothing that he will give for the office will this desire or the correspondent endeavour be encreased. By nothing that in the shape of pay he can be enabled to receive can it be diminished.

Q. The quantity of pecuniary sacrifice a man is willing to make in order to obtain the office, is it a conclusive test of his relish for the functions attached to it?

[a] *Unprecedented*—the objection of one who is unable to judge of conduciveness to the end: only wishes to hear what has been done: and concludes it to be therefore right.

---

[1] MS 'it'.

[2] The obligatory or unobligatory effect of the verdict of a jury is discussed in Ch. 9, §2, p. 66 above; see also p. 59n.

A. Absolutely taken it is: relatively and comparatively taken, comparison had between the highest bidder and the next highest, it is not. The reason is that it is by want of pecuniary ability, and not by inferiority in the scale of relish, that the bidder next to the highest is prevented from being the highest.[1]

Q. What are the particular objects or public benefits the receipt of which it is the object of the plan thus proposed to secure to the public?

A. In this case as in all others in which Office is concerned, the maximum of appropriate aptitude in conjunction with the minimum of expence at the public charge.

Q. In what way does this plan contribute to the securing of the maximum of appropriate aptitude, as above?

A. By making manifest the degree of relish or good liking which has place in the breast of each Candidate with reference to the nature of the Office, benefits and burthens taken together. If he will give any thing for the aggregate, the more in value he is content to give, the greater it is evident is the value he sets upon whatsoever it is that he is to receive. So, if he will not give any thing for it but insists on receiving over and above the benefits attached to it, something in the character of an equivalent for the service rendered by taking upon him the duties of it, the less he requires to be given to him, the greater it is alike evident is the value he sets upon such benefits as are attached to it.

[1] A fragment on this theme is at UC clx. 36 (24 May 1822): 'Location of functionaries by superiority in the scale of pecuniary competition in the case of certain offices, viz. Offices not requiring appropriate scientific aptitude, or in Offices although requiring scientific aptitude, in case of equality of altitude in the scale of scientific competition.

'Objection—exclusion of Candidates all but such as are furnished with property in the shape of capital to a certain amount, all but the relatively and comparatively rich.

'1. A most strongly probative circumstantial and presumptive evidence of relish for the function in question, and consequent appropriate aptitude in respect of all its branches taken together, is the smallness of the recompense or retribution, if any, which the Candidate is content to receive in compensation for his taking upon himself the obligations attached to the Office. To exclude pecuniary competition in the shape in question on the occasion in question is to divest the public in its character of Master of this important security for appropriate aptitude on the part of its servants.

'2. The money and time expended on the acquisition of the requisite degree of appropriate aptitude is so much capital employed in the construction of the psychological machinery necessary to the performance of the work belonging to the Office. No reason can be assigned why to enable them to obtain the matter of subsistence and abundance by the use of machinery in this form—of capital applied to this branch of industry—capital should in the shape of a bounty be bestowed upon any description of persons any more than to enable them to do the like by the use of machinery and capital applied to any other branch of industry. If it were right that, at the expence of all, the government should give capital to the few for the purpose of its receiving this application—so would it be that capital should thus be given for the purpose of every other application that could be named: instead of leaving a correspondent chance of correspondent eventual profit to all such as out of their own stock shall be at the same time able and willing to purchase it by the making of the necessary advance.'

Q. Is this the only means by which, in the instance of any Office, the possessor of the maximum of appropriate aptitude taken in the aggregate can be obtained?

A. No, certainly. In what instance so ever personal examination as applied to all the several Candidates can have place, that mode of ascertainment should likewise be employed.

Q. What is the most apt mode of making application of the principle of Competition to the purpose of obtaining on the part of a Public Functionary the maximum of the aggregate of appropriate aptitude?

A. The first points to be ascertained are: [1.] the duties attached to the Office: 2. the emolument and benefit in all shapes attached to it. The sort of instrument and the only instrument by which these duties can be adequately made known is a book [in which] all the services exigible at the hands of the functionary in virtue of his Office stand expressed, and which to answer this and all other purposes will require to be printed and published.

Competition is either in the line of offers made of pecuniary sacrifice or by manifestation made of personal aptitude.

In both cases let notice be given of the existence of this Code and where copies of it may, and at what price, be had: due time being allowed for the consideration of it. Add notice of the day and place at which, and the interval of time at which, *tenders* will be received.

At the time appointed, let the several Competitors, or say Candidates, make their appearance together in the presence of the Functionary or Functionaries appointed for that purpose. The separate offers, with the names of those by whom they have been respectively made, [having been received], competition may thereupon commence and be carried on in the ordinary mode of Auction, termed in English, Auction—in French, *à la folle enchère*. Question having been put to each competitor in the presence of the rest: whether a copy of the Code belonging to the Office has been received and read by him?

On the other hand, let the aggregate emolument or benefit which in all its branches is attached to the Office form part of the Code: the emolument together with the times at which the successive portions of it shall be receivable and a specification of the several conditions respectively necessary to be fulfilled ere the several receipts can take place.

Q. Suppose the claim to superiority in the scale of pecuniary offer to be decided in favour of one man, and superiority in the scale of personal aptitude, as indicated by public examination, in favour of another: to which of the two shall the Office be adjudged?

A. It seems necessary that the ultimate decision should be referred to some arbiter or number of arbiters. If it be to a single person in that character, that person is thereby the patron of the Office—the patron in respect of location: and for responsibility sake, a single patron appears to be in this case preferable to any other number of patrons, supposing them in all other respects all of them equally apt.

Q. Why so? how is it that the comparatively unimmediate and circumstantial evidence afforded by the mere circumstance of relish for the business—relish as thus indicated—evidence which applies not to any Office more than another, but only to all Offices taken in the lump, countervail[s] the more immediate and direct evidence afforded by the proof which examination is capable of affording in relation to each individual Office, whatever it may be?

A. Because that Office can scarcely be mentioned in relation to which every element of appropriate aptitude can by any course of examination, antecedently to experience of his conduct in the Office, be brought to view.

Q. The choice being after all thus left to the patron, to what use is all this complication, all this machinery, since after all he is left free to make his choice just as if no such machinery had been employed?

A. The use is not inconsiderable. The use of it is to fasten upon him the more effectually the requisite responsibility as towards the power of the Public Opinion Tribunal. To the members of it, it will be manifest in favour of which of the two Candidates the one indication operates, in favour of which of the two the other. The patron will judge which of the two is on the whole the most apt—affords the fairest promise—and the public will judge whether his judgment is apt. His reputation in respect of appropriate knowledge and judgment will in all cases be staked upon the result, and in some cases even in respect of appropriate moral aptitude.

Q. In the case of the two branches of the Military department, namely the Land Service and the Sea Service, supposing the power of location to be in the hands of a single functionary and he not belonging [to] the military profession in either branch, appropriate knowledge and judgment being thereby rendered necessarily deficient, what course can be safely taken for the supply of such deficiency?

A. Suffrages as many as can be obtained of the several functionaries of all ranks belonging to those departments respectively, these suffrages to be collected in the secret mode, and the results communicated to the patron, with or without communication made to other members of the Executive department: but the results not to be obligatory on him.

Q. Why secret?

A. Because only in proportion as they are secret is it possible they should be free: in the instance of each individual, the genuine expression of the real opinion of that same individual.

Q. Why should not the result of the suffrages be obligatory on the non-military patron?

A. Because if it were, the tendency of the institution would be to place the government in the hands of men belonging to the Military department, and thus render it a Military Aristocracy.

CHAPTER 12. CONCLUSION

In the arrangements here proposed to be taken in the character of securities for the aggregate of appropriate aptitude on the part of public functionaries in all the several situations, there is nothing very novel, nothing in any considerable degree wide of the usual road, the customary track, of government practice. There is little or nothing that is not already in practice in certain instances. In what cases? even in those in which it is the undoubted and indubitable desire of the individuals in question that appropriate aptitude should actually have place. This then is the rational cause why in these instances the arrangement has been resorted to. In the instances in which it has not been resorted to, what has been the rational cause why it has not been resorted to? What but the opposite and correspondent cause? namely that it has not been the desire of persons in the commanding situations in question, in the patronage possessing situations, that in the correspondent subordinate and patronized situations appropriate aptitude in all its points should have place: but that on the contrary it has been their desire that in those same patronized situations appropriate aptitude with reference to the business of those same situations should be at its minimum. Such would not be their desire were it not, in their conception at any rate, their interest: and that according to the conception commonly entertained by men in relation to their interest, it is in governments of a certain class the interest of men in the patronizing situations that such appropriate aptitude be at its lowest point in the scale will be shewn in another place.[1]

Under the form of government in question, it is the interest and accordingly the practice of rulers so to establish their arrangements with respect to the location of functionaries in official situations, that to the entrance of individuals occupying the lowest level in the scale of appropriate aptitude the utmost possible facility may be afforded. Conclusion. Therefore that form of government is with relation to the only right and proper end of government an unapt or bad form of government. So *a converso*. The form of government in question is [a] bad form of government. Hence among its practices is that of giving every possible facility to the admission of inaptitude in its highest degree into a large proportion of the whole number of its offices.

[1] See *Constitutional Code*, I (*CW*), Ch. VI, §31, Arts.25–41, pp. 123–9.

APPENDIX.

Indication of certain False or Erroneously supposed Securities for appropriate aptitude in relation to divers Official Situations

CHAPTER 13. EXCLUSIONS USUALLY PUT UPON CERTAIN CLASSES EXCLUDING THEM FROM PARTICIPATION IN THE EXERCISE OF THE SUPREME CONSTITUTIVE POWER BY RIGHT OF SUFFRAGE[1]

Q. Are there any, and, if any, what description of, persons which the greatest happiness of the greatest number requires to be excluded from the faculty of contributing by their votes to the location of the functionaries invested with the supreme operative power as above?

A. Yes: all such in whom such properties have place as render them deficient in respect of any of the several elements of appropriate aptitude: moral, scientific, judiciary, or active.

Q. What, if any, are those properties by which an individual, with reference to the function in question, is rendered destitute of the requisite and indispensable portion of moral aptitude?

A. None whatever. In the case of a public functionary possessing of himself a share in the supreme operative power, the branch of inaptitude opposite to moral aptitude is neither more nor less than the disposition to sacrifice to his own personal interest the universal interest. But if an equal share of the constitutive power in question is in the hands of every member of the community in question, the aggregate of the several personal interests is itself the universal interest.

Q. What, if any, are the circumstances by which, with reference to this function, a member of the community is divested of the requisite and indispensable portion of intellectual aptitude?

A. Yes [there are two]: namely 1. Immaturity in respect of age. 2. Destituteness or insufficiency in respect of that branch of art and science, of appropriate scientific aptitude, which is necessary to enable the constitutive functionary to form a judgment in relation

[1] The material in this chapter was originally intended for inclusion in 'Identification of Interests': see the Editorial Introduction, p. xxviiin above.

to the aggregate appropriate aptitude, absolute and comparative, of a person proposed for the situation of member of the body of supremely operative functionaries, in a word the art of reading, with the addition of the art of writing as applied to the signature of his own name: provided alway that in a number sufficient to constitute an interest not disagreeing from the universal interest, members endowed with this branch of art and science are in a condition to exercise the function.

Q. What in the scale of age is the point below which the greatest happiness principle requires that immaturity with reference to this function be presumed?

A. That point below which persons in general are regarded as not possessed of knowledge and judgment sufficient to enable them to take the general direction of their own conduct.

Q. What is that age?

A. On this point, fixation can not be other than in a great degree arbitrary and casual. Custom may therefore be allowed to determine. Under Rome-bred law, the age thus fixt is five and twenty years; under English-bred law, one and twenty. One and twenty seems full long enough, five and twenty much too long. Reason silent or hesitating, custom should on every occasion decide the scale. By departure from custom, disappointment is produced: and by disappointment, disquietude, uneasiness, pain.

Q. Does the greatest happiness principle require that the female sex should be excluded from a participation in this function?[1]

A. Not any more than males. No: unless persons of the female sex are not members of the community—if their happiness forms no portion of the universal happiness—their interest of the universal interest: or the state of their minds such as to demonstrate them to be irremediably incapacitated from giving direction to their own conduct without detriment to their own interest.

As to intellectual aptitude, no reason has ever been assigned why, in respect of that branch of appropriate aptitude, this half of the species ought to be deemed inferior to the other. Of experience—of experience as far as it goes—as applied to the highest situation in the scale of operative power, the decision is more in favour rather of the female sex than of the male. In no two male reigns was England as prosperous as in the two female reigns of Elizabeth and Ann.[2] As to Ann, whatever was the cause, it was more prosperous than that of her

[1] Fragments headed 'Females', dealing with some of the topics discussed here, are at UC clx. 85–8 (29 May 1822).

[2] Elizabeth I (1533–1603), Queen of England and Ireland from 1558; Anne (1665–1714), Queen of Great Britain and Ireland from 1702.

immediate male predecessor,[1] a man as unamiable as she was amiable. In intellectual aptitude, Elizabeth of England shewed herself in an incontestable degree superior to her immediate successor and even to the nearest of her male and adult predecessors.[2] If Ann was weak, she was not more so than her two immediate successors, both males.[3] If Mary[4] put men to death for what was called religion, so did her father, and so did her next male successor:[5] if Queen Mary put men to death for what was called religion, so did Chief Justice Hale, the saint and hero of English lawyers, for what was called Witchcraft.[6]

As to intellectual aptitude considered as applied to the field of thought and action at large, two points require to be considered: in the first place, among writers for example, in how small a degree the superiority is on the side of the male sex; in the next place, how small is the number of those of the female sex whom laws and institutions have left unexcluded from the competition in comparison of those whom they have excluded.

They might be unapt for exercise of supreme operative power or a share in it, and yet not be so for exercise of constitutive power in relation to supreme operative power. But they can not be unapt for exercise of supreme constitutive power, i.e. constitutive power with relation to supreme operative power, and at the same time apt with relation to supreme operative power.

Under the greatest happiness principle no reason can be assigned why the aggregate means of happiness should be less in the case of females than in the case of males. In domestic concerns, males derive greater power from physical force: here then is a means of injury: for security against it, if in respect of political power there be a difference, it should be rather in their favour than in the favour of males.[7]

[1] William III (1650–1702), King of England, Scotland and Ireland from 1689.

[2] James VI (1566–1625), King of Scotland from 1567, and as James I, King of England and Ireland from 1603, and Henry VIII (1491–1547), King of England from 1509 and King of Ireland from 1541, respectively.

[3] George I (1660–1727), King of Great Britain and Ireland from 1714, and George II (1683–1760), King of Great Britain and Ireland from 1727.

[4] Mary I (1516–58), Queen of England and Ireland from 1553.

[5] Henry VIII and James I respectively.

[6] The Marian persecution of 1555–8 resulted in nearly three hundred burnings for heresy. Sir Matthew Hale (1609–76), Lord Chief Baron of the Exchequer 1660–71, Chief Justice of King's Bench 1671–6, presided over the trial of two women accused of witchcraft at Bury St. Edmunds on 13 March 1665. On their conviction, he sentenced them to be hanged and they were executed on 17 March 1665. (See Howell, *State Trials*, vi. 687–702.)

[7] Bentham expanded on this point in the marginal summary: 'From their right to equality as to happiness, if admitted, will follow their right to equality as to power considered as an instrument of happiness, so far as the nature of species and sex permitts. To constitute equality in their favour, for every necessary inferiority they should have a compensation. In domestic concerns, inferiority of physical force renders them inferior in power. So, as to exercise of military function. So, under the military government of males they are not likely to be placed in

Q. Does not the consideration derived from custom present a sufficient reason for the exclusion here in question?

A. Certainly not: for the times in which custom had its commencement were times of barbarian immaturity, inferior to the present in all points bearing relation to government. Forms of government in general, and the feudal form in particular, had their origin in war. In war, necessity gave the command of all to a single chief; in peace, which in those days was never free from apprehensions of war, habit and prudence concurred in keeping it in the same hands. The female sex, at all ages less fit for war than the male, is during the time of fertility rendered in a more particular degree unfit by the weaknesses attached to gestation and parturition and lactation.

When monarchical despotism received for the first time its mitigation from a sort of humble and servile[?] democracy operating by delegation, it was because the continually experienced impossibility of extracting money time enough from unwilling contributors drove them into the practice of trying to extract it from willing ones, who thereupon were raised [to] a certain degree of importance, and in return for money receive[d] a certain degree of effective power disguised under the appearance of humble influence. These male slaves, heads of the several families, possessed a small degree of appropriate aptitude, their female slaves, their female relatives, none. To the males of each family, the fatigue and perils of journeys to and from the seat of husbandry and traffic to the seat of power were endurable, to the females unendurable. From a delegated assembly composed of males and females promiscuously, nothing but confusion and ridicule could have ensued. Thus it was that political power in all its forms and degrees came to be engrossed by the males.

Q. Can practical good in any form be mentioned as likely to be produced from the admitting the female sex into a participation of the supreme constitutive power?

A. Yes. The affording encreased probability of adoption to legislative arrangements placing sexual intercourse upon a footing less disadvantageous than the present to the weaker sex.

Q. On the occasion of any new Constitution framed in [the] present time would it, think you, be contributory to the greatest happiness of the greatest number, that a set of legislative arrangements directed to this end should be proposed?

A. No. In no political state that I know of should I think it at present

Civil Offices. Hence, from executive power in almost all its branches they will stand excluded. Also from share in supreme legislative power by contemplation of the confusion and corruption from mixture of sexes. Hence, greater the demand for equal share in constitutive power with reference to supreme operative.'

expedient to make any such proposal. Before the state of the legal system had been made on almost all other points contributory in the highest degree to the greatest happiness of the greatest number, scarcely could any prospect be afforded of [its][1] being rendered so as to this. The contests and confusion produced by the proposal of this improvement would engross the public mind and throw improvement in all other shapes to a distance.

Q. Are there no other descriptions of persons—are there no other classes—which the greatest happiness principle would exclude from a participation in this power?

A. No: and for this simple reason once for all, namely that there are no other classes in the instance of which the utmost good obtainable from discrimination would countervail the evil resulting from contestation. No matter how flagrant the inaptitude on the part of a few individuals, by such inaptitude no perceptible inaptitude could be produced in the aggregate result.

Q. What? not criminals? not even convicted criminals? not even convicted criminals whose crimes have been of the deepest die?

A. In some cases, their respective sentences might oppose a physical bar to their admission, and that bar an insuperable one. But physical bar apart, no adequate reason can be assigned for the application of political ones. Take the reasons following:

1. By moral inaptitude, though it were in the highest conceivable degree, no bar is applied in this case. See above.

2. In respect of moral aptitude and inaptitude, between the most mischievous and eminent of those who have been consigned to legal punishment and those by whom in the exercise of legislative and judicial functions they have been consigned to it, there is no such difference as self-partiality and prejudice have hitherto been so in unison in the declaration of: at any rate in any political state other than that of the Anglo-American United States, and what difference there is would not upon examination be found in favour of that side on which it has almost universally been imagined to be.

[1] MS 'this'.

CHAPTER 14. FALSE SECURITY FOR APPROPRIATE APTITUDE, MORAL, INTELLECTUAL OR ACTIVE. DIVISION OF THE SUPREME OPERATIVE POWER INTO TWO OR MORE BODIES[1]

The supreme operative body one and undivided: operating all the Members of it at the same time in the same place, with the exception only of sections of itself, called Committees, appointed by itself, for various purposes, as occasion calls.

Q. Why undivided?

A. Because by division would be produced evil in divers assignable shapes; good in no assignable shape: evil, even on the supposition that the number of sections into which it is divided is the least number possible, namely two: and from every addition to the number of two, the mass of evil would receive encrease.

Q. What are those evils? What are the shapes in which in this case evil would have place?

A. 1. Delay. 2. Complication. 3. Expence. All uncompensated. Delay and complication, inevitable and certain: expence, perhaps not inevitable, but by usage rendered probable.

Q. Delay—in what more particular shapes has it evil for its effect?

A. The arrangements whatsoever they are which, on all occasions taken together, are the ultimate results of the operations of this body must, for the purpose of the argument, be supposed good: conducive to greatest happiness: on the contrary supposition no such body ought to have place. Now what is certain is that in case of the existence of two such independent bodies, after the arrangement in question has been fully discussed, discussed by as many as feel disposed to take a part in the discussion, in one of those bodies, it will be liable to be discussed over again in the other. Let there be but one body,

[1] For the relationship of the MSS used in this chapter to 'Anti-Senatica', published by C. W. Everett in *Smith College Studies in History*, xi (1926), 207–67, see the Editorial Introduction, pp. xxv–xxvi above.

A fragment containing the following aphorisms on the theme of this chapter is at UC xliv. 17 (20 May 1822): 'The supreme operative body should act without division.

'[1.] It should not act in so many as two bodies: even though the Members were located by the best compounded set of locators, i.e. Electors—much less in *more* than two.

'2. Much less should it be composed of two or more indistinctly operating bodies: each taking cognizance of the same measure after the other.

'3. Still less should enter into the composition of it a body of men, located by a Chief Functionary, or set of Chief Functionaries, established for the purpose, sitting for a long term of years or for life.

'4. Least of all should enter into the composition of it a body of men succeeding to one another in the way of genealogical succession.'

whatever can be found by any one to be said on the subject will be said in that one body—let there then be two bodies, either the same things will be said in both, or of those things which are to the purpose some will be said in one only, others in the other only: or while in one of them every[thing] is said, in the other nothing will be said. Evils are in the first case, useless repetitions and time lost: in the second case, in each of the bodies judgment deduced from partial and insufficient data: in the last, delay produced by the transition from body to body and back again, and no other effect, therefore no good, produced.

Q. What are the more particular and immediately sensible, the more tangible, evils included under the word *complication*?

A. Opakeness. Want of transparency, disturbance given [to] the transparency of the whole business: hence facilities afforded throughout for the secret and successful operation of sinister interest. On each occasion those whose sinister interest is affected by the measures oppose of course whatsoever obstruction is in their power: the forms of proceeding of the two chambers are not the same in both: so many diversities, so many latent means of obstruction: out of these diversities, a sort of science is formed with its correspondent art: those to whom the business [is] most familiar turn the science and the art to their own account, and employ it in the creation of mischievous obstructions such as the advocates of the measure were not aware of, not prepared for, and are thence unable to prevent.

But if the texture of the business is thus more or less rendered obscure and undiscernible by those to whom by office it obtains, much more effectually is it concealed from the eye of the people at large in their character of members of the Public Opinion Tribunal: and thus the tutelary counterforce opposed by the popular or moral sanction to excess of force on the part of the political including the legal sanction is diminished: the controul exercised by the people in the character of constituents over those official functionaries in question in the character of their Agents is weakened and rendered less efficient.

Thus it is that throughout the whole political machine, every part that does no good does mischief.

Complication is a Jungle in which sinister interest has its lurking place.

When the political system in its whole expanse is reduced within the smallest dimensions possible, and in every part of it rendered as transparent and clearly understood as possible, still there will be many to whose conception, though equally interested in it, the whole has never presented itself; among those to whom it has presented itself, there will be many to whom in many parts of it no sufficiently clear conception of it will have been formed, and in readiness for every occasion, retained in mind. But only in proportion as it is known and understood in time can it be productive of any good effects it aims at; and in so far as it is unknown to, or not understood by, those whose interest is concerned in the knowing and understanding of it, evil is the sure effect of it.

Q. In what way is it productive of addition to expence?

A. If the Members of either of the two Chambers receive at the expence of the community compensation in a pecuniary shape, so much compensation to the functionary, so much expence to the public: the compensation, and thence expence, perhaps not necessary: but by custom rendered probable, and until trial has demonstrated the needlessness of it, unavoidable.[1]

If it be established that there are to be two chambers, out of this single circumstance spring questions swarming [with][2] doubts and difficulties. With respect to the whole field of legislation taken together, shall each have the initiative, or shall one of them alone, and which, have the initiative, and the other the negative?

Or with relation to certain parts of that field, shall the initiative be possessed exclusively by one and which of them? Here then comes the necessity of lines of demarcation, and thence not only of certain complication, but continually probable dissention and contest, amiable or hostile.

Lest the additional chamber should be regarded as useless, some special reason must be found for the institution of it. For this purpose the division of the branches of appropriate aptitude is brought to view and assumed to be applicable. Both being assumed to be provided in sufficient amount with appropriate moral aptitude, the advantage in respect of appropriate active aptitude is the supposed attribute [of] the one, in respect of intellectual aptitude, of the other, in which case to render it the more imposing, the varnish of antiquity will be spread over it, and wisdom will be the name given to it. Meantime for rendering wisdom, whatever is meant by it, more abundant in one chamber than in another, the contrivance is to require that in that which is to be the wisest, the Members shall not any of them be of less than a certain age.

First as to age. Only in so far as moral aptitude has place, is intellectual contributory, or otherwise than detrimental, to the aggregate of appropriate aptitude: in so far as his object is particular and sinister interest at the expence of universal interest, the more knowledge and judgment a man has, the more mischievous he will be.

[1] In the margin, Bentham noted at this point, 'See Part II, Expence minimized', but this particular topic is not discussed in the surviving MSS.

[2] MS 'without'.

But in so far as there is any difference, youth has much better pretension to the being regarded as the seat of appropriate moral aptitude—of *virtue* if that is to be the word—than a more advanced age has. In a ratio which is the inverse of the degree of altitude in the scale of age, the mind is susceptible of that degree of excitation, in the French phrase *exultation*, of which self-sacrifice, sacrifice of immediate self-regarding to social interest,[a] is the result.

In so far as regards intellectual aptitude, needless with reference to this its professed purpose is in the present case this security for appropriate intellectual aptitude. Take any age for the age short [of] which deficiency in the article of wisdom is to be regarded as preponderantly probable: say for example 21 years of age. By no such deficiency can any sensible evil be produced otherwise than in the case in which the individuals labouring under it compose a majority. But that in any number approaching to a majority, these supposed unripe minds should have place in any body constituted as that in question is here proposed to be, is altogether improbable. Were it even life at large that were in question, the long[er] a man's life has been, the more numerous will have been the opportunities which his appropriate aptitude, whatever it be, has had of making itself generally manifest. But if this is true as applied to life in general, more particularly true will it be as applied to political life, and to political life with a view to that department and that grade.

In disproof of the utility of a Second Chamber there appears this argument—this dilemma.

If there be a state of things in which, by the danger of precipitation, a demand is made for a retardative in this shape, it should be at a time of the establishment of the Constitution or immediately after. Why? because at that time the stock of experience is smallest: the stock of experience, and thence the means of forming a mature and well-grounded judgment in relation to the several points. But this is exactly the season in which the demand for dispatch is at its maximum: and here a cause of acceleration, supposing it possible, being the thing in demand, instead of it a cause of retardation is provided. In process of time, the demand for extraordinary dispatch being satisfied, or regarded as being satisfied, then, if at any time, comes the good, if there be any, from retardation and encreased maturity of judgment in particular instances, unalloyed by the inconvenience of universal retardation at a time when extraordinary and universal acceleration is the thing in demand. But at this time, a general encrease of maturity of judgment has been derived from

[a] *Gallicé, dévouement.*

universal experience. The evil from universally applied retardation remains, as before: and for the good producible in particular instances by encreased maturity of judgment, the demand is lessened: lessened in proportion to the quantity of experience which in the mean time has accumulated.

Prodigious is the mass of complication—useless, needless and mischievous complication—produced by limited and indistinct views.[1]

At the first concoction of the system, surplusage in this form is unavoidable—the grounds of action remain as yet in a state of obscurity. But sooner or later that which is superfluous comes to be discerned and distinguished from that which is really necessary: thus it is that upon an all-comprehensive survey, these the superfluous and useless matters may be cleared away and conciseness and transparency substituted to obscurity, diffuseness and turbidness.[2]

The greater the number is of the seats of authority through which a useful measure [must pass][3] ere execution and effect can be given to it, the greater the number of stages at which sinister interest may apply itself to encounter and obstruct it.[4]

Q. What can have been the cause or causes why a second chamber has been added to the first?

Answers. 1. The supposed probability or fear of precipitation, and the hope of obviating it. 2. The principle of imitation—authority-begotten prejudice.

Q. The evil of precipitation (its degree of probability taken into account), does it seem to be of such a magnitude as to warrant the application of such an institution in the character of a preventive remedy?

A. Hardly. For: 1. the evil of additional delay is an evil that applies

[1] The meaning of the remainder of this paragraph is obscure and therefore has been excluded. In the corresponding marginal summary, Bentham wrote: 'seen, the particular possible evil: not seen, the general state of things by which it is rendered inefficient'.

[2] In the text, Bentham noted at this point:'☛ Try whether a list can be made of the cases in which useless complications have had place, and the instances classed. 1. Stages of Election. 2. Stages of progress for a law. 3. Causes of exclusion: 1. in an Elector: 2. in a witness: [3.] in a candidate for useful instruction.' There is no further discussion of these topics in the 'Economy as applied to Office' MSS.

[3] The addition is suggested by the marginal summary: 'Seats of authority through which a measure must pass the more, places at which sinister interest may retard or deteriorate it the more.'

[4] There is no text corresponding to the following marginal summary, which belongs here: 'Under a corrupt form of government having for its end in view sinister interest, places of stoppage may incidentally be of use: why—measure sinister, members negligent and postponing this occupation to all other interested and pleasurable ones, the more places at which stoppage may be made, the better the chance that some idler who would not have opposed the measure a first day, will a second, and so on.'

itself to every measure. 2. So does the evil of complication—in every individual case the existence of [each][1] one of them is certain.

As to the *good*, the only case that affords an inlet to it is that in which a pernicious measure, which would have passed had there been but one Chamber for it to pass through, is prevented from passing by being thrown out by the Second Chamber. To be on sufficient grounds assured that in this case preponderant good has been the result of the operation—if this instrument has had preponderant good for its result—two distinguishable points must be established: viz. 1. that the law or measure, if carried into effect, would have been pernicious: 2. that had there been no Second Chamber, it would not have been thrown out in the First. For as to this latter point, a state of things not incapable of being realized is—that, on being assured that the measure will not pass the Second Chamber, many of those who would otherwise have opposed it in the First Chamber, are by one consideration or other kept back from meddling with it.[a]

Cause 2. Principle of imitation—authority-begotten prepossession or prejudice.

Antecedently to examination performed with a distinct view of the right and proper end in view belonging to the subject, and the relation borne to it by the several arrangements that present themselves as capable of being contributory to it, in the character of means, comes necessarily in every line of action, observation of the arrangements that actually have been made to take place in such cases as appear parallel to the one upon the carpet.

Thus, in the establishment of legislative bodies. Number of chambers, what shall it be? Look round the field of civilization. In so many political states, number of chambers, two or more: in so many others, if any, no more than one: natural conclusion without further reflection:— therefore two or more are better than one: more especially if the condition of the community in which two or more are observed is with reference to that in question more familiar and better known than any other.

In the Anglo-American Union, in the Constitution of the Congress, the example of Great Britain might naturally, at the time of the

[a] Note that of the addition of a Second Chamber, if the number of its members is greater than those of the First Chamber, an effect which may with any degree of frequency happen is—that a measure shall be thrown out by a minority of the whole number of members voting in relation to it. ☛ Give here a feigned case.[2]

[1] MS 'every'.

[2] In the marginal summary, Bentham commented, 'Try this on the U.S. Congress members', but no material appears to have been written.

framing of the Constitution, have been regarded as constituting of itself a sufficient warrant for a Second Chamber, the Senate. In the Constitution of the Mother Country, evil points really existing, and in the self-emancipated Colonies acknowledged to be evil, in abundance. But in the list of these evils, it was not necessary that the existence of a Second Chamber in the mere character of a Second Chamber should be placed: accordingly in the list on that occasion it appears not to have been generally placed: whatsoever evil was ascribed to the existence of a Second Chamber in that case was naturally ascribed to the particular composition of it: to the situation of the locating functionary, and to those other points of inaptitude that have been already brought to view: the sinister interests and privileges possessed by the Members and the utter absence of all dislocative power in relation to them.

In proportion as the result of the division or rather multiplication of barriers that must be passed through ere a measure reaches the end of its career is favorable to factitious delay, factitious delay is resorted to in preference to argument. But it is in the nature of argument, on the supposition that the end pursued is the universal interest and not particular interest—that the further from being preponderantly beneficial a measure is—the more likely it is to be put aside by argument; the more highly beneficial, the less likely to be thus put aside: whereas factitious delay contributes according to the length of it—contributes in the same proportion in the one as in the other, to put aside the best and the worst.

If in consequence of precipitation, a measure the effect of which is upon the whole preponderantly evil receives the sanction of law, the evil is not incapable of being removed by a subsequent law:— whereas whatsoever is the sum of the delays produced in all measures without distinction by the dilatory system remains for ever uncompensated.

True it is—that where by reason of precipitation, a measure productive of a balance on the side of evil receives the sanction of law, so long as the law remains unrepealed, the evil continues on the encrease. But, by the supposition, being, as it is, indebted for its existence to precipitation and nothing else—being such that had it not been for the precipitation, it would not have passed, but would have been rejected—rejected before the evil had begun to shew itself—still more surely will the system be rid of it, now that the correctness of the general anticipative judgment has been demonstrated by experience.[a]

[a] By a natural enough operation of the imagination a Senate, with its veneration-preaching denomination, is apt enough to be presented in the character of a deposit

For the formation of a well-grounded and well-matured judgment on this question, [take][1] the body of experience already obtained in the Congress of the Anglo-American United States. Take any year or any number of years: take an account of the whole number of laws passed and rejected within that time, and say:

1. Total number of laws introduced into the Senate from the House of Representatives, so many.
2. Whereof passed, so many.
3. Rejected, so many.

Then take in hand the number of those rejected and say:

4. Introduced and passed in a subsequent Session, so many. Of these, unless some special and adequate reason to the contrary, it ought to be assumed that they have upon the whole been, and continue to be, of a beneficial nature.[2]
5. Of those rejected, pernicious upon the whole upon a present view, if any, so many.
6. Of those rejected, pernicious as above, but which had it not been for the existence of the Senate would, it is now supposed, have been rejected by the Chamber of Representatives, so many.
7. Of those rejected, deemed, now upon a maturer view of the subject, beneficial upon the whole, so many.

or treasury of undefined and undefinable wisdom in the shape of a set of recondite maxims: a sacred deposit, transmitted from hand to hand like a secret in factitious religion, in magic, or in trade: a security against improvident change and the evils liable to be produced by it. Illusion, all this. By no supposed useful instrument of direction and guidance can any useful effect be produced any further than, by its being committed to writing, a permanent shape can be given to it. By a *rationale* attached to the text of the several articles in the Code, this instrument of guidance would be given of course. In that its form, it is, from first to last, before adoption and after adoption, open to all eyes, subject to discussion and contestation, to amendment, and if there be sufficient cause, to abrogation.

Attached to any political body whatsoever, any such eulogistic appellative would naturally be cherished as an instrument of power peculiar to that body and an instrument in the display of which it would feel peculiar gratification—it would be like the flowing robe and yard-long beard of the Magician on the Stage, the sacred vestments of the Superior Judges in England and of the Priest almost every where: in a word, whatsoever comes from such a source would receive attention and probability of adoption beyond what on the score of utility would be due to it.

---

[1] The addition is suggested by the marginal summary: 'Plan for forming a well-grounded estimate of the balance on the side of good or evil from a Second Chamber, taking U.S. for example.'

[2] In the marginal summary, Bentham inserted an additional stage in the calculation as point 5: 'Remain rejected, so many.' Thereafter points 5, 6 and 7 of the text are numbered 6, 7 and 8 respectively in the marginal summary.

Such is the plan recommended to each individual for the formation of his own particular opinion.

Supposing the balance in the account of aptitude to hang exactly even, the consideration of expence will suffice to turn it, and the scale with the Second Chamber in it will kick the beam.

Case 1. The members of the Second Chamber located not by the adult portion of the whole community voting in districts in the way of Election, but by some individual in the State: an individual who by this function alone, were no others added to it, would be rendered the Chief in the State: possessing one half of the supreme constitutive power: at any rate if, with this power of location, that of dislocation were conjoined: dislocation performed by time, at the end of the functionary's life or at the end of a certain number of years.

In the endeavour—the constant endeavour—to sacrifice [the] universal interest to his own private interest would the whole power of this functionary be occupied. To every arrangement by which at the expence of this sinister interest the universal interest were endeavoured to be served, the opposition of these his creatures might justly be regarded as sure: here then would be a sure and certainly effectual power of *resistance* to every thing good, to every thing tending to the introduction of improvement or removal of abuse. But to this defensive power is attached an active and aggressive power sufficient to enable the possessor sooner or later to effect for his own private use the consummation of the sinister sacrifice. By the expectation of receiving for self or connections an office thus important, the functionaries occupying the several seats in the other Chamber would sooner or later be gained over in sufficient number to place the whole fabric of the government on a footing sufficient for the consummation of the sinister sacrifice for the joint benefit of all the partners in the aggregate mass of sinister interest: namely [1.] the Chief by whom the Members of the second Chamber are located: 2. the Members of that same second Chamber: and 3. the Members of the first Chamber, notwithstanding their being located by the people at large in quality of their constituents.[1]

Case 2. The Members of one of the two Chambers located by a Chief functionary, and upon the death of each of them a successor to him located by genealogical proximity with relation to him: further additions, with or without such genealogically located successors, being capable or not capable of being made by the Chief functionary of the time being and his successors.

[1] In the marginal summary, Bentham added: 'For the course by which they would extract the money, see Ch. | | below.' For such a discussion see Ch. 2, §§6–8, pp. 20–5 above.

Here the sinister sacrifice is of the same sort and effected by the same means: but still more burthensome.

Not only a particular class of men is established, but a particular race, sharing among them a particular and sinister interest, continuing and operating in a state of everlasting hostility to the universal interest: the unprivileged people at large, objects of unassuageable hatred and contempt to the members of this privileged class: of hatred for the resistance which, in so far as regard for personal security allows, they can not but oppose to whatever measures they see operating to their prejudice: of which measures, for the purpose of depredation and oppression in all shapes, there can never want a continual encrease: contempt for the inability[1] under which the authors of the oppression will see the victims labouring: and for the magnitude of those deficiencies which it is the constant endeavour of the oppressors to encrease.[2]

In these sentiments of unassuageable hostility, [of] the members of the privileged race, their progeny will, from generation to generation, be imbued: and as generations multiply, the interest-begotten prejudice, begotten by this sinister interest, will acquire an ever-encreasing force. In regard to this right to do wrong, the longer the continuance of it has been, the more strongly confirmed on the part of all those who share in it and enjoy it will be the persuasion that it is a natural one. A system of theology will be framed for the support of it. A God will be created to whom will be assigned the office of creating two races: two races of essentially different substance under the same form and appearance: one to command, the other to obey: one to be in a state of undisturbed felicity, the other in a state of unmitigated and hopeless wretchedness.

In regard to whatsoever presumptive evidence may have been considered as afforded by precedent and authority, this consideration requires to be kept in mind—namely that, in no instance antecedent to the formation of the Constitution of the Anglo-American United States has the existence of a Second Chamber had for its cause any such consideration as the affording a security against precipitation.

The example in view in that case has been the example of England. But in that case, of the two Chambers, the Aristocratical Chamber,

[1] i.e. 'incapacity for resistance' as per marginal summary.

[2] In the text, Bentham noted at this point, 'Reference to some paper in which the evils of Aristocracy are depicted in detail', and added in the marginal summary: '☛ See *Members unapt* etc.' Bentham wrote material under this heading between December 1821 and February 1822 for use in *Codification Proposal addressed . . . to All Nations Professing Liberal Opinions*, London, 1822, but which he excluded from the published work. The surviving MSS (see UC lxxxiv. 73–191) contain comments on the sinister interests of aristocracy within a more general discussion of the sinister interests of rulers.

the House of Lords, was the Chamber first established:— established, or at least continued, by the Monarch, under the pressure of necessity because no sufficient means of bringing the people under permanent subjection to his own power was ever in his hands. In this state continued the Government from the time of the Norman Conquest till the days of Henry the third.[1]

In the days of Henry the third was laid the foundation of the Second Chamber, the House of Commons. Founder in the first instance, Simon de Montford, one of the Lords by whom a contest with the King was for some time kept up.[2] Second Founder, the King himself. Probable causes of foundation two: 1. Encrease of facility for obtaining money: consent on the part of the contributors being found a readier and more copiously effective instrument than force. 2. Hope of allied counterforce against the apprehended superior force of mutually confederated Lords.[3]

Since the restoration of Monarchy, the exclusive initiative in money matters being recognized as belonging to the House of Commons, the place of Second Chamber, considered as a source of negatory power, has been occupied by the House of Lords.

But in this case, by what consideration has the revived and continued existence of the Second Chamber been produced?[4] By any apprehended danger of precipitation on the part of the House of Commons? No. But the particular and sinister interest of those sections of the supreme operative power, all of them acting in confederacy against the universal interest.

No part in either instance had any such cause as the fear of evil from precipitation, and the hope of excluding it by delay, in the formation of either House. By force alone till t'other day were laws and institutions ever established; by force they have been established: by hopes of gain, the reasonableness of them has been pretended to be proved. Where is that institution so atrocious, of the excellence of which, whatever is meant by excellence, demonstrations have not been procured in abundance by the influence of that same all-powerful motive?

[1] Henry III (1207–72), King of England from 1216.

[2] Simon de Montfort (1208?-65), Earl of Leicester, one of the leaders of the Baronial Movement of 1258–65, eventually defeated Henry III at the battle of Lewes (14 May 1264) and took him prisoner. Montfort's death at the battle of Evesham (4 August 1265) was followed by the restoration of royal authority. He was traditionally regarded as the founder of Parliament because of his innovation of summoning two citizens from every borough to the Parliament held at London in January 1265.

[3] Bentham, in his interpretation of the development of Parliament, seems to have been following David Hume, *The History of England, from the Invasion of Julius Caesar to The Revolution in 1688*, 8 vols., London, 1763, ii. 210–11, 265–78.

[4] The House of Lords was abolished in 1649, but began to meet again in 1660.

Against the presumptive evidence of aptitude thus derived from authority and custom, subsequent events have furnished other sources of counter-evidence.

Since that time the following are the Constitutions which have been framed, or with amendments been revived, each with no more than one Chamber for the seat of the supreme operative power:

1. The Spanish Government—a mixt Monarchy.[1]
2. The Portugueze Government—a mixt Monarchy.[2]
3. The Chilian Government—a Republic without a Monarch.[3]
4. The Columbian Government—a Republic without a Monarch.[4]
5. The Buenos Ayres Government—a Republic without a Monarch.[5]
6. The Haiti or St Domingo Government—a Republic without a Monarch.[6]

In these several Governments, does there appear reason to believe that by the non-existence of a Second Chamber, whether by means of precipitation or any other cause, evil in any shape has been produced?

[1] The Constitution of 1812, which had been overturned in 1814 but restored in 1820, vested the legislative power in the Crown and a single-chamber Cortes.

[2] The Constitution of 1821 vested the legislative power in a single-chamber Cortes, subject to the suspensive veto of the Crown.

[3] The Constitution of 1818 instituted a legislative Senate of five members and five deputy members, all nominated by the Supreme Director.

[4] Bentham perhaps had in mind the Congress of Angostura (1819) which acted as the supreme legislative body of the emerging state. The permanent constitution which was proclaimed in 1821 by the President, Simon Bolivar (1783–1830), vested the legislative power in two chambers, a Senate and a House of Representatives.

[5] The Law of Elections of 1821 established the Junta of Representatives as the legislative body of the province.

[6] Bentham's reference here is not straightforward. The Constitution of Haiti of 1806 vested the legislative power in a Senate, but this constitution was ignored by the President-elect, Henri Christophe (1767–1820), who in 1807 adopted a constitution consisting of himself as President and a Council of State of nine members whom he nominated. The Senate declared Christophe an outlaw, and elected Alexandre Sabes Pétion (1770–1818) as President. There were thus two rulers with separate governments administering different parts of the territory, and civil war was waged by their respective adherents until hostilities were suspended in 1810. In 1812 Christophe had himself proclaimed King of Haiti with the title of Henry I, but facing rebellion committed suicide in 1820. Meanwhile in 1816, Pétion modified the constitution of 1806: the legislative power was vested in a Senate and a House of Commons, and he himself was elected President for life. In 1818, on Pétion's death, Jean-Pierre Boyer (1776–1850) became President, and on the death of Christophe he united Haiti under his rule. The Spanish having been expelled from Santo Domingo in 1821, Boyer invaded and in 1822 extended the Haitian Constitution of 1816 to the whole of the island. Bentham therefore seems to be referring to the Constitution of 1806 which was supported by Pétion, but revised by him in 1816.

CHAPTER 15. DISPOSITION OF THE WHOLE MASS OF SUPREME POWER ACCORDING TO DIVERS PHANTASTIC THEORIES[1]

By the form of government above-described as being the only apt one, the supreme power is located in the hands of those whose interest it is to exercise the powers belonging to it in such manner as shall be in the highest degree contributory to the greatest happiness of the greatest number of the members of the community to which it is applied: in a word a Delegated or Representative Democracy, a Democracy operating by Delegation.

To the interests of those who participate in the powers of government in States in which the mass of power is differently disposed of, this form is more or less unsuitable.

Of each government, it is a maxim on the part of the rulers that the form of it is not merely the best, but the only good one. For producing in other minds a persuasion of the truth of this position, or at any rate for the purpose of persuading others that such is the persuasion of him by whom the argument in question is employed, a theory more or less different is employed in each government, adapted to that form which is there established. In each government, a problem susceptible of the same general description in all of them is proposed and undertaken to be solved. Four words suffice for the expression of it. Whatever is, is best, or the same [in] seven, viz. Every thing is as it should be.

I. As to a pure Monarchy, or say pure Despotism. Under a government of this sort, as the form of the government is superlatively simple, simple to the perfection of simplicity, so is the argument or theory by which it is proved to be the only good one. The essence of it has of late years been compressed within the compass of one word—*legitimacy*. It is the result of a theory according to which the Almighty Being has in each political community placed, or at least ought to have placed and ought to place, a human being, who, being a copy of himself, and invested with his attributes, ought in all things to be served with the same all-comprehensive and indiscriminating obsequiousness as himself.

II. Under a government which, being likewise Monarchical, is not in the above sense altogether pure, the people having or appearing to

[1] For the relationship of the MSS used in this chapter to 'Anti-Senatica', published by C.W. Everett in *Smith College Studies in History*, xi (1926), 207–67, see the Editorial Introduction, pp. xxv–xxvi above.

have in the composition of it a share more or less considerable, the argument is not quite so simple.

In this case, for the solution of the problem divers theories have been invented and are occasionally employed.

They may be thus enumerated and denominated:

1. The Balance Mechanical theory.
2. The Diagonal Mechanical theory.
3. The Chemical theory.

To the support of one and the same mixt Monarchy or apparently limited Monarchy have all these several theories been employed: employed with unceasing industry, and each of them with universal satisfaction to all those who, by sinister interest, interest-begotten prejudice, authority-begotten prejudice or the force of the mixture, have been and continue attached to it. This is, as every one knows, the English Monarchy.

Of all these several theories, England has the honor of the invention. But if they are good for the persuasion and satisfaction of Englishmen, they may be alike good for the persuasion and satisfaction of the subjects of any other mixt Monarchy, to the rulers of which it may happen to think it worth their while to seek in words, and such words, a support for that military force which in such governments renders logic needless.

Of each of these theories a brief exposition follows.

§1. *Phantastic theory the first. Legitimacy*[1]

This theory consists in the use of a particular word—legitimacy.

In this word is tacitly involved a proposition: namely, Every Monarchical Government is legitimate. Therein is involved another—No Government that is not Monarchical is legitimate.

By legitimate, in so far as it has a meaning, seems to be meant—such as ought to find obedience on the part of those, whosoever they are, whom the Monarch is disposed to treat as his subjects.

Ask why the members of the community in question, how extensive so ever it be—ask why the hundred million, if there are so many of them, ought to suffer themselves to be disposed of at the will and pleasure of one man amongst them, as cattle are disposed of at the pleasure of their proprietor, if any answer be given the most intelligible is *custom*.

[1] Bentham's original, but abandoned, draft of this section is at UC xliv. 16 (24 May 1822).

In this word then is involved this proposition—namely, Whatsoever is customary is right: whatsoever is customary is apt, right and proper to be done and suffered.

According to this theory, among the Members of the Community, suppose it the custom for all but one to be by that one made constantly unhappy: this state of things is apt, right, proper, legitimate. Why? because it is customary.

Custom has been stiled the Law of Fools.[1] So far as regards Government, with as much propriety might it be stiled the *Law of Knaves*, or the Law of Knaves and Fools. It is a law in the establishment of which the initiative function has had rulers in the character of Knaves for its functionaries; the Consummators, the people in the character of fools.

In a Monarchy, the greatest happiness of the Monarch is in the opinion of the Monarch, the sole right and proper end of government.

In the opinion of the Monarch, the greatest happiness of the Monarch requires that the greatest happiness of all but that one be, on every occasion, made a sacrifice to the happiness real or supposed of that one.

When in support of the claim of a Monarch to whatsoever share of power he happens to be possessed of—unlimited or limited—argument, or any thing that shall wear the appearance of argument, is employed, it resolves itself into one or other of the three propositions following:

1. It has been the custom for the Monarch to exercise such his power: and, in Government, whatsoever is customary is right.

2. In a Monarchy, the Monarch is the only person whose happiness has any claim to regard.

3. The happiness of the people has a claim to regard. It may even be admitted, that the greatest happiness of the community at large is the only legitimate end of government. But to the admission is tacked this condition: namely, that it be admitted on the other side that the Monarch is the only proper Judge of that which on each occasion is in the highest degree contributory to the greatest happiness of the community at large.

[1] In the margin, Bentham noted: 'See Ch. 2. Exclusions from Constitutive power. 1. *Females*.' In a fragment headed 'Females' at UC clx. 86 (29 May 1822), he wrote: 'There is a custom which is reason's offspring. There is a custom which is reason's enemy. The first offspring is legitimate and has open eyes that not only bear the light but love it: the other is spurious and eyeless: that blind custom which, conscious of having reason for its enemy, and seeing in that enemy, should he but gain entrance, an irresistible one, bestirs itself with all its mite to shut the door against [him]. Custom has by some been called the law of fools: when such has been the definition given, it is this custom and this alone that has probably been in view, and so far as that is the case, this appellation seems unexceptionable.'

This last theory is the one that seems to possess the best claim for currency.

To the profession of benevolence, it adds the assumption of matchless and even exclusive wisdom. By it, the Monarch is presented to view in the character of the Vice-gerent and present image of the Divinity. He is the God whom the Latin Poet Juvenal portrays to us:

> Permittas ipsis expendere Numinibus quid
> Conveniat nobis, rebusque sit utile nostris.
> Nam pro jucundis aptissima quaeque dabunt Dei.
> Carior est illis homo, quam sibi.[1]

All this is perfectly true in every eye to which it has been revealed by superhuman power, that there exists such a God upon earth and that, in the Monarchy in question, the Monarch whoever he be, is he.

In it is moreover tacitly involved, the theory of which more open profession is made in *Thibet*: namely, that this everliving though earthly God is, in all ages and generations, one and the same mind, by which one mind bodies in endless succession are in infinite number at different times animated.[2]

All this is perfectly true in every mind to which, as above, it stands revealed. But all this is at the same time perfectly false in every mind to which it does not stand revealed.

To every such supernaturally privileged mind, it calls on every occasion for passive obedience and non-resistance. But in the case of every mind not thus supernaturally privileged, it calls for resistance: resistance on the part of each according as power and opportunity presents itself, and by means, without any exception, afforded the promise of being most effectual.[3]

[1] 'You should leave it to the powers that be to provide what suits us, and what will be useful for our affairs. For instead of what is pleasing, the gods will give us what is most suitable. Man is dearer to them, than he is to himself.' Juvenal, *Satires*, x. 347–50. Bentham deviated slightly from the usual rendering of the passage.

[2] An allusion to the Dalai Lama, who enjoyed both religious and political authority, and who was considered to be the reincarnation of a deity.

[3] Bentham did not go on to discuss the theories employed in support of a mixed monarchy.

SUPPLEMENT TO ECONOMY AS APPLIED TO OFFICE

Apt location of power

1. The greatest happiness of the greatest number requires that with reference to the possessor or possessors of the supreme operative power, the *constitutive* power be in the hands of the greatest number: viz. of *apt* hands: apt in respect of literary acquirements.

2. The greatest happiness of the greatest number requires that the supreme *operative* power, Legislative and Super-Executive, should be in the hands of a corporate body, the Members thereof located by Election performed by so many assemblages of such of the Members of the whole community as are endowed with adequate appropriate aptitude, relation had to such their function: the assemblages being determined by the local Districts which they inhabit and each Member being elected by the apt inhabitants of one such District: no inhabitant deliver[ing] his vote in Districts more than one: each such Member being stiled a Deputy, or say a Delegate, of the People: and the whole Assembly, the Congress of the Deputies of the people: or say for shortness the Congress.

3. The greatest happiness of the greatest number requires that, the supreme Legislative power being in the hands of a Congress composed of the Deputies or Delegates of the People located as above, the supreme Super-Executive power be in these same hands. Principle: Anarchy-inhibiting principle.

4. The greatest happiness of the greatest number requires that the powers of the Delegates of the people be exercised by the whole number sitting and acting in an undivided body: no other divisions having place but such as are effected by that same body itself: by its forming, for example under the name of Committees, Sections out of itself, each Section subordinate and responsible to the whole. Principles: 1. Delay-prohibiting principle. 2. Expence-prohibiting principle. 3. Complication-prohibiting principle.

5. The greatest happiness of the greatest number requires that no functionary be located by chance: much less by birth: in no case otherwise than by nomination or election.

Q. Why not by chance?

A. Suppose a certain individual endowed with the maximum of appropriate aptitude, chance renders the location of that individual improbable in the ratio of the number of individuals to whom chance admitts a possibility of admission to one.

Q. Why not by birth?

A. Take for example the case where the whole of the operative power in the highest grade, Legislative and Super-Executive, is in a single hand. Taking birth for the efficient cause of location, i.e. in the line of generation, proximity to the last individual located, the improbability of the maximum of the aggregate of appropriate aptitude will be at the highest pitch, more particularly in respect of moral aptitude: the probability will be on the side of the maximum [of] that branch of inaptitude which corresponds to and is opposite to appropriate moral aptitude.

6. The greatest happiness of the greatest number requires that the hand or hands in which the supreme Executive power is placed be subordinate to the supreme Legislative body: namely 1. by power of cessation: 2. by power of command on pain of punishment: 3. by power of punishment: 4. by power of dislocation: but not 5. by non-concurrence. Principle of exclusion of Anarchy, Anarchy-inhibiting principle.

Q. The supreme Legislative power and the supreme Super-Executive power, why in the same hand?

A. For simplicity of conception suppose the Supreme Executive power to be in the hand of a single functionary. If he were not displaceable by the supreme Legislative functionary or body of functionaries, their power might by him be reduced to impotence. If he were not punishable by that same Legislative body, he might, before the dislocation could be effected, produce mischief indefinitely intense, extensive and irremediable. He might for example put to death the members of it in any number. If, so far as depended upon their power and the orders given in consequence, he were dislocated, he might refuse to submitt to those same orders.

7. The greatest happiness of the greatest number requires that the Office of Supreme Executive Functionary be in the hand of a single individual: stile him for example Supreme Director of the Commonwealth. Reasons: 1. Responsibility-securing principle. 2. Expence-minimizing principle. 3. Complication-inhibiting principle.[1]

[1] In the marginal summary, Bentham added at this point: '8. Supreme Judicial power be it single-seated: viz. in a Minister of Justice.'

Securities—Rationale

Saving special and sufficient reason to the contrary, all political functionaries ought to [be] placed and at any time displaceable by those for whom they are functionaries.

Analogous case, trustees in general under systems of law in general.

Special and sufficient reasons to the contrary are:

1. Want of time on the part of the people at large: want of time for the operation and the enquiries requisite to the forming of a sufficiently grounded judgment on the subject of the several proposed Candidates.

2. Comparative want of appropriate intellectual aptitude in relation to certain functions and situations, in comparison with certain individuals whose appropriate aptitude has been established by appropriate and public examination.

3. Want of ***responsibility*** in comparison of individuals individually taken in whose instance the existence [of] appropriate aptitude has been established as above.

By the people at large in the character of possessors of the supreme constitutive power the location and dislocation of a functionary is capable of being performed in the immediate way, or by the intervention of an intermediate locator, or any number of ranks of intermediate locators.

The unimmediate mode in any degree ought not to be employed in any case except in so far as by sufficient counter-reasons as above the immediate mode stands inhibited.

An unimmediate mode through a less number of intervening stages is preferable to an unimmediate mode through a greater number of intervening stages.

Reason 1. The probability of inaptitude is augmented at each stage—the augmentation is as the number of the stage: of aptitude in the lowest or immediate rank the good effect may be defeated by inaptitude in the rank next above. So many stages, so many sets of persons, to each of whom it may happen that corruption shall apply itself.

Reason 2. Complication augmented—with its general bad effects.[1]

[1] In the text, Bentham noted at this point: 'See *Complication*.' Though no extended discussion on this theme appears to have been written for 'Economy as applied to Office', the following fragment, in the hand of Richard Doane, but with an addition by Bentham, is at UC xliv. 7 (5 May 1822): 'What are the effects of complication?

'A. As such, good effects it has none.

Legislature fractionized—Rationale

The Supreme Legislative power, why in a fractionized state in the simple mode[1] rather than in a single individual.

Reasons.

1. Were it in the hands of one only, there could be no sufficient security that by that one any attention would be bestowed upon any part of the business—that any all-comprehensive and undiscontinued exercise would be given to his power.

2. Whatsoever exercise were given to his power, there could be no security that any adequate reasons would be given in justification of it, nor therefore that it would be such for which such justification could be given.

3. Nor yet, that for explanation or justification of his several operations any all-comprehensive and undiscontinued and clear, correct and compleat evidence of them would be put upon record and published.

4. Because as there would be no Debates, so neither would there be any of those auditors by whom, on the occasion of the Debates in a public Assembly, observation is made of the deportment as well as of the language of the Debating Members: and whose presence and presumed attention constitutes a check upon such persons as, with or without commission from the constituted authorities, may happen to make a practice of taking minutes of the Debates.

5. Because in any way in which he could be elected the inconvenience attendant on such Election would be much greater than where in a numerous Assembly each Member has for his Electors the inhabitants of a particular District.

6. By each Elector's vote taken by itself the effect produced would be so small that in general it would scarcely in his eyes be worth the trouble of giving it.

'What are its bad effects?

'A. Perplexity, error, and deception by fraud: delay of useful measures.

'1. Perplexity. By some persons the system is gazed at, they are bewildered by the aspect of it, they see not the effects of it and know not how to act in consequence.

'2. Error. By others false conceptions are formed in relation to it, they take wrong measures in consequence and experience suffering in some shape or other, or cause others to experience it in consequence of those measures.

'3. Deception produced by fraud. Those by whom the structure of the system is thoroughly understood take advantage of those perplexities and those errors and turn them to their own account. Among the errors which they observe in it, they give continuance and increase to all those by means of which they are enabled to promote their own interest at the expence of all those in whose breasts those perplexities and misconceptions have place.'

[1] MS orig. 'why in a numerous Assembly'.

7. To the comparatively few persons whose situation it would suit to deliver a vote, the importance of the Office in question would be so great that by the contest for it the passions produced would be proportionably great.

8. If the time he continues in office were long, the power purposely attached to it would suffice to enable him to add more <and> more power to it till at last he would become despotic, and secure it to himself for life, be his government ever so unapt.

9. Because, supposing the territory and population considerable, the territory of the State will include districts having different interests produced by different states of things: each requiring a representative particularly acquainted with them.

Fractionization of Power—Rationale

Why not give to the division of the power a complexly fractional mode having for one of its elements a single functionary, say a Monarch?

Answer.

Because if his will is not constantly overborne, the mass of power, money and other external instruments of felicity attached to his situation will never be exposed to diminution, yet at the same time will always be susceptible of encrease: they will therefore be continually upon the encrease, which can not but be at the expence of the common stock of the whole community.

But the instruments of felicity as applied to his own person are instruments of corruption as applied to the several members of the co-ordinate body or bodies whose power contains whatsoever share of Supreme Operative power is not directly his: by this means they will sooner or later be led to join with him in the consummation of the sinister sacrifice, thus converting the government into a virtual despotism under the forms of a mixt and thereby limited Monarchy.

If the sole initiative is in the Monarch, of course he will never originate any measure the effect or tendency of which will be to diminish his share in the abovementioned pretious mass: and his endeavour to give encrease to it will be uninterrupted, and by every past encrease, facility is given to every succeeding encrease.

Maximizing responsibility—Rationale

Q. The institution by which the supreme operative power is lodged in hands more than one, and the number of those hands so large as it usually is, is it reconcileable with the principle of individual responsibility, and, if yes, how is it?

A. In the cases in which the principle of individual responsibility is here proposed to be applied, the business is performed in secret: by one functionary and by him alone, no other person, unless as here proposed by special appointment, being privy to it. Hence the absolute need of special appointment for giving publicity to his acts, and the reasons on which they have been [grounded] in so far as the nature of the case admitts of it.

But in the case of the proceedings of a deliberative Assembly such as that by which the supreme operative power is exercised, the numerousness of the Members does not exclude but rather augments the individual responsibility in the persons of the several Members. The part which on every occasion is taken by each is to a certain extent actually made known, and by appropriate arrangements may be made known to an indefinitely greater extent.

Advocative class—merely Judicative class—under these two classes the whole population of a deliberative Assembly may be comprized: Advocative class, those by whom speeches are delivered as well as votes: Judicative, those by which votes alone are delivered and not speeches. Each man of each class to a certain extent is unavoidably known—each to the utmost possible extent ought to be made known—by his respective works: the man of the Advocative class by his recorded speeches as well as votes: the man of the Judicative class by his recorded votes.

IDENTIFICATION OF INTERESTS

§ 1. *Identification of individual with universal interest in the breasts of functionaries: and in particular in the possessors of the Supreme Constitutive power. In what it consists*

In the instance of each such individual, this identification would be compleat, on every occasion if in consequence of the man's conduct, whatsoever good befalls the whole community, good, in the same proportion, befalls him: as also whatsoever evil befalls the whole community, in the same proportion befalls him. Instrument of identification in this case, say equal or proportionable participation in good and evil.

Opposition of individual to universal interest would be compleat, on every occasion if in consequence of the man's conduct, whatsoever good befalls the whole community, evil in the same proportion befalls him: as also whatsoever evil befalls the whole community, good in the same proportion befalls him.

On each occasion if, according to the estimate taken by him at the moment of action, good in net quantity will befall him in consequence of his taking that line of conduct which he proposes to himself to take, he will take it accordingly: in the opposite case, not: this estimate, supposing it to be in favour of the affirmative side: in this case, the line of his conduct will be on that same side: that which has been proposed by him to himself to be done will be done accordingly. In this state of things, if in consequence of what he has so done, good having or not having [in fact][1] befallen him, good to a net amount befalls the whole community, the identification of his interest with that of the community at large will have been compleat.

As between each individual and the whole community, identification of interests has place, in so far as when in consequence of any act on his part, or any other event or state of things, good in any shape happens to him, good in the same or any other shape happens to the whole community; or in so far as evil happens, evil: and in so far as in consequence of that same cause, good happens to the community, good happens to him, or in as far as evil happens to the community, evil happens to him.

As between individual and the community, identification of interests is constituted by communion in good, or by communion in evil, or by communion in both kinds.

[1] The addition seems necessary to clarify the meaning of the passage.

§2. *Necessity of this identification to greatest happiness*

The greatest happiness of the greatest number requires that on every occasion, to the greatest extent possible, this identification shall have place: insomuch that on every occasion on which, in consequence of the line of conduct taken by him, the happiness of the whole community receives encrease, his own happiness shall receive encrease likewise: as also that in so far as in consequence of the line of conduct taken by him, the happiness of the whole community experiences diminution, his own happiness should receive diminution likewise.

The efficiency of the influence capable of being exerted by him on the happiness of the whole community being given, the conduct of the individual will upon the whole be contributory or detrimental to the happiness of the whole community according to the degree in which, in the view by him taken of it, this identification has place.

Take any proposed act of his, and suppose it upon the whole contributory to the happiness of the whole community: if in his estimate of the matter it will add to the net amount of his own happiness, he will do that act: otherwise, not: suppose it detrimental to the happiness of the whole community: if in his view of the matter it will add to the net amount of his own happiness, he will do that act notwithstanding.[1]

§3. *Opposition of rulers' to subjects' interest, trustees' to principals' interest—its detrimental consequences with relation to greatest happiness*[2]

Correspondent and opposite to identification of interests as between a functionary and the community at large, is oppositeness of interest of the functionary with reference to the interest of the community at large—in proportion as such repugnance has place, such identification fails to have place.

On the part of men in general, and public functionaries in particular, repugnance of particular to universal interest, thence, on the part of public functionaries in particular, repugnancy of interest to duty, may on the one hand be the work of the laws and institutions without delinquency in a legal sense, or the work of delinquency in a legal sense in disconformity to laws and institutions.

[1] This sequence of MSS was originally continued by UC xxxiv. 88–9 (24 May 1822), but which Bentham later decided to exclude.

[2] Related fragments are at UC cxiv. 13–15 (27 May, 7 June 1822).

In the first case, the evil is at its maximum, the difficulty of purging the community of it being at its maximum: and on the part of those by whom the powers of government are exercised, moral turpitude is accordingly also at its maximum: a demonstration is thereby afforded that the root of the evil is in the form of the government: and that till the texture of the government is changed, the nature of the case admitts not of any effectual remedy.

If the root of the evil is in the very form and texture of the laws, it is so because by those on whom that texture has all along been dependent, it has been conceived to be their interest that the evil, whether by them created or no, should under them have continuance: in this case, the evil has therefore the correspondent and continued action of their will for its proximate cause.

In so far then as in consequence of such repugnance and such sacrifice of universal to particular and sinister interest, depredation and oppression in its several other shapes has place, depredation and oppression are carried on with impunity, and the scale on which they have place is the very largest scale: the whole number of members of the community, with the exception of those to whom the self-constituted and self-licensed depredators and oppressors are please[d] to grant exemption, being in a state of continual sufferance as well as subjection under it.

If in its texture the government be such as to be, throughout the whole extent of the field subject to it, productive of such effect, every act, whether on the part of a functionary or on the part of an unofficialized individual, in so far as any act is exercised, the effect of which is to give support and continuance to the government, is an act of hostility to the people, the support and encrease of whose happiness is the only right and proper end to which the texture and conduct of the government could have been directed.

§4. *Modes of inaptitude on the part of rulers, in so far as such oppositeness has place*

In so far as such repugnance has place, and evil doing and delinquency have place on the part of the people at large, or if on the part of public functionaries, only on the part of a small proportion, those in the highest grade not possessing any share in the profit, in no shape but that of intellectual aptitude will appropriate aptitude be wanting to the extirpation of the evil: and for the furnishing of that requisite, appropriate and correspondent information will naturally and commonly suffice, and any hand how obscure so ever may suffice for the communication of it, and thence for the production of the desirable effect.

But when it is by the highest functionaries themselves that the sinister profit is reaped, the root of the evil lies in the scantness, or rather the utter absence, of all appropriate moral aptitude. Information, however apposite and compleat, would be of no use: by them it is either possessed already and studiously forborne to be profited from, or if not at this moment possessed by them, but at the next moment will be received, will be altogether sure of being in like manner not neglected—but received with abhorrence, and a determination more and more strenuous to avoid as far as possible the putting it to use and giving the whole community the profit of it.

§5. *In case of extensive oppositeness, sole remedy against misrule, change of form of government: change of functionaries, useless*

In this case, every man thus tormented must either lie down as motionless as he can under his torment, or rise up—and in conjunction with as many as he can get to join with him, rise up, and endeavour to rid the country of the nuisance:—to substitute to a form of government having for its effect as well as its object the sacrifice of the universal interest to the interest of the rulers, a government which for its object at least shall have the causing the line of conduct of the rulers to coincide with that marked[?] out by the universal interest and thereby by their official duty.

Where the government is thus in its very essence, form, and texture, in a state of opposition to the universal interest, altogether useless is every such pretended remedy as consists in the substituting to the existing set of rulers [a new set of rulers][1] acting under the same form of government: placed in the same situations with their predecessors, impregnated with the same sinister interests, acting under the same *temptations*, acting under the same insensibility to the counterforce of all tutelary sanctions, the universal nature of man suffices to secure their pursuing the same sinister course.

The whole Official Establishment is in that case in the state of a ship infected with the plague.

[1] The addition is suggested by the marginal summary: 'receiving the same situations, new rulers receive the same sinister interests with the old'.

§6. *Exemplifications of corruption having the form of the government for its causes*

I. As to War.

It is the interest of the greater number that, unless for the purpose of national defence against injury, war should not against any nation be at any time carried on. If in any political community the official establishment is so constituted and circumstanced that the members of it in general, and in particular the chief functionary on whose acts the movement of the whole machine principally depends, will by means and in consequence of war receive, either in the shape of money or in the shape of power, profit to themselves, their particular and sinister interest is thereby served and promoted at the expence of the universal interest: the form of government is a corrupt one—not fit to stand but fit to be extirpated: on every occasion that appears favorable the sinister sacrifice will be resumed, and carried on as far as circumstances will admitt, until the point of consummation is reached or by the subversion of the government is prevented from being reached.

In every such case, a pretext is in readiness: whatever you may say or think, the war was not avoidable. This may be true or not true. But what is at all times true, that in the government of the community in question, whatever it be, matters may be so arranged, that by no war in which it has any part shall the mass of official profit, of official profit in any shape, receive encrease.

Such for example is the texture of the Government in the Anglo-American United States.

Such for example is not the texture of the Government in England.

II. As to forced contributions to all purposes in general.

It is the interest of all the members of the community taken together that the quantity of money levied by forced contributions shall at all times be as small as possible.

If in any political community the official establishment is so constituted and circumstanced that the quantity of money at the disposal of those on whom the movement of the machine principally depends, the quantity of money at their disposal, whether in the way of immediate enjoyment or in the way of expenditure, receives from the encrease of such forced contributions encrease rather than diminution, here is another conclusive token of radical and incurable corruption in the texture of the Government.

In case of war, for example, that which on this or that occasion it may not be in their power to prevent is the encrease in the necessary and unavoidable amount of these same forced contributions. But that which it is at all times in their power to prevent is their reaping in either shape from any such encrease, any encrease in the aggregate mass of profit reaped by themselves.

III. So as to Judicature, the state of the Judicial Establishment and the state of the Law of Judicial Procedure, the branch of law in the giving execution and effect to which the function of the members of it in a more especial manner appertains.

It is the interest of all the members of the community taken together, that to the purpose of affording redress to all wrongs, the force of the laws should, under the direction of the several members of the Judicial establishment, be as far as possible at the disposal of all persons by whom wrong in any shape has been suffered: that it shall not in any case be itself employed as an instrument of wrong, and that the redress and support so obtained by individuals be obtained by them with as little delay, vexation in the form of forced expence, and vexation in every other form, as possible.

If then in any political community the correspondent branch of the Official Establishment be so constituted and circumstanced that by those functionaries on whom the movement of this part of the machine principally depends, the quantity of money received to their own use, whether in an immediate way or in the way of patronage, is encreased, either by imposition having in effect the denial of redress for wrongs, or by contributing to the employing of the force of the law as an instrument of wrong, or by giving encrease to the quantity of delay, expence or vexation in other shapes, as the means and the only means of giving encrease to the quantity of profit reaped by themselves out of the expence, here is another exemplification and conclusive token of radical and incurable corruption in the texture of the government. Every Judge who, out of needless delay, expence and vexation, organized or continued to be produced by himself, reaps profit in either of the above two shapes[1] to himself is a corrupt Judge: every functionary who, bearing a part in that supreme operative power of the country, would have it in his power either to put an end to the corrupt profit thus reaped by the Judge, or at least to employ his endeavours towards the doing so, neither does so nor employs any such endeavours is himself a corrupt functionary, accomplice before and after the fact in the corrupt practice of the corrupt Judge.

In this instance as in the former one,[2] so long as the system of

[1] i.e. either in an immediate way or in the way of patronage.

[2] It is not clear to what former instance Bentham was referring, but it may be the example of war in point II above.

Judicial Procedure, by which factitious misdecision, delay, expence and vexation in other shapes, to the profit of the Judge has been created, remains as it is, remains unpurged of these corruptions, or rather, reform being plainly impossible, unextirpated, the quantity of such factitious delay, expence and vexation, can not in any very considerable proportion by any single exertion of it[1] be diminished: yet what is at all times in his power is to afford indication of the quantity of abuse which in this shape is continually generated: to use his endeavours towards the framing and obtaining the sanction of law for a set of arrangements by which all such factitious abuse would be extirpated: but more especially the abstaining from being a partaker in reaping as above any such profit to any amount or in any shape as may accrue from that corrupt source.

In England, the whole Judicial Establishment has at all times been in this radically and all-pervadingly corrupt state. In the situation of the Judges, the profit from this corruption has been and is greater than in the situation of the Judges in any country upon the face of the earth: money being in certain judicial situations reaped by these means in greater quantity without fear of the law, under the protection of the law and by the application of the law itself to this flagitious purpose, than in any other country has ever been reaped by any Judge, without the known allowance of the law—of those on whom the state of the law depends—and by acts of delinquency committed at the hazard of their respective fortunes and reputations.

Including the profit which in all imaginable shapes they are in the habit or expectation of receiving from the Chief functionary in the event of [their doing] and in proportion to the extent to which they do his will, the profit which, with all partakers in the legislative power for their accomplices and protectors, the Judges receive from this corrupt source is so great, that to receive at the hands of individual suitors money which in their situations men are forbidden to receive, to receive thus in disobedience to law and therefore at the peril of undergoing punishment in consequence of evidence afforded by those by whom they had been corrupted, would be an act of too palpable imprudence to be ever committed by a functionary in any such situation. On their part not the smallest probability of acceptance for any such offer having place, while punishment might by any such offer be brought down on the head of him by whom it had been made, by no individual is any such offer ever made.

Hence comes all that boasting which, in the mouths and pens [of] the admirers, real or pretended, of the English Constitution, is so

[1] i.e. of the power of the supreme operative functionary.

undefatigable. Through one particular channel never is the matter of corruption received by the functionaries in the superior grades of the department. Why? because through other channels they are saturated with it, in so far as by the matter of greed man is capable of being saturated—through other channels they are thus saturated with it, and through this particular channel it is altogether out of their power to obtain it.

In the Anglo-American United States, the Members of the Judicial Establishment, if in any degree at all corrupt, are not so in any degree worth considering in comparison of what is above. But, though in a degree of enormity much less than in England, factitious misdecision, delay, expence and vexation, have place in their system of substantive law and in their system of adjective law, otherwise called Law of Judicial Procedure, it being derived from that same corrupt and corruptive English source. From all this corruption, the profit whatsoever it be which is thus derived, it is by the professional retinues of the law, by such of the lawyer tribe as are enlisted in the service of individual suitors, that it is reaped: these men, the receivers of the corrupt profit, and the men belonging to the legislative department in the several states, as well as in the central state, and by whose connivance and inaction it is continued to be reaped, these are the men whom they have for their accomplices.

Of corruption in this form, which, with the addition of that in which it has place in the case of Slave buying and Slave holding, may be stated as constitut[ing] the only form in which any thing to which the name of corruption can with truth and justice be attributed has place in that political state, the efficient cause is the predominant influence of the lawyer tribe in the legislatures of these several states. In the *Codification Proposal*,[1] the baleful magnitude of this sinister influence on that as yet matchless seat of good government has been brought to view.

§7. *Different ways in which this security applies to the situation of supreme constitutive and that of supreme operative functionaries*

The course most conducive to this identification of interests on the occasion of the establishment of the supreme constitutive power is one thing: the course most conducive to this same end on the occasion of the establishment of the supreme operative power is another thing. For giving to the supreme constitutive power the best form possible,

[1] See *Codification Proposal*, pp. 70–1, 73 (Bowring, iv. 578, 580).

for placing it in a set of hands better disposed than any other set can be, nothing more is requisite than the placing it in the hands of individuals disposed each of them to take that course which in his judgment is most conducive to his own individual interest: so disposed, he will be disposed to take that course which is most conducive to the universal interest: for the universal interest is nothing else but the aggregate of all individual interests. So far as depends upon *disposition*, the constitutive power therefore can not be placed in any other set of individuals so aptly as in that set of individuals of the aggregate of whose several individual interests the universal interest is constituted: and this set of individuals will at all times be the same, with the additions of the changes effected by birth and immigration and the substractions made by death and emigration, neither of them such as to require any changes in the plan of provision in consideration of the change thus made in the mass of those for whose interest provision requires to be made. Nothing can be more simple than this plan: nothing more surely effectual with relation to the only right and proper end.

So far then as regards the supreme constitutive power, that which the legislator has to do is—not the taking men by selection and rendering the aggregate of their individual interests in a state of identification with relation to the universal interest, but the taking at once that class of individuals the aggregate of whose interests constitutes the universal interest—the taking those individuals belonging to this all-comprehensive groupe, and lodging the power in their hands.

Altogether different is the plan that for the accomplishment of that same end requires to be pursued on the occasion of the location of the supreme operative power: the quantity and quality of the powers with which those individuals shall be invested in whose hands the exercise of whatsoever operative power shall come to be placed, the designation of which shall have been effected by those in whose hands the supreme constitutive power is located or rather remains located. For the accomplishment of the universal end in the case of the possessors of the supreme constitutive power, the provision made can not be well-adapted otherwise than in so far as facility is left or given to each individual to make what in his eyes is the best provision possible for his own individual interest: in the case of the possessors of the supreme operative power, unless in so far as the utmost difficulty is opposed to his endeavours to make what in his eyes is the best provision possible for his own individual interest, to the detriment of the interest of the other individuals of that same community, that is to say in so far as mutual incompatability and competition have place, making provision for his own interests to the detriment of theirs. In the first case, the power left in or brought into existence needs no limits: no limits that could be applied to it could have any tendency to secure to the exercise given to it the most perfect conduciveness to its end: in the other case it requires to be applied to it the strictest limits which in any direction can be applied to it, consistently with its retaining amplitude sufficient for its giving accomplishment to that same end.

In regard to the possessors of the supreme operative power, the general description of their power must be that their power extends to every thing—is all-comprehensive—that in virtue of it they are at liberty and have been empowered on all occasions to do whatever they please in relation to all persons and all things appertaining to the community in question. But on the other hand, to confine the exercise of this power within the limits corresponding to the universal end, an adequate counter-power or counterforce must be established: this is the power reserved or given to the creators of their power, the possessors of the supreme constitutive power, to be the annihilators of it whenever they please. This being established, so long as in the eyes of these creators, that pursuit in which these same creatures (being human creatures) are sure to be engaged—namely the pursuit of their own particular happiness, is carried on no otherwise than through the medium of the universal happiness and the share they have in it—no otherwise in a word than by the pursuit of the universal happiness in consideration of the share they have in it, so far will the possessors of the supreme constitutive, governed as they are each of them by his regard for his own interest, suffer the possessors of the supreme operative power to continue to exist in such their situation, and to go on in such their course. But no sooner is it understood or believed that, in the pursuit each one of his own happiness, these possessors of the supreme operative power concurr in a course of action detrimental to the aggregate happiness of these same possessors of the supreme constitutive power, than by their act to the existence of such their rebellious creatures and unfaithful agents a period will be put. Of the general nature of the counter-power or limitative power proper to be applied to the general power conferred on the possessors of the supreme operative power, this is the least [incorrect][1] description that can be given in thus small a number of words. But for rendering the description accurate, certain modifications will require to be added—modifications the expression of which will come in due course.

[1] MS 'correct'.

In the construction of this part of the machine, the first mentioned power[1] performs the office of the main spring in a watch; the other[2] that of the regulator in a watch. Without the regulator, the main spring would do too much: without the main spring, the regulator would do nothing: viz. one with one another and antagonizing with one another, in so far as they are aptly proportioned to each other, they will do that which is required.

§8. *Identification, how effected*

If it were possible, each constituent would cause to be chosen such a Candidate as would sacrifice the interests of all the constituents to his: each Candidate, his own personal interests and connections out of the question, rather than not succeed, [would] engage himself to that same constituent to make that same sinister sacrifice, and, rather than not have his vote and interest in the next Election, perform that engagement. Thus it is with all the constituents having votes for the seat attached to that District. But, certain points common to all excepted, the interests of all these several constituents are in a state of opposition to one another: the interest of no one can be promoted without the sacrifice of the interests of all his competitors and opponents, without the sacrifice of all these adverse interests. To recommend himself to all, what is possible is—to promote the interest of each in those points in which it is not opposed by any other interests: this accordingly is what he does.

At the same time, among the points which all the interests of the inhabitants of a certain District have in common are some which are at variance with the interests of all the several inhabitants of all the several other Districts. The Delegate of that District, how then will he comport himself? He will give his vote and interest in favour of the inhabitants of his own District as to these same points. But in respect of the result of the voting, what is the evil consequence of this? None whatever. For the interests of the inhabitants of all the other Districts being adverse, this endeavour of his will be of no effect: the arrangements which are favorable to the interests of the inhabitants of all the Districts, or at least to the majority of them, these are the arrangements which on each occasion will be adopted and carried into effect.

In this way, in the instance of each individual such part of the whole mass of his happiness as is not adverse to the happiness of any other

[1] i.e. the supreme operative power.
[2] i.e. the supreme constitutive power.

individual will be, in so far as depends upon the agency of the government, secured to him: the correspondent part of his interest will be provided for: the correspondent part of his desires, of his wishes, will receive its gratification: while all such portions of happiness as he could not be made to enjoy without depriving others of happiness to greater amount will not be given to him: the correspondent part of his interest will be left unpromoted: the correspondent part of his desires, of his wishes, left ungratified.

On this plan, the identification of each man's individual interest with the several individual interests of all the other members of the community has place as far as the nature of man permitts.

The identification of interests of rulers taken in the aggregate with that of subjects taken in the aggregate is as compleat as possible. For in regard to the supreme operative power, it is in hands chosen by themselves: and in regard to the supreme constitutive power—that constitutive power which[?] is so with relation to the supreme operative power, it [is] in their own hands—so far as concerns that branch of power they are themselves rulers: not the less rulers for being subjects: not the less subjects for the being rulers.

This then in a word is the perfection of government: that all rulers should be subjects: rulers only to certain purposes, subjects to all others: in that case subjects can not suffer but they must suffer with them. But if there are any rulers who are not on any occasion subjects, then all suffering is on the side of subjects, no suffering, in so far as it is in their power to prevent it, on the side of rulers.

Behold now how the matter stands in the case where supreme and uncontrouled power is in hands any otherwise circumstanced.

1. Is it in the hands of one alone and no more than one? he, ruler to all purposes and on all occasions, subject on none?

The only individual for whose happiness any provision is made for his own sake is that one: to the happiness of other individuals no regard paid but in so far as it happens to them to be special objects of his sympathy, or as it seems to him necessary instruments to his happiness: and then only because, and in so far as, if they had less happiness, they might not serve so effectually in the character of instruments to his.

2. Is it in the hands comparatively speaking of a few? of any class that has an interest separate from that of those that are not rulers. The result is much the same. The number of the partners in the stock of factitious happiness is greater: but the condition of those who are not partners is much the same. Of the means of happiness as much as may be is taken into the hands of the ruling class: as little as may be is left in the hands of the non-ruling class, among whom are the

productive classes by which the whole stock of those means has been produced.[1]

Taking men in private life, for the management of a man's own concerns, if he be not in a state of mental imbecillity, who would think of proposing for a man's trustee any other man than himself? who would think of proposing that the trustee thus placed by himself should not be removable by himself? So in the case of half a dozen men, a dozen, a hundred, a thousand taken together. But if in the case of a thousand, why not in the case of the million, the 10 millions? at what number is the aptitude of this arrangement to cease, the inaptitude, the absurdity, of any other arrangement, to cease?

To produce this identification the situation to be operated upon—the situation to the fashioning of which the operations of the legislative hand must be directed—is that of the supreme operative functionary or functionaries: matters are to be so ordered that on every occasion on which a functionary of this class uses his endeavours to promote his own interest at the expence of the other members of the community taken in the aggregate, the least evil that can happen to him is to see these endeavours become unavailing: here then is an evil the prospect of which, supposing the arrival of it eventually certain, will be sufficient to prevent any such endeavours from being employed: but to render the identification compleat, to provide for the event of the prospect of this minimum of evil not being found sufficient, the prospect [of] an ulterior mass of evil may require to be added.

§9. *Means of identification. Non-reeligibility of supreme operatives*

First as to moral aptitude.

As a security for moral aptitude, the usefulness of an arrangement of this sort is obvious and seems incontestable: in the situation of ruler a man's continuance is for no longer a time say than a year: in the situation of subject his continuance is for the whole remainder of his life—is it probable that for such short-lived power, a man will in general feel disposed to barter away security to an indefinite amount, that for so little power, he will forego so much security?

Objection 1. Insufficiency.

The reason however is not quite so conclusive as it will be apt to appear. By obsequiousness to interest and thence to the will of the

[1] In the marginal summary, Bentham added at this point: '☛ Note here the controul produced by rulers' fear of appeal to people in case of disagreement among one another.'

Supreme Executive functionary in his character of giver of good gifts, a Member of the Supreme Operative body may obtain for his connections desirable situations to an indefinite value: situations of more or less value according to the value set upon his talent and connections by that Chief. By the same means, so will every other Member, or at any rate a majority of them. But having this opportunity of converse with each other, not only those of each such body will thus form particular connections, but so will the quondam Members of the several successive bodies. There then will be gradually formed a particular aristocratical interest common to all the individuals by whom the supreme situation in question has ever been occupied: and notwithstanding his exclusion from the situation to which each Member was indebted for this particular and sinister interest, the particular and sinister interest itself will remain, and will remain distinct, and prevent the all-embracing and salutary identification from being so perfect as could be wished.

Objection 2. Inconsistency with the supposition of appropriate intellectual aptitude on the part of the Electors.

Applied to the situation itself in general, and to the aggregate number of those by whom it is occupied, the relevancy of the objection can not but be admitted.[1] If among the quondam Members there be any who contribute to the formation of this aristocratical interest, who they are will be generally known: known on evidence which, though not in a sufficient degree probative for the purpose of subjecting a man to positive and direct punishment in any shape under that name, will be sufficiently so to cause a man to be subjected to the sort of negative inconvenience consisting in the not being a second time placed in possession of the lot of power of which the supposed unapt exercise has been made.

Now comes the objection that bears reference to intellectual aptitude. Intellectual aptitude depends upon experience, appropriate

[1] In the text, the following sentence appears at this point: 'But, in the appropriate intellectual aptitude which can not consistently be said to be wanting on the part of the Electors—[in] their judgment, guided by their knowledge, produced as it is by apposite observation and experience—an answer to the objection may be found.' This however seems inconsistent with the sense of the passage. The remainder of the paragraph is an explanation of the objection, not an answer to it. The marginal summary supports this interpretation: 'By supposition, [the electors] are apt to choose a representative antecedently to their experience of him: much more after such experience. In Assembly No. 1, suppose sinister influence of aristocratical interest observed in a Member: to Assembly No. 2 he will not be returned. Evidence not sufficient for punishment may be quite sufficient for non-reelection.' It is unclear whether Bentham neglected to answer the first two objections, or whether he accepted their validity. Bowring claimed that at the end of 1821 or beginning of 1822 he had changed Bentham's mind in favour of non-reeligibility (see Bowring, x. 528–30). Bentham may however still have had some reservations on the matter.

intellectual aptitude upon appropriate experience. In the early days of a Constitution, the demand for appropriate experience is in a particular degree urgent, and at the same time the supply in a particular degree scanty. In such a state of things, any such an idea as that of making any defalcation from the supply, and in particular a defalcation to so vast an amount, can it be a defensible one?

Answer. In an intellectual point of view, the importance of the supply is admitted. But two counter-observations present themselves.

One is that the utility of appropriate intellectual aptitude, its conduciveness to the greatest happiness of the greatest number, depends upon the state of the functionary's mind in respect of appropriate moral aptitude. If his disposition be to minister to the sinister sacrifice, not promoted but detrimented is the universal interest by whatsoever advantage he may be in possession of in respect of intellectual aptitude.

The other observation is that if the proceedings of the supreme operative body have that publicity which is capable of being given to them and can not consistently be refused to them, the advantage which in point of appropriate knowledge is possessed by one who has been a Member though it be for ever so great a length of time in comparison with one who is a new Member[1] will not upon examination be found so considerable as might naturally be imagined. A person placed by the free suffrages of so large a section of the whole community is not likely to have been inattentive to the proceedings of antecedent legislatures. Whatever acts have been passed, by him have been at all times at his command: so likewise the substance of whatsoever in the way of discussion and debate has been said in the appropriate place on the occasion of these acts: known to him in a word has been and is not only whatsoever has been done, but the rationale of whatsoever has been done.

The question here is as to that which is in his power, supposing inclination not deficient: for let inclination be deficient, compleatly ineffective may have been all the opportunities of information that any the longest continuance in the situation can have afforded. England can afford examples in any number of two bodies[2] containing Members who, after continuing half a century in the situation, die in it without any the smallest particle of appropriate information over and above the nothing they were in possession of at their first entrance into it.

[1] MS 'possessed by one who is a new Member in comparison with one who has been a Member though it be for ever so great a length of time'. The syntax has been emended in order to make it consistent with the evident sense of the passage.

[2] i.e. the House of Lords and the House of Commons.

Nor yet is the advantage afforded in this particular by long continuance or frequent re-entrance to be set down as amounting to absolutely nothing. But that which it will principally consist in is acquaintance with the dispositions and habits of the individual persons of whom from time to time the body has been composed. Rather to the individual functionary than to the interest of the community at large is this advantage of use: what answer can be given with best prospect of effect to such or such an opponent: among colleagues on the same side, in what shape or shapes from this one and that one, on this or that occasion, may assistance with most probability be expected.

Of the true interests of the whole community, knowledge may as effectually be obtained out of the body as in it: if what the French [call][1] the *carte du pays* be in any considerable degree material, it will be in a party view: the active aptitude to which it will afford assistance and support is the aptitude to afford support to your own party and annoyance to the opposite ones.

The Tactics of the Assembly will here be apt to present itself as a part of the field in relation to which appropriate experience may in a particular degree be of use. But if that has been done which can not consistently have been omitted, neither in respect of this branch of information will the condition of him who has been for any length of time a Member of the body be very materially different from that of him who, not having been a Member, has such adequate inducements for the acquisition of this stock of knowledge. In the English House of Commons may always be seen an individual or two who, in a peculiar degree of acquaintance with those usages and decisions from which the existence of corresponding rules and imaginary ordinances are to be inferred, and among which rules, the offspring of corruption and absurdity, the stock of really useful and honest rules are drowned, beholds his grounds of pretension to a situation in which factitious dignity of immense altitude is added to a mass of pecuniary emolument, the excessiveness of which forms an apt match to the excessiveness of the whole official establishment of which it forms a part.[2]

Another reason that pleads in favour of non-reeligibility is the

[1] MS orig. 'if what is called'.

[2] The Speaker of the House of Commons, as the first commoner, had been ranked next to the peers of the realm, both in and out of Parliament, since the time of the Glorious Revolution (1 W. and M., c.21). His salary had been fixed at £6,000 per annum by Act of Parliament in 1790 (30 Geo. III, c.10), but other perquisites included an official residence with coals and candles during his term of office, the cash equivalent of a service of plate of 2,000 ounces (in 1790 worth about £1,000) and an outfit allowance of £1,000 each time he was elected, an allowance for stationery of £100 per session, and two hogsheads of claret annually.

advantage that will accrue to the aggregate of the public mind by the perpetual infusion made of a fresh stock of political knowledge and experience into the aggregate mass of the population.

The advantage which in respect of skill in judicature results from the institution of a Jury, whether it be a Jury with an obligatory verdict, a Jury with an unobligatory verdict, or a silent Jury hearing without pronouncing a verdict, will be brought to view in another place.[1] That which to a certain extent is done already by the one institution in the department of judicature, would by the other be done in the department of legislation.

The advantage which the bulk of the population may be expected to reap in the article of moral character and conduct from such diffusion of political knowledge and the habit of attention to political subjects is neither less important nor less manifest than in the article of intellectual vigour.

In England, since the time when, by the question concerning parliamentary reform, minds least elevated in the conjoint scales of power and opulence have to so great an extent been led to apply themselves to the subject of legislation, the improvement that has had place in respect of moral conduct has been matter of observation and proportionable satisfaction to all those whose age has placed the means of observation in their power.

Such in a word has been the effect in every country which has had the good fortune of witnessing the existence of this same cause. Witness Ireland during its golden age, France, Spain, Portugal, Naples, Piedmont.[2]

Against deficiency in point of intellectual aptitude so far as depends on experience, another security might be afforded without prejudice to that afforded against want of moral aptitude by the non-reeligibility principle. At any time antecedent to its dissolution suppose the Assembly to elect out of its own Members, a body composed of three,

[1] For a discussion of this topic see 'Principles of Judicial Procedure, with the outlines of A Procedure Code' in Bowring, ii. 149–50.

[2] Each of these countries had experienced revolution or some degree of constitutional reform. The French Revolution of 1789 had culminated in the abolition of the monarchy and the establishment of a republic. In Spain a military revolution in 1820 had forced Ferdinand VII to adopt the liberal constitution of 1812, which he had himself overturned in 1814, while a liberal constitution on similar lines had been established in Portugal in 1821. An uprising in Naples in 1820 had overturned the Bourbon monarchy and led to the establishment of a constitution based on the Spanish model of 1812, though the old regime had been restored by Austria in March 1821. This Austrian intervention gave rise to a short-lived revolution in Piedmont in March 1821 prompting the abdication of Victor Emmanuel I (1759–1824), King of Sardinia from 1802 to 1821, and the granting of a liberal constitution by the regent Charles Albert (1798–1849), afterwards King of Sardinia from 1831 to 1849. The new monarch, Charles Felix (1765–1831), King of Sardinia from 1821, restored order with the aid of Austrian troops. For Ireland see pp. 146–7 below.

five, or some other odd number of persons, whose function should consist in communicating appropriate information in all shapes in and to the Assembly next succeeding. So long as they have not the right of voting, there seems no reason why the members of this delegated body should not possess the right of speaking: the right of speaking on the same footing with those by whom the right of voting is possessed.

Here, it is true, would be influence: still however it would be but that sort of influence which is exercised by understanding over understanding, the power and effect of acting not being affected by it.

§ 10. *Objection: deficiency in respect of intellectual aptitude*

Taken in the aggregate, the people neither do any where possess, nor are capable of being made to possess, appropriate knowledge sufficient, nor thence appropriate judgment sufficient, to qualify them, respectively each of them, for contributing by his vote to the location of a Member of the supreme operative body, in which provision shall be made for the promotion of his (the Elector's) share in the universal interest.

Answer. This objection applies not, unless the case be, that in some other quarter indication has been given [of] a person or set of persons in whom there has place appropriate intellectual aptitude to a greater degree, in conjunction with appropriate moral aptitude in an equal degree: or at any rate in so high a degree superior in appropriate intellectual aptitude, and in so low a degree inferior [in] appropriate moral aptitude, as to be superior in the aggregate of appropriate aptitude. Of no such person or set of persons can indication have been or can be ever made.[a]

1. The power shall it be lodged in a single hand? See how this situation stands in respect of appropriate moral aptitude. It is the interest of the greatest number that the external instruments, or say means, of felicity be distributed in a manner as near to equality as is consistent with general subsistence, general abundance in the character of a security against accident, and general security in all its shapes. It is the interest of a ruling one that these same instruments be, to an amount as great as is consistent with his own security, in all shapes accumulated in his single hand.

[a] Of the three branches of appropriate aptitude, active aptitude does not belong to the case—in the case of the people in their quality of Electors, no demand for active aptitude has place: by this circumstance is the situation of supreme constitutive functionary distinguished from the situation of supreme operative.

Such is his interest: so says the nature of man. Such in all places at all times has been his endeavour. So says history.

2. The power shall it be lodged in the hands of a few, in the hands of any number in such sort intermediate between one and all as to have in common one with another an interest distinct from that of all? In the main, the answers are still the same.

3. The power shall it be shared between the one and the few? In the main, the answer is still the same.[1]

4. The power shall it be lodged in a tricompound body, composed of the one, the few and the delegates of the people—or rather of a small portion of the people, this being the only individual exemplification that has ever been made of the tricompound thus described? In the main, the answers are not materially different. Neither the share engrossed by the one, nor the share engrossed by the many, of the external instruments or means of felicity, will be in quite so large a ratio to that left in the hands of the people at large as where they have no share at all in the supreme operative power. But still in respect of moral aptitude, there will here be great deficiency: in respect even of intellectual aptitude, there will be great deficiency: what intellectual aptitude there is being engrossed by the endeavour to add to the excessive share of the instruments of felicity possessed by the one, and to the excessive share possessed in partnership by the few: and whatsoever be the share possessed by the people, the whole endeavour and the whole of the stock of knowledge, judgment, and active talent, will be employed in the augmentation of the shares engrossed by the one and the many, which is as much as to say in the diminution of the share left in the hands of the people at large, those included by whom the whole stock of these instruments is at all times produced.

On the part of the people appropriate aptitude in the shape of moral aptitude is at all times at a maximum: on the part of the one, at all times, as above, at a minimum.

In the shape of intellectual aptitude, it is at all times naturally on the encrease. By exertions on the part of the supreme operatives directed to this end, it is susceptible of great and continual encrease: but even without any such endeavours it has been found sufficient.

In so far as the power of the one and the few has been predominant, the object towards which on this occasion the endeavours of govern-

[1] Bentham marked the remainder of the paragraph for exclusion: 'But if there be a difference, it will be found to consist in this—namely that under the joint dominion of the one and the few, the degree of appropriate aptitude in the rulers is, in respect of moral and intellectual aptitude both, inferior to that in which it is under the dominion of the few without the one: and that accordingly under this composite form of government the condition of the people has been worse than under that same simple one, viz. the undivided dominion of the few.'

ment have actually been directed has been to diminish on the part of the people the degree of appropriate intellectual aptitude, to diminish the aggregate stock of knowledge or to keep it diverted into other channels; to diminish in relation to this department the stock of true, active knowledge: in the room of true conceptions to substitute false, fallacious and mischievous ones: to implant in their minds the persuasion that, instead of that minimum which really has place, the heart of the ruling one is the seat of the maximum of moral aptitude: and in the breasts of the sub-ruling or jointly ruling few, that same element of appropriate aptitude has place in proportion to their respective altitudes in the conjoint scales of power, opulence and factitious dignity.

§11. *Objection: on the part of the people, time for appropriate intellectual aptitude deficient*

On the part of the people at large, the whole quantity of disposable waking time is unavoidably preoccupied by labour for subsistence, and a small quantity of recreation. In the field [of] appropriate aptitude on the part of members of the supreme operative body is comprized the whole field of legislation, little less than the whole field of thought and action. For the possession of aptitude for the forming a correct judgment concerning the aptitude of each such Member on the occasion of Election, concerning the aptitude of each Candidate for the office of Member, an Elector must himself be possessed of correspondent and equal aptitude: neither of the whole people, nor of any number approaching to a majority, can any such aptitude with any approach to truth be predicated.

Answer. This deficiency constitutes no objection any further than in so far as greater sufficiency can be shewn to have place as above in some other quarter, coupled with that equality in respect of moral aptitude without which superiority in intellectual aptitude is detrimental, and not contributory, to superiority in the aggregate of appropriate aptitude.

To this point applies the distinction between aptitude self-seated, and aptitude derivative, say aptitude borrowed.[a] Aptitude through advice is within the reach of the least instructed: no one but has time for taking the opinion of one whom general estimation points out as the best qualified for giving such advice of all who are within his reach.

Of aptitude *self-seated*, an all-comprehensive and rationalized Code,

[a] *Aptitude empruntée*, French.

a sort of work of which these very pages exhibit a part-performance—would suffice of itself to confer upon all possessors of the art of reading a stock in a prodigious degree greater than has ever yet been in the possession of the best instructed minds. This being taken for the standing table, the transactions of the day as reported in the Newspapers of the day would furnish to the mind of the people its daily bread.

By those by whom the breast of a single individual is proposed as being the most apt seat for the supreme operative power, the supreme constitutive power being left in the hands of chance operating through genealogical consanguinity, neither can the relevancy of the distinction between self-seated and borrowed aptitude be consistently denied, nor yet the sufficiency of borrowed aptitude.

In Monarchies in general, aptitude with relation to the exercise of the supreme operative power is regarded as possessed by the Monarch at an age far less mature than that at which for the first time an individual is regarded as competent to the management of his own affairs. Why? because he is environed by those who are in so high a degree able to afford to him a full supply of advice of the very best quality: his deficiency in self-seated aptitude finds a supply, and that an adequate one, in derivative aptitude, derived as it is from such transcendently apt sources.

The source of information being the same, intellectual aptitude is not acquired without mental labour: the quantity of labour is proportioned to the force of inducement. In the Monarch class, inducement to mental labour is less than in any other: less in proportion to the smallness of the need there is of it. Of a Monarch, the whole time is spent in the enjoyment of the pleasures of power, none in acquiring aptitude for the exercise of it: and what is thus true of the one is with inconsiderable variation true of the few.

In the Monarch class, instances of mental incapacity have place in a number some thousand times greater than in all classes taken in the aggregate. Down [to] the very moment at which it is regarded as absolutely necessary to the surrounding company of advisers that he should be placed under confinement, or in a state of banishment, deprived either of his power or of his life, he acts with the benefit of such advice, and remains in the eyes of all his subjects the same perfect and inimitable seat and model of appropriate moral, intellectual and active, and, in full, all-exalting aptitude.

Thus stands the question on the ground of general argument. How stands it on the ground of particular experience?

Look to the Anglo-American United States. For upwards of 40 years last past, the supreme operative power in the hands of the

Delegates of the people. During this or any former time, no where appropriate aptitude so nearly approaching to consummation: appropriate aptitude in all its branches: no where the degree of aptitude possessed, purchased at so small an expence: expence in all shapes. No where on the part of the people, considered in their capacity of subjects—no where so great a measure of felicity, no where so great a measure of good morals, efficient cause of all such portion of felicity as depends not on physical, but on political, causes.

In all places at all times, not in the inverse but in the direct ratio of the quantity of power left in the hands of the many has been the aggregate of appropriate official aptitude, the moderateness of official expence, the stock of actual felicity and intelligible virtues.

Even when instead of the tranquilly and equally elected Delegates of the people, the supreme constitutive power, coupled with as large a portion of supreme operative power as men chose to assume, has been in the hands of self-appointed individuals: these representatives coming in from all classes promiscuously, and all of them actuated by one and the same interest, the universal interest, the whole community, instead of that scene of universal disorder and universal mischief which has been so constantly assumed to be the neverfailing and necessary consequence of such [a] state of things, has been a scene of universal innocence, universal tranquillity, universal felicity and universal moral virtue:— a scene forming in all those particulars the most striking and perfect contrast with the state of things in that same country in all former times, and in all subsequent times down to the moment in which the pen is moving on this page.

This state of things is the state exhibited by Ireland for about five years between the year 1777 and the year 1783: time during which the regular government of the country lay at the mercy of a body of volunteers, self-appointed, self-clothed, self-subsisting, self-armed, self-trained.[1]

[1] The Volunteer movement was formed in 1778, in response to the possibility of a French invasion, for the purpose of home defence and the maintenance of law and order. Volunteers were usually expected to provide their own equipment and uniforms, while Catholics were in the main discouraged from enlisting, so membership tended to be limited to the more affluent and was overwhelmingly Protestant. Nevertheless, at the height of the movement, there may have been as many as 40,000 Volunteers organized into corps of between 30 and 100 men, each of which elected its own officers. In addition to their military function, the Volunteer companies formed themselves into political associations to press for constitutional reform, and helped secure the legislative independence of the Irish Parliament in 1782. They then turned to the questions of parliamentary reform and tariff reform. A National Convention, composed of delegates elected by the Volunteers, met at Dublin in November 1783 and agreed to a scheme of parliamentary reform. The proposal was presented to the House of Commons by Henry Flood on 29 November 1783, but was rejected by a large majority. A further reform bill and a motion in favour of protection were both defeated in the Commons in March 1784, whereupon the Volunteer movement began to lose its impetus.

That such during that length was the state of that country is attested by the unanimous testimony of the contemporary historians of all parties, without a single dissenting voice: so depicted by all, but in the most glowing colours by Hardy, adherent, personal friend and intimate, representative in the legislative body, biographer and panegyrist of the Earl of Charlemont, by whose exertions more than by any other cause that golden age was made to give place to the anterior iron one.[1]

Not many years had elapsed when by another creature of the same creator, in the grand and most notorious of all theatres of political corruption, a speech was made, a speech which may be seen in print, declaring the utter impossibility of that very state of things which in that very place had as above been exemplified in all eyes—the certainty of the destruction of all property in a state of things under which, during that same period, all property had existed in a state of security never exemplified in that same country, either before or since.[2]

[1] Francis Hardy (1751–1812) was not a nominee of James Caulfield (1728–99), fourth Viscount and first Earl of Charlemont, but was returned to the Irish House of Commons for Mullingar from 1782 to 1800 on the interest of George Forbes (1760–1837), sixth Earl of Granard. He was however closely associated with Charlemont, and was the author of *Memoirs of the political and private life of James Caulfield, Earl of Charlemont*, London, 1810. Bentham seems to have regarded the failure of the National Convention to secure parliamentary reform as the decisive moment in the decline of the Volunteer movement. He was especially critical of the role played by Charlemont, who had been elected president of the Convention (see Bowring, iii. 618). After the scheme recommended by the Convention had been rejected by the House of Commons, Charlemont was determined to bring its proceedings to a conclusion as quickly as possible, and it disbanded rather tamely with a call for petitions in support of reform to be presented to Parliament. Hardy's description of Charlemont's part in the adjournment of the Convention is in *Memoirs of Charlemont*, pp. 263–80.

[2] In the marginal summary, Bentham made it clear that he was referring to Henry Grattan (1746–1820), who from 1775 to 1790 had been returned to the Irish House of Commons for the borough of Charlemont on the interest of the Earl of Charlemont. At the time Bentham was writing, a comprehensive edition of Grattan's speeches had just been published: see *The Speeches of the Right Honourable Henry Grattan, in the Irish, and in the Imperial Parliament*, ed. H. Grattan, 4 vols., London, 1822. It is possible that Bentham had in mind Grattan's speech in the Irish Commons on 21 January 1785 in the debate on the address to the King, where he denounced the activities of the Volunteer movement in the previous year, claiming that it had been reduced to something of a popular and radical rump (see i. 210–13).

SUPREME OPERATIVE

§1. *Reasons all-comprehensive for not locating the supreme operative power, or any portion of it, in the hands of a Monarch.*
Case I. The Monarch absolute: appropriate aptitude would thereby be minimized. Cause of inaptitude in the aggregate

Opposite and correspondent to the several elements of appropriate aptitude are the several parts of relative inaptitude.

The elements of appropriate aptitude may be thus designated: 1. appropriate moral aptitude; 2. appropriate intellectual aptitude; 3. appropriate active talent.

Appropriate intellectual aptitude may again be considered as having two branches:—[1.] appropriate knowledge and 2. appropriate judgment.

The causes of these several modifications of relative inaptitude may be thus summed up or designated: 1. sinister interest. 2. interest-begotten prejudice. 3. original weakness, understand intellectual weakness. 4. authority-begotten prejudice.

By sinister interest understand every particular interest by which, it being opposite to the interest of, that is detrimental to the greatest happiness of, the greatest number, a man is prompted to sacrifice to it that all-comprehensive interest.

Such sacrifice may be termed the sinister sacrifice.

By prejudice understand erroneous prepossession: prepossession in the case where it is regarded as erroneous.

It is in sinister interest that the relative inaptitude which corresponds to appropriate moral aptitude has its cause.

It is in interest-begotten prejudice, original weakness and authority-begotten prejudice that that modification of relative inaptitude which corresponds to appropriate judgement has its cause.

Interest-begotten prejudice, though by the supposition it would not have had existence but for sinister interest, may where it does exist be in any proportion more mischievous—in a proportion to any amount greater, contributory to the sinister sacrifice—than sinister interest itself. To the number of persons capable of being infected with the sinister interest there are certain limits: to the number of those capable of taking up and retaining the interest-begotten prejudice there are no limits: by a change of circumstances, the particular interest in question may cease to operate in the direction and character of a sinister interest: it may operate in the opposite direction and thus become a right and proper interest: whereas prejudice when once formed may continue to any length of time inflexible, contributing so long as it has place to the sinister sacrifice.

Notorious are the instances in which, by thousands and ten thousands, by prejudice in its various modes, men have been led to sacrifice each of them his own unquestionable interest while contributing to the sacrifice of the universal interest at the altar of monarchical and aristocratical despotism.

§2. *Objects of general desire: external instruments of felicity etc. what*

To every man the several external instruments of happiness are, in so far as they are regarded by him as being within his reach, so many objects of desire: each of them in the greatest quantity in which they present themselves as obtainable.

To the present purpose these may be all of them comprehended under one or more of the [six][1] following denominations: namely, wealth, power, factitious dignity, superior reputation, vengeance and ease: factitious dignity in countries in which it is to be had: vengeance incidentally in case of ill-will excited: ease, in so far as compatible with the pursuit and enjoyment of the several preceding objects.

By no man can these objects, any one of them, be enjoyed but in some way or other at the expence of all other men: manifestly in case of competition: and there is not any one of them that is not at all times an object of universal competition.

§3. *Cause of Monarch's moral inaptitude, his sinister interest. His right and proper interest is overpowered by his sinister interest*

These objects of general desire it is the interest of every man to possess, and enjoy, and in so far as is consistent with enjoying, retain in his possession or at his command, in the largest quantity possible.

This being the interest of every human being, this therefore, if the Monarch be a human being, is the interest of the Monarch.

The legitimate interest of the Monarch is his share in the universal interest.

The sinister interest of the Monarch is his particular interest.

Opposite, irreconcilably opposite, to the universal interest is the Monarch's particular interest: it is therefore in every part of it a sinister interest.

[1] MS 'five'. Bentham subsequently added 'superior reputation' to the list, but neglected to alter the total.

It is the interest of all that by each of them the matter of subsistence, the matter of abundance, security in all its shapes or branches, be possessed and enjoyed in the highest degree possible; so equality in so far as consistent with subsistence, abundance and security of all.

It is the interest of the Monarch that by all the other members of the community, means of subsistence and the matter of abundance should be enjoyed in so far as the quantity of his money and of his power are encreased thereby, or at any rate not lessened. But it is his interest that their share in the aggregate of the matter of abundance be lessened at all times in whatsoever degree is necessary to give to his share any the smallest degree of encrease.

In regard to power, it is their interest that in any hands the quantity of it should be a minimum, consistently with their possession of the maximum of the four elements of general felicity above mentioned, namely subsistence, abundance, security and equality. It is his interest that the quantity of power in his hands, and therefore that so far the quantity of power in existence, be as great as possible: that in quality of subjects, all beside himself should be in all things subject to his power, and that there should be no power any where except what has been derived from him and can at all times be resumed by him at pleasure.[1]

Security bears reference to evil, and can no otherwise be understood than by reference to it: security is security against Evil. Evil may be considered in respect of its nature, or in respect of its source.

Sources of evil are the operations of nature: the operations of human beings considered in the several characters of internal adversaries: and external adversaries: internal adversaries are termed misdoers: their acts, in so far as productive of evil, misdeeds. Misdoers are either non-possessors of political power or possessors.

It is the interest of every member of the community to possess in the compleatest degree security against evil from all these several sources: against misdeeds by individuals at large and against misdeeds of functionaries.

Exception excepted, it is the particular interest of the Monarch that

[1] There is no text corresponding to the following marginal summary, which belongs here: 'Interests as to factitious dignity. I. Universal that there be none: because 1. By each man's exaltation is produced every other's humiliation. 2. By factitious dignity, power is encreased. 3. By power, faculty of obtaining money at the expence of others. 4. The source by which factitious dignity is more easily obtained than power or money is most apt to be that which is service to the particular and thence sinister interest of the Monarch. [II.] Monarch's interest that there be of factitious dignity the maximum, and the highest his own.' The fourth point of part I does not appear in the marginal summary on the text sheet, but has been added by Bentham to the marginal summary sheet (UC xxxviii. 108).

the maximum of security should be enjoyed by all the other members of the community in all these several branches. But it is his interest that against his own power, including that of all other functionaries in so far as the exercise of their respective powers is not unconformable to his will, there shall be no security.

It is in a word his interest that in all points in which any contrariety has place between his particular interest and the universal interest, a sacrifice of the universal interest to his particular interest shall have place. This sacrifice may be termed a sinister sacrifice—in the present instance, the Monarch's sinister sacrifice.

Whatsoever arrangement produces a net addition to the sum of his happiness, it is his particular and sinister interest that it shall accordingly take place, whatsoever be the defalcation thereby made from the greatest happiness of the greatest number.

Power on the one part is constituted by, correspondent and proportioned to obedience, active and passive, on the other.

In respect of power, it being the Monarch's interest that his portion of it be as effective and comprehensive and irresistible as possible, it is his interest that on the part of the rest of the community [obedience][1] be as abject, devoted and comprehensive as possible.

The interest of the Monarch being thus decidedly and exclusively adverse to that of the rest of the community, it is the interest of every community in the first place that there should be no such functionary: in the next place that if there is, his power should be as small as possible.

So, as to his opulence: for the whole of it operates in augmentation of his power.

So, as to his factitious dignity: for the whole of it operates in augmentation of his power and thereby of his opulence, of his opulence and thereby of his power.

The power of the Monarch therefore depends upon and is proportioned to the sacrifice which the greatest number are in the habit of seeing made without resistance or discontent in each man of his own interest and that of the rest to the interest of that one individual functionary.

It depends therefore upon and is proportioned to their neglect of their own interest.

This neglect will be the more entire in proportion to their intellectual weakness.

Intellectual weakness is composed of, is constituted by, and proportioned to: 1. ignorance in respect of every thing by which,

[1] MS 'it'.

whether in a beneficial way or a pernicious way, their interest is affected. 2. misconception and thence error in so far as the effect of it is to produce in their minds the opinion that the interest of the Monarch is the same with theirs, or that it is not irreconcileably opposite to theirs, or that in so far as it is opposite to theirs, it is either probable or possible that he should be disposed to make sacrifice of it to theirs.[1]

If for want of such a support his own individual security be lessened, it may be his interest to allow to a portion of his subjects a mass of power being in such sort dependent on his own as not liable to be taken back again by himself. The persons to whom such partially independent power is allowed become thereby members of a particular body—of that sort of political body which is stiled an aristocratical body: or in one word an aristocracy.

If there be any other sinister interest the continuance or establishment of which would be subservient to his own sinister interest, it is his interest to give, as the case may be, existence or support to it.

So likewise, as to interest-begotten prejudice, authority-begotten prejudice, and original relative intellectual weakness.

Under a Monarch, in so far as sinister interest operates with effect, bad government is the result: bad government, or in one word misrule.

§4. *Monarch's moral inaptitude continued. Sinisterity of his interest as applied to the several specific ends of government*

A community of interest (it may be said) has place between a Monarch and his subjects: and this community of interest will suffice for securing them against ill treatment at his hands: nay: for securing to them the best treatment in his power. True. There is a community of interest between a Post-master and his Post-horses: but this community of interest suffices not for saving them from an untimely death at the end of a life of torment. The interest which a Monarch has

[1] On the marginal summary sheet (UC xxxviii. 110), Bentham inserted an addendum: 'Means of continuing and encreasing relative appropriate intellectual weakness by delusion. 1. All matter of corruptive influence operates as matter of delusive influence. 2. So, all interest-begotten prejudices. [3.] Appropriate instruments of factitious dignity: 1. Habiliments—Personal decorations. 2. Local decorations. 3. Ceremonies. 4. Eulogistic appellatives applied to pernicious dispositions. Ex.gr. Loyalty: ill-will towards the many.

'Appropriate errors: errors particularly favourable to Monarch's sinister interest. Notion that happiness and exemption from misery in a future life depends on degree of obsequiousness to Monarch and his sinister interest. Like notion for producing obsequiousness towards all sinister interests linked with the Monarch's. Notion of a natural association between aristocratical superiority and virtue, the opposite being the real one.'

in common with his subjects is not sufficient to render him in general so well disposed towards his subjects as a Post-master is to his Post-horses. By the horses nothing is usually done by which irritation and hatred towards them are produced in the breast of the Master. By the subjects much is constantly done by which hatred and continually renewed irritation is produced in the breast of the Monarch.

Spite of whatsoever there is in common between the two interests, in the breast of every Monarch the tendency of his disposition is at all times and in all places to produce the greatest infelicity of the greatest number. Such is every where the tendency necessarily produced by his situation: and such every where, except in so far as accidental circumstances have risen up in opposition to such tendency, has been, and so long as a Monarchy exists upon the face of the earth will be—the effect.

The more particularly the several shapes in which interest has place in the two situations are examined into—the several departments in the field of legislation to which it applies are examined into, the less numerous and extensive the seats of coincidence, the more numerous and extensive the seats of opposition as between the two interests will be seen to be.

[I.][1] Take in the first place the two immediately subordinate ends of the Constitutional Code: 1. Maximization of appropriate aptitude on the part of functionaries; 2. Minimization of the expence attached to the employment of them.

1. As to expence. With relation to the interest of the Monarch, distinguish the aggregate of the expence into two portions: Portion 1: that in respect to which his profit is equal to the expence: of this portion the whole being to him so much profit. Portion 2: that in respect of which his profit, though not equal to the expence, is in proportion to it encreasing as the expence encreases.

2. Next as to appropriate aptitude. In a Republic, appropriate aptitude means aptitude with reference to the greatest happiness of the greatest number. In a Monarchy, appropriate aptitude means aptitude with reference to the supposed greatest happiness of number *one*. But in the imagination and judgment of this same number *one*, the greatest happiness of this same number one will consist in the subserviency of all other wills and of the conduct of all other persons on each occasion to the will of this same number one. But what may happen and has continually been happening is—that while in the breasts of the greatest number of his subjects, infelicity has been

[1] In order to clarify the enumeration of this sequence of text, Bentham's arabic numerals identifying the various branches of law have been altered to roman numerals.

continually on the encrease, the will of number one has been continually [done] by all.[1]

[II.] Take in the next place the four immediately subordinate ends of the Non-penal or distributive branch of law: Subsistence, Abundance, Security and Equality, in so far as the less important are compatible with the more important, maximized.

1. Subsistence. This it is true it is his interest they should have: that is to say such of them as are in a condition to work and can be made to work: for man can not work any longer than he lives.

But it is the interest of the greatest number that whether able or not able to work they should live, in which is included the having subsistence.

2. Abundance. This also it is his interest they should have: and the greater the quantity they produce and thence have, the greater the quantity which it will be in his power, as it can not fail to be in his inclination, to get out of them for himself. But so long as by any act of his, any addition how small so ever [is made], which could not otherwise be made to the stock of the matter of abundance, to the stock of this pretious matter, passing into and through his hands, how great may be the quantity which by this same act is taken out of their hands or prevented from finding its way into them will, to this same personal interest of his, be matter of indifference.

3. Security. Security is *for* body, mind, reputation, pecuniary property, power, condition in life: it is against injury at the hands of external evil-doers, internal evil-doers not being functionaries, and internal evil-doers being functionaries. Security against external evil-doers, i.e. against foreign enemies, his personal interest prompts him to maximize, so far as no expectation of profit presents itself from the restriction or diminution or destruction of it. But that which he is continually upon the watch to get is—an augmentation of the mass of the external instruments of felicity in his hands at the expence of other communities: and by means of war, that is murder upon the largest scale, this he never can get but by the diminution and to so much the destruction of the security of his subjects as for the several possessions above enumerated.[2]

As to security against misdeeds on the part of functionaries—security against the abuse of his own power—the very idea of it is intolerable—as if in his hands power were capable of being abused! as if wrong could be done by him by whom no wrong can be done—by

[1] MS 'continually doing by all and done'.

[2] There is no text corresponding to the following marginal summary, which belongs here: '[It is the monarch's interest that the people should not possess security] against evil-doers whom, though not functionaries, he is inclined to favour.'

him, by whom that which if done by another would be wrong is, by the mere circumstance of its being by him that it is done, converted into *right*.

4. *Equality*.[1] In a Republic, the instrument of felicity thus denominated is watched and guarded with peculiarly anxious care. It is prized not only as being in its own character an instrument of felicity, an instrument for producing the greatest quantity of internal felicity itself out of a given quantity of the external instruments of felicity, but an instrument of security for security itself: in particular for securing all the several instruments of felicity to all the Members of the community against invasion on the part of such of them as are in the situation of public functionaries.

But to the Monarch the very word is an object of abhorrence. To give admission to it in the list of fit ends of the distributive branch of law, is at once to put an exclusion upon his office: to shut the door of the Official Establishment against his office. Of all the imaginable instruments of felicity that can be named, not one is there in which he can endure the idea of seeing any other member of the community possessing an equal share.

In particular not so much as an equal share in the protection of the law:—in the benefit derived from the services of the Officers belonging to the judicial department, directed, as they are or ought to be, to the securing to every Member of the community his proper share in the aggregate stock of the external instruments of felicity, against evil, in the several shapes in which it is endeavoured to be excluded by prohibition and punishment attached to the several misdeeds by which it is liable to be produced.

[III.] Take in the next place, the Penal branch of law. Immediately subordinate ends: beneficial effect of the distributive branch of the law maximized; punishment minimized.

With regard to Civil or say Distributive branch of law taken in its several sub-branches or specific branches, as above, it has been [seen] how far in the situation of Monarch his particular interest is accordant and coincident with the universal interest, how far opposite to it.

1. First then as to the maximization of the beneficial effects in question. So far as the above-mentioned coincidence has place, it is his interest that the universally beneficial effects may, by all imaginable means, and by this principal means in particular, be

[1] There is no text corresponding to the following marginal summary, which belongs here: 'Equality. Greatest happiness etc. requires that so far as consists with security, subsistence and abundance, this instrument of felicity be maximized. Because by whatsoever A has less than B, A loses more than B gains.'

maximized. But so far as instead of coincidence, opposition has place, this same particular interest of his requires that the amount of these same beneficial effects be minimized: or, in other words, that none such have place, but that the opposite evils have place.

2. Next and lastly, as to the minimization of punishment. So far as by the infliction of punishment, misdeeds on the part of any individual, in or not in the situation of functionary under him, tending to promote his particular interest—vengeance and ease included—would be repressed, his interest requires that no punishment at all be inflicted: or if any, none beyond the least possible.

So far as by the infliction of punishment, acts tending to the security of individuals against misdeeds the commission of which is required as above by his particular interest, and thence [restricting] his power of evil-doing, would be prevented,[1] or any gratification afforded to his appetite for vengeance, or any security afforded to his ease against disturbance, his particular interest requires that punishment be maximized.[2]

So much as to the several external instruments of felicity, and proper subordinate ends of government.

Now as to the internal.

I. As to Moral Virtue: or speaking with relation to felicity, moral aptitude.

This his interest prompts him to maximize on the part of his subjects, viz. so far and so far only as by the possession of it they are disposed to do his will and contribute to the advancement of his particular interest.

But at the same time this his interest renders him desirous to minimize, in so far as by the possession of it men are disposed to thwart his personal interest in all its several branches, preferring their own interests respectively to his.

II. Next as to intellectual virtue with relation to felicity, say intellectual aptitude.

In proportion as knowledge and sound judgment as applied to the field of legislation encrease, this opposition of the interest of the Monarch to the rest of the community becomes manifest and with it the want of virtue, moral as well as intellectual, betrayed by the obsequiousness by which any such Office in the Official Establishment

[1] The syntax in MS, 'by his particular interest would be prevented, and thence his power of evil-doing restricted', contradicts the evident meaning of the passage by suggesting that it is the interest of the monarch that punishment be inflicted to restrict his own power of evil-doing.

[2] In the text, Bentham noted at this point: 'For particular exemplifications, see the above-mentioned *Sketch*.' Bentham was apparently referring to 'Sketch of English Law considered in relation to the proper ends of Government' (see p. 160n below), a work for which no MSS appear to have been written. It is not mentioned previously in 'Supreme Operative'.

is suffered to have existence: the Office which may be stiled that of Malefactor General.

For the diminution and if possible destruction of virtue in this form, he sees before [him] two resources: the extinction, and the perversion of it.[1]

§5. *By locating supreme operative power in Monarch's hands, the inaptitude opposite to moral aptitude would be maximized*

The inaptitude opposite to appropriate Moral aptitude is in this state of things at its maximum. In pursuance of the self-preference inherent in human nature, the end of his government will be the greatest possible happiness of his individual self. This object, according to whatever happens to be his notion of it, he will pursue without regard to the happiness of the greatest number, at the expence of that happiness, and to the sacrifice of that happiness. His sinister interest having no right and proper interest to serve as a check to it, the force of his power having no counterforce to check it and keep the action of it in a state of conformity to the public interest, his desire to make on all occasions the sinister sacrifice will find no power in a condition to oppose it, will on every occasion find ample means for the gratification of it, and the sacrifice will at all times under his government be consummated.

He will accumulate under his own grasp all the external instruments of felicity, all the objects of general desire, in the greatest quantity possible: all at the expence of and by the sacrifice of the felicity of the other members of the community.

[1] The marginal summaries are more detailed than the final six paragraphs of text in this section, and pursue a divergent line of argument: 'Specific ends consisting in the encrease of felicity so far as depends on its internal instrument: viz. inward Virtue: or say with relation to felicity, internal aptitude. This virtue is 1. Moral—viz. Effective benevolence. 2. Intellectual: viz. Self-regarding prudence. Within these two all others are includible.

'I. Effective benevolence. This too his particular and sinister interest, as above, requires to be excluded in so far as incompatible with it: and the opposite vices or modes of inaptitude (with reference to greatest happiness) maximized.

'For the arrangements made to this effect, see below *Sketch of English Law considered in relation to the proper ends of Government*.

'II. Intellectual virtue: including sound judgment and useful knowledge: sound judgment i.e. 1. self-regarding prudence: 2. extra-regarding ditto.

'This too, in its above branches, his particular and sinister interest, as above, requires to be excluded, in so far as incompatible with it: and the opposite vices (here say *infirmities*) or modes of inaptitude etc. maximized. For exemplifications see *Sketch etc* as above.

'Conclusion. Such the predominance of the sinister branch of Monarch's interest, that the right and proper branch can never suffice to prevent or considerably retard the consummation of the sinister sacrifice.'

All around him being below him, dependent all of them on his pleasure for whatsoever portion of felicity they are suffered to enjoy, he find[s] in none of them any desire to oppose his will in any of the above particulars, in all of them the disposition and the endeavour to give accomplishment to it. He finds them joining one and all in the assurance that his greatest happiness is the only right and proper end of government: that if the happiness of any other individual is a fit object of regard to him or any one else, it is only in so far as the happiness of the individual servant may chance to be an object of regard and sympathy to the universal master.

In the eyes of this one Member of the community, all the others will be objects of regard on a footing similar to that [which] working cattle are in the eyes of the proprietor. On the part of an ill-tempered Monarch the treatment experienced by them will be that sort of treatment which is experienced by cattle at the hands of an ill-tempered Master. The best that can happen to them in the hands of the best-tempered Monarch is to be treated upon as good a footing as cattle are treated upon by a good tempered Master.

But in the hands of the best-tempered Monarch they never will in any instance be treated upon as good a footing as in the hands of a good-tempered [Master] it is common for his cattle, say his horses for example, to be treated. His horses will be continually in his presence: in the event of their being ill-treated by the negligence or malice of a servant, the ill-treatment they have suffered will manifest itself by visible signs: by the appearance of their suffering, the sympathy of the Master will be called into action. Knowing that the quantity of service he can obtain from them without prejudice to their appearance is limited—and that so sure as he endeavours to obtain any more their appearance and their value in his eyes will be deteriorated—he will never work them to excess. No determined and permanent resistance to his will being ever opposed by them and the inferiority of their minds to his being manifest, they will on no occasion be the objects of his ill-will or of his anger: among trained horses there is no such thing as a determinately and constantly rebellious horse.

On not near so good a footing are subjects in the eyes and hands of the best-tempered Monarch. Of the whole number of them, no more than a very small part at the utmost are ever under his eye: those who are worst-treated, those whose sufferings are greatest from the treatment they receive under his government, are never, especially while enduring that treatment, under his eye. Of this whole number there will always be a large portion by which his ill-will, his anger, will continually be called forth. By every obstruction afforded by any one of them to the fulfilment of his will, his anger will be called forth, and such obstructions howsoever kept under by fear and hope must notwithstanding be universal and continual.

Whatsoever quantity of the external instruments of felicity he happens at any time to have in his hands or at his immediate command, he is never satisfied with it. He never can be satisfied with it so long as he sees around him any other of those instruments that are not equally at his command. In his desires are included those of all the persons attached to his immediate service: and of those desires there are not any that are or ever can be compleatly satisfied.

Seeing that his gain in happiness never can have place but by means of loss to them, and that of every such gain, loss to them to a prodigiously greater amount is a never-failing accompaniment, what he can not entirely avoid the perception of is—that of the suffering thus produced by him, ill-will to an amount more or less considerable in the instance of every such sufferer is liable to be the consequence. Among them in a large though never exactly determinate proportion he beholds so many enemies: by the contemplation of enmity on their part, enmity on his part is produced. For the gratification of this enmity, as well as for keeping down resistance, and securing against non-payment the continually encreasing quantity of the instruments of felicity exacted by him at their expence, the afflictiveness of the penal laws is continually screwed up to the highest amount that is thought to be consistent with their efficiency. Thus it is that in the very best-tempered Monarch by far, the greatest number of the rest of the community have an enemy, and that enemy an essentially implacable one. If under such a Monarch such is their condition, what must it be under an ordinary one?

As in their own Monarch all subjects have an enemy, so have they in every other. Betwixt every Monarch and every other there exists a powerful cause of sympathy: in no instance ever could or ever can that cause have failed to be more or less productive of effect. In the instance of all of them, on one and the same set of principles is grounded that obedience by which their power is constituted, and in proportion to which it has place: disposition the effect of habit: habit the effect of force, fear, corruption, delusion, sinister interest, interest-begotten and authority-begotten prejudice. By every other throne he sees shaking, if the shock be from within, he feels the shock communicated to his own. By one another they are stiled brothers; and on that one occasion they are sincere. They have a common interest: and that interest is paramount to every other interest.

While to one another all Monarchs are objects of sympathy: to all Monarchs all subjects are objects of antipathy, of a sort of compound sentiment, made up of fear and hatred and contempt. On the part of all Monarchs there exists something like that which women and children are apt to feel for a toad. In the breasts of all Monarchs there accordingly exists at all times a natural alliance, defensive and offensive, against all subjects.

As between injurer and injured, the man on whose part antipathy toward the other is most apt to cease is he by whom the injury has been sustained: the one on whose part it ceases with greatest difficulty, if it ever ceases at all, is he by whom the injury has been inflicted.

Monarchs, it may be said, are apt to go to war with each other: and when with any two Monarchs this happens to [be the] case, the subjects of each should in that Monarch who is the enemy of their Monarch, that is of their natural enemy, have a friend. But in practice this is not the case. The war one Monarch carries on with another Monarch is a war of rivalry but it is not a war of enmity: every Monarch is to every other Monarch an object of respect: and where there is respect on both sides, no rooted, no decided, enmity can be said to have place on either side. Between Monarch and Monarch war is upon the largest scale that which between professed pugilist and professed pugilist it is upon the smallest scale. Many a Monarch has given up to a brother Monarch, and freely too, domains which he might have kept if he had pleased. No Monarch ever gave up freely to his own subjects an atom of power which in his eyes could be retained with safety. War is a game: a game of backgammon. Between two players at the game of war there is no more enmity than between two players at backgammon. [In][1] the breasts of the players at war there is no more feeling for the men of flesh and blood, than during the game at backgammon on the part of the men of wood there is for one another or themselves.

Not merely in the exercise of his political power—not merely in the public part of his life, but in the private part of his life, the natural tendency not to say the constant effect of his situation is to place [him][2] not at the top but at the bottom of the scale of moral worth, and this whether the influence of the self-regarding principle or that of the purely social principle—namely sympathy—be considered. By the purely self-regarding principle, the more urgent the need a man feels himself to have of the kindness and free good-will of others, the more strenuous and steady will be his exertion for the obtaining it: the less the need, the less strenuous. The kindness and free good-will and thence as occasion calls the good offices, the services, of others are,

[1] MS 'On'.
[2] MS 'it'.

where power of remuneration is wanting, no otherwise to be obtained than by demonstration of the like kindness, in effect and in endeavour, [on] a man's own part as towards them: the stronger a man's need of the effective benevolence of others, the stronger the inducement he has for the manifesting effective benevolence as towards them: an inducement which, in this way, self-regarding prudence suffices to afford: the less the need, the less strong the inducement. But the Monarch is of all men the man who by a vast amount has least need of kindness and free good-will and free good offices and free services at the hands of others—of the fruits of effective benevolence unmixt with those of self-regarding prudence. For whatsoever good things it be that in other situations men are indebted for to effective benevolence, it is in his power to command, in part by his punitive power, in other part by remunerative.

So the more extensively a man feels himself exposed to ill treatment at the hands of others, the stronger is the inducement he has to bestow good treatment upon them, for the purpose of averting from him the effects of such their ill-will: the less extensive the exposure, the less the inducement. But the Monarch is of all men the one who stands the least extensively exposed to ill-treatment at the hands of others: he is in a more especial degree guarded against it by the punitive branch of his power, and again by the remunerative, the immensity of the assistance and support which, in the way of purchase, and without need of kindness on their part, it puts him in a condition to command on every occasion at the hands of others.

Of this state of things, of this circumstance belonging to his condition, the result has been already stated. To place not, according to the vulgar mode of designation, at the summit, but at the lowest point in the scale of moral worth, him whose place in the scale of power is at the summit.

If the current mode of estimation is in so strange a degree erroneous, where shall the causes of the error be looked for? The reason is given in two words—*corruption* and *delusion*.[1]

Thus it is that to every practical purpose, in the situation of Monarch, inaptitude in that branch which stands opposed to appropriate moral aptitude should in all places and all times be regarded as consummate. Be the man who he may, that thing whatever it be by the contemplation of which no uneasiness is produced in his mind, that thing, be it what it may, it is not possible he should have any

[1] In the text, Bentham noted at this point, 'For the application of them see | |', but failed to provide any reference. For a discussion of corruption and delusion see 'Constitutional Code Rationale', Ch. 3, §§5–6, pp. 252–67 below.

desire to remove. Be the sufferers among his subjects ever so numerous—be the sufferings of each ever so intense, ever so long protracted, seen or unseen, no uneasiness capable of procuring a relaxation of those same sufferings can ever find entrance into a breast so situated. Why? because experience being altogether wanting, no conception of those same sufferings can ever have had place in any such high-seated breast. In a word—to sympathy of *affection*, correspondent sympathy of *conception* is indispensable.

§6. *Anti-social affections towards the people the result of Monarch's sinister interest*[1]

To no Monarch can the subject many have ever failed, or ever cease, to be objects of contempt and hatred: contempt, on the score of their deficiency in respect of those instruments of enjoyment which he has been suffered by them to heap up upon himself at their expence, and on the score of the intellectual weakness manifested by their patience under a course of unceasing injury: a patience produced by the conjunct power of force, intimidation, corruption and delusion exercised by him on their minds.

In so far as by the consum[m]ateness of their patience his contempt of them is rendered proportionably consummate, no such affection as that of hatred takes place: there is no cause for it. But, no sooner is the patience seen to give way to impatience than the contempt begins to give way, and hatred to take its place: and the less intense the contempt is, the more intense is the hatred. To a certain degree hatred can never fail to have place: for, his desires being constantly and necessarily insatiable and encreasing, no gratification which their patience and obsequiousness are ever disposed to afford, or are so much as capable of affording, can ever keep pace with him. But when, the united powers of force, intimidation, corruption and delusion beginning to fail, depredation and oppression have on their part produced discontent, and in the train of discontent, disaffection, [and] disobedience, resistance and insurrection have in his imagination become visible, then it is that, in proportion to the fear excited by the prospect, contempt diminishes and hatred swells.

In proportion as, by the apprehension of resistance as above, fear is produced in the Monarch's breast, a diminution more or less

[1] The text for this section originally formed one long note to a passage in *Codification Proposal*, but Bentham eventually decided to exclude it from that work (see his remark of 21 November 1821 on the corresponding marginal summary sheet at UC xxxviii. 109). A preliminary draft of some of this material is at UC cxiii. 78v.

considerable in the quantum of the sacrifice which he has been in use to make of their happiness to his own—a degree of relief from the burthen imposed by depredation and oppression—is a consequence not altogether incapable of taking place. Of such fear, true it is that a proportionable degree of hatred can not fail to be the result: and of hatred, if exclusively listened to, the result would be—not the lessening but the encrease of the sinister sacrifice:—not alleviation but aggravation of the burthen. Here then in the Monarch's breast will be a conflict: a conflict between the two affections—the self-regarding and the antisocial. In proportion as the self-regarding prevails, alleviation of the burthen will be the effect, which whether produced or no will at least have been aimed at: in proportion as the antisocial prevails, aggravation will be the certain consequence. Most commonly it is the antisocial that prevails: and thus it is that tyranny grows unendurable and revolution ensues. It may seem almost a paradox to speak of the antisocial affection as capable of prevailing over the self-regarding affection: to say that in any instance it does so, is as much as to say that in that instance a Monarch hates his subjects more than he loves himself. But to put a restraint upon the antisocial affection requires self-restraint:—it requires self-command and the more used a man is to command others the less used he is to command himself. When he *visits* (as the phrase is) the objects of his hatred it is still to his love of himself that he administers its gratification, though in a different shape.

So in the case of the limited Monarchy. In the breasts of the sub-ruling few, as towards the subject many, are produced the same antisocial affections—contempt and hatred—as in the breast of the Monarch, and by the same causes: hatred towards the Monarch having, however, incidentally place in their breasts, and, by the apprehension of it, operating in encrease of that fear on his part to which the subject many are indebted for whatever alleviation their burthen ever experiences: hatred of the Monarch, in proportion as the burthen intended principally for the subject many presses upon them, the sub-ruling few, or as the share allotted to each man out of the plunderage fails of coming up to his expectations.[1]

Remains, as the only form of government under which the subject many are not, in the breasts of the ruling few, objects of dissocial affection in any shape—Representative Democracy: in particular, *that* which, for these forty years, has stood exhibited in the Anglo-American United States: original number, thirteen: now, August

[1] The MS from which the remainder of this section is taken (UC xxiv. 449v) is a copy made by John Colls from Bentham's original draft at UC cxiii. 32v (23 August 1821), but which bears deletions, emendations and additions in Bentham's hand.

1821, encreased to twenty-three.[1] Here instead of contempt and hatred on one side (not to speak of the other) may be seen by every eye that can endure the sight, respect and love on both sides. Of this felicity, the cause is—that, while the whole of the *operative* power of the government is in the hands of a comparatively small number, the whole of the *constitutive* power, with reference to that same operative power, is in the hands of the many: those by whom the several branches of the operative power are exercised being, with or without [intermediate][2] agency, not only appointed, but with certainty and promptitude removable, by those by whom the abovementioned constitutive power is exercised: for it is of such power of appointment and removal that that same constitutive power is composed.

Thus it is that as, in an absolute Monarchy, on the part of the rulers, that *inaptitude* which is the *opposite* of appropriate moral aptitude is consummate, so, in a representative democracy, framed on the principle of virtually universal suffrage, appropriate moral *aptitude* itself is consummate. Under a limited Monarchy, according to the extent of the limitations, and the situation of the hands by which they are applied, the degree of moral inaptitude on the part of the sub-rulers may admitt of some depression: namely in consequence of any influence which the subject many may chance to have in the choice and on the conduct of those same sub-rulers: but, at the very best, in so far as in their eyes competition has place, the happiness of the subject many will still with certainty and constancy be sacrificed to the happiness of those same sub-rulers.

§7. *So, inaptitude opposite to intellectual aptitude*[3]

The branch of inaptitude opposed to appropriate intellectual aptitude is also in this case at [its][4] *maximum*. In respect of moral aptitude the condition of the Monarch as such being that which has been described, the consequence is—that towards the greatest happiness of the greatest number, all that in the situation in question could be done by intellectual aptitude if raised to its maximum would be the preserving that same greatest number from such infelicity as should in

[1] Maine was the twenty-third state to be admitted to the Union on 15 March 1820. By the time this passage was written, however, Missouri had become the twenty-fourth state, having been admitted to the Union on 10 August 1821.

[2] MS 'immediate' is a mistranscription made by Colls which Bentham failed to correct.

[3] i.e. by locating supreme operative power in the monarch's hands, the inaptitude opposite to intellectual aptitude would be maximized.

[4] MS 'his'.

the eyes of the Monarch not be contributory to his own felicity. But by the care taken of his own felicity at the expence of theirs, infelicity on their part may be raised to a height to which no limit can be assignable.[a]

But in comparison of other men who have had the advantages of what is called a liberal education, intellectual aptitude is in the situation of Monarch, by unchangeable causes, placed at the lowest pitch.

Of the two branches of intellectual aptitude, appropriate knowledge is that in respect of which the deficiency is less considerable and less uniformly exemplified. In the situation of Monarch, as in every other situation, man is necessarily for a length of time more or less considerable, by the infirmity attached to immaturity of age, placed in a state of subjection. During his continuance in that state not only knowledge at large, but knowledge in some sort and degree appropriate, is injected into the infirm and unresisting mind. Knowledge? but of what sort?

The answer is—no matter of what sort. This answer is the only proper one. In respect of moral aptitude, the condition and situation of the royal pupil being what it is, any vacuity in his mind, even supposing it ever so perfect, can scarcely be matter of regret: the knowledge, supposing him to have any, the sound judgment, supposing him to have any—could not in that situation be applied to any other purpose than the giving extent and promptitude to the sinister sacrifice.

It being thus certain that into a receptacle so situated no sort of matter contributory to the greatest happiness of the greatest number could keep its place even if injected, which is what it never would be, it may accordingly be stated as a matter not worth thinking about, with what rubbish the receptacle, which in an opposite state of thing[s] might be stocked with matter contributory to the greatest happiness of the greatest number, may happen to be filled. As [in] no considerable degree could good be produced by any such injection, so neither could any evil; good could not in any considerable degree be lodged, so on the other hand neither could evil. Take for example

[a] Take for example the case of Frederic the Great, King of Prussia. See the state of the people under his government as depicted by Sir Charles Hanbury Williams, Diplomatic Resident of England at his Court, in the Appendix to The Earl of Orford's Memoirs, London, 1822.[1]

[1] Extracts from the correspondence of Sir Charles Hanbury Williams (1708–59), while Envoy-extraordinary at Berlin (1750–1), describing the court of Frederick II (1712–86), King of Prussia from 1740, were printed in Horace Walpole (1717–97), fourth Earl of Orford, *Memoires of the last ten years of the Reign of George the Second*, 2 vols., London, 1822, i. 517–24.

indication given concerning the best-adapted means for promoting the only interest which can be the object of regard—means for giving the maximum of extent and promptitude to the sinister sacrifice. A scheme of instruction, by which all such pernicious knowledge would be excluded, would it not be preferable, it may be asked, to a scheme in which it were comprized? The answer is—No. For in this way the supply afforded by others, the supply afforded by the servant, whoever he happens to be, whose destiny it is to hold the seals of office when the royal pupil holds the sceptre, this supply will at all times be perfect, this cup will at all times be full, and by no quantity which has his breast for the seat of it, can any addition ever be made.

To the situation of Monarch it belongs to find *will*: to the situation of Minister it belongs to find knowledge, to find judgement, and if need be to find invention, such as on each occasion shall be necessary and sufficient to the giving accomplishment to that will. But to do so requires a degree of exertion, of mental labour, much beyond the greatest quantity which in the situation of Monarch it is consistent with human nature to bestow: this being admitted, it follows that from no stock of appropriate knowledge which in the situation of Monarch the mind of man is capable of finding room for can the mass which will be applied to the business of government receive encrease.

One thing of which the non-injection is matter of certainty is soon stated: this is the axiom by which the greatest happiness of the greatest number is stated as the only justifiable end of government. That no such position could by any preceptor be placed before the royal pupil in the character of a true one is sufficiently evident, for in this position, among others the content of a Constitutional Code, is included this: namely, that no such office as that which he is destined to fill ought to have place in any community, and that the only good act capable of being done by any one who is in it is to suppress it, to strike it out of the Official establishment, or to abolish the system of government of which it forms a part, to substitute a representative democracy to the whole of the system of government of which it forms a part. No such advice will the preceptor ever give. Various are the inducements, it need scarce be observed, any one of which would abundantly suffice to produce this negative effect: to the community the advice would be unavailing, for in no case would the pupil follow it: to the pupil, it would be unpleasant: to the prospects of the preceptor, ruinous.

The only right and proper end of your Government is your own greatest happiness—take this commodious axiom substituted to the other incommodious one, the two latter inconveniences are avoided, while to the interests of the community at large no damage is done, forasmuch as by any advice to the opposite effect, so many words and minutes employed in giving expression to it would be thrown away.

So necessarily and so intensely afflictive is the treatment which, through system and cool reflection, from the most successful results of sound judgment, subjects are almost sure to receive at the hands of the most intelligent Monarch, that any ulterior suffering they may stand exposed to from mental derangement in the same quarter may be thought scarce worth adding to the account. But by the extraordinary proportion of the individuals known to have laboured under malady in this shape, aid may be afforded towards a right conception of the character of the class, and the effect produced on the mind by power in excess.[a]

[a] In England—number of individuals in present life Anno 1821: 1.,...,...
In ditto number known to labour under mental derangement Anno | |: | |,...
Proportion of sane to insane: | |
In Europe, total number of Monarchical families: | |
Among whom those containing within these | | years individuals known to be labouring under mental derangement or under a degree of imbecillity such as to prevent them from taking any regular cognizance of the business of the government.[1]

I. Monarchical families known to have contained Monarchs known to be labouring under mental derangement:

1. England—George 3.
2. Naples.
3. Sardinia.
4. Prussia.
5. Russia—1. Peter 3. 2. Paul 1.
6. Spain—Philip 5. Charles 4.
7. Sweden—Gustavus.
8. Denmark—Christian.
9. Portugal—Mary.
10. Austria.
11. Saxony—Augustus King of Poland. See Walpole's Memoirs: Sir Charles Hanbury Williams, Diplomatic Letters.[2]

II. Monarchical Families not known to have contained Monarchs known to labour under mental derangement:

1. France.
2. Bavaria.
3. Netherlands.

[1] In the marginal summary, Bentham supplied figures for some of the blanks: 'To judge of the effect of political situation in this case on intellect, note among Monarchical families the proportion of insane to sane: say 11 to 3 as per Table. Sane to insane at large as 12 millions to not half.' According to the census of 1821, the population of England and Wales was 12 millions. If Bentham was suggesting that the number of insane in this total approached something close to half a million, his estimation seems extraordinarily high: according to returns compiled by *The Select Committee appointed to enquire into the State of the Criminal and Pauper Lunatics, in England and Wales, and of the Laws relating thereto*, 1807, there were 2,398 insane persons under custody, though the report did warn that these figures were probably deficient and understated the full total. Contemporary estimates suggested that the true total was about 8,000 (see Sir Andrew Halliday, *A General View of the Present State of Lunatics, and Lunatic Asylums, in Great Britain and Ireland, and in some other kingdoms*, London, 1828, pp. 90–1).

[2] Of the monarchs identified by Bentham, the following were regarded as having been insane: George III (1738–1820), King of Great Britain and Ireland from 1760; Peter III (1728–62), Emperor of Russia from 1762; Paul I (1754–1801), Emperor of Russia from 1796; Philip V

In this extraordinary case, if the mischief to which the community is exposed is not so great as in the ordinary one, the absurdity of submitting to it is more flagrant, and the depravity, moral and intellectual taken together, manifested on the part of a nation which submitts to it, at the same time but too incontestably demonstrated. In every Monarchical state, the probability always great—great in the proportion of several to one—that at any given period the fate of all its members will be in the hands of a madman!

Look now to the Electors of a President of the Anglo-American United States. Of their placing a Madman in the situation of Chief functionary, from this moment to the end of time, by what numbers shall the degree of probability be represented?

The curious circumstance is—that down to the moment when the condition of the sufferer is too manifest to be any longer concealed from the public eye, those same features of superhuman excellence, in all its shapes in general, and in that of consummate wisdom in particular, will still be his, by the unanimous testimony of all who hope for any good thing or fear for any evil thing at his hands: by the unanimous voice of these hypocrites, ecchoed by the unanimous chorus of these dupes. In him the priests will continue to behold the most religious, the lawyers the most just, the Diplomatists the wisest, the Courtiers the most gracious, all these in chorus together with the hireling writers, in one word, the best of Monarchs present, past or future.

Every Monarch is a Slave-holder upon the largest scale, and in that relation, each correlative is corrupted by the relation he bears to the other. Under a Monarchy, the population is composed of the insulters and the insulted; of the corrupters and the corrupted; of the deluders and the deluded: of bullies and cowards, of hypocrites and dupes.

(1683–1746), King of Spain from 1700 until his abdication in 1724, and again from 1724; Charles IV (1748–1819), King of Spain from 1788 until his abdication in 1808; Gustavus IV (1778–1837), King of Sweden from 1792 until his abdication in 1809; Christian VII (1749–1808), King of Denmark and Norway from 1766; and Maria I (1734–1816), Queen of Portugal from 1777. The other instances are not so straightforward. In the case of Naples, Bentham perhaps had in mind Ferdinand IV (1751–1825), King of Naples, and as Ferdinand III, King of Sicily, from 1759, and as Ferdinand I, King of the Two Sicilies from 1816, who, though not insane or imbecillic, was ill-educated and considered loutish and indolent. Though no Habsburg ruler of the eighteenth or early nineteenth centuries was regarded as either insane or imbecillic, the heir apparent to the Austrian throne, later Ferdinand I (1793–1875), Emperor of Austria from 1835 until his abdication in 1848, was generally known to be mad. In the case of Saxony, according to Williams, who was Envoy to Dresden 1747–50, 1751–3 and 1754–5, it was not Frederick Augustus II (1696–1763), Elector of Saxony from 1733, and as Augustus III, King of Poland from 1733, who was weak-minded, but the Electoral Prince, Frederick Christian (1722–63), Elector of Saxony from 1763 (see Walpole, *Memoires of the last ten years of the Reign of George the Second*, ii. 467–8). No Sardinian monarch of the eighteenth or early nineteenth centuries, nor any Prussian king up to this time, was regarded as either insane or imbecillic.

When once the human race is rid of the two congenial plagues, Monarchy and Slave-holding—with how contemptuous a sympathy will not the present generation be regarded by all succeeding ones?

If where the Monarch is a madman, the people are not worse afflicted than they are seen to be, it is because in the name of the Madman it is not by the Madman himself that the determinations are taken by which the operations of government are directed, but by a knot of Courtiers whom accident has thrown in his way in such sort as to have become chosen by him to be made the instruments of his will in the several departments; or rather, and what is more simple, some one of them who has had the good fortune to persuade him, to produce in his mind the notion, that by the choice of that one instrument his desires are likely to receive a more extensive gratification than by the choice of any other individual: among those several desires, the desire of ease acting always with predominant influence: acting as it were as President of the Council of Desires—which individual is then Prime Minister exercising the powers of the Monarch, and easing him of the whole detail of the cares of government. Certain subject matters there are on which the titular Monarch and the operative Sub-Monarch are at all times and in all places agreed of course: the accumulating in the hands of the Monarch of the external instruments of felicity in as large a mass as possible, in particular power, money and means of vengeance: at whose ever expence on each occasion the accession is to be made: whether at the expence of his own subjects, or the members of a foreign State, or of both together, as so far as war is the occasion can not but be the case. Master and Servant in this behold the common end; and to the Servant it belongs to provide the means, to provide the labour.

Thus far they are sure to agree.[1] Meantime the occasions for disagreement can never altogether be wanting. With the Monarch the first object is of course to provide for his personal gratification. But for this no funds which it is in the power of the Minister to provide can ever be sufficient. Buildings suffice of themselves to create an appetite the satiation of which is impossible. To add factitious to natural unpleasantness in one single spot during a course of years cost France under Lewis the 14th. a sum—recollection is not able to state in what degree below or above the whole expence of government during that time.[2]

[1] There is no text corresponding to the following marginal summary, which belongs here: 'As to army, disagreement none. To Monarch a toy, to him and Monarch it is the most efficient of all instruments of the sinister sacrifice.'

[2] An allusion to the palace and associated works at Versailles built between 1669 and 1710 by Louis XIV (1638–1715), King of France from 1643.

SECTION 7

The whole stock of the external instruments of felicity, the whole of the allotment attached to the Official Establishment, is regarded by the Minister as being at his disposal. But the Monarch has in both sexes his associates in, and living instruments of, pleasure in all its forms—in a word his favorites. These favorites are not themselves men of business or women of business. But each such favorite is himself or herself, as the case may be, the centre of a circle of dependents among whom men of business and men desiring to be men of business are abundant. A vacancy takes place and now comes the contest: the contest between the Monarch's dependent and the Minister's dependent.

Meantime the process of depredation and oppression goes on in its course: the torment of the people goes on encreasing: encreasing and in such sort that it communes itself even to the Royal or Imperial breast.

How so? is it that in that breast there is or ever did exist or ever can exist any real sympathy for the misery of the people? Not until it has first existed in the breast of his bronze similitude. But, be the Palace where it may, the discontented swarm in it. Next to none can have all they wish for: and every one who can not have all he wishes for is more or less discontented. So many discontented persons, so many eventual talebearers and accusers of the Minister, watching every occasion that affords a promise of being a favorable one. A class of misdeeds the idea of which is at all times, in every state of things, of a nature to excite in the royal breast a sentiment of displeasure is every considerable depredation in the benefit of which he has not, either in his own person or in that of a favorite, any share. A misdeed which in ordinary times, in the ordinary state of things, is not of a nature to produce any such displeasure, is a misdeed productive of human suffering which, whatsoever be the amount, does not present itself as pregnant with any disturbance to his ease, which threatens not to be productive of any consequence of an unpleasant nature to his royal self: of any thing worse than suffering, how great soever may be the amount of it, on the part of the people. But by those by whom injury—injury in all its forms—day by day [is] done to millions, and to many of them in its worst forms, no certainty can ever be obtained but that among the millions whom oppression has wounded there may be some one into whose hand despair may have put the dagger of assassination: but that while so many thousands are throwing away their lives in the endeavour to destroy by thousands strangers none of whom have done them any injury, some one may stand up and turn the instrument of death against an individual against whom there is no other means of defence, whose whole life from beginning to end is an undiscontinued act of injury to the millions whose lot has cast them under his feet. Fear of personal safety is therefore of necessity among the attendants at every throne. When by the lips of an aspiring talebearer hints are given of the suffering endured by the oppressed people, Fear presents of course to Imagination the connection which so inconveniently has place between the production of human misery and the endurance of it.

Meantime, whether sanity or insanity be the state of the Monarch—whether in the acts to which the name of the Monarch is affixed, the judgment and the individually applied will have any or no part, be the whole tenor of the government more or less predatory, more or less oppressive—the suffering of the people more or less evident—the conduct and frame of mind of the Monarch present, in all statements which have any pretension to the character of authenticity, the same aspect of unrivalled and unvaried excellence. For the bodies of two Monarchs, two portraits, both indeed beautiful, but beautiful in two different forms, are found necessary: but for the minds of the two, one and the same portrait always serves, is always found sufficient.

In England, of the so many hundreds of laws passed every year, not one is passed in and by which the King does not join with the sham representatives of the people and the too real representatives of the people, in declaring himself to be Most Excellent.[1] By the universal declaration of all who join in the devotion in a Church of England Church—and by an unrepealed Law of Elizabeth all are punishable who omitt to join in it—every English King is most gracious, every King is most religious.[2] Gracious alike he who never smiles and he who sometimes smiles: religious alike the bigot and the unbeliever: the infidel with a mask, and the infidel without a mask. Sunday after Sunday, Charles the second while amusing the Lords in waiting with the pleasantry of which religion was the standing object, Charles the second who was really the most gracious of English Kings, heard

[1] An allusion to the enacting formula inserted in Acts of Parliament between the preamble and the provisions: 'Be it enacted by the King's most Excellent Majesty, by and with the Advice and Consent of the Lords Spiritual and Temporal, and Commons, in this present Parliament assembled, and by the Authority of the same, That. . . .'

[2] The *Book of Common Prayer* included 'A Prayer for the High Court of Parliament, to be read during their session' amongst the prayers and thanksgivings 'To be used before the two final Prayers of the Litany, or of Morning and Evening Prayer'. This contained the words: 'Most gracious God, we humbly beseech thee, as for this Kingdom in general, so especially for the High Court of Parliament, under our most religious and gracious King at this time assembled. . . .' The Act of Uniformity of 1559 (1 Eliz. I, c.2) authorized, with a few modifications, the form of worship contained in the *Book of Common Prayer* of 1552, and prohibited all others under penalty. The prayer in question, however, was first used in the Fast-day Service of 1625, and then included in the *Book of Common Prayer* of 1662, which was enforced by the Act of Uniformity of 1662 (14 Car. II, c.4).

himself proclaimed by consecrated lips in the same breath the most religious.[1]

Of all these lies the creature[2] has the benefit, whether in the exercise of his power he be or be not occasionally disturbed by his creator: and thus it is that, for a time more or less considerable, whether the creator be sane or insane, so long as the insanity remains unconspicuous, the powers of government may continue in exercise without much perceptible difference worth thinking of.

§8. *How far in a Monarchy misrule has for its cause moral, how far intellectual, inaptitude*

The amount of misrule and its effects being given, a standing question, a question that on each occasion presents itself is—as to how much of it is owing to moral inaptitude, how much to intellectual: how much to sinister interest, how much to prejudice, whether interest-begotten or derived from other causes. The question however is a matter rather of curiosity than of use: of use to the purpose of affording guidance to practice. Take this or that anti-popular arrangement at pleasure: if not its creation, its preservation at any rate is the work of the sinister interest. Independently of the sinister interest, be the institution, [be][3] the arrangement, be the phantasm of the imagination ever so absurd, go back far enough, you may always find honest absurdity, honest intellectual weakness, sufficient for the creation of it. How can it be otherwise? since among the people at large notions fraught with absurdity are not without example, notions which being adverse to the interest of those by whom they are entertained can not have had for their cause sinister interest, at any rate can not have had correct conceptions of particular interest.

But so long as it is by the sinister interest that the causes of evil are supported and maintained, whether it was in the moral part or in the intellectual part of the mental frame that the evil had originally its rise matters nothing to any practical purpose. Many are the instances in which that which at first sight will present itself as the result of intellectual weakness will on scrutiny be seen to have been the genuine fruit of sinister interest: and the more closely the mechanism

[1] Charles II (1630–85), King of England, Scotland and Ireland from 1660. The source of the anecdote has not been traced. Bentham, however, was familiar with *Bishop Burnet's History of His Own Time*, 2 vols., London, 1724–34, in which Burnet was critical of Charles II's behaviour at religious ceremonies (see i. 93).

[2] i.e. the minister.

[3] MS 'let'.

of misrule is scrutinized into, the more extensively will this genealogy be seen to have had place.[1]

One universally-applying maxim, the genuine fruit of the sinister interest, serves as a means of preservation to absurdity in every imaginable shape. 'Though the absurd institution or arrangement is not productive of any immediate advantage to yourself,' says the modern Machiavel to his patron, 'preserve it notwithstanding: for though the existence of it does not serve, the abolition of it would disserve, your own particular interest: to justify the abolition it would be necessary to bring into action some position, conformable to reason and subordinate and subservient, bearing a reference more or less obvious, to the all-comprehensive and universally applying principle—the greatest happiness principle. But by homage paid to that principle, you put arms into the hands of the adversary: when the absurd arrangement from which you derive no advantage is disposed of, presently after enters the adversary and proposes the abolition of an absurd institution and arrangement from which you do derive advantage—thereupon for a ground for the proposition, out comes this position which, you yourself having made use of, and paid homage to, you can not oppose, or elude the force of, without rendering your insincerity and the corruptness of your disposition manifest, without betraying and laying open to view the corruption with which your whole frame of mind is impregnated.'

Be this then the rule acted upon in all cases—whatsoever institution or arrangement is adverse to the universal interest is the result of the rulers' particular and thence sinister interest. In few instances indeed, if in any, will the position be wrong in theory—and where it is wrong the error will not be productive of any evil consequence in practice. Not so, if the cause being sinister interest, the effect is ascribed to a mere error of the understanding, to a derangement in the intellectual part of the machinery. In this case, it is to the curing men of their error that all your exertions will be directed: to the changing into converts the opponents you have to deal with. Full of this conception, you will keep labouring and labouring till you are tired: while you are labouring, the adversary is laughing at you in his sleeve.

Another bad consequence. So much for your adversary—the corruptionist. Now for the bystanders, in the character of members of the Public Opinion Tribunal.[2] Seeing that even in your opinion, all its

[1] In the margin, Bentham noted, '☛ Give examples', but none appear to have been written. In the marginal summary, he also commented at this point: 'Generally interest has been the cause in the minds of the few governors: weakness in ditto of the subject multitude.'

[2] In the margin, Bentham noted: 'See further on Ch. | |, §| |.' For a discussion of the public opinion tribunal see 'Economy as applied to Office', Ch. 9, pp. 56–76 above, and 'Constitutional Code Rationale', Ch. 5, pp. 283–98 below.

hostility notwithstanding, the fault if any is in the understanding of your adversary, not in his will, in the intellectual part of your adversary's frame, not in the moral, they in their impartial situation can not think less favorably of him than you do in your hostilely partial situation: along with you, in their expectation of his [. . . ?], they will keep looking for the time when, in consequence of the rectification of his judgment, his conduct will be rectified, which time, the cause of the wrong not being in that place, will never come. All this while, had the real seat of the wrong been known to them, they might have acted accordingly. Seeing the adversary in his true colours, they might have joined with you in acting upon him in the only quarter in which from this time to the end of time he can be acted upon with effect: they might have acted on his fears.

Whatsoever talent and whatsoever industry there is in that situation being employed in keeping the sanction covered by a veil as impenetrable as possible, no wonder if on many an occasion it should succeed in hiding itself from most eyes.

Behold now an example of the mischief to the people from the imputing to error the result of sinister interest. True cause of the excess in Military Establishments, King's sinister interest; erroneously supposed cause, erroneous supposition of the necessariness of the actual magnitude to the purpose of defence against foreign aggression.

In the several civilized communities, the Rulers why at such vast expence to subjects and thence to themselves do they persevere in straining till the cords of it are ready to burst their military force? their military force in both elements. When in this way they have done each of them his utmost, there will they be all of them with their respective masses of force bearing one to another a certain proportion: keeping thus the same proportion they might divide each of them his force by the same divisor, say two, say ten, say a hundred, and the quotients being in the same proportion, the security would on the part of each of them be the same. Some number of years ago, did this idea occur to me—I know not how many except that it must have been before my eyes had applied themselves with any closeness to the constitutional part of the field of law: my good fortune, I know not exactly in what way, saved me from the disappointment and loss of time which a proposition of so Utopian a cast would have had for its fruit.[1] Yes: were it merely as instruments for the defence of the community and the territory against foreign aggression that an army is kept up: but

[1] Bentham was referring to the scheme developed in MSS written in 1789 (see UC xxv. 26–58, 106–35) and first published in Bowring, ii. 546–60 as 'Plan for an Universal and Perpetual Peace'.

besides that it is kept up: 1. for the defence of the country against its inhabitants: 2. for the defence of the Monarch, his instruments and his favorites and his dependents against resistance to legalized depredation, oppression and vengeance: 3. it is kept up as a toy for the Great Baby to play with: 4. it is kept up by each [Monarch] as an instrument for the gratification of vanity, vying with the vanity of every other: and how ill any of these purposes would be served by retrenchment is sufficiently obvious.

While the sinister interest continues on its present footing, to propose any thing that would be beneficial to the community upon a sufficiently extensive scale to be worth thinking of is not simply useless, it is positively pernicious. It is a certificate that on the part of those on whom acceptance depends, a disposition to act in conformity to the universal interest has place: a certificate which neither is, nor by possibility can be, true. The persons to whom it is addressed are those on whose exertions depends the only state of things in which any thing good that depends on government can ever be brought into effect. In this same certificate therefore is contained the implied assurance that such exertions are not needed. Of the existence [of] this persuasion on the part of the projector, a proof is thus given much more conclusive and impressive than could be given by any positive and direct assurance expressed in words: in this case the existence of the persuasion is indubitable: for it is upon the ground of it that the man himself has acted.

In England, this hopelessness of every thing good has never been a secret to the Whigs. Accordingly put to them any thing good, their advice is of course—'Under the present Administration, your plan is hopeless: it is a good one, and by them no good proposal will ever be adopted. By us all good proposals will be adopted: if you wish any thing good to be done, look to us.' What is true is that there is not any ground for hope from their antagonists: what is not true is—there is ground of hope from themselves. In them there would no more be either power or will to do good than in their more fortunate and prosperous adversaries.

§9. *Which inaptitude most adverse to universal interest?*

In the order of importance, moral aptitude stands before intellectual: each being understood in all degrees in any of which it is likely to have place. In so far as moral aptitude is deficient, by intellectual aptitude and active talent, both or either, in proportion to the degree in which [they are] present, appropriate aptitude taken in the aggregate will, instead of being encreased, be diminished. In proportion as appropriate moral aptitude is deficient, the disposition of the man and the tendency of his endeavours will be to make sacrifice of the universal interest—the greatest happiness of the greatest number—to his own particular and sinister interest: to that part of his own happiness which he purchases or thinks to purchase at the expence of his fellow Citizens.

Opposite to appropriate intellectual aptitude and appropriate active talent stand degrees of inaptitude, the operation of which would have for its consequence a greater defalcation from the mass of appropriate aptitude taken in the aggregate than could be made from the most compleat absence of appropriate moral aptitude. By the mere care of ministering to his own happiness, a man possessed of a certain degree of intellectual aptitude and active talent would be led to make better provision for the happiness of his fellow citizens than would or could be made by a man in whom intellectual aptitude or active talent were to a certain degree deficient, although he were at the same time endowed with the highest conceivable degree of appropriate moral aptitude.

Of men by whom, on a throne or elsewhere, great power has been exercised, no one perhaps was with relation to the work of legislation lower in the scale of appropriate moral aptitude than Napoleon Bonaparte.[1] Yet in virtue of the appropriate intellectual aptitude which with relation to that work he possessed, he has by means of that body of law of his called the *Cinq Codes*[2] rendered to France not only a prodigiously great service, but greater service by far than was ever rendered by any of those Monarchs whose disposition was least adverse to the happiness of their fellow citizens, a Lewis the 16th.[3] for example, or an Alexander the first.[4] Lewis in his simplicity never thought of giving them a tangible and an all-comprehensive rule of action: Alexander at one time tried at it, and, as will presently be seen, failed.[5] Napoleon had in his hand the plan of an all-comprehensive body of law, having for its end in view the greatest happiness of the

[1] Napoleon Bonaparte (1769–1821), First Consul of France 1799–1804, Emperor of the French 1804–14.

[2] These codes were *Code Civil* (1804), *Code de Procédure Civile* (1806), *Code de Commerce* (1807), *Code d'Instruction Criminelle* (1809) and *Code Pénal* (1810).

[3] Louis XVI (1754–93), King of France from 1774.

[4] Alexander I (1777–1825), Emperor of Russia from 1801.

[5] In 1801 Alexander I had established a Commission on Laws in order to codify the laws of Russia, but its work had not been brought to a conclusion. It was eventually replaced in 1825 by the Second Section of His Imperial Majesty's Chancery, established by Nicholas I (1796–1855), Emperor of Russia from 1825. A new code of Russian law eventually came into force in 1835. Bentham did not discuss this topic further in 'Supreme Operative'.

greatest number, with a rationale. Tallyrand had the merit of putting that plan into his hand. His appropriate intellectual aptitude made him applaud it: 'c'est un ouvrage de genie' were his words. His want of appropriate moral aptitude made him put it aside. It would have suited the purposes of those over whom he ruled: but it would not have suited his own purposes. The hands he looked for were such as would and could frame a body of law that should suit his individual purposes: and no difficulty of course could he find in meeting with such hands.[1]

Hence, instead of the clear and steady light he might have had, in the shape of an interwoven rationale, deduced all along from the principle of utility, from the principle of the greatest happiness of the greatest number, he had on each occasion in the shape of a detached dissertation an *ignis fatuus*, consisting of vague-generality gas, twinkling aloft in a region or regions of unmeasurable altitude.

Now a word as to interest-begotten prejudice.

Though among prejudices the most mischievous would not perhaps have had existence had it not been for the corresponding sinister interests, yet especially when considered [in] the character of a cause of inaptitude, a prejudice in this or that shape may perhaps be found more powerful in its action, and thence more pernicious, than the corresponding sinister interest. To the number of those who are capable of possessing a share in a sinister interest, there are determinate limits: limits applied by the very nature of the case: for suppose it shared in by the greatest number of the members of the community, the interest is by the supposition, by the very definition, not a sinister but a right and proper interest. But to the number of the persons capable of being under the dominion of a prejudice, whether interest-begotten or inbred, there are absolutely no limits.

It is by their own sinister interest that in England all Monarchs have of course been at all times led to sacrifice to that particular and thence sinister interest, the interest of all their fellow Citizens. It is by a conjunct sinister interest that their several subordinates in the several departments of government have by the possession or prospect of shares in the profit of the sacrifice been at all times prompted to give support and encrease to that same sinister sacrifice. It is by that same interest that they have been led to nourish in their own breasts the corresponding prejudice by which this sinister sacrifice never ceases

[1] The plan in question was Bentham's own *Traités de législation civile et pénale*, ed. Étienne Dumont, 3 vols., Paris, 1802 (see *Deontology together with A Table of the Springs of Action and The Article on Utilitarianism*, ed. A. Goldworth, Oxford, 1983 (*CW*), p. 48n). Bentham repeated the story in *Codification Proposal*, pp. 14–15 (Bowring, iv. 543–4) and again in conversation with Bowring (see Bowring, x. 565). Charles Maurice de Talleyrand-Périgord (1754–1838), French Minister for Foreign Affairs 1799–1807, had met Bentham in 1792, remained interested in his work and encouraged Dumont in the publication of *Traités*.

to be represented as a right and proper one. At the time of James II,[1] in all these minds by the sinister interest was begotten the desire and endeavour to sacrifice to the particular and sinister interest of the ruling one, for his own benefit and that of the few that were ruling under him, the interest of the many. By that same sinister interest was begotten in an unascertainable but probably not inconsiderable proportion of these same minds, the prejudice according to which this same sinister sacrifice was a right and proper sacrifice: and that accordingly it was, on the part of every individual, matter of duty to contribute by obedience and obsequiousness without reserve, to the utmost of his power, to that same sinister sacrifice: a duty the fulfilment of which had for its enforcement the three great Sanctions, the popular or moral, as well as the political, and still more unreservedly than the political, the religious.

In those days, the quantity of the matter of wealth continually at the disposal of the Monarch and of itself, without need of any endeavours on his part, acting, as in these hands it does in every country, in the character of matter of corruption, was in comparison of the quantity of that same matter in the same hands[2] so small, that the number of individuals governed by it would not have been sufficient for carrying the sinister sacrifice to the pitch to which it was then carried, would not have been sufficient without the aid of those whose conduct was engaged in that same direction by the correspondent interest-begotten prejudice, as above they not being partakers in the sinister interest. But as matters stand at present, so vast has been the addition made in the interval to the quantity of the matter of corruption as above, that even without the aid of the corresponding prejudice, the sinister interest would suffice for engaging in the sinister sacrifice a number sufficient for the consummation of it.

Not only by the extent of which it is susceptible—by the unlimitedness of the number of those who are capable of sharing in it—is interest-begotten prejudice preeminently pernicious in comparison of the correspondent sinister interest, but also by the firmness of the hold which it takes on the mind. Those who are engaged to [the] course in question by no other tie than that of sinister interest, may by sinister interest operating in an opposite direction be in a moment engaged in a course directly opposite: whereas when once the mind is engaged in the trammels of prejudice, although it may have had its origin in sinister interest, there is no saying with what pertinacity and for what length of time it may not persevere in that same course:

[1] James II (1633–1701), King of England, Scotland and Ireland from 1685 to 1688.

[2] i.e. in the hands of the present monarch, namely George IV (1762–1830), King of Great Britain and Ireland from 1820.

persevere, in spite of the opposite action of ever so strong a force of interest—of interest in which ever direction operating.

Frenchmen who being without prejudice, and at the same time preferring to his share in the universal interest each man the share he had in possession or expectancy in the particular and sinister interest of the ruling few, might in [their][1] attachment have vibrated any number of times between a Capet and a Bonaparte:[2] while the multitude of those who, having no chance or expectations of advancement in the event of the restoration of the antient regime, persevered in their attachment, remained of course, if there were any such, attached to the old regime [by interest-begotten prejudice],[3] and would still, at any time, expose themselves to a danger more or less considerable, for the purpose of restoring it.

In so far as his conduct is determined by prejudice alone, he is what in English is termed a man of *principle*: a man of principle, in contradistinction to a man whose conduct is determined by what in his eyes, says the correspondent phrase, is *his interest*: and a man of principle he may be—this appellation may when applied to him be a proper one, even in the case where the attachment in question had, even in the breast of this same man, no other origin than a sinister interest.

In coarse but concise and expressive and impressive language, dupes in any number may be made and kept so by a comparatively small number of knaves, and while by the current of sinister interest the knaves are driven and bandied about from side to side, the dupes may by their prejudice be kept steady all the while in a uniform and consistent, howsoever erroneous and pernicious, course: steadily engaged in giving their support to the sinister sacrifice.

Hence it is that in every country in which Government has for its actual end in view the sinister sacrifice, in every country in a word but that of the Anglo-American United States, no small anxiety is shewn to secure in the hands of the government to the exclusion of all other hands the function of instruction: the power of fastening the minds of men to the yoke. Hence that preeminently powerful and equally pernicious instrument of depravation, moral and intellectual, a

[1] MS 'his'.

[2] Capet was the name of the family which had held the throne of France since 987. The Bourbons, the ruling dynasty at the time Bentham was writing, were a younger branch of the family who had succeeded in 1589. Bentham was alluding to the struggle in France between the supporters of the ancient monarchy, and those of the republic and later the empire, during the Revolutionary and Napoleonic periods.

[3] The addition is suggested by the marginal summary: 'By sinister interest Frenchmen might have been induced to vibrate between Capet and Bonaparte, while by interest-begotten prejudice others were induced to remain steady to Capet, braving every danger.'

religious establishment: an instrument with which the few in the character of teachers are made knaves, that the many in the character of learners may be made fools and made to submitt.

§10. *By their relation to the Monarch, correspondent moral inaptitude is fixt in the breasts of all his subordinates, i.e. Ministers and favorites*

Seen above, the frame of mind given to man by that situation: seen him above in disposition—in preparation. Behold him now in action. In the field of society, of political life, action can not be without instruments. Behold now his instruments.

Instruments real and corporeal, three: the Soldier, Lawyer, Priest: instruments fictitious, incorporeal, nominal, four: force, fear,[a] corruption, delusion: with these incorporeal instruments, the one by the hands of his corporeal instruments works.

For the sake of an always questionable and at the utmost imponderable and comparatively inconsiderable addition to his own felicity, to give existence, unquestionable existence, to human suffering in all its shapes and in quantity immense and indefinite, this is the course of action which at every moment of his life the sinister interest inseparably attached to his situation urges him to: power being in adequate quantity always in his hands, this, such as has been mentioned, is the result.

Their felicity being by their situations dependent on his will, such as his interests are, such are theirs. By his interest he is rendered the enemy of all who are subject to his power: his interest being made theirs, people find these too added to the number of their enemies: in these the people feel so many subordinate enemies whose function consists in giving accomplishment to the inimical wishes of the arch-enemy.

Arch-forciant[b]—Arch-terrorist—Arch-Corrupter—Arch-Deluder[c]—this he is by the mere virtue of his situation, without need of action on his part, without need of so much as *volition* on his part, without any such interruption to his ease: they in their several situations Sub-forciant, Sub-terrorist, Sub-Corrupter, Sub-Deluder.

As to the corporeal instruments, each of them contributes in his own particular way to the common end, the fulfilment of the

[a] Synonyms: terror—intimidation.

[b] English lawyers have in their language a *deforciant*: a man by whose force some other man is put out of the possession of something that of right belongs to him.

[c] Synonyms: Forcer-General–Terrifier, Intimidator-General–Corrupter-General–Deluder-General.

constantly sinister will of the people's irresistible and implacable enemy. In one way or other, on one occasion or other, all these several incorporeal instruments of misrule operate in their hands: but by this or that corporeal, this or that incorporeal instrument is most handled, by this or that other corporeal, this or that other.

1. As to the Soldier. Manner in which in a Monarchy he contributes to the fulfilment of the sinister and irresistible will—to the performance of the sinister sacrifice.

Force and intimidation are the incorporeal instruments which, in the more direct and intentional way, the Soldier is occupied in the making application to the all-embracing and constantly pursued purpose. But by his pay and other e[mo]luments he is added to the Monarch's stock of the instruments of corruption: while by the place he occupies in the vast Puppet-shew apparatus of which he is one of the puppets, and the glitter with which he is invironed, he contributes at the same time to the amusement of his owner, the great baby, and to the delusion of the subject many, fascinating and setting to work their imagination, perverting their judgment, and from the power and splendor which they see, causing them to infer the existence of the excellence, moral and intellectual, which they imagine.

2. Next as to the Lawyers. External are the enemies against whom the force and intimidation by which the Soldier operates are principally and most avowedly prepared: but incidentally, as often as occasion calls, force has for its destination the being employed against the subject citizens in the character of most natural, most constant and nearest enemies. As to the scale, the force which it is his destination to apply is in each individual instance applied upon the largest scale. The enemies to which that force is applied which is at the command of the Lawyer are no others than these same internal enemies, and in its application to them it operates upon the smallest scale: if the scale is to a certain degree enlarged, that force which has been lodged in the hands of the Soldier is called on.

Force and intimidation are the only instruments to the use of which the operations of the Soldier are purposely directed. Of corruptive influence he sees no need: of delusive influence as little.

Delusion is the instrument for the application of which the faculties of the lawyer are principally applied with most energy and most constancy.

By the force of his imagination he creates a sort of God or Goddess upon Earth, a sort of Divinity which he calls Common Law. Of this Goddess the principal and unavoidable occupation is in finding pretences for giving fulfilment to the Monarch's sinister will as evidenced by his sinister interest: to lodge in the hands of the

Monarch the external instruments of felicity in the largest quantity, to exercise for that purpose the arts of depredation and oppression—all this for the benefit of the Monarch: his[1] subordinate occupation, subordinate in profession, principal of course in design and will, is to exercise the same arts for his own benefit.

The Common Law, not having any existence, can not serve as a justification for any thing. In the face of the whole people who, in so far as they have courage and energy to open their eyes, see that it has no existence—that by the appellation Common Law nothing that has any existence is designated—in the face of the whole community, the existence of this Goddess is on every occasion asserted, and to this Goddess are ascribed the two wills to which execution and effect are to be given—the will of the Monarch and the will of the Judge. While for the benefit of the sinister interest of the Monarch, the Judge has been inflicting evil on the people to a certain superior degree, the Monarch connives at his inflicting evil for his own benefit in a certain inferior degree.

3. Now as to the Priest. In him may be seen another of the Monarch's corporeal instruments, of whom delusion is the principally employed incorporeal instrument. Force, physical force, belongs not to his province. Intimidation, yes. But it is by delusion that the intimidation is produced. The Divinity sprung from the brain of the Lawyer is Common Law. The Divinity sprung from the brain of the Priest is Religion. The business of the Lawyer is to do in the first place the will of the Monarch, in the next place his own: these are the two ends of action, the principal and the subordinate. In this the business of the Lawyer and that of the Priest agree. What difference has place between them lies in the means: in the different forms and degrees of the intimidation they employ. By the Lawyer as such the scene of the terrors he holds out is confined to the present life: the Priest provides a life of his own invention, a life which he fills with an all-comprehensive instrument of intimidation—a life filled with torments in intensity and duration infinite. The lawyer in the bitterest of his inflictions left the victim unbereft of hope: hope of seeing the termination of them in death: this last consolation is torn from him by the Priest: the tyranny of the lawyer is taken in hand by him, improved upon to the highest degree—and from finite, the suffering and the despair are rendered infinite.

A life filled with torments in comparison of which the most excruciating torments known by any man's experience would be consummate pleasure is by one general positive rule declared to be

[1] Bentham has mistakenly changed the subject of the sentence from 'Goddess' to 'the lawyer'.

the lot of every thing in the shape of man. But to this general [rule], in some indeterminate small number, exceptions may peradventure be found. To take his chance for constituting one of these exceptions, the first thing a man has to do is to do in all things, as far as lies in his power, the will of the Monarch, to the production of human misery in what quantity soever it may happen to it to be directed.

In respect of moral frame of mind, widely different are the effects which in a Monarchy are produced in the three professions.

The Soldier stands by himself. Force and intimidation, the instruments he applies, are no other than those without the eventual application of which the best government could no more have existence than the worst. Neither corruption nor delusion does it belong to his province to apply: neither of the one nor [of] the other instrument is the application expected at his hands: neither the one nor the other is it natural or frequent for him to seek to apply: delusion in particular is much more likely to find in him a contemner than a practicer.

Between the Lawyer and the Priest, the similarity of situation and thence of frame of mind is close and intimate. In governments in a state either reputed or called semi-barbarous, they have been united in the same person. In England, Priests were for a long time almost the only Lawyers. The coif, once the covering of the priestly tonsure, [is] still an ingredient in the composition of the masquerade dress with which the Lawyer, when placed in the Judicial Office, bears evidence [of] the primæval association to this day.

In the Mahometan religion, the Priest if not the only lawyer is at any rate the only Judge. In England the instances become daily more and more abundant in which the subordinate Judicial situation of the local Judge called Justice of the Peace is added to the function performed or not performed of the Priest.

In so far as for relief from their suffering the mind of [the] people can find a place for hope, the situation and natural character of the Soldier is the chief if not the only source that can be found for it. The great instrument of democratical government, the great support of the universal interest against all particular and thence sinister interests—the force of the popular or moral sanction brought into action by the Public Opinion Tribunal—has every where and at all times found far more sensibility to it in the breast of the Soldier than in the breasts of either of those workmen who work with delusion for their tool.

Accordingly, when on those great occasions on which, against oppression by Monarchs, the interest of the subjects has found effectual supporters, Soldiers have been so by thousands, Lawyers and Priests, only no otherwise than by *units*.

§11. *Monarch's incorporeal instruments: 1. Force: 2. Intimidation: 3. Corruptive influence: 4. Delusive influence*

Of the sinister sacrifice, the chief instruments may stand expressed in these four words: namely, 1. Force. 2. Intimidation. 3. Corruption. 4. Delusion.

Force, namely physical force, incidentally and in case of necessity, and to the extent of that necessity, applied, is an instrument the use of which is of the essence of every government: [of] a government which has for its object the greatest happiness of the greatest number, not less than [of] a government which has not for its object the happiness of any other than the ruling one.

The like may be said of intimidation: namely fear of punishment: from which is inseparable in case of necessity, and to the extent of the necessity, the actual infliction of punishment.

Not so corruption. By corruption understand the application of the matter of reward to any sinister purpose.

In every mixt Monarchy that is ever presented to view by that appellative, there has been a set of men deputed by and acting under the name and in the character of representatives of the people and actually delegated by a portion more or less considerable of the people and professing to act as trustees for the people, supporting to the best of their power the interest of the people. In a mixt Monarchy, by corruption is meant a breach of that same trust produced by the possession or expectancy of the external instruments of felicity in some shape or other at the hands of the Monarch or of one another in consideration of such breach.

In the case of a pure Monarchy, there being no functionaries appearing and professing to act in the character of trustees of and for the people, there is no demand, no room, for corruption in that its ordinary sense. If by corruption be meant depravity, or destruction wrought in any other way to the happiness of the people, there is indeed corruption plenty: but in this case corruption is not used in the same sense as in a mixt Monarchy containing a body of men professing to be Representatives of the [people].[1]

So again as to Delusion. In a pure Monarchy there is indeed delusion plenty: instruments of felicity operating as instruments of delusion upon the minds, upon the imaginations, of the subject many. But in a pure Monarchy there is no such demand for, no such need of, delusion as in a mixt Monarchy. Force and intimidation, with or without corruption, suffice for the production of the effect.

[1] MS 'body'.

§ 12. *In support of Monarchy, non-existence of all reasons drawn from the greatest happiness principle. Irrelevancy or senselessness of all arguments on that side*

In no instance, at no time, has any attempt been made to shew that by the substitution or by the addition made of the Office of Monarch to the Office of member of a body of Delegates chosen by the great body of the people, any addition has been made or can be made to the greatest happiness of the greatest number. In no instance can any such attempt have ever been taken into consideration but the utter impossibility of success must immediately have manifested itself.

In no instance has the attachment to any such form of government been placed upon any firmer or better ground than that of blind prejudice: in no instance will it ever be endeavoured to be placed upon any other than that ground.

In corruption and delusion, in the conjunct force of these two instruments of evil, has at all times been and at all times will be the only trust.

§ 13. *Case II. The Monarch limited: the Monarchy limited or mixt. In a limited Monarch, moral inaptitude is still more flagrant than in an absolute Monarch*

In this situation compared with the forementioned the causes of enmity are more active: of resistance the symptoms are continually obtruding themselves on observation. Though on every occasion the office is out of hazard, on every occasion a contest with circumstances of irritation has place.

To moral inaptitude in the shape of cruelty is in this situation necessarily added immorality in the shape of insincerity and deception. The Representation of the people is [in] a state of corruption—the people themselves are in a state of delusion. If the Representation were not in this state of corruption, no such Office as the Kingly Office could continue. If the people in a vast proportion were not in a state of delusion, no such Office as is the Kingly Office could continue.

Of that mass of the external instruments of felicity which otherwise might be, and in the situation of absolute Monarch would be, employed by him in the endeavour, how vain so ever, to make an ulterior addition to his own felicity, a portion more or less considerable must be employed in the keeping in a state of perpetual corruption, and perpetual subserviency to his sinister interest, the

Delegates, real or pretended, of the people, in securing on their part a constant breach of such their trust. In these men, the people, in so far as they see clearly, behold their enemies: subordinate depredators under the orders of the supreme depredator, and before all things occupied with him in the exercise of depredation at their charge. In the eyes of the Monarch they are at the same time his enemies: partly because the quantity of the matter of depredation seized by them is never adequate to his desires, partly on account of the vast share which he finds himself under the necessity of abandoning to them, in consideration of that part which, in fulfilment of the sinister contract, it is necessary should be performed on their part, or his will could not be done.

At all times, until the *Old man of the woods* has been shaken off from the shoulders of *Sinbad* in every wood upon the earth,[1] in every Monarchy one and the same option, and that in both parts a disastrous one, will be presenting itself to the Monarch's choice: the option between magnitude and stability. In some eyes, encrease of stability will be seen provided for in the expedient of imparting a share of power either to a Representation of the people alone, or to a self-representing Aristocratical body, or to both together.

§ 14. *Effects of the conjunction of sinister interest between the Monarch and the Aristocracy subordinate to him*

In the situation of an Aristocracy, the general description of sinister interest is the same as in that of a Monarchy.

In so far as in any community there exists a body of men distinguished from the rest by a peculiarly large proportion of the general mass of the objects of general desire in any shape, a corresponding aristocratical body or aristocracy has place. Of aristocracies in one and the same community, there are accordingly or may be [seven][2] different sorts.

[1.] Aristocracy more or less lasting constituted by operative power belonging to the legislative branch, or derived by means of Election, real or pretended, from the body of the people.

[1] For the story of Sindbad and the old man of the sea see R.F. Burton, *A plain and literal translation of the Arabian Nights' Entertainments, now entituled The Book of the Thousand Nights and a Night*, 16 vols., Benares, 1885–8, vi. 50–3. Bentham's description of the old man of the sea as the 'old man of the woods' may not have been altogether fortuitous. Richard Hole, *Remarks on the Arabian Nights' Entertainments; in which the origin of Sindbad's voyages, and other oriental fictions, is particularly considered*, London, 1797, p. 151, suggested that the old man of the sea represented an orang-outang, a word which is derived from the Malay phrase meaning 'man of the woods'.

[2] MS blank.

[2.] Aristocracy constituted by official power belonging to the executive branch—aristocracy of power.

3. Aristocracy constituted by factitious dignity—aristocracy of title.

4. Aristocracy constituted by present opulence—aristocracy of wealth.

5. Aristocracy constituted by power, dignity or opulence of a man's ancestor—aristocracy of birth or ancestry: aristocracy of landed opulence: ditto of monied opulence.

6. Aristocracy constituted by official power, factitious dignity, present opulence and hereditary opulence in the hands of the Clergy.

7. Aristocracy constituted by the influence of talent employed in the political field of government.

In these several shapes, any or all of them, the matter of aristocracy may be lodged and united in the hands of one and the same individual.

Relation between the Monarch's interest and the interest of the Aristocracy in its several branches. Interests how far coincident, how far conflicting—how far and how reconcileable and reconciled

I. In respect of money. It is the interest of the Monarch as above that the quantity of money in his hands and at his disposal, extorted from those by whom it has been produced and from those into whose hands with their free consent it has passed, should be as great as possible.

So is it the interest of the aristocracy in the aggregate, with the exception of such part of it as is extracted from them and thus at their expence.

II. As to power. It is the interest of the Monarch as above that the quantity of power in his hands and at his disposal be as great as possible.

So is it the interest of the Aristocracy in the aggregate, with the exception of power in any shape from which any sensible defalcation may be made from their own security: in particular from their own security as against misdeeds committed to their prejudice by the Monarch or any instrument of his.

III. As to factitious dignity. It is the interest of the Monarch as above that the quantity of it be as great as possible: in a Monarchy the whole stock of it being in one way or other his: either condensed in his own person, or at his disposal.

It is the interest of the Aristocracy taken in the aggregate that the quantity of it be as great as possible: since the greater the aggregate mass, the greater in possession or in contingency will be each member's share.

On the other hand, it is the interest of each member taken separately, not only that upon a level higher than his own, but upon the same level with his own, a quantity of this aliment to pride and vanity be as small as possible: since by every addition to the number of those who are sharers with him, the value of his own share is lessened.

Means of conciliation

By the very nature of the conflict, indication plain enough is given of the means—the effectual and exclusively effectual means—of conciliation.

As to *money*, the larger the share allotted and given up by the Monarch to the Aristocracy, the larger the quantity they will be content to see him take.

The same observation applies to power, and without any difference worth remarking.

The same observation again applies to factitious dignity, without any observations or exceptions other than as above.

In all these particulars, much more valuable in their eyes will naturally be the sinister interest which they share with the Monarch than their share in the universal interest. By the nature of the human mind, on the occasion of every bargain of this sort, the Aristocracy are disposed to accept of terms more or less disadvantageous to themselves. Offices with the emolument and power attached to them, with or without the addition of factitious dignity, come all in a lump: taxes creep on gradually: and at the outset no man sees the amount to which they are destined to swell. Whatsoever be the real value of each man's chance, his own good opinion of himself, together with the confidence most men have in their own good fortune—that confidence by which lotteries are filled—suffices for swelling to excess the value of it in his eyes.

As to power, by every portion he concurrs in giving to the Monarch, the Aristocrat gives up a correspondent portion of his own security: of his own security against abuses of that same power: abuses of a power which never has been nor ever can be used without being abused. He augments the degree of humiliation to which it may be necessary to him to subject himself. But whether advantageous or not in reality, few are those in whose eyes a bargain of this sort does not appear to be so: those as towards whom it is necessary for him to be obsequious and humble are the few, perhaps the very few: whereas those on whom his power imposes the necessity of being, or the disposition to be, humble and obsequious as towards him, are a countless multitude—and thus it is that many a man who would not have been corrupted by avarice is corrupted by pride and vanity.

Thus it is that to every member of an aristocracy howsoever

composed, the great body of the people naturally and generally are the objects of a mixt affection composed of aversion and contempt. In the breast of the aristocrat this affection is naturally stronger than even in that of the Monarch: for in his elevated situation, the Monarch is placed out of danger of receiving from the lower orders those rubs to which the members of the aristocracy, by their lesser elevation, stand exposed.

Thus it is that among aristocrats the number of those who would give up any of their privileges is still smaller in proportion than of Monarchs who would give up their crown. Behold a certain well-matched pair of houses.[1] Think whether in either of them [it is][2] natural that for one who would embrace in preference representative democracy as in the Anglo-American United States to absolute Monarchy carried on as in Austria, there should not be more than a hundred who would prefer absolute Monarchy as in Austria to representative democracy as in the United States.

§15. *Case III. The Government an Aristocracy.* *In this case, the features of inaptitude being in the main the same as in the case of a Monarchy, secure the same result*[3]

In every political community, every member has a share in the aggregate interest composed of that of all the members of the community taken together—in a word in the universal interest.

But in every community, every member has a particular interest in which the rest of the members have no share—and on every one of a multitude of occasions this interest is liable to be in a state of opposition to the universal interest; in such sort that on each such occasion his felicity can not receive encrease, but the aggregate felicity of the rest of the members must in a certain proportion undergo decrease—this particular interest, when and in so far as thus circumstanced, may be stiled, and commonly is stiled, a sinister interest.

On each occasion, every man's conduct is the result of his interest if there be but one interest that on that occasion is operating upon his mind, or if there be more than one of that which in his view of the matter is on that same occasion the greater, or say stronger, interest. To this interest it will naturally, not to say necessarily, be his

[1] i.e. the House of Lords and the House of Commons.

[2] MS 'is it'.

[3] Bentham remarked that the material which he designated for use in this section (UC lxxxiv. 155–6) was 'Not exclusively relevant' (see UC xxxiv. 11), but failed to provide any alternative.

endeavour to give effect, whatsoever may be the effect on all other interests put together.

In every community, all such individuals as whether by determinate portions of political power or other means are in the exercise or possession of means peculiar to themselves in kind or degree of influencing the conduct of the rest, constitute thereby a sort of community within the universal community: it may be stiled the community of the ruling and otherwise influential few.

As such this particular community possess, and each member of it possesses, a particular interest which on a multitude of occasions is liable and apt to become a sinister interest.

Of the influential few, such as are simply influential and not of the number of the ruling few, the influence is in the ordinary state of things comparatively inconsiderable: it is exerted in subordination to, and in the same direction with, that of the ruling few: but occasionally it may happen to it to find itself in a state of opposition to that generally stronger interest: and to act in opposition to it with more or less effect.

Under every form of government but one, the power of the ruling few, if it is not already at its maximum, is continually on the encrease until it has arrived at its maximum, or by resistance on the part of the subject many has been lessened or utterly destroyed.

When this power is at its maximum, the interest of the subject many, or what comes to the same thing the universal interest, being compleatly overborne, is compleatly sacrificed to that of the ruling few: the aggregate felicity of the ruling few is swelled to its maximum; the aggregate felicity of the subject many reduced to its minimum.

§ 16. *Effects of the conjunction of sinister interest between the Monarch and a Legislative body, superordinate, co-ordinate or subordinate in relation to him*

A Monarch, whose power is subject to limitations, will be, in as far as any probability of success presents itself to his eyes, continually occupied in the endeavour to shake off these shackles, and render himself absolute: and this with the greater energy if having been originally absolute, he has been under the unpleasant predicament of sitting still while these shackles have been forced upon his hands: and at the same time he will extract for his own use from the purses of his subjects money in the largest quantity that seems obtainable without preponderant difficulty and uneasiness on his part.

The Representatives of the people will in like manner seek the encrease of their own felicity, by means of the above and all other instruments of it, at the expence of all at whose expence if encreased it must be encreased—at the expence of their constituents and the rest of the people, and at the expence of the Monarch, except in so far as they may think they see the necessity of his assistance for the compassing of their designs against the people: and for securing it, sacrifice to him whatsoever the purpose requires to be sacrificed: the money of the people, including their own share in it, and even in a proportion more or less considerable their own peculiar power, if necessary. It will be the endeavour of each to keep himself fixt in his seat for as long a term as possible: it will [be] the endeavour of each and of all to render themselves as independent of the people in every respect as possible.

So in regard to money: an article which can not come into the pockets of either sort of functionary without being taken out of the pockets of a more or less unwilling people, every atom so taken producing to those who lose it suffering to much larger amount than enjoyment on the part of those who gain it.

This money—this object of continual and ever unsatiable desire, the Monarch can never obtain it without the Representatives of the people, nor the Representatives of the people without the Monarch: he and they will thus be perpetually linked together in a sort of partnership, a community of sinister interest.

The Monarch as such will have at his disposal, with exceptions to a comparatively small amount, all the masses of money and power, with or without those of factitious dignity, which are attached to the several public offices and public functions by the exercise of which the powers of government are exercised. As the magnitude of his power is in the direct ratio of the aggregate value of these several offices and functions, it will be among the objects of his endeavour to give every practical encrease to the number of them and to the value of each: including of course the preserving it from decrease.

The Representatives of the people will on their parts be desirous in like manner each of them to give unbounded encrease to his own felicity by obtaining to the largest amount in respect of value these and all other instruments of it.

The Monarch, for the purpose of satisfying such his desires, will at all times be in readiness to impart to these several Representatives of the people, or at any rate to a sufficient number of them, these same objects of general desire.

The Representatives of the people on their parts will in like manner be at all times in readiness each of them to receive at the hands of the Monarch to the greatest amount obtainable these same objects of desire: to receive whether by their own hands or by the hands of others whose interest in that respect is identified or linked with theirs makes to the purpose in question no material difference.

But to satisfy such their desires, respectively they must on their part be ready to contribute, be seen to be ready to contribute, and upon each favorable occasion must contribute accordingly, each of them to the fulfilment of the corresponding desires on the part of the Monarch. Of these desires, there is not any that to them can be unknown or dubious. By accident with respect to this or that particular object, yes: but with respect to the aggregate of all in general, no: without any individual communication on his part to any of them, they know each of them what it will be agreable to him he should do towards satisfying his desires as he himself does. Each will be disposed to receive as much as he can obtain: and to each the Monarch will be disposed to give in proportion to whatsoever it may in the eyes of the Monarch be his power to contribute to the satisfaction of his desires: to contribute by vote, speech, and influence.

Relation between the Monarch's interest and that of the legislative branch of the Aristocracy

Note that upon the legislative branch of the Aristocracy depends immediately or unimmediately the whole stock of the objects of general desire that at the expence of the whole community shall have place.

It is the interest of the Monarch that for the preservation and augmentation of his own portion of money, power and factitious dignity, enjoyed at the expence of and by the correspondent sacrifice of the universal interest, after deduction of what is consumed by his individual self for his personal enjoyment, it be made to operate upon the possessors of the supreme legislative power in the way of corruptive influence.

It is the interest of each individual of this branch of the Aristocracy, that this matter of corruptive influence be received by him in the greatest quantity possible: received by him whatsoever in that sinister direction and to that sinister effect may be the operation of it.

In so far as this effect is produced, every act by means of which a sacrifice of the interest of the greatest number is made to the particular and sinister interest of the ruling few is an act of hostility to the people: an act of hostility on the parts of both corrupter and corrupted: on the part of the corrupted, an act of perfidy and treachery to their Constituents: by whom, in proportion as they see the effect produced, resentment and ill-will as towards the agents can not but be entertained.

To obviate as far as may be such resentment, it is the interest of both the contracting parties to join in whatever measures convey the appearance of a desire to render such hostility and perfidy impracticable, and this interest will be strong in proportion to the real inefficacy and apparent efficacy of such pretended preventives.[1]

To produce such corruptive effect, what can in no case be necessary is any communication on the subject between the one party and the other.

By no interdiction therefore of any such communication can the quantity of the effect be lessened.

To know what on each occasion is the wish of him, who ever he be, at whose disposal the good things wished for are, the situation occupied by him says as plain as words can speak. No man in the situation of a representative of the people ever has been so stupid as to entertain a doubt about it.[2]

Yet every now and then comes a man with a proposed Bill in his hand having for its professed object the prevention or lessening of corruptive influence by punishing all particular communication between man and man for any such purpose. Of any such proposed law, what is the object? To lessen the evil it professes to lessen? No: but to give establishment and encrease to it. To convey to men without doors the notice that within doors a desire to apply an effectual remedy to the evil has place, and thus to obtain a misplaced confidence, to cause a betrayer to be regarded as a saviour: in the next place, in the assured inefficiency of the pretended remedy to engage men in the habit of acquiescing in the sight of the evil under the notion of its being an irremediable one. That in the nature of things it is an irremediable one is not true: for the example of the Anglo-American United States affords a compleat disproof of the truth of it. But that it is irremediable under any such Government as the present English or the present French is unquestionably true. For to render the conduct of the other constituted authorities in a state of compleat subservience to the will of the Monarch, determined by the

[1] There is no text corresponding to the following marginal summary, which belongs here: 'Course contributory to this purpose, joining in prohibitory and punitory arrangements inhibiting particular communications for such compact. By this course, the amount and effect of the corruptive influence is not really diminished: though an appearance is produced perhaps of an actual diminution, at any rate of a wish and endeavour to effect it.'

[2] There is no text corresponding to the following marginal summary, which belongs here: 'By the uncertainty, what will satisfy the Monarch etc., the exertions of the Representatives are made greater than they would be if the quantity that would satisfy were liquidated. By interdiction of acceptance, no diminution of corruptive influence is effected. Gift to a man's relatives can not be interdicted: and from gift to relative a man may receive as much advantage as from ditto to himself.'

sinister interest of the Monarch, all that is necessary is to give to the representatives, real or pretended, of the people a certain length of continuance in their situations, placing at the same [time] at the disposal of the Monarch a mass of the objects of general desire to a certain amount: and not only is the quantity actually in hand in the one government or the other sufficient for this purpose—but so would [be] a very small part of it.[1]

Suppose the body of men who act as representatives of the people; suppose the mode of electing them so arranged as that they should in fact be the deputies or say delegates of, as being chosen by, the greatest number, elected in the only mode in which such elections can be free and the persons who are said to be chosen any thing better than impostors and usurpers; suppose the term of their continuance in their situation so short, as that by the shortness of it a virtual power of displacing them is lodged in the hands of their constituents. To speak concisely and in the language of English Constitutional law, suppose them chosen in the way of Radical Reform, by and with virtual universality, effectual secrecy, practical equality, and annuality, semi-annuality, or bienniality of suffrage. The Monarch continuing in his possession the whole or any considerable portion of the Corruption Fund as above described.

Such an arrangement, would it suffice to cause the greatest happiness of the greatest number to be taken for the actual end of government as it is in the Anglo-American United States? would it in a word suffice for the prevention of the sinister sacrifice?

Antecedently to direct experience, no assured answer seems warrantable. But the probability seems on the side of the negative.

A Representative of the people who by speech, vote, or absentation had on this or that occasion lent his concurrence to the sinister sacrifice will at the next Election be displaced. Be this the case ever so constantly. By any such connection between delinquency and punishment, how should the delinquency be prevented? In itself the situation of representative of the people is worth nothing: but by the undue obsequiousness in question it might always in the existence of a majority be really made worth something: and in default of eventual possession, expectancy without possession would be equally effectual:

[1] There is no text corresponding to the following marginal summary, which belongs here: 'Sure but sole remedy: 1. Causing the alledged representatives of the people to be really chosen by the greatest number. 2. Causing them to be displaceable by non-reelection after a short time of service. 3. Minimizing the matter of corruption within their reach. [4.] Abolishing the office of a Chief functionary irremovable by the people and with the whole or a great part of the Official Establishment etc., in the character of a corruption fund, at his disposal.' Points 2 and 3 do not appear in the marginal summary on the text sheet, but have been added by Bentham to the marginal summary sheet (UC xxxviii. 112).

the possession would be received by many: the expectation would be entertained by all: and be the man who he may, so long as there is any other human being whose interest is either by self-regarding interest or sympathy identified with his, the temptation would not be taken away even if in his own person he were rendered incapable of receiving any part of the corruption fund in any part of the remainder of his life.

If by this means the end were fulfilled, it would be in a less immediate way. The people seeing their Representatives constantly unfaithful, would at length open their eyes—they would see that to expect to see any ruler or set of rulers sacrifice their own particular interest to the universal interest, they having it in their power to reverse the sacrifice, is among the most palpable of all imaginable absurdities: instead of kicking against the pricks they will rise with one accord and to a form of government which can not by possibility have for its object the greatest happiness of the greatest number, the only legitimate end of government, substitute one that has.

§ 17. *Corruption may be made compleat by institution without need of individual acts of corruption*

Under every form of government in which no constitutive power in the hands of the subject many has place, the sinister sacrifice is already in a state of completion.

Under a form of government in which, with relation to a portion and no more than a portion of the aggregate of the operative power, the constitutive power is in the hands of the subject many in quality of constituents, the portion of operative power being in the hands of individuals deputed by them in the quality of representatives, the sinister sacrifice is continually making, the quantity of it continually upon the encrease, until it has arrived at the point of consummation, the mixt government becoming if not in form as well as effect, at any rate in effect, a pure one.

When as above no more than a portion of the operative power is in the hands of the deputed representatives of the people, placed in those hands by the exercise of a correspondent constitutive power, a small quantity of external instruments of felicity—objects of general desire—if lodged in hands not displaceable by the subject many, suffices, sooner or later according to circumstances, for the production and consummation of the sinister sacrifice.

For this purpose it is not possible to say what would be the least quantity sufficient: a quantity much smaller than the smallest that has ever yet been exemplified would suffice: amply sufficient would be the quantity in the hands of the President of the Anglo-American United States if that functionary were not, as he is, placed and displaceable by the subject many.

Considered in respect of its tendency, by its action on the desires of the deputed representatives and trustees of the subject many, to produce on their part a constant sacrifice of the universal interest in the continued violation of such their trust, the quantity of the external instruments of felicity thus stationed may be stiled the matter of corruptive influence, or more shortly the matter of corruption: it is composed of the matter of reward, that is to say the matter of good in any shape, in the case where and in so far as applying itself to this evil purpose.

The course taken by the matter of corruption while occupied in the production of this evil and sinister effect may be thus conceived.

The hands in which as above it is lodged may be the hands either of a single individual—a Monarch; or those of a number of individuals—an Aristocracy:[a] or in any proportion it may be divided between both. For facility of conception take the simplest case, and let the hands be those of a Monarch.

Considered in themselves, the objects of general desire thus lying at his disposal are comprisable under one or other of three denominations, namely money, power, and factitious dignity: money say as being shorter and more familiar instead of the matter of wealth in all its shapes.

Considered in respect of the occasions on which or the form in which they are disposed of thence, they are either Offices, Commissions, Donations or Dignities. Of an Office the value and influence is composed either of power, or of money, conferred by it on the official individual placed in it—a Commission is a name [given] to Offices in certain departments and to Offices the existence of which is short and transient in any department. A Dignity is a sort of evidence and token of a certain degree of favour and estimation in which the dignitary is held by the Monarch: and the favour of the Monarch being the

[a] In the original Greek, Aristocracy is the power of the best: for such they would of course be stiled: stiled by themselves and by all who looked for favour at their hands. In fact they are every where and necessarily the worst: to render them such, this very power of contributing towards the sinister sacrifice—accompanied as such power can never fail to be with the correspondent desire and the act—is amply sufficient: if in any community they are in any degree better than a distinguishable and considerably extensive proportion of the whole, it must be in virtue of that intellectual culture by the want of which alone those who are destitute of any share of operative power can be rendered worse in a moral sense than those who respectively have a share in it.

immediate source of all the good things as above which are at his disposal, it operates in the eyes of the subject many in particular as an earnest of the matter of good in all its other shapes.

No sooner is any such mixt system in existence than the influence of the people, and with it the welfare of the people, is diminished at both ends.

The representatives of the people can not by their own single power extract for their own use any of those instruments of felicity at the expence of the people. But either for their own use or, what comes to the same thing, for the use of their connections, with the concurrence of the Monarch, through the medium of one or other of the several possessions above-mentioned, they can extract them in any quantity.

Money in particular they can thus obtain in any or all of the four several forms: necessary emolument attached in necessary quantity to Offices and Commissions useful and at the same time needful: money attached to these same possessions in a quantity neither needful nor useful: pecuniary emolument attached to Offices and Commissions which, though not useless in their natures, are in respect of their number needless: money attached to Offices which, though not without functions annexed, are altogether useless: money attached to Offices without functions, called in England, where they are so abundant, *Sinecures*.

At the disposal of the Monarch to a vast amount on the whole are, in the least expensive Monarchy, good things in all these several forms. But to place in the hands of any such irremovable and irresponsible functionary [the disposal of good gifts][1] in any considerable quantity, while the Members of the body of the Representatives of the people, whose concurrence is necessary to every law and every considerable exercise of the functions of the Executive department, are in a condition by their own hands or other hands which are virtually their own to receive them, is to establish a fund for the corruption of those same deputed Agents and Trustees of the subject many.

From the first establishment of such a fund down to the compleat consummation of the sinister sacrifice—the compleat conversion of this mixt government or limited Monarchy into a pure despotism, no one act that can be punished or even made known as an act of bribery or corruption is necessary. That in order to give encrease to the mass of the instruments of felicity at his disposal the Monarch is at all times

[1] The addition is suggested by the marginal summary: 'Representatives, without whom [the Monarch] can not extract the money, being able and necessarily willing to receive at his hands, by theirs or their connections', such good gifts, to place the disposal in such hands is to establish a fund of corruptive influence.'

willing and desirous to impart to every individual whose assistance is necessary to that encrease can not be made more certain by any thing he says to any body than it would be otherwise is exactly as certain as that he is a man: to make this known exactly as useless would any such speech be, as to make it known that he is a man would be the sticking upon his back a placard saying this is a man.

On the other hand, exactly in the same case are in their situation the Representatives of the people.

To establish a system of corruption as compleat and effectual not only as history can exemplify but as imagination can conceive, any one act of intercourse between the Corrupter General or any agent of his on the one hand and any Representative of the people on the other hand is not awhit more necessary than to carry on the business of [a shop it is to the][1] Shopkeeper to any extent to keep running out of the shop with goods in his hand and, laying hold of passengers as they go by, call upon them to become purchasers.

To establish any such form of government is therefore to establish a partnership concern—leading partner, the Monarch, junior partners, the representatives of the people: Articles of the Constitution, articles of the partnership: stock or subject matter of the partnership, whatsoever portion of the substance of the people can by any instruments or sources or device be extracted and applied to the use of the several partners in such proportions as circumstances, as the state of the concern, shall from time to time prescribe.

A thousand little sources or channels of detail are continually springing up as it were of themselves. All these put together are as nothing in comparison of the two vast torrents, wars and distant dependencies.

Wars are at the command of the Monarch every where, distant dependencies only in particular situations, though the usefulness of them to every such partnership has rendered them numerous in the extreme.

Distant dependencies have to this purpose their value not only in their own separate character, but as sources of war.

Wars likewise on their part have their value not merely in their own character, but in case of what is regarded as success and good fortune, in the character of sources of the acquisition of distant dependencies: being in both characters as conducive to national health and felicity, as a bloody flux is to individual health.

[1] The addition is suggested by the marginal summary: 'To establish a compleatly efficient system of corruptive influence, no special intercourse between the parties is necessary; no more than to carry on the business of a shop, it is necessary to Shopkeeper to address himself to passengers individually.'

Here then may be seen a sort of perpetual repetend, shall it be called? or circulate?—from distant dependencies flows war: and from war, distant dependencies.

A few words suffice to bring to view the manifest and undeniable truth, that from both these main sources flow of necessity the several minor rills abovementioned, Offices, Commissions, Pensions.[1]

Except in a rare and shortlived state of things, under no form of government, that of the Anglo-American United States excepted, or one not essentially different from it, is it possible that by the aggregate power of the [legislative] body,[2] the greatest happiness of the greatest number should be the object to the attainment of which the exercise of that power will have been directed: they are to a certainty under the dominion of a particular and sinister interest.

Towards the directing the rule of action towards that exclusively justifiable end what is possible is that in a favorable conjuncture a body of law having for its end in view that same object may be presented to the notice of the whole people: in which case, those among whom the power of legislation is shared may, by fear of the ill opinion and resentment of the greatest number, be engaged to adopt such universally beneficial measures as if left to themselves no one of them would have originated.

The favorable conjuncture in question is this:—when, after a long course of misrule, a new set of men, by means of the support given to them or expected to be given to them by the great body of the subject many, have come into possession of the aggregate powers of government: exercising them at the same time in such sort as to let the great body of the people into a portion more or less considerable of that power: divesting thereby the former rulers of a correspondent share: either of the whole of the power they had been possessed of, or of a more or less considerable part of it, leaving them in the possession of the rest, or giving to them a newly modified portion in lieu of it.

In this state of things, the minds of the persons from whom the change had divested more or less of their power would of necessity be in a state of continual irritation and hostility towards all persons in

[1] A sheet of MS is missing from the sequence of text at this point. A copy of the corresponding marginal summary is at UC xxxviii. 114: 'How people are drained of liberty, and power of resistance to the other drain [i.e. the drain of money]. As the drain of money with the oppression necessary to it encrease, their suffering encreases. They see themselves betrayed by representatives, injured by them and monarch: thence continually encreasing dissatisfaction, discontent, expression of ditto: endeavour in this or that shape to secure themselves against endless encrease.'

[2] MS 'of the body on whom the sanctionment of the work in question depends'. In *Codification Proposal*, Bentham envisaged that the codes of laws produced by individual draftsmen would be presented to the legislature of the state for acceptance or rejection. The alteration clarifies the passage in the context of 'Supreme Operative'.

whom they viewed the authors of their loss: and to them among the subject many would be added not only all those who felt or supposed themselves partakers in that loss, but all such others [in] whose instance habit had produced an attachment to the existing government and suspicion and aversion towards every new one: nor was there ever any government so hostile to the happiness of the greatest number as not to have derived from the force of habit the benefit of an attachment to itself at the hands of a portion more or less considerable of that number.

Here then between the rulers under the old government and the rulers under the new government, say between the former and the new rulers, whatsoever were the colour worn by language and external deportment, would in so far as mind was concerned—desires, intentions and secret endeavours—be a state of civil war: the old rulers striving to regain their lately lost power; the new rulers labouring to retain, give stability, and as far as possible encrease to theirs.

So long as this concealed civil war continued, the new rulers, whatsoever were the share of power avowedly assumed by them, can not but feel themselves in a state of effectual dependence, more or less strict, on the support and thence on the good will and good opinion of the people: in each mind would remain impressed an apprehension more or less intense lest the people instead of continuing their support should turn against them: in which case to the power at present in their possession might succeed not only impotence but actual suffering: and this either at the hands of the people themselves or at the hands of the former rulers. Thus hostile to them would of course be the disposition and conduct of the people in proportion as they saw or suspected that by the new rulers endeavours were used to advance their own particular interest at the expence of the universal interest of the people, in imitation of, if not in conjunction with, the former rulers.

Thus far then, and during the continuance of this secret war between the former and the new rulers, between the new rulers and the people a natural alliance will have place.

By that love of power, so extensively prevalent in every human breast, the new possessors of it might naturally enough be rendered more or less insensible to such their dependence: in which case proportioned to such insensibility would be their endeavours, either on their own bottom alone or in alliance and conjunction with the former rulers, to fix a new yoke upon the necks of the people. But whatsoever might be the view taken of it, this dependence whatever it were would not be the less effective.

No sooner is this civil war terminated than the late combatants become natural allies: the sense of insecurity with the accompanying hostility and fears having subsided on both sides, on both sides men are left to yield to the universal propensity, the irresistible propensity planted by nature in the heart of man, the appetite for power together with all those other external instruments of felicity of which it is itself an instrument.

The alliance which at first had place on the part of the new rulers and the people against the former ruler or rulers now gives way to an alliance between the former rulers and the new rulers against the people. In terms more [or][1] less explicit a treaty of alliance is now formed, and in this treaty is included a partition treaty: subject matter of the partition, so much of the annual produce of the labour of the productive classes as by any means can be wrung from them.

Under the former system, this mass of produce was a mine worked by the Monarch alone for his own account alone. By the partition treaty, certain branches of the Aristocratical interest are let into partnership with the Monarch: the mass in question becomes the subject matter and stock of this partnership: and hence forward it is for the account of Monarch and Co. that the mine is worked.

By the Constitution that has been formed and sanctioned, the articles of this treaty and thereby the articles of this partnership have been established. Of the profits, so much is allotted to the head partner for his private use, for his own consumption and that of his domestic servants and other personal dependents; so much is allotted to Offices, which under their own names or those of their respective connections are to be distributed among the junior partners: of these Offices, the emolument is theirs in the way of possession and permanent enjoyment; his, to the whole or the greatest part, in the way of patronage: of patronage with the incidental and transient enjoyment attached to the act of donation, and the permanent power that results from the right and habit of exercising it.

Peace restored, the alliance and the partnership formed, the condition of the Monarch will be found by no means so disadvantageous as at first it threatened to be. In the article of power, he has been a loser: but in the article of security, he has been no small gainer. Under the new system, even the people find their condition less disadvantageous, less miserable, than under the former one. Under the former one, their condition was that of beasts under a blind and inconsiderate master: under the new system, it is that of beasts under a more or less discerning and calculating master. Under the

[1] MS 'of'.

single master, their powers were exhausted in a short time: their powers were brought to the utmost degree of exhaustion: under the partnership, the process may go on for a length of time more or less considerable before it is consummated.

§18. *Sinister sacrifice, when consummate*

Where there exists any one functionary who is not in the ordinary way of election displaceable immediately or unimmediately by the greatest number, he at the same time having at his disposal the objects of general desire to an amount more or less considerable, this person is thereby in a condition to prosecute with effect his own sinister interest at the expence of the interest of the greatest number, at the expence of the universal interest.

In the instance of every government that has an irremovable chief, such is the condition of that same irremoveable chief.

Every government which amongst its functionaries numbers an irremovable chief is a Monarchy: if amongst the other functionaries there is not any one who is not at all times displaceable by this one, the Monarchy is a pure Monarchy: if there be any one or more functionaries who are not thus displaceable, a mixt Monarchy.

Whether the Monarchy be pure or mixt, the interest of the Monarch is essentially a sinister interest.

Of every mixt Monarchy, the perpetual tendency is to become a pure Monarchy: and in case of tranquillity, sooner or later such tendency can not consistently with the nature of man fail of being carried into effect.

Of the sinister interest when coupled with adequate power capable of giving effect to its tendency, the ultimate effect may be stiled the consummation of the sinister sacrifice.

The consummation of the sinister sacrifice has place when by no addition made to the quantity of the matter of wealth endeavoured to be exacted for his own use from the other members of the community, further addition can actually be made: when taxation has arrived at its *ne plus ultrà*.

In every pure Monarchy, taxation is at every point of time at its *ne plus ultrà* with reference to that time.

In a mixt Monarchy in which taxation has not yet arrived at that point, it is still tending towards that point. It may have arrived at that point and still continue a mixt Monarchy. But as in this case there will be a continual striving to add to the quantity of wealth collected by taxation, and on the part of the people a correspondent repugnance and reluctance, in the course of the endeavours to surmount that reluctance there will be many continual additions to the quantity of power: till at length all power of resistance being taken from all the other members of the community, the mixt Monarchy will be passed into a pure one.

For any length of time the forms of the mixt Monarchy may remain and will be likely to remain: but the condition of the people will not be in any respect the better for these forms. The forms of mixt government remained under the tyrant Cæsars.[1]

§ 19. *Arguments in favour of a Mixt Monarchy—their irrelevancy and nullity*

For proving the aptitude of their principle, the Corruptionists have two emblems: as if an emblem were a proof. Its aptitude—but with reference to what end? for that it has any aptitude with relation to the greatest happiness they dare not venture to assert: at any rate in any direct terms: the falshood would be too palpable.

Of these emblems, one may be stiled the mechanical, the other the chemical.

The mechanical emblem is that of the *balance*. Good government, say they, requires that of supreme direction there should be two powers of equal force, antagonizing with each other: as the two scales, with the weights in each, do in the balance: power in the one, that of the Monarch: power in the other, the power of the people. If of the one power the force is exactly equal to that of the other, the scales will be exactly upon the same level, and motionless: in which case good government takes place of course. Should the Monarch be inclined to give to his power a greater effect than is produced [by] the interest of the people, he will not be able: for in the opposite scale is lodged the power of the people which will prevent it. Good. But should the people be inclined to give to their power a greater effect than is produced by the power[2] of the [Monarch],[3] they will not be able: for there is the power of the Monarch, which will prevent it. By this principle, if interests are to be taken into the account, just as much care is taken <of> the interest of the one, as of the interest of any number <of> millions.

[1] The Roman Emperors of the Julio-Claudian dynasty (27BC-AD68) were careful to retain the institutions of the republic as a cloak to their own power.

[2] MS orig. 'interest'.

[3] MS 'people'.

Let it be assumed that at any moment taken at pleasure, that equi<pon>derance has been the one thing needful and that the aptitude <. . .> has been proved by it: still the proof would not <. . .> the better, for the next ensuing moment the equiponderance <. . .> must have been at an end, the scale with the power of the <. . .> it must have kicked the beam: and remained <. . .> at present.

Instead of the two scales, let them put three—instead of the bilance (so improperly spelt in English balance) they make their machine a *trilance*, still their proof will not be any better: the scale with the power of the people in will be on one side of the point of suspension, both others on the opposite side.

Another emblem of the mechanical kind has sometimes been employed to this same purpose: but it is not so familiar and accordingly seems to have given way pretty generally to the balance: the place it is borrowed from is not the shopkeeper's counter, but the natural philosopher's close-locked cabinet—after having been once brought out, it seems therefore by common consent to be suffered to lie on the shelf.

Two forces impelling a body at the same time in so many different directions: the directions, one of them that in which [it is] acted upon by the interest of the people: the other that in which it is acted upon by the interest of the people. Borrowing infallibility from the mathematician, the politician proves to you that whatever be the direction thus taken by the body, it can not [but] be that in which it is acted upon by the interest of the people. This is what he gets by his mathematics. Instead of two of these impelling forces, let them take three or thirty, the matter will not on their side be much mended.

Of the chemical emblematic proof, the essence is contained in the word mixture. Wherever there is mixture, there is good government. Look into a certain House,[1] there you will see mixture: mixture of classes, and of classes having each of them a separate interest. Whatever were the elements of the composition, its goodness should in some measure, one should think, depend upon the proportions and upon the security there is that whatever aptitude there is in the proportions is not mere matter of accident, but will be preserved: but of this, nothing is said: you must grant that they are, in an altogether sufficient degree, well-adapted to the purpose: that same purpose which by any other than this so conveniently flexible description is not mentioned. Another misfortune is that among these classes, that which has in it the interest of the greatest number has no place. But to the Orator or the writer this little deficiency produces no uneasiness,

[1] i.e. the House of Commons.

for the greatest number being no better than a mob, whose place is in the kennel, their interest is an object too dirty to be any thing better than an object of disgust to his hearers or his customers.

The men who profess to take these images as proofs are not ideots. What then are they?

Balance of power principle—its incompatibility with greatest happiness principle

No man or body of men, other than the greatest number themselves, ever took for the object of government the greatest happiness of the greatest number: no body of rulers other than that same greatest number, or if a less number, a number actually subject to their effectual influence.

Applied to different branches of aggregate political power, the notion for the conveyance of which the phrase a balance of powers is employed is compleatly misapplied. No sooner is the phrase understood than the notion meant to be conveyed by it is seen to be compleatly erroneous and delusive.

Suppose the equiponderance to have place any one moment, the next moment puts an end to it.

At the foot of every throne is a fountain of corruptive influence: and the stream of it a perennial and ever-encreasing one.

An equiponderance [exists] between two interests, the universal interest and a particular interest naturally and materially opposite to that same universal interest. Of such a state of things, supposing it capable of continuing, what will be the result? that nothing will be done for the advantage of the particular interest that is prejudicial to the universal interest. True: but not less so that nothing will ever be done for the advantage of the universal interest that is prejudicial to the particular interest, its antagonist.

No such conceit could have been entertained by any one in the character of a means for the advancement of the greatest happiness of the greatest number: by the utterance of it, sufficient proof is afforded that in the mind of the utterer no such desire as that of giving encrease to the greatest happiness of the greatest number, in preference to an equal share of happiness to the several individuals composing the smaller number, could with him have place.

At a given moment, suppose the equiponderance to have place: to the prejudice of the ruling one, there is nothing that can destroy it: to the prejudice of the interest of the subject many, every change that is capable of having place suffices to destroy it. On the one hand, any one new office in the gift of the ruling one suffices to destroy it: on the other hand, so does any one regulation by which the liberty of public discussion is narrowed: for it is only by means of and in proportion to the liberty of public discussion that the greatest number, the subject many, can give employment to whatsoever power may have been professed to be given to them, or learn how to give employment to it [to] their advantage.

Not only a plausible pretence for new offices may at all times be made, but a real and irresistible demand for new offices will frequently have place. Every addition to the military establishment is a cluster of new Offices. Every new distant dependency acquired is a cluster of new Offices. Every war is an immense and indefinitely extensive cluster of new Offices. Every instance of preparation for war creates a cluster of new Offices. In a mixt Monarchy, there is no end to the incidents each of which is capable of giving and in the habit of giving birth to so many clusters of new Offices.

Every intimation given of a fact prejudicial to the reputation of an individual possessed of a certain share of power or influence produces an endeavour to restrain the liberty of public discussion: and the endeavour is the more strenuous, the more uncontrovertibly true the imputation is, and the more disreputable the conduct that has been imputed.

So, every opinion in the field of government or religion contrary to any of those to which the force of government has been employed to give currency.

Thus it is that in a mixt Monarchy in a time of domestic tranquillity, the power of the Monarch is perpetually on the encrease until the mixt Monarchy becomes a pure and absolute one. Into the scale which contains the power of the Monarch, power is continually pouring itself from the fountain of corruptive influence: out of the scale which contains the power of the people, power is continually made to flow by the pressure by which the liberty of public discussion is forced out.

In the field of an all-comprehensive Code is included the field of operation of every modification of the Monarchical interest and every branch of Aristocratical interest. By alliance with the most powerful of all particular and sinister interests, the Monarchical, there is not any branch of the Aristocratical interest that is not capable of receiving advancement at the expence of the universal interest.

For every Office or other political good thing in the gift of a sharer in the Monarchical or in any branch of the Aristocratical interest, for every such good thing in possession there are perhaps twenty expectants: for every corruption-eater, twenty corruption-hunters: every such Office is therefore the source and centre of an atmosphere of corruptive influence.

Two and twenty millions a year is the amount of a part of the Offices and other good things in the gift of the Monarch alone:[1] not to speak of those which are in the gift of so many branches of the Aristocratical interest, all of them in a state of the closest alliance with the Monarchical interest. To find the aggregate amount of the force of corruptive influence, what multiplier shall we take as representative of the number of men corrupted by expectancy in addition to the number of those corrupted by the possession of all these several good things? Look over the Book exhibiting the Official establishment,[2] count the individual offices, thus may you get the number of those corrupted by possession: multiply that number by the multiplier fixt upon, thus will you have the number of those corrupted by expectancy. But if corrupted by the Monarch or by any branch of the Aristocracy, every man who of himself is rich or otherwise powerful is of himself the source of an atmosphere of corruptive influence.

Difference between Rod-of-iron men's and Corruptionists' arguments[3]
One thing the Monarchists of both classes—the rod-of-iron men and the corruptionists are agreed upon—this is that the Monarch, whoever he is, is most excellent. Most excellent—in what? in regard for the greatest happiness of the greatest number? No: [not][4] of this have they ventured any of them to assure us. The contrary would have been too palpable: not regard, but disregard for that object is on the part of that man of all others at once sure and conspicuous: demonstrated by the unchangeable nature of man, demonstrated by all history and all experience.

On this occasion distress of argument has drawn the Corruptionists into a self-contradiction which the rod-of-iron men have had no need to hamper themselves with. Most excellent? If so, in which of the three branches or elements of appropriate aptitude? aptitude with relation to the ever-unspecified end. Is it the moral branch? O yes—though the contrary as above stands demonstrated, that they will of course stickle for, the Corruptionists as well as the rod-of-iron men. But here the two divisions split. Ask them how it is with the idol in respect of appropriate intellectual aptitude and appropriate active talent, the answer is—not only not above par, but below it: below it, and to a degree which stations him on at least as low a level as that of

[1] It is unclear how Bentham calculated this figure. Perhaps he had in mind the sum of the supplies granted for the services of the year, which in 1820 had amounted to £20m., and in 1821 to over £19m.

[2] See for instance *The Royal Kalendar: and Court and City Register*, or *The British Imperial Calendar*.

[3] i.e. the supporters of pure monarchy and the supporters of mixed monarchy respectively.

[4] MS 'neither'.

a child in leading strings. Is there so much as a single act that he is capable of doing, so much as a single determination that he is capable of taking, by the guidance of his own judgment? Oh no: nothing can the great baby ever do but under the direction of his dry-nurse. Oh but the great baby may turn off his dry-nurses and choose fresh ones as often as he pleases: and if it has happened to the great baby to soil his sheets, the cast-off dry-nurse may be made to pay for it.

This supposition, howsoever exaggerated, has more of truth in it than most of their other principles. But what would be said of that man who for the management of his own affairs, [or][1] of the affairs of any individual for whom he had any regard, should choose an agent who, in his opinion, was thus deficient?

On one point the two parties are not so widely at variance. As to the dress of the baby and the furniture of the baby-house, they are pretty well agreed. The Monarch has an article of dress belonging to him called a crown: he has an article of furniture belonging to him called a throne. Neither of these implements would be fit for use had it not a certain splendor, and moreover a certain lustre, if there be any difference. Instead of splendor or lustre, if you are an Englishman, be careful not to say *glitter*: if you do, the emblem will be spoilt by it: the proof will be unconclusive. This proof may be stiled the *Jeweller's* proof; this principle, the Jeweller's principle. Of this proof—of these implements with these their attributes, the rod-of-iron man agrees as to the usefulness, nor will he bate one mite of them: but as to the needfulness, the indispensableness, it is not his way to lay quite so much stress upon it as the Corruptionist does. The less the force, the more urgent the need of delusion as well as of corruption.

In what way is it that these implements with their attributes contribute towards the ever-necessary and indubitable and never-defined effect—the superlative excellence? Is it by constituting it, by causing it to exist? Is it by causing the subject many to believe it exists when it does not, when it is not that quality that exists but its opposite? That this delusive quality has place, to the disgrace and sad affliction of the species, is as yet but too true. Wherever they see the external instruments of felicity heaped upon one object, there they fancy they see excellence: excellence, moral or intellectual, or both together: and on this vitiated state of the people's visual organs is the dependence of their adversaries of both classes for the success of the imposture.

How long will men be gulled, or affect to be gulled, by such impostures?

[1] MS 'of'.

All the misery under which men groan in all Monarch-ridden states, compared with the felicity which they enjoy in the Anglo-American United States, [has it][1] any other cause?

§ 20. *Case IV. Government a Representative Democracy. In this case, appropriate aptitude is in all its branches consummate*

Whatever be the form of government, a man will prefer his own felicity to that of all others put together: his wish and upon occasion his endeavour will be [to] get into his own hands all the several external instruments of felicity in the greatest quantity possible. For this purpose, his wish and upon occasion his endeavour will be, at the expence of all others, to committ depredation to the greatest extent possible. But upon every occasion that presents itself as favorable, this depredation will, at the hands of all those at whose expence it is exercised, produce the endeavour to escape from it—in a word [preserve themselves][2] from it—and to that end, in so far as it seems consistent with personal safety, resistance. But even by such endeavour at evasion, much more by resistance, on the one part, anger will be produced on the other: thereupon partly for securing the faculty of exercising the depredation, partly for the gratification of the passion of anger, oppression will be added, and by whatever causes it is produced in any the slightest degree, the disposition and the habit of exercising it in the greatest degree which circumstances admitt of will be continually on the encrease. Thus it is that by the innate propensities of man's nature, propensities necessary to the very existence of the species, every man is rendered, at least in desire and wish, and upon occasion in endeavour, a depredator and an oppressor.

In the situation of Monarch, the joint powers of his incorporeal instruments of misrule supply a man with corporeal instruments sufficient to enable him to grant to these desires the requisite correspondent gratification: and thus it is that the power being added to the desire, the correspondent effect is produced: the correspondent effect in the present case, the unquestionable sacrifice of the real felicity of the greatest number, of the millions, to the questionable felicity of this *one*.

In the instance of each individual member of that same community, whatever it be, this same sinister desire, the desire of making to the

[1] MS 'have they'.
[2] MS 'self-preservation'.

profit of his own happiness, the sinister sacrifice, has place: but in the instance of no such individual has the power any place: to his purpose the incorporeal requisites are wanting: and these being wanting, the corporeal instruments are so too. In his endeavours to secure himself against depredation and oppression, each man finds all others in general disposed to become co-operators and supporters: for against depredation and oppression at his own expence, no one of them can find any means of security but such as can not but afford the like security to other individuals in general. Accordingly in this case the power being added to the desire, the corresponding good effect has place. But in any endeavours he might use to exercise depredation and oppression at the expence of others in large multitudes, no man, who, not having the incorporeal instruments, has not at his command the corporeal ones, will find co-operators and supporters in number and force adequate to the purpose: accordingly in this case, the power not being added to the desire, the corresponding evil effect does not take place.

Though in all breasts these same propensities must be acknowledged to have place, and in all men the correspondent desires have place accordingly, and upon occasion to a greater or less extent become productive of correspondent acts, yet the difference between the strength of the desire in the one situation and the strength of the desire in the other situation is prodigious. In the case of those desires which have for their object corporeal gratification or exemption from corporeal suffering, the force of the desire is not taken away or lessened by the absence of hope, or say by the absence of expectation of the power of gratifying them: witness the desires of hunger and thirst. But in the case of those desires which have for their object any such complex good as is denoted by the appellations of *power*, or *money*, in the quantities attached to political situations, the absence of the corresponding expectation is capable of keeping the desire in a state in which it is compleatly inefficient, and even to the individual himself, for want of attention to what passes in his own mind, imperceptible.

Thus it is that the existence, not only of gratification, but even of desire itself, may depend upon a union with power. In the Anglo-American United States, Bonaparte might have been a Washington:[1] in France, a Washington might have been no more than a Bonaparte. In the breast of Washington, he being a man, it can not have been but that the desire of depredation or oppression or both, to be exercised on the large scale, must at times have had place, and been more or

[1] An allusion to George Washington (1732–99), President of the United States 1789–97.

less troublesome. Why? because the power of affording, to a greater or lesser extent, gratification to such desire could not have been wholly unaccompanied by hope. But, of the greater number of those by whose suffrages Washington was located in the situation which gave him the power of being what he became, take any one at random, no probability of his having ever been actuated or even troubled by any such desire will be found in his instance. Why? because in his breast there can not have been any hope of gratifying it.

Now then in a representative democracy, take any one member of the community, acting in the situation of a functionary of the constituent class, acting in the exercise of the supreme constitutive power—that power which is such with relation to the supreme operative. His desire is to afford to himself security against depredation and oppression: such being his ultimate desire, his intermediate desire is—to see located in the situation of his Representative, a man who, appropriate desire and power in all shapes included, appears to him likely to contribute in a degree more than any other man would to his possession of that same security: such is [his] desire, and such accordingly is his act:—the act by which he gives his vote.

Meantime his desire is—or at least in a certain case would be—to exercise and cause to be exercised for his own benefit, depredation and oppression to an indeterminate amount at the expence of all other men without distinction, and in particular at the expence of his fellow-citizens. But towards the gratification [of] this desire, he sees not among any considerable number of his fellow-Citizens, and in particular among the Candidates for the seat in question, any one to whom he can look to with any expectation of finding co-operation and support. What follows is—that having no expectation of promoting by his vote that particular and sinister interest which either is peculiar to himself, or can not be shared in with him but by a comparatively few, he restricts his endeavours to the employing of it in giving support to his share in the universal interest: to that interest which finds in every other voter an interest by which he is urged to contribute his endeavours towards the accomplishment of that same all-comprehensive and universally beneficial end: he gives his vote to that Candidate whom by all means taken together he expects to find willing and able to contribute in a greater degree than any other to the accomplishment of it.

In a representative Democracy, the Anglo-American United States for example, suppose a man by individual frame of mind, seconded by political Office, placed in a situation capable of inspiring him with the expectation, and through the expectation with the effectual desire, of putting himself in possession of some new mass of power, by means of which, at the expence of the greatest number of the members of the community, some great plan of depredation or oppression, or both, might, for his benefit, be carried into effect. Take for example, the President: and let the desired mass of power, pregnant with the faculty of exercising depredation and oppression in a manner gratifying to the oppressor, be the acquisition of the power given by the Constitutional Code to the President to be exercised by him over a territory subject to the United States, and not as yet admitted to a share in the Supreme Operative power over the whole, by sending Representatives of its own to the Supreme Operative Assembly, the Congress.[1] Suppose him possessing the support of a party, each individual toiling to be a sharer with him in the expected benefit. By no such party, under the existing Constitution, could any such effect be produced, without its constituting a majority in the Supreme Operative body—the Congress, and that majority persevering to join with him, the head, in this same pursuit, and that for a length of time in which several Elections would be. But an enterprize of this sort could not be carried into effect [without], nor present any means conducive to the purpose other than that of, a war—a war of aggression begun and continued and ended for that purpose. But of this war, all the Electors in the United States to the number of perhaps more than a million would have to share in the expence: while in the benefit, supposing it attended with any, a very small proportion of that number could have any expectation of being sharers. By concurring in the Election of a Representative, if any such there were disposed to concur in the prosecution of this so extensively pernicious scheme, each Elector would be concurring in a sacrifice of his own share in the universal interest: and this without any tolerably well-grounded prospect of promoting to any thing like an equal amount, if to any amount, any such supposed share of his in the particular and sinister interest.

There seems not therefore any the smallest probability, that in the situation in question, and by means of the instrument and source of power in question, it should ever enter into the head of any man to accomplish by means of a majority of votes the acquisition of any power of depredation and oppression—any power of misrule, any

[1] Bentham seems to have had in mind the case of Florida, which Spain ceded to the United States in July 1821. The President, as Commander in Chief, was able to establish a military regime in a ceded or conquered territory without the prior consent of Congress. In this instance, however, the President was directed to do so by Congress by an Act of 3 March 1821. An Act of Congress of 30 March 1822 established a territorial government in Florida, thereby terminating military rule, and authorizing the territory to send a delegate to Congress.

such power as that of carrying on government in the manner in which it is carried on elsewhere.

But if it could not in the situation of President, much less could it in any other situation. Much less could it in the situation, for example, of Governor in any one of these same United States. For in comparison of the power of the President of all the States, the power of Governor in that State in which he has most power is inconsiderable.

By Colonel Burr, who had been Vice President, and if he is to be believed, had the option of being President, the Representative Democracy of the United States was to have been improved into an absolute Monarchy; absolute Monarch, Colonel Burr. Improved? Yes: but how? by free Votes? by the free Votes of those by whom he had been freely made President? Oh, no: in how great a degree so ever conducive to the greatest happiness of the greatest number, by any such means the change was even in that breast in which the desire was strongest, and as the endeavour proved, not far from hopeless. Oh no: to the throne of the Anglo-American United States, the road he had pitched upon passed through the throne of Mexico. In his view, Mexicans were sheep, his own countrymen, lions. First he was to have been Emperor of Mexico. On the backs of the sheep, he was to have been brought home to subdue and tame the lions.[1]

§21. *General conclusion.*
In every Government but a Democracy, men are governed by their enemies, and those everlastingly implacable ones. Consequent Evils, all those producible by the consummation of inaptitude[2]

In every form of Government in which the possessors of the supreme operative power have not the great body of the people for their constituents, the situation of every possessor of or sharer in the supreme operative power is that of an enemy of the people.

In an absolute Monarchy, the situation of the Monarch is at all times that of an enemy to the people.

[1] Aaron Burr (1756–1836), Vice-President of the United States 1801–5, was responsible in 1805–7 for hatching a conspiracy in the western part of the United States. His objectives were never clarified, but it was alleged that he intended to overthrow Spanish power in Mexico, unite the conquered country with the western states and territories of the United States, and found an imperial dynasty. In 1807, on account of his activities, he was tried on a charge of treason, but acquitted, then tried on a charge of misdemeanour, and on a technicality again acquitted. Between 1808 and 1812 he toured Europe, where he became closely acquainted with Bentham.

[2] The section title continues, 'Comparative prosperity of England no objection to this', but no corresponding material has been indicated on the plan and none appears to have been written.

In a limited Monarchy, limited by a body acting as [a] Representation of the people, spurious or genuine, the situation of the Monarch is at all times that of an enemy to the people.

In a limited Monarchy, limited by a so stiled Representation of the people, spurious or genuine, the situation of a Representative of the people is that of an enemy to the people.

In a limited Monarchy, limited by two bodies, one composed of the Representatives of the people, spurious or genuine, the other of a set of men succeeding to one another upon the principle of genealogical succession, thereby rendered a perpetually existing Aristocratical body, the situation of every Member of that body is at all times that of an enemy to the people.

A people governed in any one of all these ways is a people governed by its enemies.

In comparison of that of a people governed by its own Delegates, the condition of a people governed in any of these ways will of necessity be, at all times, an infelicitous one.

Willingly to contribute to the support of, or even to submitt to, a government constituted in any of these ways, so long as any better is in prospect, in conjunction with a prospect of or probability of its accomplishment, is willingly to act in the character of an enemy of the people.

§ 22. *Monarchy continuing, the most perfect Representative system is inadequate to the prevention of misrule*

In the opinion of a considerable and gradually encreasing number of the people, the system of government as carried on in England is so bad—so adverse to the greatest happiness of the greatest number, that a man desirous of contributing his endeavour to that same greatest happiness can not without inconsistency fail of being desirous of seeing brought about a change: a change of a nature to add to that greatest happiness by substituting good to what is evil in the frame of government as it exists at present.

For this purpose, two changes are continually brought to view: one under the name of Parliamentary Reform, the other under the name of Revolution. By Parliamentary Reform is meant a change in the mode in which the people are said to be represented: by causing the men who, under the name of Representatives of the people, exercise a principal share of the power of government to be located and dislocable by the great body [of] those whom they are said to represent instead of a comparatively minute portion of it. By

Revolution is meant locating in the situation of King of this political State an individual different from him by whom it is filled at present.

As to the answers, they have already been given in generals and in substance. But as the mind finds a convenience and a relief in having before it its own conceptions in a determinate form, the following positions may upon the whole not be without their use.

First as to Parliamentary Reform.

Parliamentary Reform has been proposed in two modes: one stiled radical: the other stiling itself sometimes moderate, sometimes temperate.

By radical reform is meant the substituting to the Commons House as at present organized a House of Commons organized upon the principle of a Representative Democracy—but leaving in full possession of their power the Monarch and the House of Lords.

By moderate reform is meant the taking the power of the House of Commons out of the hands of the present Oligarchy and placing it in a regular and equal sort of Aristocracy, leaving King and Lords in possession of their power as in the former case.

If no good fit to be satisfied with or no permanent and adequate remedy to the existing evils could be brought about by radical reform, still less could it by moderate reform.

Note now the change that would be brought by radical reform: supposing no other change effected than that which is expressed.

1. The King would remain. Therefore so long as he retained his power, no change could be effected that were adverse to his interest. But every change that would be beneficial to the interest of the people, contributory to the greatest happiness of the greater number of them, would it has been seen be adverse to his interest. For his existence it has been seen is incompatible with the greatest happiness of the greatest number: unchangeably adverse to their interest. Therefore the King alone would suffice to prevent any considerable good from being done, any effectual remedy from being applied. Take in turn the whole catalogue of abuses. Look over it from beginning to end. Not one is there in the continuance of which he has not an interest: not one of them is there which it would not be against his interest to part with. Not one of them is there which on any reasonable ground he could be expected to part with if he could help it. The King, were he alone left, would suffice to shut an everlasting door against all remedy.

2. The House of Lords would remain. But of all the Members of that House, there can not be one who, so long as he is one, will not be a sharer in that sinister interest which, as has been seen, stands irremovably attached to the situation of Monarch. The House of Lords

alone would therefore suffice to shut an everlasting door against all remedy.

But if for this purpose, the King by his single force, as also the House of Lords by its single force, would either of them suffice: much less can they fail to suffice by their conjunct force.

'Yes'—(it may be said)—'Reform, if radical, will suffice: it will suffice without further change. Not in any shape, and in particular not in this shape, can Parliamentary Reform have been brought about, unless and until both King and Lords have been brought into acquiescence. But the use and only use of this Reform is to remove the existing abuses: in this one point is concentrated all the effect looked to from it: the powers sufficient to produce the cause will be sufficient to produce the effect.'

Answer. No: it will not suffice. By the supposition, the office of King will remain: the power of the King will remain untouched: the power of the Lords, their veto, will remain untouched. But from the office of King a quantity of the matter of wealth, all of it operating upon the Representatives of the people in the character of matter of corruptive influence, is inseparable: in a large proportion it will suffice to prevent the abolition of the mass of depredation and oppression at present established: and whatsoever it is not able to prevent the immediate abolition of, it will suffice to bring back in a longer or shorter course of time. To produce this effect not so much as a single act that can with propriety be called an act of corruption (it has been shewn) is necessary: not so much as a single act of that sort on either part.[1]

To confirm the existence of the Kingly office would be to sanction a principle opposite to the only justifiable end of government. It would be [to] continue in the hands of a functionary, the hostility of whose interest to the universal interest has been shewn as well by theory to be necessary, as by recent experience to be radical and unchangeable, the power of giving effect to that same sinister interest.

You who propose the continuance of the state of things by which the mischief has been done, by what means is it your expectation that the reform you propose should be effected? You who propose the accomplishment of an end, how is it that you can avoid proposing the adoption of the means, the only means, by which it can be effected? Parliamentary Reform or any reform you can make or think of—will it change man's nature? Finding in every office an appetite for power as intense as in dogs an appetite for bones, will the word *reform* extirpate it?

[1] In the text, Bentham noted: '☛ A list being made of their pernicious powers, here repeat it or refer to it.' No such list appears to have been written for 'Supreme Operative'.

No such Reform can be carried into effect but by a power sufficient to go further, and abolish the Office of him with whose means of happiness the greatest happiness of the greatest number is incompatible, and the power of that unelected fraction of the Sovereign Assembly whose particular and [sinister] interest is not less at variance with the universal interest than the particular and sinister interest of the Monarch.

Leave the two Offices untouched—you leave an injured King and an injured House of Lords. Now leave where you find him a man enraged with the sense of that which in his view is injury, and you leave him with the means of self-reinstatement and vengeance in his hands. Easier, much easier, is the whole of the work than this same half. The whole is eminently simple: the half is as eminently complicated.

Leave the half in existence, you leave unremoved all the moral filth, all the intellectual absurdity, which defiles it: the same system of shameless and indefatigable lying. The lies you can not leave untouched, but the same practical inferences which have been at all times deduced from them will continue to be deduced. You cannot leave in office a King but you leave in Office a functionary who can not do wrong: that is to say who has, by the universal declaration of all who have at any time thus spoken of him, possessed and exercised the power of converting into right whatsoever wrong his sinister interest and vices ever prompted him to committ. You can not continue the office in existence without endeavouring to give perpetuity to by far the foulest system of immorality as well as the grossest system of absurdity that the art of man ever engendered.

When on the part [of] King and Lords acquiescence has in any way been produced, to leave them in possession of their power is to leave them with arms in their hands, in a condition to fight the matter over again. Very generous this: indeed, but to whom? To the one and to the three hundred: to these hundreds, generous: but to four times as many millions, still more ungenerous.

The sources of waste and corruption are here all of them indicated and enumerated and delineated. Dry them up all, dry them up without exception, to all this mass of evil you may substitute the opposite and correspondent good with a sacrifice comparatively inconsiderable of existing interests and expectations. Keep one of them undesiccated, for every one so left undesiccated you defray a proportionable mass of existing possessions, you defeat a proportionable mass of existing expectations.

On Revolution considered as a remedy against misrule, a syllable is almost too much. Suppose it effected, what good would be effected by it or with it? Suppose the present King removed, where should be found a better? No where in the ordinary course of events: already we are threatened with a worse.[1]

Proposed in the character of a remedy, Revolution supposes the cause of the evil to lie in the individual. But it does not lie in the individual—it never has lain in the individual: it lies in the species: the species must be extinct or nothing is done.

As well might you think of doing away the mischief of the Inquisition system by dislocating one Grand Inquisitor and locating another in his place: or that of the Press-licensing system by removing one licensor and locating another in his place.

By no man surely by whom Revolution has been mentioned can it have been seriously meant to be proposed. One of the flowers of Oratory, in this character alone has the word Revolution ever shewn itself.[2]

Think not that because the bringing the present system of corruption to the present degree of perfection, the sinister sacrifice to its present vicinity to the point of consummation, it has taken up [134][3] years, reckoning from the Revolution, whatever small and inadequate defalcation from the mass of abuse could be made by Parliamentary reform alone, could have any such continuance. At the Revolution, taking the requisite time for it, there existed the possibility of screwing up the amount of the depredation to 800 millions. But in addition to these 800 millions, could another 800 millions be added in the same time or in any time? Oh no, all that stock has been expended.[4]

[1] George IV was the present King, and Frederick Augustus (1763–1827), Duke of York and Albany, heir to the throne.

[2] There is no text corresponding to the following marginal summary, which belongs here: 'By change of Monarch remedy can no more be applied than by change of Ministry.'

[3] MS '132'. Bentham was counting from the Glorious Revolution of 1688 to the date of his writing, 1822.

[4] Bentham was alluding to the National Debt, which had its origins in the wars of the 1690s, and which, according to the *Finance Accounts for the year ended 5 January 1822*, then stood at £802m. The argument in the marginal summary diverges from that in the text at this point: 'Think not that because after the Revolution in 1688 it has taken up 134 [years] to bring the sinister sacrifice to its present pitch, it would take up the same time to reproduce the quantity of evil removed by a second Revolution now. Suppose all the sources of waste dried up, the quantity of expenditure necessitated by moral obligation, by regard for greatest happiness, would supply a fund of corruptive influence sufficient to restore in a few years as much waste as had been defalcated.'

§ 23. *Concluding Aphorisms*

1. In the scale of appropriate moral aptitude[a] a man's altitude is, naturally speaking, inversely as his altitude in the scale of prosperity, meaning that which is composed of the contiguous and conjunct scales of power, opulence and factitious honor.

2. So, in the scale of appropriate intellectual aptitude: necessary external means of information being supposed equal.

3. So, in the scale of appropriate active aptitude.

4. On all three accounts taken together, the place of the absolute Monarch will, in the aggregate of the three scales of appropriate aptitude, naturally be at the lowest point.

5. The place of the limited Monarch will naturally be at a point above that of the absolute Monarch, but below that of a member of a purely Aristocratical government.

6. Among limited Monarchs, the place of each one in the aggregate scale of appropriate aptitude will be inversely as his altitude in the scale of prosperity, and in particular as his altitude in the scale of power: directly as the quantity substracted from his power by the aggregate of the limitations applying to it.

7. The place of a Member of a purely Aristocratical government will naturally be above that of a limited Monarch, but below that of an average individual not belonging to the class of those functionaries among whom supreme rule is shared.

8. In the particular scale of appropriate moral aptitude, the place of a Member of a purely Aristocratical government will naturally be even below that of the most mischievous of those designated by the common appellative of malefactors: and the importance of this branch of appropriate aptitude being in comparison of the two others so much greater, thereby also in the aggregate scale of appropriate aptitude.

9. The place of the Member of a supremely operative Representative body in a Representative [democracy] in the aggregate scale of appropriate aptitude will naturally be above that of an average individual taken from the class of non-functionaries.

[a] Aptitude with relation to the functions of a functionary of government in a government having for its ground the greatest happiness principle.

SUPPLEMENT TO SUPREME OPERATIVE

In a limited, say rather a mixt, Monarchy, the Aristocracy are not in practice co-equal with but dependent on and instruments of the Monarchy

In England the Borough-mongers are under the King, not the King under the Borough-mongers.

The King (it has been said) is in a state of subjection to the Borough-mongers. The party by whom this notion is adopted is the party of the people: it is on every occasion assumed, and argued upon as a principle. In relation to it, two questions will here present themselves. 1. Is it correct? 2. If incorrect, what is the cause of its currency?

Question 1. Is it true? Answer. It is untrue. That the two powers act not in constant union, thus far is true. But, on each occasion whatsoever be the course taken by the union, it is by the will of the King, not by the will of any [other] power, that that course is determined: not by the will of any other power whatsoever be the situation of it, or by what name so ever denominated.

By Borough-mongers are meant the aggregate of the several individuals by whom the seats in the Commons House are filled. The cause why this denomination is employed will be mentioned in its place.

What is here assumed is—that the Lords House in its corporate capacity is in practice in a state of subjection to the Commons House. Thus much is true, manifest and undisputed.[1]

What is also assumed is that in a very large proportion the occupiers of the seats in the Commons House are located by individuals who have seats in the Lords House. This also is manifest and undisputed.

The simple truth of the matter is this. It is by force and intimidation that the conduct of the people at large is determined. It is by corruptive influence that the conduct of the majority in each of the two Houses of Parliament is determined: in the House of Commons in the first instance, and then in the House of Lords: the will of the Lords following of course that of the King and the Commons.

But the matter of corruption—on whose will does the application of it depend? On that of the Minister. And the Minister—on whose will does his existence in that situation depend? On the King's.

[1] In the text, Bentham noted, '☛ Quere whether to state the proofs', but no material appears to have been written.

Let the King give to what man he will the disposal of the matter of corruptive influence, the will of that individual is sure to be done by the majority in both Houses.

Events may happen—events which for a time may make the King see a convenience in substituting to a Minister more agreable to him, a Minister less agreable to him. But in this temporary exception there is nothing that detracts from the truth, to all practical purposes, of the general rule. In this there is nothing more than what is every now and then happening in the most absolute governments, that of Turkey not excepted.

Be this as it may, the fact is—that whatsoever is done, it is with the King's will that it is done: in each instance it may or may not have originated in the King's will: but in whose will so ever what is proposed originated, if it be against the King's will, it is not done.

The question here is—what in this respect is the general and habitual course of the government. Of the few exceptions that by careful inquiry might perhaps be found, the effect will rather be to prove the rule than to disprove it. No Monarchy so absolute, but that exceptions in this or that instance might be found in it.

Of the absoluteness of the King's power, a conclusive proof was that which was held up to view in a Commons House Debate in the Session of 1822.[a] Motion by Mr. Brougham: object of it, holding up to view what is called the influence of the Crown: that is to say the absoluteness of the King's power in respect of giving determination to the proceedings of the two sets of functionaries who in profession and form are sharers with him in the supreme operative. Proof this. The Prime Minister is the nominee and instrument. When once a man has been decidedly located in the situation of Prime Minister, the Commons House, a vast majority of it, vote according to his will, after having but a few days before, namely when he was not Minister but in opposition, voted against it.

Instances have happened in which the King has discarded a Minister whom he had rather have kept, and placed a Minister whom

[a] June 1822. Black Dwarf, July 3 1822.[1]

[1] On 24 June 1822, in the House of Commons, Henry Peter Brougham (1778–1868), created Baron Brougham and Vaux in 1830, had moved, 'That the Influence now possessed by the Crown is unnecessary for maintaining its constitutional prerogatives, destructive of the independence of parliament, and inconsistent with the well government of the realm' (for his speech see Hansard, *Parliamentary Debates*, vii. 1265–99). Bentham based his account in this and the following paragraph and the accompanying note on an article entitled 'Historical Characteristics of "The Working of the System" in the House of Commons', published in *The Black Dwarf* of 3 July 1822 (ix. 13–16), which carried extracts from and a commentary on Brougham's speech.

he had rather not have appointed. True: but the Minister who was not agreable to him never for any considerable length of time has he been kept in Office.[a]

In England ever since the accession of the first English-born King since the Revolution, viz. George the 3, there has been a party in opposition to the Minister of the King's choice, and thereby to the King. The Ministry for the time being they have never been able to attack without attacking in some part or other the system of abuse and sinister sacrifice, and thereby and so far serving the cause of the people. But in so far as they have so done, they have been giving constant offence to the King, while their more prosperous antagonists have been occupied in the doing of his will in so far as it has been done. In the very nature of their situation they could not therefore do any thing against the King and his Minister without doing something for the people, and professing some principle by which a sort of continual warrant could be afforded for whatsoever they were doing. This principle however never could be the greatest happiness principle, since by that, if followed up with any consistency, the grand and universal and constant object of their wishes would be reduced to that which would be nothing in their eyes. Prevented then from being either Absolute Monarchists or Democrats, they have been all along confined to a middle course by which they were determined to be Aristocrats. According to them the form of government must remain the same: for to their interest the preservation of it is not less necessary than to the interest of the men in power, their antagonists.

[a] Anno 1806. Lord Grenville, Mr. Fox and Mr. Addington were in Office together.[1] Lord Grenville and Mr. Fox were men disagreable to the then King: Lord Grenville on one account; Mr. Fox on another: Lord Grenville from his personal demeanour: Mr. Fox from the too great popularity of the principles professed by him. Mr. Addington was a man found to be agreable to a King, whosoever the King were. A favorable opportunity for getting rid of them was watched for, and found. Lord Grenville was dismissed: Mr. Fox was dismissed. Mr. Addington was retained. It was the desire of Lord Grenville that the oppression under which the Catholics had so long been suffering should be removed; this was also the desire of Mr. Fox. But the will of the King was opposite and inflexible. He refused to adopt the measure, and rid himself of the authors.[2]

[1] In the Ministry of All the Talents, which came into office in February 1806, William Wyndham Grenville (1759–1834), first Baron Grenville, was First Lord of the Treasury, Charles James Fox (1749–1806) was Foreign Secretary, and Henry Addington (1757–1844), who had been created Viscount Sidmouth in 1805, was initially Lord Privy Seal and later Lord President of the Council.

[2] George III forced the Ministry to resign in March 1807 over the issue of Catholic emancipation. Fox in fact had died in September 1806, while Sidmouth, though supportive of the King on this question and eager to remain in office, was excluded from the incoming Portland administration.

But the hands in which the power is must be different: they must be their hands: and when in their hands, the form must be such as will keep it there: an Aristocracy of which they are Members must be not only continued: but strengthened: strengthened in such sort that to displace them shall be no longer in the King's power. Such accordingly was the object of the East India Bill brought in by Charles Fox in the course of the short reign to which this Bill put an end. The object of it was to transfer the Patronage of that government into their hands.[1]

By the will of the Minister have the wills of the majority in both Houses been at all times determined: and such will be the state of wills, so long as the government remains in the form it wears at present. Why? because such is the state of interests—of interests and of the means of affording satisfaction to the correspondent desires.

[1] The Fox-North Coalition, which formed the administration from April to December 1783, was dismissed from office by George III when Fox's East India Bill, which was denounced as an attempt by Fox to appropriate for himself the patronage of the East India Company, was defeated in the House of Lords.

CONSTITUTIONAL CODE RATIONALE

CHAPTER 1. FIRST PRINCIPLES INDICATIVE OF THE FOUNDATION OF THIS PROPOSED CONSTITUTIONAL CODE[1]

§ 1. *First principles described in general terms*

To whatever portion of the field of thought and action the literary work in question belongs, it has been found convenient, and is accordingly usual, to place at the beginning of it some opinion or opinions, embracing in their extent the whole of the portion in question, or as large a portion of it as may be.

On this occasion a number of mutually related expressions are found needful or convenient, and accordingly in fact are usually employed.

Take for example—First principles—Leading principles—First lines—Outlines—Positions—Axioms—Aphorisms.

If in writing, in the composition of the work, the design be to recommend a certain course of action as ought to be, or say proper to be, pursued for the attainment of a certain end, thereupon come certain other words and phrases of correspondently extensive import. Of this sort are Ends—Objects of pursuit—Means—Obstacles—Helps—Counterforces acting in opposition to the obstacles.

Where the object of the inquiry and discussion is what is the course of action which with relation to the field in question is proper to be pursued, a necessarily concomitant object of regard throughout is—the course actually pursued: pursued in the community which the writer has in view.

If the course actually pursued is on all points the same with the course proper to be pursued, it is well: and unless on the supposition that in default of apposite warning and instruction a departure, to an extent more or less considerable, may have place, any work on the subject in question would be useless, and by him in whose opinion such coincidence has place can not consistently be undertaken.

In regard to some of the above expressions—viz. ought to be done—ought not to be done—is proper to be done—is not proper to be [done]—one matter of fact there is which on every occasion it may be of use to the reader to have in mind. This is that every thing of which any such expression can be in an immediate way the expression is a certain state of mind on the part of him by whom the expression is

[1] An earlier draft of this chapter, dated 26–7 July 1822, is at UC xxxvi. 80–5. Other related fragments are at UC xxxvi. 78–9 (21 July 1822) and clx. 237 (22 July 1822).

employed: the state of his mind with relation to the subject matter of the discourse whatsoever it happens to be.

This state of mind will be the state of one or more of his intellectual faculties—in one word his understanding—or the state of his sensitive faculties—in one word feelings—or the state of his volitional faculties—in one word his will, his desires, his wishes.

Thus in the case at present on the carpet. When I say the greatest happiness of the whole community ought to be the end or object of pursuit in every branch of the law—of the political rule of action—and of the constitutional branch in particular—what is it that I express—this and no more: namely that it is my wish, my desire, to see it taken for such by those who in the community in question are actually in possession of the powers of government: taken for such, in such sort that on the occasion of every arrangement taken by them in the exercise of such their powers, their endeavour shall be to render such their course of action contributory to the attainment of that same end, conducive to that same end, contributory to the obtainment of it. Such then is the state of that faculty in me which is termed the will: such is the state of those particular acts or modifications of that faculty which are termed wishes or desires, and which have their immediate efficient causes in corresponding feelings—in corresponding pleasures and pains such as on the occasion in question the imagination brings to view.

In making this assertion I make a statement relative to a matter of fact, namely that which at the time in question is passing in the interior of my own mind: how far this assertion, this statement, is correct, is a matter on which it belongs to the reader, if it be worth his while, to form his judgment.

If, admitting the existence of this desire on my part, it be his desire to learn from me how it happens to have place, in other words what are the efficient causes, I am ready to give him the information he desires, if in his estimate it be worth his while to receive it.[1]

Such then being the desire, truly or falsely expressed by me, but at any rate expressed by me—in his breast has that same desire a place? If so, then may it be worth his while to apply his intention to the course herein marked out by me under the notion of its being correspondent and contributory and conducive to the attainment of that same end. On the other hand, if so it be that that same desire has no place in his breast, on that supposition, generally speaking, it will be a useless trouble to him to pay any further attention to any thing contained in it.

[1] Bentham added at this point, 'Here give in a Note the three efficient causes', but none appears to have been written.

To this observation one exception it is true there is, and it is this: namely that, if the end in view which it is his wish to see pursued is different from this, it may be of use to him to take note of the arrangements here proposed as conducive to the end pursued by me, for the purpose of taking or rec[om]mending such different and opposite arrangements as may prevent the attainment of the end proposed by me and procure or promote the attainment of that other end, be it what it may, which is more agreable to his wishes: say for example, the greatest happiness of some one member of the community in question, or of some other number smaller than the majority of the whole number of the members.

So again when I say—in the breast of every ruler, on the occasion of the arrangements taken by him in the field of government, the actual end or object of pursuit has, in the instance of every such arrangement, been his own greatest happiness, and that in such sort as that wherever in his judgment there has been a competition between his happiness and that of all the other members of the community in question taken together, he has on each occasion given to his own happiness the preference over theirs, and used his endeavours to give encrease to his own happiness, in whatsoever degree the aggregate of their happiness may in his judgment be lessened by it,—in saying thus, what I have been doing [is] exhibiting the state of my own mind viewed in another point of view: viewed as it were in another part of it—my judgment, the judicial faculty. I have given that as my opinion: an opinion of which I am prepared to bring to view the efficient causes.[a]

[a] While I am a-doing, I observe another law-writer who, on the score of my so doing, taxes me with egotism, or to use another word, with Dogmatism: meaning by dogmatism the doing something which it is his wish, his desire, should not be done.[1]

In answer to this charge what I say is—that either a man must do thus, or he must forbear to write at all: for that it is not possible for man to write without doing thus.

But on this occasion what I say is not confined to self-defence against the charge of Dogmatism—it has for its object the giving warning against that form of discourse on which the imputation expressed by the word Dogmatism does really and properly attach.

In saying as above the proper end of government is the greatest happiness of all or, in case of competition and to the extent of the competition, the greatest happiness of

---

[1] The author in question was Jean Baptiste Antoine Hyacinthe Blondeau (1784–1854), the French jurist, who in his work *Essais sur quelques points de Législation et de Jurisprudence*, Paris, 1819, p. 47n, had written: 'Cet auteur [Bentham], qui, dans le chapitre II de ses *Principes généraux de Législation*, combat avec tant de force les Dogmatiques, nous paraît avoir lui-même admis, comme un dogme, ce principe: *les Lois doivent avoir pour but l'intérêt général*.' The essay 'Principes généraux de Législation' formed the first part of *Traités de législation civile et pénale* (i. 1–145); Blondeau may however have had in mind Chapter III, see especially i. 21.

§2. *First principles enumerated*

1. Position—Axiom. The right and proper end of government in every political community is the greatest happiness of all the individuals of which it is composed.

Say in other words, the greatest happiness of the greatest number.

In speaking of the correspondent first principle, call it the greatest-happiness principle.

In speaking of this end of government, call it the right and proper end of government.

2. Position—Axiom. The actual end of government is in every political community the greatest happiness of those, whether one or many, by whom the powers of government are exercised.[1]

In general terms the proof of this position may be referred to particular experience, as brought to view by the history of all nations.

This experience may be termed *particular* inasmuch as the particular class of rulers is the only class concerned in it to which it bears reference: this may be called the experimental or practical proof.

For further proof reference may be made to the general, indeed the all-comprehensive, principle of human nature. The position which takes this fact for its subject may be termed an axiom and the expression given to it is as follows.

the greatest number, it seems to me that I have made a declaration of peace and good will to all men.[2]

On the other hand were I to say the proper end of government is the greatest happiness of some one, naming him, or of some few, naming them, it seems to me that I should be making a declaration of war against all men, with the exception of that one or of those few.

Be the subject what it may, unless it be allowed to me to say what in relation to that subject are my judgments, my feelings or my desires, I can not say any thing in relation to it: and as to my judgment on each occasion, not giving it as on every occasion I do for more than it is worth, it seems to me that it is on my part no unreasonable claim to be allowed—free from every imputation conveyed or endeavoured to be conveyed by the word Dogmatism—to be allowed to give it.

This being the basis on which all legislation and all morality rests, these few words written in hopes of clearing it of all obscurity and ambiguity, of all doubts and difficulties, will not, I hope, be regarded as misapplied or applied in waste. On no other occasion shall any thing said by any other writer be taken by me for the subject matter of disputation.

---

[1] In the marginal summary, Bentham added: 'Corresponding principle: Rulers' object-indicating principle. Corresponding end or object: sinister end or object.'

[2] Luke 2: 14.

CHAPTER 1

In the general tenor of human life, in every human breast, self-regarding interest is predominant over all other interests put together. More shortly thus, self-regard is predominant: or thus, self-regarding interest is predominant over all other interests put together: or thus, self-preference has place every where.

This position may to some eyes present itself in the character of an axiom: as such self-evident, and not standing [in] need of proof. In other [eyes] as a position or proposition which, how clearly so ever true, still stands in need of proof.

To deliver a position in the character of an axiom is to deliver it under the expectation that either it will not be controverted at all, or that he by whom it is controverted will not, in justification of the denial given by him to it, be able to advance any thing by which the unreasonableness of his opinion or pretended opinion will not be exposed. Of this stamp are the axioms laid down by Euclid.[1] In the axioms so laid by him, nothing of dogmatism will, it is believed, be found.

For the satisfaction [of] those by whom this last account of it is preferred, reference may be made to the *existence* of the species as being of itself a proof—and *that* a conclusive one. For, after exception made of the case of children not arrived at the age at which they are capable of going alone, or adults reduced by infirmity to a helpless state, take any two individuals, A and B, and suppose the whole care of the happiness of A to be confined to the breast of B, A himself not having any part in it, and the whole care of the happiness of B confined to the breast of A, B himself not having any part in it—and this to be the case throughout, it will soon appear that in this state of things the species could not continue in existence, and that a few months, not to say weeks or days, would suffice for the annihilation of it.

Of all modes in which, for the governance of one and the same individual, the two faculties could be conceived as placed in different seats, sensation and consequent desire in one breast, judgment and consequent action in another, this is the most simple. If, as has with less constant truth been said of the blind leading the blind, both would in such a state of things be continually falling into the ditch,[2] much more frequent and more speedily fatal would be the falls supposing the separation to have place upon any plan more complex: suppose the care of the happiness of A, being taken altogether from A, were divided between B and C: the happiness of B and C being provided for

[1] The celebrated geometrician, who lived at Alexandria during the reign of the first Ptolemy (323–283BC).

[2] Matthew 15: 14; Luke 6: 39.

in the same complex manner: and so on, the greater the complication, the more speedy, could there be any difference, would the destruction be, and the more flagrant the absurdity of a supposition assuming the existence of such a state of things.[1]

Note that if in the situation of ruler the truth of this position held good in no more than a bare majority of the whole number of instances, it would suffice in the character of a ground for practice: in the character of a consideration by which the location of the several portions in the aggregate mass of political power should be determined: for in the way of induction, it is only by the greater, and not [by][2] the lesser, number of instances that the general conclusion can reasonably be determined: in a word, mathematically speaking, the probability of a future contingent event is in the direct ratio of the number of past instances in which an event of the same sort has happened to the number of those in which it has not happened—it is in this direct ratio, and not in the inverse.

If human beings were so circumstanced, if such were the condition of human beings, that the happiness of no one being came in competition with that of any other—that is to say, if the happiness of each or of any one could receive encrease to an unlimited amount without having the effect of producing decrease in the happiness of any other, then the above expression might serve without limitation or explanation. But on every occasion the happiness of every individual is liable to come into competition with the happiness of every other. If, for example, in a house containing two individuals, for the space of a month there be a supply of food barely sufficient to continue for that space of time the existence of one of them—not merely the happiness of each but the existence of each stands in competition with, and is incompatible with, the existence of the other.

Hence it is, that to serve for all occasions, instead of saying the greatest happiness of all, it becomes necessary to say the greatest happiness of the greatest number.

If however instead of the word *happiness* the word *interest* is employed, the phrase universal interest may be employed as corresponding indifferently to the interest of the greatest number as to the interest of all.[3]

[1] Bentham noted at this point, 'See Appendix No. 1. Dissertation on Self-preference: proving the necessity of it in the human and every other sensitive being', but no material under this heading appears to have been written.

[2] MS 'in'.

[3] Bentham noted at this point: '☛ Insert relation between the import of the word *happiness* and the import of the word *interest*.' For a discussion of this relation see for instance *An Introduction to the Principles of Morals and Legislation*, ed. J.H. Burns and H.L.A. Hart, London, 1970 (*CW*), pp. 12–13.

CHAPTER 1

In the eyes of every impartial arbiter, writing in the character of legislator, and having exactly the same regard for the happiness of every member of the community in question as for that of every other, the greatest happiness of the greatest number of the members of that same community can not but be recognized in the character of the right and proper, and sole right and proper, end of government: end, or say object of pursuit.

For the designation of the opposite or reverse of what is right and proper, the adjunct sinister may, in consideration of the mutual relation borne to each other by the two terms taken in the original physical sense, be expressed.

Accordingly, in so far as between the happiness of the greatest number and the happiness of any lesser number any competition and incompatibility has place, if the greatest happiness of the greatest number be taken for the only right and proper end of government, the happiness of any lesser number, coming into competition and being incompatible with the happiness of the greatest number, may be stiled a *sinister* end of government: end, or say object of pursuit.[1]

If, as above, so it be, that, in the situation of a ruler, whatsoever that situation be, the conduct of no man can at any moment reasonably be expected to be determined by any interest that at that same moment stands in opposition to that which in his conception is his own individual interest, [it][2] follows that for causing it to take any direction in which it will be subservient to the universal interest, the nature of man, the nature of the case, affords no other method than that which consists in the bringing of the particular interest of rulers into accordance with the universal interest.

Here then we have a third principle of the first rank in addition to the two former ones.

Call it the Means-prescribing, or Junction-of-interests prescribing, principle.

To make a third, e'en join the former two.

The first declares what ought to be: the next, what is: the last, the means of bringing what is into accordance with what ought to be.

Meantime this junction of interests, how can it be effected? The nature of the case admitts but of one method, which is the destroying the influence and effect of whatever sinister interest the situation of

[1] There is no text corresponding to the following marginal summary, which belongs here: 'Correspondently every particular interest the advancement of which is incompatible with ditto of the universal ditto, a sinister [interest]. The sacrifice of every such sinister interest to the right and proper interest, the right and proper sacrifice. The sacrifice of the right and proper interest to any sinister ditto, a sinister sacrifice.'

[2] MS 'in'.

the individual may expose him to the action of: this being accomplished he will thereby be virtually divested of all such sinister interest: remains as the only interest whereby his conduct can be determined, his right and proper interest: that interest which consists in the share he has in the universal interest, which is the same thing as to say that interest which is in accordance with the universal interest taken in the aggregate.

Be the act what it may, there are two modes in either of which a man may be divested of the interest requisite to his performance of it: one is the over-powering the force of whatsoever body of interests may be acting on him in a direction tending to engage him in the performance of it, in other words destroying the effect of all sinister interests by the application of a preponderant right and proper interest: this is the direct mode. The other is—the divesting him of the power of performing that same act. For that which in his own eyes it is not in a man's power to perform, it can not in his own eyes be his interest to endeavour to perform: it can never be a man's interest to expend time and labour without effect. Considered in its application to a man's interest, this mode may be termed an *indirect* mode.

Thus it is that by one and the same arrangement, application may be made to both the will and the power: at the same time and in either mode, the requisite junction of interests is capable of being effected or secured.

A question that now immediately presents itself: [how] is it that to any individual, supposing him invested by the Constitution in question with the supreme power, any inducement can by that same Constitution be applied of sufficient force to over-power any sinister interest to the operation of which, by his situation, he stands exposed? Inducements operating on interests are all of them reducible to two denominations—punishment and reward. Punishment in every shape his situation suffices to prevent his standing exposed to: so likewise reward. For being by the supposition invested with supreme power, the matter of reward can not be applied to him in any shape in which he has not already at his command whatsoever it would be in the power of the Constitution by any particular arrangement to confer on him. To him who has the whole, it is useless to give this or that part.

To a question to this effect, the only answer that can be given is sufficiently manifest. By reward an individual so situated can not be acted upon: for there exists no other individual in the community at whose hand he can receive more than he has in his own. By punishment, as little—for there exists no individual at whose hands he is obliged to receive or will receive any such thing.

The result is that in a Monarchy no such junction of interests can be effected, and that therefore by no means can Monarchy be rendered conducive to the production of the greatest happiness of the greatest number: nor therefore, according to the greatest happiness principle, be susceptible of the denomination of a good form of government.[1]

[1] The marginal summary expands on the text at this point: 'Under a pure Monarchy, the sinister sacrifice is unintermittingly performed. The greatest happiness of one is the end constantly aimed at: the greatest happiness of the greatest number constantly sacrificed. The force of his share in the universal interest continually mastered by ditto of his separate and sinister interest. The sinister sacrifice constantly performed to an indefinite amount. To an indefinite extent, Misrule substituted to Good Rule.'

CHAPTER 2. THE JUNCTION OF INTERESTS, HOW EFFECTED: OR SINISTER INTERESTS, HOW OVERPOWERED

For the effecting of this junction—for the removal of those obstacles to the greatest happiness of the greatest number—the following are the expedients which the nature of the case presents to view.

1. Rendering the possessors of supreme operative power eventually punishable for any abuse of it: i.e. for any act whereby the sinister sacrifice is to any amount effected or endeavoured to be effected.

This expedient supposes the existence of another: namely the lodging of the supreme operative power in more hands than one: the taking it, considered as a whole or aggregate, into shares: and that in such sort as to give to one individual one share, to other individuals in whatever number, to each of them another share, in other words to break this integer into fractions: or say in a single word, to *fractionalize* or fractionize it.

If it be in such sort fractionized as that an individual whose share is so large as to preserve him at one time from being subjected to punishment may at another time have no power at all, or at any rate no power such as to preserve him from exposure to punishment, the problem is accomplished. And in such an arrangement there is nothing either unexampled or peculiarly difficult: nothing but what is familiar in practice.

Resource 2. Placing, to the greatest possible extent, in the situation of rulers those over whom rule is to be exercised.

Could this expedient be employed—employed and with advantage throughout—no need would there be of recourse to any other. But this would be—not government, but the absence of all government. For a time at least it might serve for hundreds: it could never serve for millions.

Two circumstances are seen at once, either of which suffices to render it physically impossible.

1. To act in concert, it would be necessary the whole multitude should at the same time be in the same place, and that in such sort that each one should be within sight and hearing of all the rest.

2. It would be necessary for them to give to the business of government, and in particular the business which consists in settling in what manner the matter of subsistence and abundance, in proportion as it comes into existence, shall be disposed of, the time necessary to the bringing it into existence.

Hence the need of *deputation*: an operation by which the supreme operative power and the supreme constitutive power are detached from one another: the supreme operative being committed to the individuals deputed, deputed to exercise it in the character of trustees: the supreme constitutive, exercisible with relation to these same possessors of the supreme operative power, being reserved in the hands of those over all whom, individually taken, this same supreme operative power may notwithstanding be exercised.

In the supreme constitutive power may be considered as comprized two perfectly distinct and instantly distinguishable powers—the supreme locative and the supreme dislocative: the power of placing in the situation in question the individual in question, and the power of displacing him—of removing him out of it. In point of fact, the power of displacing is capable of being lodged in hands different from those in which the power of placing the individual in question is reposed. It is even capable of being withheld altogether from every human hand: in which case it is exercised by death. But in point of expediency, how inadequate to the purpose of the required junction of interests the first of these powers can not but be, unless accompanied by the other, and that other placed in the same hands, is sufficiently evident.

In this way is done upon an all-comprehensive scale, that which is every where permitted to be done upon the smallest scale. In the instance of no individual, the case of acknowledged imbecillity excepted, infancy for example or insanity, is any objection made to the permitting any individual to place the management of his affairs in the hands of another in quality of trustee, and thus to place them at one time, and take them out again at any other time. That which is unquestionably right in the case of each—why it should be otherwise than right in the case of all, it rests with him to say who in this latter case takes upon him to condemn it.

In the case of Monarchy, the locative function is placed in the hands of blind chance under the name of *birth*, the dislocative in no other hands than those of death. Why in the one case blind chance, in the other case death, should be regarded as affording a better probability of relative aptitude than is afforded by human judgment, judgment exercised by those who have the strongest interest in the correctness of it, is among those questions which look for an answer.

Objections will be considered in another place.[1]

On the scale of private life, only on one or other of two suppositions is either the power of location or the power of dislocation with

[1] In the margin, Bentham noted at this point: 'See | |.' For a further discussion of Bentham's views on monarchy see 'Supreme Operative', pp. 149–226 above.

reference to a trustee denied to the principal. The one is—that of mental infirmity on his part: and on that supposition, regard for his own happiness requires that both the one and the other power should be refused to him. The other, that of moral untrustworthiness: and on that supposition, whether the power of location has or has not been possessed or exercised by him, regard for the interest of those for whose sake the power of location has been exercised requires that the power of dislocation—at any rate the absolute power—should not be exercised by the same hands. Why? because if it were, the application of the power given to the trustee to the purpose in question could not be secured. This is the case where, for the purpose of securing the liquidation of a debt, the property of a debtor is placed in the hands of trustees one or more, till the liquidation shall have been accomplished.

By the division thus made of the power, the will is likewise operated upon—and the junction of interests, the bringing of the personal interest of the functionary into accordance with the universal interest, promoted. In so far as his situation is an object of value in his eyes, and in so far as his continuance in it or his return to it or to a similar one is felt by him to be dependent on those of whose interest the universal interest is composed, in so far is his individual interest brought into accordance with the universal interest.

On what occasion soever applied, for what purpose soever applied, to whomsoever applied, whether it be punishment or reward that is applied—either this junction of interest is effected—either the separate interest of the individual is brought into accordance with the universal interest, and thereby with his share in it, or the purpose whatsoever it be, so far as concerns the effect meant to be produced on the conduct of that same individual, is not effected.

Expedient 3d. Confining and keeping confined within the narrowest limits consistent with its sufficiency with relation to the right and proper all-comprehensive end of government, the mass of supreme operative power possessed when, as above, separated from, and placed in subordination to, the supreme constitutive power. Say—minimizing supreme operative power.

In what distinguishable shapes supreme operative power exists or is capable of having existence will be seen in due place.

So likewise, in what distinguishable ways it is capable of being confined, as above.[1]

Reasons. The less the quantity of power with which a functionary is armed, the more easily will it be for the legislator to deal with him, in

[1] In the margin, Bentham noted at this point: 'See | |.' For a discussion of this topic see 'Economy as applied to Office', Ch. 4, pp. 30–9 above.

such sort as to keep his individual interest in a state of accordance with the universal interest: the less easy will it be for him to find accomplices for any measures adverse to the universal interest; and the more sensibly will he feel [his] dependence on the good opinion and good will of those whose interest composes the universal interest.

Expedient the 4th. Corroborating and employing to the utmost advantage every such force as the nature of the case renders it possible to employ in the character of a counterforce serving as a check upon the legal power lodged in the official hands in question: viz. the power of the popular, or say moral, sanction: the power of the functionaries in question being the power of the political, including that of the legal, sanction: the power of the popular, or say the moral, sanction as applied by the fictitious tribunal denominated the public opinion tribunal.

All human sources of power being already brought upon the carpet, the force here brought to view in the character of a counterforce to that of the possessors of the supreme operative power can not be any thing else than the power of those whose interest composes the universal interest: their power considered under a somewhat different point of view, and designated accordingly under another name.

In the situation of possessors of the supreme constitutive power with relation to the possessors of the supreme operative power, those whose interest composes the universal interest were brought to view in the character of legislators: in the situation here in question, the same persons, the same functionaries if such they may be stiled, are presented to view in the character of judges. Neither of the one power nor of the other, nor of both together, though lodged in the same hands, is there in this case any danger of abuse: in the case of [each][1] power, making the most of it for the advancement of their own interest is in this case the very course that is most desirable.

When of this natural counterforce such advantage is made as is capable of being made, the effect is that in case of misdecision or misrule in any shape an appeal has place, has place of itself and without formality, delay, vexation or expence, from the possessors of the supreme operative power to their creators, the possessors of the supreme constitutive power, in the character of Judges.

Even in the very sink of corruption, where all functionaries are corrupt—rendered necessarily so by the very form of government—even in such an atmosphere, this tribunal, fictitious as it is, is not altogether without force: by this force it is, and no other, that all that evil has been prevented which as yet remains undone: if in so

[1] MS 'every'.

pestilential an atmosphere, in which what is called religion has its effect, and understanding and will labour under the avowedly desired prostration of strength, this antiseptic is not without its effect, what would it be under a pure one?

How to employ this counterforce to most advantage will form a particular subject of enquiry in another place.[1]

Expedients for effecting the junction of interests recapitulated:[2]

1. To those whose interest composes the universal interest give or leave as much power as possible.

2. To those whose interest is not the universal interest but in its very nature adverse to the universal interest give as little power as possible.

3. Keep on foot, in the character of a power prepared when occasion calls, a power superior to their own, the power of those whose interest is the universal interest, in readiness to act upon them in the character of Judges and punish them with dishonor and loss of office in their character of legislators.

When these things are accomplished, all things are accomplished by which any thing can be done towards keeping the interest of the possessors of supreme operative power in accordance with the universal interest: that is to say, if the word *duty* be worth employing, in accordance with their *duty*.

To this same denomination—viz. bringing the less principal interest into accordance with the more principal interest—is referable whatsoever in private trusts is done in the view of securing probity on the part of trustees.

So likewise whatsoever is done for the purpose of minimizing the evil produced by the misdeeds of those against whom, under the general denomination of malefactors or say criminals, the force of punishment under the name of punishment is applied by that branch of the aggregate mass of law which is distinguished by the name of penal law. Were it not for the punishment, the particular and sinister interest, correspondent to and created by the appetite whatsoever it be in which the misdeed had its source, would stand unopposed, and produce conduct opposite in the way in question to the universal interest. Comes the legislator with his penal law: punishment being attached to the misdeed, the sinister interest finds itself thereupon encountered and opposed by another interest operating in a direction favorable, or at least supposed to be favorable, to the universal interest—to the universally right and proper interest. If, at the moment of decision, in the eyes of the individual in question, in all

[1] See Ch. 5, pp. 283–98 below.
[2] This phrase is taken from the marginal summary.

dimensions or elements of value taken together—namely intensity, duration, propinquity, certainty, purity and fecundity—the value of the mass of looked for pleasure which constitutes the temptation is greater than the value of the punishment opposed to it by the penal sanction added to the force of the other sanctions, the misdeed is committed notwithstanding: if not so great, the particular and sinister interest is overpowered and rendered inefficient by the united force of the sanctions, and conduct is determined by that interest which is in accordance with the universal interest, as above.

CHAPTER 3. OF RULE—ITS NATURE—PRIMARY MODIFICATIONS, THEIR RESPECTIVE ENDS IN VIEW—SUBJECT MATTERS—INCORPOREAL INSTRUMENTS, CORPOREAL INSTRUMENTS—AND EXPENCE

§ 1. *Rule in general—its general nature and primary modifications*[1]

1. First as to its nature. By the word rule, and its synonym government, in the sense in which it is employed where the subject of discourse is Constitutional law, is commonly meant the exercise of political power upon the largest scale in respect of extent: upon a scale commensurate with the whole number of those human beings who are considered as members of the community in question: with the whole number of those whose interest constitutes the universal interest.

To exercise power upon that scale is to exercise rule—to exercise the power of government.

2. Next as to its primary *modifications*. By these, understand those which are expressed by the names of the two opposite qualities *good* and *bad*: both of them, in so far as they have any determinate meaning, bearing reference to the felicity and infelicity, the happiness and unhappiness, of the sensitive beings whose interest is in question.

The beings by whom the power in question is exercised being in both cases sensitive beings, *good rule* and *bad rule* can not but have this in common—namely their being directed throughout to some end. This end will in every individual case be found capable of being designated and brought to view by one general expression: namely human felicity, or say human happiness.

Unless some end in view considered in the character of a standard of reference be taken into account, the epithets *good* and *bad* will be designative of nothing but the state of human affections in relation to the subject matter to which these qualities are respectively attributed: namely of the affections of him by whom these same epithets are employed.

By a good thing, he who speaks of it means that by the idea of which a sentiment of approbation—a sensation of the pleasurable kind—is excited in his mind: by a bad thing, that by the idea of which a

[1] Earlier drafts of this material are at UC cxiii. 138 (30 July 1822) and cxiii. 139–42 (17 August 1822). Other related fragments are at UC xxiv. 433v (17 August 1822) and cxiii. 143, 145 (18 August 1822).

sentiment of disapprobation—a sensation of the painful kind—is excited in his mind.

Rule being on the present occasion the subject matter of the discourse, by *Good rule* that which the author means is—that one of these two primary modifications of rule which he approves of. The only rule, the only government, which he approves of is that which has for its *end in view*, or in other words its object of pursuit, the greatest happiness of the greatest number of the individuals of whom the community in question is composed. The idea of a government keeping this end in view and taking this same end for its object of pursuit is to him a pleasurable one: the idea of a government which, keeping or not keeping this end in view, takes any other end for the object of its pursuit is to him a painful one.

Taken according to the above description of it, Good rule being that rule which has for its end in view, or say object of pursuit, the greatest happiness of the greatest number of the beings of whom the community in question is composed, bad rule, or say misrule, will be that rule which has for its end in view or object of pursuit not that greatest number, but some lesser number.

The persons by whom the rule is exercised being sensitive beings, as such taking respectively for their end in view and object of pursuit their own happiness, they will of themselves compose this lesser number, the greatest happiness of which is the end in view or object of pursuit in the case of this same bad rule: compose it, or at any rate be comprized in it.

Of those by whom at any given point of time the rule is exercised, the end in view or object of pursuit should be, can not (it will be seen) but be, in the case of each individual, his own individual happiness. But what will also be seen is that by this circumstance it is not rendered impossible but that of the whole system of government under which they act the end in view or object of pursuit may be the greatest happiness of the greatest number.

§2. *Good Rule and Misrule—their primary Operations*

First as to Good Rule. Its all-comprehensive operation, in one word maximizing felicity: of this all-comprehensive operation, primary modifications: maximizing positive felicity: minimizing positive infelicity.

The greatest felicity of the greatest number being here the common end in view, or say object of pursuit, this object divides itself naturally into two opposite and correspondent branches—positive felicity, or say pleasure in all its several shapes; negative felicity, or say exemption from pain in all its several shapes. And note that without negative felicity in perfection, there can be little positive.[1]

Correspondent to these branches of felicity will be the primary modes of operation having the maximization of it, as above, for their common end or object in view.

In the case of Good rule, the description of these opposite and mutually correspondent operations will be altogether plain and simple: mode of operation the first, maximizing positive felicity: mode of operation the second, maximizing negative felicity. But to maximize negative felicity is to minimize positive infelicity: yet whatsoever may be the accordance in the ultimate result, the two modes of operation will to a large extent be found perfectly distinguishable.

In the account of good government, felicity, positive felicity, positive good, is the *profit*; infelicity, positive evil, is in bookkeeper's language the *loss*, in ordinary language the expence, taking in the utmost latitude of its signification the word *expence*.

In no private business, whether in the shape of production or mere exchange, can profit be obtained without loss, or otherwise than by means of loss. As little can it in the business of government: the evil produced for the attainment of the good is the loss—the expence: the good produced by the application made of that same evil is the profit.

In the account of Good rule, the greatest number of the members of the community being here the persons whose felicity is the end in view, the profit to them is in the ratio of the happiness added to them, to that of the happiness substracted from them—the success of the business is directly as the balance on the happiness side in favour of the greatest number of the members.

Not so in the case of Misrule: the persons whose greatest happiness is the end in view and object of pursuit are the lesser number, the ruling one or the ruling few: the success of the concern is in this case as the balance on the happiness side in favour of those few, whatsoever be the balance in favour of the greatest number: or even if instead of a balance in their favour, there should be a net loss. The expence being the whole of it defrayed by the subject many, while the profit is reaped by and carried to the account of the ruling few, hence it is that while the profit to the one side is continually on the encrease, the expence, which is so much loss to the other side, will at the same time be continually receiving a correspondent encrease: and thus

[1] In the text at this point, Bentham inserted the following note, but it is unclear where it should be placed: 'Good being used indifferently to signify pleasure or exemption from pain, and an instrument or efficient cause of pleasure or of exemption from pain: evil, to signify pain or loss of pleasure, or an instrument or efficient cause of pain or loss of pleasure.'

instead [of] minimization, maximization will be the operation performed upon the expence.

§ 3. *Subject matters of operation and distribution*

The end in view in the case of all rule being felicity, namely in good rule the greatest felicity of the greatest number, in the case of misrule the greatest felicity of the favoured few, felicity and its opposite, infelicity, will in respect of intention and endeavour be the subject matter of distribution in both cases: other subjects howsoever denominated no otherwise than in consideration of the felicity or infelicity of which they are regarded as the productive instruments.

These will be to be distinguished in the first place [into] those which are elements of felicity—elements of a pleasant, or say a beneficial, nature, say in one word *benefits*: and those which are elements of infelicity—elements of an unpleasant, or say burthensome, nature:—in one word *burthens*.

In the distribution of both these fruits of rule—the sweet and the bitter—all rule as such is necessarily occupied. In the case of good rule, it is with satisfaction on the part of the rulers that the sweet fruits are distributed, with regret, and only under the rod of necessity, the bitter ones.

The sweet ones will be found comprizable under one or other of two denominations, power and wealth: the bitter ones under two correspondent and opposite ones, subjection and forced contributions.

So much for those subject matters of distribution, benefits and burthens together, which being distributed by all rule howsoever exercised can not but be distributed by Good Rule.

Remain three other distinguishable ones the distribution of which is the peculiar work of Bad rule. These are: 1. Factitious honor or dignity in all its various modifications: 2. Official ease, at the expence of official duty: 3. Official vengeance: gratification afforded by rulers to their own irascible appetite, by evil inflicted on subjects, on account of resistance opposed, or regarded as being opposed, or as having been opposed, or as being eventually about to be opposed, to their misrule.

As to Factitious honor or dignity, its incompatibility with Good rule will be shewn under a particular head.[1] It will there be seen to be a

[1] See Ch. 6, pp. 299–324 below.

production which is peculiar to Bad rule, and suffices to stamp with that character the government under which it is found to have place.

By ease at the expence of duty, understand the non-performance, or through inattention the misperformance, of the services the procurement of which for the benefit of the public was, or was pretended to be, the final cause of the institution of the office. The obligation of rendering these services is a burthen attached to the office: the benefit has for its ordinary ingredients, the power which can not but be attached to the office, and the wealth—the pecuniary emolument—which naturally is attached to it. Under the best good-rule, the universal propensity will, in the case of every official person as in the case of every other person, as on the one hand be to encrease the sum of his benefits, so on the other hand to diminish the sum of his burthens. To this propensity, under good rule a preventive or restrictive check will be opposed: a check the efficiency of which will be as the degree of goodness in the rule. Under bad rule, in some cases no check at all will be opposed, in others none but a more or less inefficient and insufficient check, the inefficiency of which will be as the degree of badness in the rule.[a]

The case in which vengeance has place is the case where on account of some pain of which the breast of the avenger is the seat, and some act imputed by him to the victim has been the cause, the avenger has conceived the wish and thence used the endeavour to see produced pain in the breast of the victim, and has succeeded in producing it. Though in this case nothing is *got* by the avenger—no benefit which is such to his concupiscible appetite obtained, gratification is however obtained for another appetite stiled of old the irascible.

Howsoever it be with the gratification, such is the intensity of the desire that Good Rule finds little, if any, less difficulty in applying efficient checks in the case of this misery-producing appetite than in any branch of the concupiscible appetite, of that appetite which has for the object of its desire not pain but pleasure. To oppose a compleatly preventive check to it, in such sort that no pain the effect of which is confined to the giving birth to this essentially impure and uneconomical pleasure shall ever be produced, will be among the neverfailing objects of Good Rule. In the case of Misrule on the other hand, the pursuit of the sweets of government in this bitter-sweet

[a] In England, for the designation of an office from which burthen in every shape has been detached while benefit in every shape remains rivetted to it, an appropriate appellative has been invented, and is in common use:—an appropriate appellative—*a Sinecure*. To the honor of giving name to this object, subject matter and instrument of misrule, the title of England is incontestable. England may be stiled the land of Sinecures.

shape will go hand in hand with the pursuit of these same sweets in their less impure shapes.

§4. *Incorporeal instruments of Good and Bad Rule*[1]

Now as to the *instruments* of Good Rule and Bad Rule: and first, of the *incorporeal* ones.[2]

The augmentation, creation or preservation of felicity being the one all-comprehensive end in view and object of desire, as to human action in every situation, so necessarily in that of all those by whom rule is exercised, felicity together with its opposite, infelicity, in their several modifications are as necessarily the subject matters of its operations. But in their several modifications these same elements are also by an equal necessity rendered the equally necessary and indispensable instruments for the attainment of that end. In no case without the elements of infelicity and felicity—only by pain and pleasure applied to them in certain manners—can sensitive beings be rendered instrumental in the exclusion of evil or the production of good, in the exclusion of pain or in the production of pleasure.

When however they are spoken of as being employed in the character of instruments, they are spoken of by appellatives different from those by which they are spoken of in the character of ends.

Force, intimidation, and remuneration. By one or other of these three denominations may be characterized all those incorporeal instruments of rule which being indispensable instruments of all rule can not therefore but be such with relation even to the best good-rule.

1. By force, understand here *physical* force—that of which the body, as contradistinguished from the mind, is the seat. Only by means and through the intervention of this instrument can those others be brought into action. Only by physical force, by whatsoever agent applied to them, can any operation be performed upon objects not endowed with sensation, in a word upon inanimate things: and in this respect many are the occasions on which this only mode of operating upon things is not less necessary to the purpose of operating with efficiency upon persons. Only by force—by physical force—can a person who, against the will of the occupant, continues in a house, be removed out of it, if neither intimidation nor remuneration are capable of being applied with effect to the purpose of affording him an

[1] Related fragments are at UC xxxvi. 189 (24 August 1822) and xxxvi. 190 (28 August 1822).

[2] Bentham did not go on to discuss the corporeal instruments of rule in 'Constitutional Code Rationale', but for this topic see 'Supreme Operative', §10, pp. 183–6 above.

inducement adequate to the purpose of causing him to remove himself.

Force, in so far as considered as being applied to the mind, and applied not without effect, is termed *intimidation*.

2. Intimidation. This is the eventually efficient cause of infelicity—the matter of evil considered as applied to the purpose in question. The most prominent and extensive instance is that in which the matter of evil is applied to this same purpose in the character of matter of punishment—evil in consideration of a man's failing to contribute to the felicity of the persons in question in the manner pointed out to him by the directive rules which the arrangements of government furnish.

3. Remuneration. This is the efficient cause of felicity, the matter of good considered as applied to the purpose in question: good, applied in consideration of a man's having contributed, or being engaged or expected to contribute, to the felicity of the persons in question in some shape and manner, and on some occasion, indicated or not indicated by government or existing laws.[a]

On this occasion, in speaking of the efficient causes of felicity considered as employed in the character of instruments of government, a material distinction will require to be made: it is that between the internal and the external instruments.[1]

[a] Among the imperfections of language may be reckoned the not furnishing a denomination which shall designate in relation to good that which is designated by intimidation in relation to evil. Intimidation is fear-exciting—what is wanted is a single word by which [hope]-exciting[2] may be expressed.

The more particularly the analogy between punishment and reward is brought to view, the more ample is the practically useful instruction that is conveyed. The more clearly it is seen, when the dispensing hand in question is the hand of government, that *to reward is to punish*, and that, as to whatsoever is above the least quantity sufficient, remuneration is depredation, [with] the less difficulty will men be brought to extend to the matter of reward whatsoever frugality they are not averse to apply in the case of punishment.

Towards the holding up to view this instructive analogy, something it is hoped has been done in the *Théorie des peines et des récompenses*:[3] but on going back to it, I should not expect to find that as much was then done as at present might be done.

[1] In the marginal summary, Bentham noted at this point: 'See above or below.' This topic is discussed in a fragment at UC cxiii. 144, 150 (21 August 1822): 'of the several instruments of felicity the whole aggregate may in the exhaustive method (see *Chrestomathia*) be divided into two groupes—namely the external instruments and the internal, the one composed of those which may be termed external and [the other] those which may be termed internal: the object of reference being in both instances the *mind*: such instruments of felicity the place of which is exterior with reference to the mind: instruments the seat of which is in the mind itself.

'Let us begin with the external instruments. These, so far [as] rule in general is concerned, may all of them be comprized under the one or the other of two denominations, namely the matter of wealth, and power: the several portions of the matter of wealth, some of them real

Intimidation and allurement are employed, both of them, by Good Rule and by Misrule. But though in this they agree, one point there is in which they are not only different but opposite. This is the quantity of the matter which they respectively employ. By Good rule, as in the one case so in the other, it is minimized: it is the least possible: by Misrule, it is maximized.

By Good Rule, intimidation is minimized. Why? Even because threatening to produce evil would be in vain, if with more or less frequency the threat were not executed—the evil produced: and because even the fear of evil is itself evil: from the fear of sufferance, actual sufferance is inseparable.

By Good Rule, allurement—prospect of remuneration—is also minimized. Why? Because in government, good is not procured but by means of evil: the matter of good by means of the matter of evil. Indeed to no small extent the matter of good and the matter of evil are one and the same thing. Witness wealth: witness power. By the receipt of wealth, pleasure, enjoyment, is produced: by the loss of it, [suffering]: and likewise in regard to power. By the hand [of] government, neither the one nor the other can be given but in proportion as it is taken.

Hence the aphorisms paradoxical in form—not less true than useful in substance. To reward is to punish: liberality is depredation. The best use that government can make of money in the hands of the lawful possessors is: to leave it where it is.

entities, corporeal instruments of felicity, others fictitious entities, incorporeal instruments of felicity, derived in the way of abstraction from real entities: power itself in every modification of it an incorporeal instrument of felicity, a fictitious entity, but not the less operative by being fictitious.

'As to the internal instruments of felicity, the different modifications of sensibility, bodily and mental, may be thus denominated. They are not, like the external ones, under the immediate command of rulers, capable of being employed in pursuit of their several ends, good or bad as the case may be: no otherwise can they be reached than through the medium of the external ones.

'By the word *felicity* the mind is unavoidably led to its opposite *infelicity*, and thereupon comes the question, what are its instruments? The answer is—the same as those of *felicity*: on the closest scrutiny scarcely will any others be to be found: none at least in which as such any separate consideration need be bestowed—corporeal and incorporeal, real and fictitious, the same entities are instruments of felicity or infelicity according to the application: the same wine in the same head may produce exhilaration or the head-ache: the same steel may cut either the staff or the thread of life.'

For Bentham's reference see *Chrestomathia*, ed. M. J. Smith and W. H. Burston, Oxford, 1983 (*CW*), pp. 218–74.

[2] MS 'fear-exciting'.

[3] *Théorie des peines et des récompenses*, ed. Étienne Dumont, 2 vols., London, 1811; see especially the second volume of this work, which Richard Smith later translated into English as *The Rationale of Reward*, London, 1825 (Bowring, ii. 189–266). Smith also translated the first volume as *The Rationale of Punishment*, London, 1830 (Bowring, i. 388–525).

An exception blunts the point, but must not be out of mind: the least sum necessary for security against evils.

Now[1] as to those incorporeal instruments of rule which are peculiar to Misrule: 1. Corruptive influence, or say Corruption: 2. Delusive influence, or say Delusion: and in the third place, Fiction.[a]

§5. *Corruption*[2]

Taken in its largest sense, the word corruption is employed to denote the *deterioration* of the subject to which it is applied—the rendering it *worse* than it was before or would have been otherwise. *Corruptio* is in Latin *breaking up*: the breaking up of the texture of the subject in question: it being understood that by such breaking up it is rendered worse. In the first instance the word was used in a physical sense: the breaking up the texture of a mass of animal or vegetable matter: from thence it came to be used in a moral sense—the breaking up for the worse the texture of the mental frame.

When the sense in which the word is used is the physical sense, no more than one object is necessarily considered as having place in the operation: namely the corruptible mass in which the change has place: by another object operating as a ferment the change may be promoted: but no such exterior object is necessary to it.

Where the sense in which the word is used is the moral sense, the idea of two objects at once is commonly presented by it: the part in which the one appears, an active part: the part in which the other appears, a passive part. The objects thus presented to view are commonly persons. In this case what is presented to view is an operation in which two persons are concerned: one, the agent in the operation corrupting the other, and thereby rendering himself a

[a] Upon a nearer scrutiny, corruption will be found included under remuneration or allurement; fiction under delusion. The division is not a logical one. Names have been made by the authours of language: of the sum of them is composed the aggregate called language. They have been made at different times and till of late before any clearness had been given to the ideas of which they are respectively the signs. But though not a logical, it is an indispensable one: for of that which is truly predicable of corruptive influence, much will be found which is not truly predicable of allurement applied to other purposes: and of that which is predicable of fiction, much will be found that is not truly predicable of delusive influence exercised by other means.

[1] This paragraph and the accompanying note are taken from UC clx. 451. This forms part of MS sequence UC clx. 451–5 (25 August 1822), which otherwise appears to have been superseded by the MSS used in §5 below (UC xxxvi. 198–203, 195–7 and cvi. 323–6).

[2] An earlier draft of this section is at UC xxxvi. 191–4 (28 August 1822). A related fragment is at UC clx. 450 (19 August 1822).

corrupter: the other, the patient in the operation, being corrupted by the former and by the having been so corrupted becoming and continuing corrupt.

Thus it is that an operation called *corruption* has been performed: and by the same word, *corruption*, the result of the operation—the state of things brought about by it—is designated.[a]

In the operation thus described, by the party corrupting *corruptive influence* has been exercised: by the party corrupted—say in one word, on the plan mentioned and recommended by Blackstone, the *corruptee*,[1] *corrupt obsequiousness* has been practiced.

In the idea thus brought to view is commonly also comprized that of an auxiliary agent, considered as being employed as an instrument by the principal one. This instrument is a quantity of what may be stiled the matter of corruption employed in that same character of an instrument. Applied in the physical sense and to a physical subject, this instrument is what is called a *ferment*. This matter employed is an instrument to act upon the mind: if it operates, it is in the character of an inducement that it operates.

An inducement is constituted either of the matter of evil or of the matter of good operating on the mind in these their respective characters.

An inducement to which the name of corruptive might without impropriety be attached is an inducement of the intimidative kind. Say for example, the fear of death: intimation being given that if the one party, namely the party meant to be corrupted, will not perform the sinister service desired at his hands, he shall be put to death: in the opposite case, not.

An instrument of this sort however is not the sort of instrument the idea of which will by the words matter of corruption, instrument of corruption, be in general apt to be excited—not of a portion of the matter of evil, but a portion of the matter of good is the sort of instrument the idea of which by any such appellations as matter of corruption, instrument of corruption, will in general be apt to be excited.

This matter of good will be some portion of the matter of which the

[a] The ambiguity and confusion produced by the denoting by one and the same word two objects so materially different and so frequently requiring to be distinguished—the performance of an operation and the state of things which is the result of it—is an inconvenience which runs through all European languages: through all such at least as have the Latin for one of their roots.

[1] See William Blackstone, *Commentaries on the Laws of England*, 4 vols., Oxford, 1765–9, ii. 140n: 'We may here remark . . . that the terminations of "-or" and "-ee" obtain, in law, the one an active, the other a passive signification; the former usually denoting the doer of any act, the latter him to whom it is done.'

external instruments of felicity are composed, namely power and wealth, with or without the addition of factitious honor, called also factitious dignity.

Distinction 1. Corruption designed, or say by design: Corruption undesigned, or say without design.

In regard to corruption—the first grand distinction—the first in the order of importance and thence in the order of place—is the distinction between that which is designed and [that which] is undesigned. By undesigned, understand that which is capable of having place without design, not that which is not in any instance the result of design: for of that which is capable of having place without design, there is not any portion but what is not altogether capable of having place with and by design, but abundantly in the habit of being so produced.

Suppose the creation of it the work of chance: nothing is more natural than that the preservation of it shall be the work of design. The weed springs up of itself: a husbandman sees it, thinks it may perhaps serve for food, finds it palatable, gathers the seed, sows it, cultivates it and propagates it.

The corruptive influence by which, in the case of bribery, an Elector of a Representative of the people in a mixt Monarchy is engaged to give his vote in favour of a Candidate by whom money is given for it, on the part of the Candidate is the work of design: on the other part, the corrupt obsequiousness is accompanied with a consciousness of the nature of the corrupting inducement to which it is indebted for its existence. The corruption in consequence of which the Representative perseveres in giving support in favour of the measures of the Monarch in that same Monarchy for a course of years, notwithstanding any depredation and oppression of which those same measures are all the time productive, may by possibility be produced on the one part without any such design, and on the other part without any such self-criminating consciousness. The Monarch in his quality of Chief Executive functionary must have subordinates in the several situations, and as seems to him with large masses of emolument attached to them: the Representative, seeing that the situations with their functions must have place and thinking that some such large masses of emolument attached to them must have place, thinks that of these good things the possession and enjoyment may as well be in his hands as in any others. The Monarch is kind and bountiful: in return for kindness and bounty, the moral and the religious sanctions join in commanding gratitude: and thus it is that without design of evil on one part, or consciousness of it on the other, corruption may do its work, and evil to any intensity, extent and duration be produced.

Distinction 2. Corruption personal, or say personally seated: Corruption systematic, or say systematically seated.

By the case in which it is personally seated, understand the case in which a determinate individual is assignable by whom portion of the matter of good constituting the temptation, the tempting inducement, has been presented to the will [of] an individual at whose hands the sinister service was desired, and the [bait][1] accordingly swallowed and the sinister service rendered—in this case stands the transaction between the Candidate and the Elector as above. By the case in which the corruption is not personally but systematically seated, understand the case in which no such individual is assignable, but the cause of the corruptive and corrupt transaction, if there is but one in question, the source of transactions of this same nature pervading the whole official establishment, is in the system or frame of government.

A system of government in which an irremovable functionary possesses an indispensable share in the supreme legislative power, and at the same time the whole or the greatest part of that branch of the supreme Executive power by which the subordinate functionaries are placed and in a proportion more or less considerable displaceable, is a system in which corruption is systematically seated. On the one part the corruptive influence of the Chief functionary, on the other part the corrupt obsequiousness on the part of the People's representatives, has its source not in the mental texture of this or that individual, but in the political texture of the system or frame of government itself. It will therefore of necessity go on in the production of the fruits of corruption, namely depredation and oppression, in a quantity continually encreasing unless and untill the form of government receive an apt and adequate sanative change.

These distinctions will be found prime in the order of importance: therefore they have been constituted so in the order of place. A condition requisite to the constituting of a determinate object of blame and accusation is—the existence [of] an individual, a determinate and assignable individual, to whom misconduct in a determinate shape may be imputed.

When the seat and source of the corruption is in the system, one only possible remedy does the nature of the case admitt of. This is the substituting to the system or frame of government in which corruptive influence thus bears irresistible sway, another from which as to all practical effects it shall stand excluded. Of this problem, the only solution will follow in its place.[2]

[1] MS 'bate'.

[2] In the margin, Bentham noted at this point: 'Add. To engage those who profit by the system to submitt to change it, nothing but imminent fear for person or property can suffice.'

In this case if the phrase *corruptive influence* be employed, it is by the laws and institutions themselves that the corruptive influence must be said to have been applied: applied to the individual in such manner as to have given birth to the sinister effect.

Dear, in this case, it may be imagined how dear—both to corrupters and corrupted—are those same laws and institutions.

In this case it is not common for complaints of corruption to have place to any considerable extent: in general, scarcely is it seen or so much as suspected that in consequence of this state of things any considerable mischief has place. Every man, as early as he has been taught any thing, having been taught to regard as objects of the most prostrate veneration and the most boundless confidence those same sources and receptacles of corruption—those same instruments of depredation and oppression—chooses in the midst of his sufferings to find the cause of them no where, than to find it there.

At the same time this is the case in which mischief has place in a quantity by far greater than in the opposite case. It has place to a greater extent, and throughout the whole of its extent it is effectually out of the reach of all cure, and even of restraint and palliation. For no one individual is perceptible on whom it is possible, without the appearance of injustice, to fix in any shape the reproach of misconduct, of misrule.

Nor yet is it true that in this case there exists not any individual on whom blame can be fixt. On the contrary, in this case, and to the whole extent of it, whosoever be at any given point of time the individuals exercising in chief the powers of government, in a word the *rulers*, on them may the blame, the imputation, of misrule be fixt. Persons corrupted, this or that individual, perhaps even those rulers themselves; persons corrupting at any rate, those same rulers.

But if neither open accusation nor so much as secret imputation can have place, still less can remedy in any shape have place. So far therefore as the corruption has place in this shape, the system of corruption, the system of misrule by means of corruption, may be said to have been raised to the very pinnacle of perfection.

The greater the extent to which corruption in this shape has place, the more probative, antecedent to all positive evidence, is the circumstantial evidence by which it is proved that on the part of the persons exercising in chief the powers of government—on the part of the persons by whom, in the whole or in part, the profit reaped from the mass of corruption thus constituted has been reaped, the corruption that has place is the fruit of design: that they know what they are about: that they are conscious, fully conscious, of the evil that has place: and that they, by being supporters, are for the time being authors of it.

In this case the corruption may be said to be *single-seated*: or borrowing an expression from Botany—*Monoec[i]ous*: the persons thus corrupted, namely the persons reaping the sinister and dishonest profit, may be said to be self-corrupters, self-corrupted: and a species of misdeed stiled *self-corruption* may be said to have place and to be habitually committed.[1]

For explanation sake, an example may here be necessary: a mixt Monarchy is the form of government from which the clearest and most impressive example will be to be found. Depredation is of all fruits of corruption the one naturally most extorted, most likely to have been the character of the sinister profit in view. In a pure Monarchy, depredation in a covered state is needless: the force and the intimidation suffice to lodge in his hands whatsoever it may please the Monarch to find there. In a representative democracy, depredation on the part of rulers is not, to an extent capable of affording an example, practicable. Remains as the most conveniently accessible fund of example, a mixt Monarchy.

Look for instance to England, and take the case of Droits of Admiralty. In this case, see the following particulars. Fruit of corruption gathered in the course of | | years, 17 millions Sterling. Shape of the profit consequently, depredation.[2]

[1] Bentham noted at this point: 'Add. Dioec[i]ous—Judge and Suitor.'

[2] The marginal summary expands on the text at this point: 'Example, Admiralty Droits. Most constantly and universally tempting fruit of corruption, depredation. Source of the corruptive depredation, war: in particular, ditto commenced without previous declaration. Arch-depredators, King and Judge: means of conveying the plunder into their hands, Judge-made Law made by former, confirmed and acted upon by present, Judges. Self-corrupters, King, Judge, concurring Cabinet Ministry, and conniving Parliament. Had a declaration of war preceded the captures, King, by Statute, stood precluded from all share. By judgment having force of law pronounced by Judges appointed by himself, King had been endowed with all captures made antecedently to declaration of war. Capturing without antecedent declaration of war, is per international law *piracy*. To obtain this booty, King and Co. commenced the war thus piratically: value of booty, 17 Millions. Would they say, the acquiring this booty was not an inducement to make the war and commence it thus? As well might a highwayman who robs passengers of money say the acquisition of it was not the inducement to what he did. To render credence capable of being given to the assertion without absurdity, indispensably necessary was the abstaining from taking the money.'

Bentham here seems to have misrepresented the question of droits. The elementary principle of Prize Law was that all prize belonged to the state, hence in England, if the Crown had made no grants of any of its rights, every prize would have belonged to the sovereign *jure coronae*. But by ancient grants the Crown had ceded a portion of its rights in perpetuity to the Lord High Admiral. All prizes captured during hostilities either in port (providing they had come into port by stress of weather or accident, by mistake or by ignorance, not knowing of war) or by non-commissioned vessels belonged of right to the Lord High Admiral, and the proceeds of such prizes when condemned in the Prize Courts became droits of the Admiralty. On the other hand, all prizes captured at sea before hostilities, whether by commissioned or non-commissioned

In general, in the composition of a mass of the matter of corruption, or say corruptive influence, operating as an instrument of misrule, the matter of good is regarded as being the sole ingredient. It is so to no inconsiderable an extent. But to a considerable and probably even greater extent, the matter of good and the matter of evil are in one way or other employed in the composition of the instrument: the matter of good operating as an inducement of the alluring kind: the matter of evil operating as an inducement of the intimidative, or say coercive, kind.

Scene, for example, a mixt or limited Monarchy. Enter the following distinguishable cases.

Case 1. In a limited, or say mixt, Monarchy, the Monarch gives a representative of the people to understand that if he will continue giving vote, and occasionally vote and speech, for such or such a number of years, in a manner satisfactory to the Monarch, he shall at the end of the time [have][1] a place worth so much a year for life. In

ships, captures at sea by commissioned ships during hostilities and captures in port where the vessel had come in voluntarily or had been driven in by the King's men-of-war, belonged of right to the sovereign, and the proceeds became droits of the Crown. Captures made before a declaration of war were therefore condemned as droits of the Crown and not droits of Admiralty. However as the office of Lord High Admiral had been in commission since the death of George, Prince of Denmark (1653–1708), and had therefore reverted to the sovereign himself, droits of Admiralty as well as droits of the Crown were paid into the Admiralty Registry to the credit of the Crown. It seems to have become common by the beginning of the nineteenth century for both droits of Admiralty and droits of the Crown to be referred to simply as droits of Admiralty, even though droits of the Crown formed a much greater proportion of the proceeds from prizes, and the distinction was scrupulously adhered to by the Prize Courts. Bentham was also inaccurate in his claim that after a declaration of war, statute law precluded the Crown from all share in the proceeds from prizes. Prize Acts, usually passed after the commencement of each war, ceding to commissioned ships, that is Royal Navy ships and privateers with letters of marque, the whole proceeds from any captures they might make at sea during hostilities, were grounded on a Prize Proclamation by which the Crown granted them its rights. The Prize Proclamation and Prize Act conferred on commissioned captors an interest in those prizes which would otherwise have become droits of the Crown, but did not confer an interest in droits of Admiralty. Furthermore, even when a prize was condemned as a droit, it was usual for captors to present a memorial to the Treasury praying the Lords Commissioners to recommend to the Crown to award them the whole or a certain proportion of the proceeds. The specific instance which Bentham seems to have had in mind was the outbreak of hostilities with Spain in 1804. On 5 October 1804 a Spanish treasure fleet was captured off Cadiz by Royal Navy frigates, an action which was followed by many other captures before the formal declaration of war on 11 January 1805. A Prize Proclamation was issued on 31 January 1805 and later a Prize Act passed (45 Geo. III, c.72). The vessels captured before the declaration of war were condemned as droits of the Crown. Upon the presentation of memorials from the captors, certain proportions of the proceeds were granted to them: the proportion varied depending upon whether the capturing vessel was a Royal Navy ship or a pirate and upon the value of the proceeds. Moreover a smaller proportion of the proceeds of bullion than of other cargo was granted. Bentham seems to have been mistaken in stating £17m. as the sum of the proceeds from droits: according to a Parliamentary paper, ordered to be printed 1 June 1818, the total sum received as droits of the Crown and Admiralty from 1793 to 1818 was £8.5m.

[1] MS 'half'.

this case the instrument of corruption and thence of misrule is composed solely of an inducement of the alluring kind, the hope of the matter of good in the shape just mentioned.

Case 2. The Monarch places a Representative of the people in an official situation with a certain mass of pecuniary emolument attached to it: but reserving to himself the power of displacing at any time the individual so placed, it being understood from experience that in the event of his speaking or voting on the side opposite to the King's, or to a certain degree neglecting to speak or vote on the King's side, such will be the consequence. Supposing all prospect of advancement out of the case, here it is of fear alone, unmixt with hope, that the instrument of corruption and thence of misrule is composed.

Case 3. The place given to the Representative of the people is a place [for][1] life: prospect of advancement out of the case as before. The inducement is here likewise of the nature of fear: it is of the coercive—the intimidative—kind. The hands from which eventual evil is in this case eventually expected are not the hands of the Monarch: the supposition they are not: they are the hands of the fictitious entity denominated *Public Opinion*, of which hereinafter: the people at large considered as sitting in judgment on the transaction. In the opinion of mankind in general, every thing to which the generic denomination of perfidy can without impropriety be applied is a fit object of disapprobation: is disapproved accordingly, and in testimony of such disapprobation is spoken of under the still more extensive denomination of a Vice. And so it is with *ingratitude*. But in this case perfidy and ingratitude are seen united: perfidy by infraction of the virtual and implied engagement; ingratitude by the non-return of good in the appropriate shape for the good received.

Meantime the tribunal of public opinion is a tribunal not unfrequently divided against itself. To give support to a bad government, or to an unapt set of functionaries under any government, is to a certain degree disreputable, at any rate in the opinions of all those in whose eyes the government or the set of functionaries are to a certain degree unapt. In this state of things, the placeman in question is thus circumstanced. Continuing to give speech or vote in favour of the King from whom he has received his place, he remains exposed to and suffering under the imputation of corruption and want of patriotism. But in so doing he preserves himself from the joint imputation of perfidy and ingratitude. The disapprobation applied to perfidy and [in]gratitude is in general more extensive, as well as more intensive, than the disapprobation attached to the habit of taking the prosperous

[1] MS 'of'.

side in the contest of politics. Of the functionary whose place is for life, the conduct will therefore for the most part not be distinguishable from that of the placeman whose continuance in place is no longer than during pleasure.

For simplification sake, all prospect of advancement has as yet been supposed to be out of the case. Seldom indeed however would this supposition be found realized. He who can not be advanced in his own person may still be advanced in the persons of individuals in any number connected with him in the way of interest or sympathy. In general therefore, to those other more prominent ties by which the conduct of the placeman for life is attached to the will of the Monarch, namely fear of the imputation of perfidy, fear of the imputation of ingratitude, is added the less prominent, but not less powerful, tie of the nature of hope—hope of further advancement for self and connections. Suppose the hope, i.e. the persuasion, to have arrived at a certain degree of intensity, fear, the stronger passion, operates in conjunction with it: into the composition of the inducement enters not merely the hope of obtaining the object of desire, but the fear of losing the chance and prospect of it.

Case 4. The place by which the Representative of the people is engaged on the side of the Monarch in opposition to that of the people is a place given not to the Representative himself, but to some connection of his, as above. In this case, if a corrupt obsequiousness to the will of the Monarch is secured, the ties by which it is secured are those of fear of the imputation of perfidy and fear of the imputation of ingratitude, as before, supposing here likewise all prospect of self-advancement out of the case. In this case the strength of the tie will not commonly be in any considerable degree influenced by the difference in respect of permanence between a place for life and place during pleasure. Suppose the principal by whom a seat in the representation is occupied, suppose him by defection subjecting himself to the imputation of perfidy and ingratitude, that for this offence of the principal the unoffending retainer should be deprived of his place is [a] state of things not very likely to be realized, nor therefore to be apprehended.

Case 5. By the exercise of an act to which punishment is annext by law, or that which in this particular has the force of law, a man stands exposed to punishment. The inducement operating as an instrument of corruption is the hope of obtaining at the hands of the Monarch exemption from such punishment. But coupled with this hope, and in the order of time antecedent to it, is fear—the fear of the punishment whatsoever it be. Here then is another instance in which to compose the instrument of corruption, or say corruptive influence, hope and fear, the matter of good and the matter of evil—hope of the one, fear of the other—are combined.

In a general point of view, the inducement, and consequently the corruptive influence, which is composed of fear is stronger and more efficient in its operation than the inducement, and consequently the corruptive influence, which is composed of hope. The mass of evil to which man stands exposed is greater than the mass of good which he is capable of receiving. Take even the case where by the same object, according to the disposition made of it, either hope or fear are produced—for example the same emolument by which at one time the hope of obtaining it, at another time the fear of losing it, has been produced—the impression produced by the fear of losing it is in general stronger than any that can have been made by the [hope of obtaining][1] it. He who possesses £100 and no more would experience more suffering from the loss of that same <£100 than> he would experience enjoyment from the ac<quisition of a further> £100: and so on whatsoever may be the ratio of loss <. . .> possession.

§6. *Of Delusion—the second of the instruments considered as employed by Misrule: and peculiar to Misrule as compared with Good rule*[2]

In the character of an instrument of misrule, delusion has place and operates in so far as, by some erroneous conception or opinion, individuals, who but for the error would not be, are operated upon in such sort that they give support to misrule: namely adding themselves to the number either of those over whom it is exercised or those by whom it is exercised.

Note here the relation between corruption and delusion. Corruption applies itself as above to the will immediately; it has no need to operate on the understanding. Delusion does not apply itself to the will immediately: it applies itself to the will no otherwise than through the medium of the understanding. In what manner the application is made will be seen presently.

Only in so far as it operates as an instrument of misrule does delusion belong to the present purpose. But by this restriction scarcely is delusion in any shape excluded: such is the need which misrule has of delusion as well as of corruption, and such the power which it has of pressing delusion in every shape into its service: of engaging it in whatsoever shape it is capable of operating, and from whatever source it is capable of being derived.

[1] MS 'fear of losing'.

[2] Related fragments are at UC clx. 435–7 (22 July 1822) and clx. 448–9 (10 August 1822).

Distinction 1. Delusion derived from the matter of corruption: delusion derived from other sources.

Note here in the first place two cases in one or other of which the whole field of delusion and delusive influence is comprehended. One is that in which delusion and corruption have the same instrument: the matter of corruption, while, by the receipt or prospect of it, it operates on the will in the case of this or that individual, may operate on the understanding of this or that other to whose will it has not happened to apply itself: operating or not operating, as it may happen, on the understanding of him on whose will it has operated with effect. The other case is that in which the effect in question, *delusion*, is produced on the understanding by instruments and causes which are not of a nature to operate upon the will in the way of immediate application: in a word to operate on it but through the medium of the understanding.

Power, wealth and factitious dignity, are examples that may serve to bring to view the particulars that belong to the first case: fallacies—fallacious arguments in general, those which belong to the other case: power, wealth and factitious dignity by the opinion, an erroneous one it will be seen to be, which it is the nature of them to cause to be entertained of those in whose possession these external instruments of felicity, objects of general desire, are, or are supposed to be, regarded as being.

The erroneous conception or opinion, no matter what be the name given to it, which it is the effect of delusion operating as an instrument of misrule to cause to be embraced, admitts of a very concise and clear description: it is the conception or the opinion that those, be they who they may, by whom the powers of government in the highest grade are possessed, are possessed of the qualities and endowments designated as above by the phrase the aggregate of appropriate aptitude, the object of tacit and implied reference being the exercise of the powers of government. Combined with this conception or opinion thus expressed in general and positive terms is moreover the conception or opinion that the degree of aggregate appropriate aptitude possessed by a man as above is in the ratio of the quantity possessed by him of the aggregate of that same splendid mass. This conception or opinion is here regarded as being erroneous: for that in truth, as to the positive position, the possession of those same instruments of felicity and objects of desire is no evidence of the possession of those same qualifications and endowments: and that, after deduction of certain excepted cases or state of things, the degree of the appropriate aptitude in question, taken in the aggregate, will naturally be rather in the inverse ratio of the aggregate quantity of those same instruments of felicity in his possession.

To announce this position is all that belongs to the present purpose: the grounds on which it stands will be successively brought to view further on.[1]

But though distinguishable in themselves, intimate to an extraordinary and deplorable degree is the connection and intercourse and association between these two instruments of misrule: by one hand or another, in one shape or another, throughout the whole field of action, false lights have been set up, and of these false lights the tendency and the object has every where been the causing men to regard those by whom the powers of government [are possessed] as being every where possessed of a degree of appropriate aptitude beyond that which is every where possible.

[Distinction 2.] On the part of him by whom the influence is exercised, as corruption, so may delusion be designed or undesigned. As of corruptive influence and corrupt obsequiousness, so of delusive influence and deluded obsequiousness may the effect be *designed* or undesigned: produced by design on the part of him by whose situation it is produced, or produced [without][2] design on his part.

On the part of him in whose instance the sinister obsequiousness is produced, the obsequiousness can not very well have for its accompaniment a consciousness of the nature of the cause by which it has been produced: the assertion of the affirmative presents itself as involving a contradiction in terms: as if it were said he is deceived and yet he is not deceived.

[Distinction 3.] As in the case of corruption, so in the case of delusion, the distinction between person-seated and system-seated is not incapable of having place. But so efficient and extensive, not to say universal, is the influence of that which is systematically seated, that for the operation of any which is personally seated scarcely is any room any where left.

As in the case of corruptive influence and corrupt obsequiousness, so in the case of delusive influence and obsequiousness through delusion, whether the creation of the sinister instrument and cause was designed or undesigned is but matter of speculation: psychological and historical speculation. What is sufficiently clear is that at this time of day, in the instance of every individual by whom any support is contributed to the preservation of the system, of every act

[1] In the margin, Bentham noted at this point: '☛ Refer to *Securities*, *Public Opinion Tribunal*, *Exclusion of Factitious Dignity*, *Supreme Operative power*.' See Chs. 4, 5 and 6, pp. 270–324 below, and 'Supreme Operative', pp. 149–226 above.

[2] MS 'with and by'.

by which any thing is done towards that effect, the designedness is sufficiently clear and incontestable. After such notice as for so many years past has been given in all newspapers, a man can no more contribute to the corruptiveness of the system, a man can no more contribute to the delusiveness of the system, without design, than without design he could go about picking pockets.

Money for supporting the splendor of the crown! Money for supporting the splendor of the crown! For crown put throne, sceptre, coronet, mitre, star—for splendor put lustre, honor, dignity—after the cry of mountebank! impostor! swindler! pick pocket! with which such demands within doors have been answered from without doors for so many years, could it be of use to any man who joins in the demand, could it be of use to him either to plead ignorance of the effects or of the design and purpose? As well might the man who, with gingerbread and fire under it, cries 'all hot! all hot!' in the streets, deny any such intention as that of selling it.

On the part of the living Joss for which the sources of glitter are demanded, the same design, the same clearsightedness, is not quite so certain. In that seat of necessitated and carefully nurtured mental imbecillity, in that seat of ever unsatisfied and unsatisfiable desire, the only object on each occasion clearly in view may be the toy for the purchase of which the money is wanted. Habituated to receive and enjoy the effects of the corruption—habituate[d] to receive and enjoy the effects of the delusion—habituated to receive the object of every wish without reflection and almost without thought—nothing has ever led him to any such course of labour as that of reflection or enquiry [into] what, after the gratification obtained by himself, may be the ulterior consequences to others, any more than into the causes by which the system of waste, depredation, oppression, corruption and delusion he was born to and is revelling in was produced. The baby who, as he is carried past the pastry-cook's, feels the saliva as it [is] called forth by the sight of a favorite cake, what should lead him to speculations about the past or future rise in the price of corn to which the cake, if bought for him and eaten by him, will according to the value of it have contributed?

By the word fallacies, those which are of a nature to be employed in a debate between parties contending for power will most naturally be presented. But others there are which, though not so apt to be employed by one such party against another, are not the less adapted to the purpose of being employed, and accordingly are [in] use to be employed, to operate in support of misrule and thence to serve as instruments of misrule.

The general predominance of self-regarding affection in man's nature over social affection, especially when applied to distant and extensive objects—of self-regarding affection alone, and still more of self-regarding and anti-social affection taken together, is a matter of fact which there will presently be occasion to bring to view under another head.[1] An abundant source of delusion is the conception or opinion by which, in men in general, greater degrees of strength are ascribed to the social affection than is generally capable of being possessed by it. Of this error, those by whom power is exercised and abused have all the benefit. For in those men in general by whom instruction is administered to others, whether in quality of instructors of youth or authors at large, the possessors of power, wealth and factitious dignity have the benefit of so many retainers and advocates.

Wherever the moral branch of the field of thought and action is on the carpet, they are continually occupied, with or without intending it, in drawing portraits. The persons who sit for these portraits belong almost invariably to the higher orders—qualities in a degree in which it belongs not to human nature to possess are there continually ascribed to human nature: qualities by the supposed possession of which the sentiments of love, respect and admiration are called forth. The use of representing these qualities as being in the elevated degrees in question possessed by men in general is that they may be regarded as being in a more particular degree possessed by those exalted individuals of whom the teachers or writers in question are or have been retainers or associates: for in vain would any thing be endeavoured to be represented as probable and credible if it were seen to be impossible.

Not one history out of a thousand—not one biography out of ten thousand—that tends not to keep the mind plunged into this error: and this is one of the ways in which the making men dupes has for its effect, and to a vast extent for its object, their being made slaves.

Examples of instruments of delusion of this class are speeches at party meetings, funeral sermons and articles in the obituaries given in periodical publications.

Existence and currency has been given to a maxim in which the mischievousness and absurdity of the artifices employed to this effect are exemplified in a more transcendent degree. This is the Latin maxim, *De mortuis nil nisi bonum*.[2] Nothing but what is good ought to be said of any one that is dead. The dead who can not be gratified by flattery are to be flattered; and why? even that the living who can be

[1] See Ch. 1, §2, pp. 232–4 above.

[2] This phrase is a Latin version of a Greek saying, *τὸν τεθνηκότα μὴ κακολογεῖν*, 'speak no evil of the dead', attributed by Diogenes Laertius (*Lives and Opinions of Eminent Philosophers*, i. 70) to Chilon, one of the Seven Sages and Spartan Ephor 556–5BC.

deluded by that same flattery may be deceived by it. Deluded? and to what further end? only that by means of the delusion they may with the less discontent submitt to be plundered and oppressed.

On every occasion the powerless, the unopulent, the undignified, are spoken and written of as less benevolent, less knowing, less judicious, less able, than they are. Why? even that while they have thus been rendered objects of contempt, less sympathy and antipathy may be excited by the oppression, depredation and contempt of which they are the destined objects: less sympathy towards the sufferers by the injury, less antipathy towards the authors of it.

On every occasion the powerful, the opulent, the dignified, are represented as more benevolent, more knowing, more judicious and more able than they are: and as to benevolence in particular, not only [more][1] benevolent than they are, but [more][2] benevolent than any human beings can be. Why? that under favour of the ascribed benevolence, they may with the less disturbance reap the united fruits of selfishness and malevolence.

As on the stage, so on the theatre of life, the fine arts club to produce the delusive effect: corruptive influence, with its sinecures, pensions, useless offices, needless offices, overpaid offices, crowns, sceptres, thrones, palaces, coronets, mitres, stars, garters, crosses, ribbons, composing all together the *apparatus aulicus*,[3] the machinery, the property, of the political theatre, furnishes the pantomime: delusive influence, standing on its own ground, furnishes words and music: all who have money, power or factitious dignity to give, every day even to satiety hear the parrot song of eulogy: the corruptionists, the knaves who are paid for it, sing recitative and air: the dupes, in quality of unpaid amateurs, join their voices and compleat the chorus.

Wealth, power and factitious dignity—the triune God of the Corruptionists' idolatry—wealth, power and factitious dignity on the one hand, wisdom and virtue on the other, are worshipped as if inseparable: rich and respectable are employed as synonymous terms.

Whatever system of religion they preach is, because they preach it, true: whatever system of morality they practice is, because they practice it, pure. Their opinions, children and slaves of sinister interest, beget and fashion all other opinions: their tastes, all other tastes: their opinions, that is to say what they profess and pass off for their opinions: for as to what are really their opinions, only from their

[1] MS 'less'.
[2] MS 'less'.
[3] i.e. 'princely equipment'. Suetonius, *De vita Caesarum*, v. 4.

interests and their practice are they ever knowable: for of what are really their opinions, considering that of no man's mind the interior is visible to any other, and that no position or assertion is more or less easily pronounced than its contrary, assertion on matters of opinion is no evidence: in the eyes of reason no evidence would it be, even in a country where perjury is not compelled by law, and that perjury notorious.[1]

Where opinion—inward opinion—is the subject, the strongest direct evidence is weak in comparison of circumstantial evidence.

§7. *Of Fictions: viz. of falshoods of the privileged kind employed by lawyers*

By fiction, in the sense in which it is used by lawyers, understand a false assertion which, though acknowledged to be false, is at the same time argued from, and acted upon, as if true.

Belonging to it are [eight][2] characteristic features.

1. It has never been employed but to a bad purpose. It has never been employed to any purpose but the affording a justification for something which otherwise would be unjustifiable. No man ever thinks of employing false assertions where the purpose might equally have been fulfilled by true ones. By these false assertions, a danger at least of disrepute is incurred: by true ones, no such risk.

2. It is capable of being employed to every bad purpose whatsoever.

3. It has never been employed but with a bad effect. The evils of which it is productive will presently be distinctly brought to view.

4. It affords presumptive and conclusive evidence of the corruptness of the act of power in support of which it is employed.

5. It affords presumptive and conclusive evidence of inaptitude in every form of government in support of which it is employed or under which it is suffered to be employed.

6. It affords presumptive and conclusive evidence of moral turpitude in those by whom it was invented and first employed.

7. It affords presumptive and conclusive evidence of moral turpitude on the part of all those functionaries and their supporters by whom as such it continues to be employed.

8. It affords presumptive and conclusive evidence of intellectual weakness and stupidity and servility in every nation by which the use of it is quietly endured.

[1] Bentham was presumably referring to the practice of oath-taking in England, for his views on which see *"Swear not at all:" containing an exposure of the needlessness and mischievousness, as well as anti-Christianity, of the ceremony of an oath*, London, 1817 (Bowring, v. 187–229).

[2] MS 'two'.

In regard to fiction, two sources of use and service require to be noted. One is, the extent of the sinister service rendered: the other is, the extent of the class of persons to whom the service is rendered.

In respect of the extent of the service rendered, the use of fiction may be distinguished into particular and general.

By particular use, understand the particular benefit which, on the occasion of each fiction, results to the class or classes of functionaries served by it: by the general use, the benefit which accrues to all of them in the aggregate from the general principle of demoralization which it contributes to establish: viz. that in regard to human actions in general, right and wrong, proper ground for approbation and disapprobation, depends—not on the influence of the action on the greatest happiness of the greatest number, but on the practice, consequently on the will, and thence on the interest, real or supposed, of the aggregate of those same particular classes. Of the establishment of this principle of demoralization, the object and the effect is—the causing men to behold, not merely with indifference, but even with approbation—in the first place, the perpetration of injustice, and in a word of political evil in all its shapes; and, in the next place, the employing as an instrument in the commission of such mischief, falshood—wilful, deliberate and self-conscious falshood—in a word *mendacity*: the practising on this occasion and for this purpose that vice which, when by individuals not armed with power it is employed to purposes much less extensively mischievous, is by these same men[1] habitually and to a vast extent visited with the severest punishment.

Now as to the extent of the class of persons to whom the sinister service is rendered. In this respect likewise the service will require to be distinguished into particular and general. Of the wilful and mischievous falshoods in question, some will be found in a more particular manner serviceable to the functionaries having the direction of the business in that particular department of Government in the business of which they[2] are employed, and in which they are employed to the giving augmentation to the arbitrary power of those same rulers, thus enabling them, with the greater efficiency, and to the greater extent, to make sacrifice of the universal interest to their several particular and sinister interests.

In every case, and throughout the whole field of Government, these instruments of misrule have had, as they could not but have had, for their sole fabricators the fraternity of Lawyers: more particularly and

[1] i.e. the classes of functionaries served by the fiction.
[2] i.e. the fictions.

obviously, such of them as have been invested with official power, principally in the situation and under the name of Judges: though in the unofficial and less formidable character of writers, authors of reports and treatises, men of the same fraternity have not been wanting in contributing their share.

The situations on which, by means of this instrument of misrule, arbitrary power is to be heaped by these same indefatigable hands are that of the Monarch, and that of the Judge. On that of the Monarch, the Chief portion: his being the only permanent one of the two situations, and that to which the subject many were at all times engaged by habit to manifest that obsequiousness on the one part, of which power on the other part is composed.

CHAPTER 4. SECURITIES AGAINST MISRULE INDICATED[1]

§1. *Evil against which the demand for Securities has place—Misrule—General description of it—its nature and cause*

The greatest happiness of the greatest number of the members of the community in question being the right and proper, and sole right and proper, end of government, misrule has place in so far as by the line of conduct pursued by the rulers positive unhappiness is produced, or any quantity of happiness that by a different line of conduct might have been produced by them fails of being produced.

Of misrule thus explained, in so far as it has its source in the conduct of the rulers, inaptitude on the part of those same rulers, relative inaptitude corresponding and opposite to appropriate aptitude in one, or more, or all, of its several branches, may be stated as the cause of it.[2]

Of relative inaptitude, that branch which is correspondent and opposite to appropriate moral aptitude has for its cause the above-explained principle of self-preference.

Of the principle of self-preference the effect is—that, as in every other situation so in that of ruler, generally speaking, a man pursues his own happiness in preference to that of all other individuals put together: in preference to, and thence, in so far as competition has place, to the sacrifice of their happiness.

The interest by which, as being a member of the community in question, he is prompted to take for his end and object of pursuit the greatest happiness of the greatest number may be termed his right and proper interest.

The interest by which he is prompted to take for his end and object of pursuit his own interest, to the sacrifice of the interest of the other members of that same community, may be termed his sinister interest.

In so far as he is considered as bound to take for his end in view the greatest happiness of the greatest number, or the happiness of any individual or individuals other than himself, his power is said to be given to him in trust: in trust, namely in the trust or confidence that it

[1] Related fragments are at UC clx. 433 (17 July 1822) and clx. 434 (22 July 1822).

[2] In the margin, Bentham noted at this point: '☛ The division of appropriate aptitude must here be inserted or referred to.' For a discussion of this topic see 'Economy as applied to Office', Ch. 1, §3, pp. 4–5 above.

is to their happiness that the exercise of it will be directed: or shortly, his power is said to be *a trust*.

In so far as instead of being directed to the production of the happiness of the greatest number, it is to the production of his own happiness or that of some smaller number, to the sacrifice of the greatest happiness of the greatest number, that the exercise of such his power or trust is regarded as being directed, such trust is said to be broken or violated, the line of conduct pursued by him is said to be pursued in breach or violation of such his trust.

In so far as, for the sake of a benefit in any shape, i.e. of an expected addition in any shape to his own happiness, a trust is considered as being violated by any man, corruption is said to have place on his part: he is said to have been corrupt, to have acted a corrupt part.

The benefit, or say matter of good, for the sake of which a corrupt part has been acted may be termed the matter of corruption—may in this case be said to act or operate in the character of matter of corruption.

Of the matter of corruption in the case of a ruling or other functionary, the several species or modifications may require to be distinguished.[1]

In general when corruption is spoken of as having place, two parties are considered as having been concerned in it: the one a party corrupting, a corrupter—by whom the matter of corruption has been administered; the other a party corrupted—say a corruptee, to whom it has been administered, and if received, by whom it has been received.

But the same effect may be and is produced in cases where no such two parties have place: where the benefit in question, being a benefit which ought to have been applied to the use of another party—say of the community at large, say of any individual [member] or individual members of it, has by the party in question, it being at his disposal, [been] applied to his own use, or what comes to the same thing, to the use of some other person or persons to whose use it ought not to have been applied.

In this case, if two parts to the act are to be considered as having place, it is by one and the same person that the two parts are acted: the same person is at once corrupter and corruptee: left hand corrupts right.

Case I. In the character of a trustee, suppose a man to have in his

[1] Bentham noted at this point: '☛ Here insert them.' This topic is dealt with in 'Economy as applied to Office', Ch. 2, §5, pp. 19–20 above.

hands money in trust to apply it to the use of another, stiled in common language his principal, in lawyers' language his *cestuy-qui-trust*. If instead of to the use of his principal, he applies it to his own use, here corruption has place, but the act by which it is performed is not very commonly called *corruption*: it is more commonly called embezzlement or peculation: it may however without impropriety be stiled an act of self-corruption.

Case II. A man having money in his hands in the character of trustee as before, a stranger suppose, by gift of money or money's worth, an annuity suppose, engages him to make it over to the stranger for his, the stranger's, own use. Here is a case to the designation of which the word corruption would commonly and naturally. be applied: corrupter, the stranger; corruptee, the trustee.

Case 3. Trustees two: Mr Foreman, and Mr Steward; principal one: Mr Bull. By one of the trustees, Mr Foreman, money is given to the other, Mr Steward: and by this gift, Steward having property of Bull's in his hands, gives portions of it from time to time to Foreman, who applies it to his own use, spending part of it, distributing other part amongst a tribe of dependents.

Here again is a case of corruption out of dispute: Corrupter, Mr Foreman: Corruptee, Mr Steward: party plundered, say by analogy plunderee, Mr Bull.

Case the first shews the way in which, in virtue of the self-preference principle, the business of government is every where carried on, has every where and at all times been carried on, and will every where be sure to be carried on, under an absolute Monarchy.

Case the third shews the way in which, in virtue of the same principle, the business of government is every where carried on, has every where and at all times been carried on, and will every where be sure to be carried on, under a limited, or say mixt, Monarchy. Foreman and Steward join in partnership, putrify the mixture, break the cobweb chains—cast off the limitations.

Case the second is interposed only for explanation sake. Under an absolute Monarchy, it has place in the situation of the Monarch's subordinates and instruments in so far as occasion serves and adequately assured prospect of impunity presents itself. Under a limited Monarchy, it would have place under the like circumstances. But to so vast [an] extent is the corrupt benefit obtainable by means of the confederacy with perfectly assured impunity, that in this way it is not natural that, with any considerable degree of frequency, the receipt of it should have place.

In the situation of absolute Monarch, a Monarch takes and applies to his own use a portion more or less considerable of the property of his subjects. Of the portion thus taken, suppose a certain portion to be taken in excess. Be the amount of the excess ever so great, can corruption to any amount be said on this account to have place? The answer will depend upon the notions that have place respecting the relation that has place between the Monarch and his subjects.

1. According to one theory, subjects were by the universal creator created for the use of the Monarch, as the cattle of each were for the use of each.[1] According to this same theory, the greatest happiness of the Monarch is the only right and proper end of Government: in so far as between the happiness of the Monarch and the happiness of the subjects no competition has place, it is well: and if so it please the Monarch to contribute any thing towards their happiness, it is so much the better. But if competition [has][2] place, so far as it has place, so far it is the happiness of the Monarch that is entitled to the preference: it is right and proper that their happiness should be sacrificed to his: and there being no one else who has power, to him it belongs to make the sacrifice.

According to this theory, it is not in the power of the Monarch to do wrong. For to whatsoever it may happen that the term wrong may be applied, it can not with propriety be applied if no portion of happiness that ought to be taken into the account is destroyed by it, or if more of happiness than of unhappiness is produced by it. But by the supposition, in the conception entertained by the only competent Judge, namely the Monarch himself, more happiness is by every act of his produced than would have been produced by the opposite act: and their happiness or unhappiness in so far as it comes into competition with his not being fit to be taken into the account, his happiness on each occasion stands alone, and on the profit side of the account.

If this theory be a right and proper one, be the conduct of the Monarch what it may—from the beginning to the end of his life be the net quantity of unhappiness produced by him ever so great, no such word as corruption or corruptness can with propriety and consistency be applied to it in any part of it. For to say that the conduct in question is corrupt is as much as to say that it is wrong: and by the supposition, to the conduct of the person so situated no such epithet as wrong can with propriety be applied. On this theory, the Monarch is incapable of relative inaptitude in that case in which it stands opposed to appropriate moral aptitude. Whatsoever is done by him is rendered moral and right by that very circumstance, rendered moral and right in whatsoever degree it would have been immoral and wrong if done by another man, or even by him at any moment anterior to that of his

[1] Genesis, 1: 26.
[2] MS 'have'.

becoming Monarch. This theory may be denominated the theory of *impeccability*.

2. According to another theory, subjects were not as above created for the use of the Monarch: on the contrary, it is the Monarch every where that was created for the use of subjects. The right and proper, the sole right and proper, end of government is accordingly the greatest happiness of those same subjects: and in so far as competition on any occasion has place, it is the happiness of the subjects that is entitled to the preference: to this happiness it is right and proper that the happiness of the Monarch should give way. But in every case, of what is in the highest degree contributory to happiness, as above the Monarch is the proper, and the only proper, Judge. As to them, neither to any of them nor to all of them does it rightly and properly belong to pass any judgment on the matter. On this or that occasion would their judgment coincide exactly with his? on this supposition it would be useless: would it in any particular be opposed to his? on this supposition it would be an improper judgment: if acted upon, it would, by the above fundamental supposition, be detrimental to their happiness. To this theory may be given the appellation of the theory of *infallibility*.

In regard to practical consequences, whether the one or the other of these theories be adopted makes no difference. Be the occasion what it may, let that which is done by him in itself be ever so wrong, in its effects ever so mischievous and productive of human misery, he being the person by whom it was done, it follows that by him it was judged to be in the highest degree contributory to the universal happiness. But as to this matter, he, by the supposition, is the only proper Judge: therefore, by the supposition, it ought to be by all others judged to be in the highest degree contributory to the universal happiness, and as such approved of and commended.

To this theory of infallibility, to render it compleatly adequate to the purpose, a further admission—the admission of impeccability—seems requisite. For instead of the greatest happiness, suppose on each occasion the object and the sole object of the Monarch to be his own happiness, and, in so far as in his judgment competition has place, his design to be the sacrificing to that same particular happiness the universal happiness, this supposed, so far would the universal happiness be from being encreased by this same infallibility, it would in an incalculable degree be diminished.

To this simple appellative, the principle of infallibility, it seems therefore that for the designation of this second theory, the composite appellative, theory of impeccability and infallibility, should be substituted.

Upon this footing[1] stands the matter in the case of an absolute Monarchy. In the case of a limited, or say a mixt, Monarchy the second alone is the theory that seems to be adopted and acted upon.

In this case, along with the division of power, a division of mental excellence has place: of the one attribute, the seat is in one place; of the other, in another. To the Monarch belongs without dispute the attribute of impeccability. For any number of years suppose it to have been the constant object of his endeavours to get into his hands the greater number of his subjects for the purpose of destroying their lives after having brought a certain portion of them to the point of death by torture, and in this design suppose him to have succeeded, in all this he would not have done wrong: either by the doing so, it having been done by him, no wrong would have been done: or in whatsoever degree wrong, though by the second supposition it was by him that it was done, by the first supposition it [was][2] not by him that it was done.[3]

Here indeed would be a self-contradictory proposition. But [to] those by whom such theories as these are maintained and acted upon, there is nothing revolting, nothing but what is agreable and even venerable, in a self-contradictory proposition. It is only by belief in self-contradictory propositions that everlasting misery can be avoided, everlasting happiness gained.

With this attribute then he must content himself. In this state of the government, so far from being infallible, in comparison of an average man so far from being above par, he is rather below par. To such a degree is he below par, such is the imbecillity of his judgment, that on no one occasion, in the exercise of his political power, is it true either that it is right and proper that he should be guided by it, or that he actually is guided by it. On every occasion it is by some one else—by some Minister of his—that the Monarch is guided. Exactly in the condition of an infant in leading strings is this impeccable person: with the impeccability, the mental imbecillity of an infant is combined.

In this deplorable state it is that the impeccable person is surrounded by a circle of advisers to all of whom it is but too natural to become misadvisers.

Happily however the disorder is not without a remedy. Happily for the grown or ungrown baby, by the side of him, whensoever it so please him, stands a composite body stiled a Parliament. The Monarch finding impeccability, it rests on the Parliament to find

[1] i.e. upon the footing of the theory of impeccability.

[2] MS 'is'.

[3] The first supposition appears to refer to the maxim that the King can do no wrong, and the second supposition to the fact that the King performed the wrongful act.

infallibility: and infallibility is accordingly found. The wisdom of Parliament? the wisdom of Parliament! of a member of that august body, when is the ear or the mouth ever tired of these awful sounds, the wisdom of Parliament. No Pope was ever more consummately infallible in spirituals than in England the King in Parliament together are infallible in temporals: and yes: and in spirituals likewise, they forming in England part of temporals.

Was it in a mad house that this theory was hatched, or in a den of thieves: a question not unapt for a debating club, were it not that under and by virtue of it all debating clubs, all meetings that can produce discussion on topics the most interesting to human happiness, are silenced.[1]

§2. *Exhaustively analytical Sketch: shewing the mutual relations of the several abovementioned securities*

As in the case of every other act, so in the case of every act of government: add the power to the will, the act takes place: take away either, the act does not take place.

The problem is—throughout the whole field of legislation, how to prevent the sinister sacrifice: leaving at the same time both the will and the power to perform the right and proper oblation: to perform whatsoever acts may be in the highest degree conducive to the only right and proper end.

In the case of a public functionary, the *will* acts on each occasion under the pressure of two opposite and conflicting interests—his fractional share in the universal interest, and his own particular and personal interest: the former is a fraction, and every where a small one: a partnership interest in a firm in which the partners are counted by millions: the latter is an integer: and the forces with which they act are proportional. Still, be the fraction ever so small, action will be determined by it if the integer be either taken out of the scales or overbalanced.

Whatsoever arrangement has for its object the prevention of the sinister sacrifice must apply itself either to the power or the will: but the same arrangement may apply itself to both.

Of the two necessarily conjunct faculties, take in hand first the power: leaving the power to do good, take away, or if that can not be done, minimize, the power to do evil.

[1] The Seditious Meetings Act of 1819 (60 Geo. III and 1 Geo. IV, c.6), one of the so-called Six Acts, had imposed restrictions on public meetings of a political nature.

CHAPTER 4

Into the composition of all power enter three elements: intensity, extent, duration. Its intensity has for its measure the magnitude of the effect produced by the exercise of it within the extent assumed by it: the extent has for its measure, in so far as it has persons for its subjects, the number of these same persons, in so far as it has things, their number and respective values: as to its duration, it has in this case the same measure as in all other cases.

In the highest rank of power, to the intensity of the power it will be seen no limits can easily, if at all, be assigned without taking away, along with the power to do evil, the power to do good, and thus leaving evil unopposed: to the extent, still less: to the duration, with the utmost ease as well as perfect safety: witness in a word the Anglo-American United States.[1]

In any rank but the highest, limits may be set to it in any of these its dimensions without any the slightest difficulty.

Power, considered in respect of the instrument by which it operates and exercises itself, is either power operating by punishment, whence fear of evil, or power operating by reward, whence hope of good. Of reward, or say remuneration, the main shape is the matter of wealth: or for shortness, putting as is not unusual the part for the whole, in one word money: by which must in this case be understood not only money, but money's worth, in a word every thing that is to be had for money. In so far as punishment is the instrument employed or trusted to, the word power is retained and employed: in so far as money is the instrument employed and trusted to, the word money or some equivalent of it is most commonly employed: and note that by being taken away, the matter of punishment may be made matter of reward: witness pardons: as likewise that by being taken away, the matter of reward may be made matter of punishment: witness fines.

When public money is placed at the disposal of a public functionary, the purpose for which it is so placed may be that of its passing out of his hands in exchange for something designed to be employed in the public service, or that of its being applied to his own use, in retribution for the services whatsoever they may be which he is regarded as rendering or about to render to the public.

So much for power taken by itself: for power and the minimization of it considered as a means of prevention applicable to the abuse of it. Now as to the other faculty—the will. By the force of that particular interest to the action of which every human breast stands exposed, every functionary is at every moment prompted as above to make by

[1] Under the Constitution of the United States, the term of office of a member of the House of Representatives was limited to two years (Article I, Section 2), that of a member of the Senate to six years (Article I, Section 3), and that of the President to four years (Article II, Section 1).

himself or to concurr in making the sinister sacrifice. If this sinister force can by any means be prevented from becoming in that way effective, it must be by the operation of some counterforce added to that opposed by his share in the universal interest: sinister force the temptation, counterforce the sanction, antagonizing with one another. As to sanctions, three of them there has been frequent occasion to hold up to view: the *political*, including the legal, the popular, or say the moral, and the superhuman, or say the religious.

1. For a counterforce to the natural, to the native, indigenous, sinister interest, [look] first to the political, [including][1] the legal. The force of this sanction is the whole of it at the disposal of the rulers: therefore in the very nature of the case it is incapable, it may be said, [of being] opposed to theirs: if for a moment it were so, the next moment they would rid themselves of it. True. But though two rulers taken singly can not be made punishable, legally punishable, at the same time and for the same cause, each of them by the will of the other, yet arrangements in considerable variety are by no means wanting in which opposition may, even under an absolute Monarchy, be opposed for a time at least to the will of the rulers, even of the supreme ruler or rulers. Wherever for example in a Monarchy, were it only to satisfy those whom it may concern that such as is expressed in a certain document is the will of the Monarch, the countersign, the name for example of some official servant of his, is regarded as necessary, this servant, so long as he continues in such his office, has a negative upon that branch of his Master's power, and possesses in conjunction with [him] a share in it.

So again in an absolute Monarchy, suppose two officials in the service of the same Monarch, in the same office or in different offices, and one of them having committed a misdeed, the other takes measures for punishing him: the misdoer being at the same time a favourite with the Monarch. To the Monarch, were he so disposed and determined to exercise it, the power of saving the misdoer from all punishment and from all prosecution can not be wanting. But this power for some reason or other, it may happen to him not to be disposed to exercise: here then may be seen another instance of a counterforce even in an absolute Monarchy opposing itself to the will of the Sovereign: a counterforce which though by adequate exertion it might always be in his power, yet for this or that cause, on this or that occasion, it is not his will, to overpower and reduce to inefficiency.

Thus have two instances of such counterforces been brought to view: both of them capable of having place even under the strongest of

[1] MS 'included'.

all governments—an absolute Monarchy. But in like manner, as these two may have existence, and actually have existence, so in any number may other such cases have existence. In the political machine, obstacles of this sort have the effect that friction has in a corporeal machine.

Thus much may suffice for such counterforces belonging to the political sanction itself as are capable of having existence and effect of operating, and not altogether without efficiency, against the supreme power under a Monarchy even the most absolute.

2. Now as to the force of the popular, or say the moral, sanction considered in respect of its capacity of operating in relation to the will of the possessor or possessors of the supreme power in the character of a counterforce. To this moral force there has [been] frequent occasion to make reference elsewhere: and in the sequel of this work, the nature of it will come to be more particularly developed.[1] What for the present may suffice for bringing it to view is the phrase *public opinion*: an object which, far so ever from being as clear as could be wished the conception commonly suggested by it may be, can not be to any eye an altogether new one. In the opinion thus denominated stand included all those by whose obedience the power of the Monarch, be he who he may, or of the rulers, be they who they may, is constituted. Let this opinion take a certain turn, obedience ceases on the one part, and with it all power on the other. Accordingly in every government but a Representative Democracy, the idea of this sanction is of all ideas that are capable of presenting themselves to a ruling mind the most disagreeable, the most hateful and afflictive. Between these two sanctions[2] in every such government a war has place, a war which, [until][3] either the form of the government be made to give way to the democratical, or the people reduced to the condition of beasts and the force of this sanction thus reduced to nothing, can never cease.

As of a constitution which has for its object the greatest happiness of the one or the few, the main object will necessarily be to minimize this counterforce or even to annihilate it, so in a Constitution which has for its object the greatest happiness of all, the great object will be to maximize it. The course that presents itself as being in the highest degree conducive and contributory to this purpose will here come to be delineated in its place: and the reception given to whatsoever shall promise to be in the highest degree contributory to this effect may be

[1] See Ch. 5, pp. 283–98 below.

[2] i.e. between the political and the popular sanctions.

[3] MS 'under'.

seen as the most instructive test of appropriate moral aptitude on the part of rulers as any that can be imagined.

3. Lastly comes the superhuman, or say religious, sanction. But of this it will be seen that to any such purpose as that of being employed in the character of a counterforce to the power of those in whose hands is the force of the political, including the legal, sanction, it is essentially inapplicable.[1] To the force of the possessors of the supreme power, be they who they may, instead of being a counter-force, it will be an instrument in their hands: instead of a check, an instrument: giving facility, instead of applying restriction, to misrule.

As to factitious honor, it is a sort of counterfeit substitute for money, invented and fabricated by governments. Money procures services, and in this the whole value of it consists: money procures services, and factitious honor procures services: factitious [honor] procures services and among them such as it is not in the power of money to reach.

Power and money, though in both instances the less the quantity that can be made to serve the better, are to the purpose of doing good the appropriate indispensable instruments in the hands of rulers: they are both of them, according to the direction in which they are made to operate, instruments of preponderant good or instruments of preponderant evil. Factitious honor, it will be seen, is purely an instrument of evil. In the hands of rulers, power and money require to be minimized: out of the hands of rulers, factitious honor requires (it will be seen) to be altogether kept.

Of this instrument, the effect every where is, and to a great extent the design can not but have been, to make a schism in the power of public opinion, and by means of a party formed for the purpose partly to corrupt and misdirect, partly to debilitate, the force of that original most efficient, or rather only, security against misrule. But of the sort of relation which thus has place between the two forces, no adequate conception can be received or formed till the nature of these two aerial and delicate instruments has been more closely looked into and more particularly held up to view.

One advantage in beginning with power on the occasion of the minimization process—one reason for proceeding in this order—may now be visible: the less the power you have to contend with, the greater your facility in such applications as you have to make to the will. Thus, as above: if the possessor of the power is at all events to keep his hold of it so long as he lives, or even so long as he remains

[1] In the text, Bentham noted at this point: 'See further on, Dissertation | |.' This topic is dealt with in Ch. 7, pp. 325–31 below.

legally unconvicted of a specific misdeed, the difficulty of dealing with him may be unsurmountable: and by a mass of power small in extent as well as intensity, evil to an almost indefinite amount may be produced: for to one lot of power thus entrenched as in a stronghold, others indefinite in number and value may be added by him. On the other hand, when it is to the dimension of its *duration* that the knife is applied, no power so ample in its other two dimensions but may be conferred with comparative safety. Witness in the Roman Commonwealth the Dictatorship: a power which, with exception of what was thus defalcated from it, was absolute Monarchy.[1]

All this while, one thing is undeniable: namely, that for the purpose of establishing, and in the endeavour to establish, security, those who establish government begin with establishing insecurity: insecurity, viz. as against those in whose hands the means of security against others are reposed. On the other hand, another thing is no less undeniable: namely that without this risk, the other, a still greater evil, can not by any possibility be avoided.[2]

Another thing is no less so: namely that by the badness of other governments, whoever you are, you are prevented from making your own, whatever it is, so good as otherwise [it][3] might be.

In this case are the civilized nations of Europe at present with their standing armies. In each foreign nation, each nation beholds a population which may every moment become a hostile one—a population of foreign adversaries: each nation is thus laid under the unhappy necessity of providing itself with a correspondent instrument of defence: to preserve itself from distant, it submitts to present servitude.

Hence it is that to other articles in the list of counterforces must be added the institution of a national Militia.

The more extensive this counterforce is—the greater the security of the nation, not only against foreign, but against domestic, adversaries: not only against the rulers and subjects of every foreign nation, but against its own rulers who ever they are.

Against these, when the quantity of armed force in this shape is at its maximum, so is this security: the security thus constituted: in a word it is entire: for in this case, the degree of efficiency with which, in case of depredation or oppression on the part of rulers, the people

[1] The dictatorship was added to the Roman constitution soon after the expulsion of the kings at the end of the sixth century BC to provide an extraordinary magistracy in times of crisis. Though the dictator, when the office was at its zenith in the fifth and fourth centuries BC, had great power, he held his post for a maximum of six months.

[2] This sentence is clarified by the marginal summary: 'Without this risk, no security against foreign enemies or unempowered malefactors.'

[3] MS 'you'.

are capable of acting in concert for the purpose of redress is at its maximum: an entire people with arms in their hands can not be employed as instruments of oppression: why? for this plain reason—that they have no victims to act against—to operate upon.

The elementary units of this force—the individuals of which it is composed—are no other than the members of the Public Opinion Tribunal. Judges with arms in their hands prepared in case of necessity to give execution to their own judgments.

A force thus circumstanced may be so organized as that while it is incapacitated from being made to act as an instrument of offence, it may be rendered compleatly adequate for every purpose of defence, and to this purpose one simple arrangement is sufficient: a declaration that, without an express law for the purpose, no part of the population thus fortified shall be obliged or permitted to move out of the territory of the state.

For providing the community with the very maximum of force in this shape, small in comparison is the utmost expence that can be necessary: expence of small arms with men to train others to the use of them—nothing more. As to pay in money, none would be necessary. As to expence in the shape of time, neither would this be necessary: for whatever is thus employed is employed in exercise as well as pastime: it may be taken out of that which, with or without exercise, would have been employed in pastime in some other shape.

CHAPTER 5. FOURTH SECURITY FOR APPROPRIATE MORAL APTITUDE IN OFFICIAL SITUATIONS, IN PARTICULAR THE ALL-COMMANDING ONES, THE COUNTERFORCE APPLIED TO THE FORCE OF SINISTER INTEREST IN THOSE SAME SITUATIONS, VIZ. MORAL RESPONSIBILITY. FIFTH SECURITY, AS ABOVE, LEGAL RESPONSIBILITY[1]

§1. *Expository matter*

The counterforces thus distinguished—responsibility in its two modes—require in the first place a joint consideration.

By moral responsibility, understand here the result of subjection—effective subjection—to the power of the popular, or say moral, sanction, as applied by the Public Opinion Tribunal.

By legal responsibility, understand subjection—effective subjection—to the power of the political, including the legal, sanction, as applied by the several legal Judicatories that have place under the Government in question.

By the term *Public Opinion Tribunal*, understand a fictitious entity—a fictitious tribunal the existence of which is, by the help of analogy, feigned under the pressure of inevitable necessity for the purpose of discourse to designate the imaginary tribunal or judiciary by which the punishments and rewards of which the popular or moral sanction is composed are applied.

A Jury, supposing the members of it located by chance, a Jury exercising its functions in the manner of a Common Petty Jury under English Judicial Procedure, may be regarded as being a Committee of the Democratical Section of the Public [Opinion] Tribunal organized.

Attached to this same word is another import which requires to be distinguished from it. A person is said to be a responsible person, not in virtue of his actual and effectual subjection to either tribunal, and in particular the legal, but in virtue of his being in such a situation,

[1] Bentham may have originally intended to consider in full in 'Constitutional Code Rationale' the seven securities for moral aptitude listed at UC clx. 434 (22 July 1822), namely minimizing (1) the power, (2) the wealth, and (3) the pay of functionaries, applying (4) legal and (5) moral counterforces to the power of functionaries, and excluding (6) factitious honour and (7) instruments of delusion. In the event, he seems only to have composed the chapters on counterforces and factitious honour.

Abandoned fragments dealing with the topic of counterforces are at UC clx. 368 (16 July 1822), clx. 374 (21 July [1822]) and clx. 375 (22 July 1822).

principally in respect of his pecuniary circumstances, that if it were the desire of government that by means of coercion he should be made to do or suffer so and so, he would accordingly be made to do so and so, namely by reason of his being in possession of benefits, in particular either money or power or both, on which it would be in the power of government at large, and the judicial branch of it in particular, to take hold, supposing it disposed to do so.

The distinction is a real and an important one. In England, the situation of King, by the avowed state of the law, is placed above the field of legal responsibility: to the purpose of exposure to punishment he can not be made to suffer, nor consequently to do any thing that it does not please him to do or suffer.

In the other sense however, he is in an abundant degree responsible—he has money enough, for example, by the seizure of which, could it be got at without his leave, he could be brought to do any thing which by any one it was desired he should be seen doing.

It is by the plenitude of his responsibility in this particular sense that he is eased of all responsibility in the general sense: so material it is that the two senses should be mutually distinguished.

In general, from the top of the scale to the bottom, the more abundantly responsible a man is in respect of sufficiency, the less responsible he [is] in respect of effectual exposure.

In respect of exposure to punishment, the King is irresponsible by law. Other situations there are that are so in effect, though by law and to outside shew, responsible: witness the Lord Chancellor, his two immediate subordinates and the twelve paid Judges.[1]

First, calls for explanation, legal responsibility: of moral responsibility, any such clear conception not being obtainable by any other means as by its analogy to responsibility with reference to the power of the law.

As to legal responsibility, to the purpose of exposure to punishment at the hands of the political, including the legal, sanction, in a Government [in which] the whole or any fractional share in the Supreme Operative power is in the hands of a single person, no such legal responsibility, it is manifest, can in his instance and at his charge have place. The situation of an absolute Monarch is therefore one in which no such responsibility can have place. The situation of a limited Monarch, howsoever limited, is therefore another—or at the least will want very little of being so.[2]

[1] The subordinates of the Lord Chancellor were the Master of the Rolls and the Vice-Chancellor, and the paid judges the Lord Chief Justice of King's Bench, the Lord Chief Justice of Common Pleas, the Chief Baron of the Exchequer and the nine Puisne Judges and Barons.

[2] In the marginal summary, Bentham added at this point: '☛ Note case of Spanish and

Under an absolute Monarch, in the instance of no other functionary under him can any such responsibility have place, unless such should be the Master's pleasure: and it will not be the Master's pleasure unless he be an object of the Master's personal displeasure, whatsoever misdeeds he may have committed to the detriment of the universal interest, and whatsoever may have been the defalcation made from the sum of public happiness.

So far as this effective irresponsibility has place, so far it is evident the power of the legal sanction can not be presented in the character of a counterforce to the power of government—the power of government in the hands of a supreme ruler or set of supreme rulers—to present it in this character would be a contradiction in terms.

But, a case not altogether incapable of having place is—at the charge of one set of his subordinates and instruments, say his subordinates in the department of finance, [the Monarch] suffers the punishment to be administered by another set of his subordinates and instruments—say the functionaries belonging to the judicial department: here then the force of one of those sets acts as a counterforce to another set, his equally and assuredly obsequious instruments.

Thus far as to an absolute Monarchy. In the case of a limited Monarchy, the state of things is not in this respect materially different. In this case likewise, the power of giving impunity to any one and every one is commonly given even by law: such is the general rule: and if in words and shew there be any exceptions, the extent given to them is extremely narrow, and even in that extent they are without substance and effect. As to this point, the main difference between an absolute and a limited Monarchy consists in this: the impunity which in a direct and open way might by law be alike conferred in both Monarchies is in an absolute Monarchy accordingly conferred in a direct and open way, in a limited Monarchy in some indirect and concealed way in preference. In a limited Monarchy, the acts of the Monarch and his instruments are necessarily in one way or other more exposed to observation than in an absolute Monarchy. Suppose then a case in which the grant of impunity would, in the eyes of the public, be in a flagrant degree repugnant to the received notions of justice, there may be a convenience in employing some indirect and covert method rather than a direct and open one for the production of the effect. A party of soldiers, for example, are set on and employed to slaughter a peaceable company of malecontents whose abstinence

Portugueze Kings under the Constitutions.' Under the Spanish Constitution of 1812 (Art. 168), and the Portuguese Constitution of 1821 (Art. 127), the respective monarchs were declared not to be subject to responsibility.

from all violation of the law has rendered it impracticable to apply to the same purpose the hand of a Judge. The Monarch, if he pleased, might first give the order to the slaughterers and then pardon them. Under the Constitution, such is its excellence, he might kill his subjects, the whole multitude of them, and the law still remain unviolated. But were this the course, sooner or later, resistance might here and there be made and disturbance be thus given to his ease: the gard for *ease* requires that a course more or less [in]direct and [un]conspicuous should be given to *vengeance*. The slaughterers might be sent out of the way, or rendered undistinguishable. Should the resources of this physical kind fail, the state of the law, Judicatories and Judicial Procedure, affords them in such multitude, and such intricacy, that the list of them, if rendered intelligible, would compose a volume.

So much as to the casc of a Monarchy.

Now as to the case of a Representative Democracy. In this case, at the charge of the Members of the supreme Operative power—of all of them without exception—legal responsibility may have place without difficulty: legal responsibility—not in name only, but in effect, namely to the purpose of exposure to punishment. During their continuance in that situation, and to the extent of the absolute majority of them, no: a proposition asserting the affirmative would be a self-contradictory one. But even during their continuance in office, the minority remain, in the very nature of the case, in a state of legal responsibility as towards and under the majority: and from and after the expiration of their authority, being on a footing no other than that of the other members of the community, they remain, each and every [one] of them, responsible in the legal sense for whatsoever they may have done—whether in that situation or any other.[1]

Thus stands the matter in regard to legal responsibility, responsibility to punishment at the hands of the administrators of the power of the legal sanction.

Look now to moral responsibility—responsibility to the purpose of eventual exposure to the punitive power of the Public Opinion Tribunal, possessor of the force and influence of the popular, or say moral, sanction: and in particular the power of the democratical [section][2] of that same invisible, yet not the less effectively operative,

[1] In the text, Bentham added at this point: 'An arrangement for that purpose has accordingly been proposed in the Text. See Articles | |.' This is evidently a reference to enactments Bentham meant to include in the main body of the code. In *Constitutional Code* he in fact went beyond this and subjected the members of the legislature to the possibility of dislocation and legal punishment after petition and majority vote to that end on the part of their respective constituents: see *Constitutional Code*, I (*CW*), Ch. V, §§2–3, pp. 29–35.

[2] MS 'sanction'.

tribunal:[1] a tribunal, like the Vehmic, invisible; but, like *that*, not the less operative.[2]

To punishment, to not altogether ineffective punishment in a certain shape, not only in [a] representative democracy, but even in an absolute Monarchy, the possessors of the supreme Operative power are capable of standing exposed. In fact in this shape, in this sense, in the most compleatly absolute Monarchy, the Monarch is always to a certain degree responsible, and feels himself so to be: though in some Monarchies, at some times, such has been the feebleness of this responsibility in the character of a counterforce to the powers of government in the highest grade, that the effect of it in respect of a cause of mitigation to the evils of misrule—of depredation and oppression—in experience has seldom in any determinate degree or shape been perceptible.

The less the mass of counterforce which, in his endeavours to promote his particular interest at the expence of the universal interest, a public functionary feels opposed to him in other shapes, the greater the need there is of his finding something opposed to such his endeavours in this shape. An absolute Monarchy is therefore the sort of government in which there is the greatest need of it, the need of it is most pressing, and in which accordingly, if in a Monarchy the end of government was the greatest happiness of the greatest number, [it] would be established with the greatest promptitude, and maintained with the most anxious care. But a Monarchy in general, and of Monarchies an absolute one in particular, is that form of government [in which] it is not possible that the greatest happiness of the greatest number ever should have been or ever should be the end of government—in which it is not possible that the end of government should ever have been or ever be any other than the greatest happiness of that one, with or without some comparatively small number of sharers. Accordingly in every Monarchy, not the maintenance, but the suppression of this same prime instrument of security to good government and good morals has been the object of the most anxious and uninterrupted care.[3]

On the other hand, for the correspondent and opposite reason, the

[1] For the division of the public opinion tribunal into two sections, the aristocratical and the democratical, see 'Economy as applied to Office', Ch. 9, § 3, pp. 68–70 above. A fragment dealing with this theme is at UC clx. 379–82 (21 July 1822). A further fragment dealing with the aristocratical section is at UC clx. 406–8, 364–5 (8, 9, 12, 16 July 1822).

[2] The Vehmic courts flourished in Westphalia in the fourteenth and fifteenth centuries. They kept no records, and in certain cases operated in secret, yet claimed to administer royal justice throughout Germany.

[3] In the margin, Bentham commented at this point, 'Note after this to account for the comparative mildness of Tuscany and Russia', but none appears to have been written.

greater the counterforces having place as above in the frame of the government itself, the less the need of this same extraneous counterforce. Accordingly in the Representative Democracies of the Anglo-American United States for example, any such security might, as far as regards government, be extinguished with least inconvenience. Accordingly at one time, partly in consideration of the annoyance to individuals, in a season of comparative inexperience, endeavours were employed to extinguish it. But the greatest happiness of the greatest number being the very end, and sole end, in view of the Government, and by every individual seen to be so, this security, far from being suffered to remain in an enfeebled state, bound in ill-considered shackles, was presently restored, and now for the universal comfort, being set down on the rock of uncontested and full experience, is established for ever in all its plenitude.[1]

§2. *Evidence and Comments*

Requisites to the bringing into action the force of the Public Opinion Tribunal—for bringing it to bear upon any pernicious act by whom so ever performed—by a public functionary or by a non-functionary, [are] two distinguishable sets of matter: namely evidentiary matter, and commentative matter, or matter of comment. By *evidentiary matter*, understand matter the effect or tendency of which is to bring or hold up to view the individual act in question, in conjunction with all the several circumstances on which the nature of its operation on the happiness of the community depends. By matter of comment, understand all such discourse the effect or tendency of which is to afford indication, true or false, correct or erroneous, concerning the operation of such act on the happiness of the community in such sort as to be in this or that way contributory or detrimental to it.

By evidentiary matter, understand on this occasion not merely such testimony as in case of trial would of itself be sufficient to form a just ground for punishment, but also whatsoever may be considered as having the effect of denunciation: for the commencement of a process is not less necessary to the conclusion of it, than the middle of it is.

All such salutary matter in both these forms, every functionary, in proportion to the power which from the nature of his situation he has

[1] Bentham perhaps had in mind the Sedition Act of 1798, passed by the Federalist dominated Congress with the intention of halting Democratic-Republican attacks on the government. The opposition argued that the Act was in violation of the First Amendment which guaranteed the freedom of speech, but before the question was decided, the Act expired in 1801. During Thomas Jefferson's presidency (1801–9), all persons convicted under the Act were pardoned.

of pursuing his own particular and sinister interest at the expence of the universal interest, sees his interest in the suppression of: an interest the strength of which is in proportion to the sinister benefit capable of being derived by him from such sinister acts. Every functionary in proportion to his power: and accordingly in a Monarchy, whether absolute or limited, the Monarch: in a Monarchy limited by an Aristocracy, the Aristocracy.

The anxiety with which the functionary endeavours to rid himself of the opposing power of this counterforce will be in proportion to the magnitude of the sinister benefit he reaps or looks to reap from such abusive exercise of the power of his office, and the intensity of his fear of the impending punishment: by every act he exercises for the purpose of destroying or weakening it, for the purpose of preventing or restraining the publication of the tutelary discourse, he manifests himself an enemy thus engaged in a course of actual hostility against the happiness of the community.

Of every such *indication*—and of every such *comment*—the effect or tendency is *defamation*: defamation with reference to the party to whom the alleged pernicious act, whatsoever it be, is thereby imputed. To oppose defamation as such, to oppose without exception or discrimination every act to which the term defamation can with propriety be applied, is to act as an accomplice to all crimes, as an instrument of all mischief, of all misery, as above.

Every such act is therefore a virtual confession of such complicity: of such hostility to the happiness of the greatest number.

Proportioned every where to the hostility of the form of government, and of the practice under it, to the greatest happiness of the greatest number will of course be the exertions made by the governors to deprive the governed of this security, to keep the governed for ever deprived of this their only security: the only security which the nature of the case admitts of.

In the sinister interest by which they are led in the endeavour to effect such suppression, functionaries engaged in giving execution and effect to the acts of a bad government, and functionaries engaged in misdeeds for their own benefit in disobedience to the good acts of a good government, are naturally joined by individuals concerned or meaning to be concerned in such pernicious acts to the repression of which the power of the legal sanction is not applicable.

To profess to be a supporter either of good government or of good morals, and at the same time to profess to be desirous of seeing defamation suppressed in a case in which the imputation conveyed by it is true, is a contradiction in terms: put the two branches of it together, the desire is a desire to see the same thing be and not be—a desire that the same thing shall and shall not have place at the same time.

One case there is, and but one, in which the effect of defamation, supposing the misdeed charged by it really committed, is—not to [encrease], but to [reduce][1] the quantity of happiness in the community. This is where the mischief produced is produced—not by the act itself, but by the disclosure of it. In this case are comprehended all those [instances] in which, for want of sufficient maturity in the public judgment, or by the influence of some sinister interest, the sentiment of antipathy has, in the breasts of the people considered as members of the Public Opinion Tribunal, turned itself against this or that act the nature of which upon the balance is not of a pernicious nature.

Examples of this case are:

1. In a community in which the public mind is infected with the disease of intolerance in matters of religion, indication of an act evidencing the entertaining an opinion contrary to that which is established or predominant.

2. Eccentricity of any sensual appetites, the sexual for example, by which no pain in any assignable shape is produced any where. Here by the supposition, by the act itself no pain, no sensible evil, is produced: but by the disclosure of it, evil to a deplorable amount may be produced: by the antipathy, though by the supposition groundless, by the antipathy called forth by it into exercise, a whole life may be filled with misery. The real enemy to the happiness of the community is not he by whom the thus obnoxious act has been exercised, but he by whom the indication of the exercise of it has been afforded. The suffering being greater, the mischief is greater in the case where the act has been than in the case where it has not been really exercised. For he in whose instance the imputation has been groundless has for his consolation that which the other has not.

3. Indication of a breach of the marriage contract, on either side, and in particular the female. Suppose the commission of it unknown, no pain is produced by it any where: the pleasure is pure. What then, when committed ought it to remain exempt from punishment? Oh no. Why not? Even for this cause: namely that without the commission, divulgation could not have place: and that by commission, divulgation is always rendered but too probable.

Those who cry out against what they call the licentiousness of the press might with much more reason cry out against all punishment without distinction, and in particular against all punishment at the hands of the legal sanction and the tribunals by which the force of that

[1] MS 'not to reduce, but to encrease'.

sanction is applied: for in no other form at once so gentle and so efficient, and in particular in no form of legal punishment, could punishment be employed in the repression of any thing that has ever been characterized by the name of crime or by the name of vice.

Punishment as applied by the legal tribunals—punishment applied under the name of punishment—attaches to such evil acts alone the mischief of which has place as well in a shape sufficiently determinate, as in a quantity sufficiently great, to warrant the application of evil in the shape and in the quantity in which it is so denominated. Punishment as applied by the Public Opinion [Tribunal], applied as it is in effect without the name, attaches itself to mischief in all shapes in which the hand of man can, without special and sufficient justification, be instrumental to the production of it.

Applied by the legal tribunal, punishment is not only thus narrow in its applicability, and thence in its use, but continually exposed to the danger of running into excess: excess from the danger of which the punishment which the Public Opinion Tribunal makes application of is altogether exempt and free.

The efficiency of the popular or moral sanction, with its Public Opinion Tribunal, can not be strengthened, but the efficiency of the law, in so far as its force is employed in augmentation of the happiness of the people, is also strengthened. In so far [as] a misdeed, which by reason of its detrimental effect on happiness is *vicious*, and thereby exposes the agent to punishment at the hands of the Public Opinion Tribunal, is moreover *criminal*—an act of delinquency against the law exposing the agent to punishment at the hands of the law—every channel through which defamation as above may be divulgated is a channel through which, in so far as the defamation takes this turn, strength and efficiency is given to the law.

Through these channels, men who in themselves are, and would otherwise remain, helpless, receive help and abatement of their sufferings: injuries and sufferings which would otherwise swell to a boundless magnitude, and rendered altogether remediless, are met by complaint, and kept within bounds: through this channel, men, who by their own indigence and the rapacity of lawyers are deprived of all help at the hands of the legal sanction with its judicatories, find a limit and thence a mitigation to their sufferings.

For suppose the act in question to be of the number of those to which punishment stands attached, as well at the hands of the legal sanction as at the hands of the popular or moral sanction, as well at the hands of the legal judicatories as at the hands of the Public Opinion [Tribunal]: this being the case, to give intimation of it to the members of the community at large in their capacity of members of the Public

Opinion Tribunal is to give indication by the light of which not only witnesses but prosecutors at the bar of the competent legal tribunal may be brought into action, and the further investigation of whatsoever relevant facts would otherwise remain in darkness produced: that which to the uncorrupted, free and ever open Public Opinion Tribunal is evidence to the purpose of conviction in an immediate way, being to the legal tribunals evidence to the purpose of investigation for the obtainment of ulterior evidence, such as suffices in the first place for a ground to accusation, and in the next place for the obtainment of such evidence as shall suffice for conviction and punishment.

Against such misdeeds, whether by the state of the law put or not put upon the footing of crimes, against such misdeeds as have in the governors, their instruments, favorites and dependents, their authors or protectors, the legal sanction, with the corresponding legal judicatories, refuses of course all redress: against all such misdeeds, whatsoever redress if any is afforded, it is by the popular or moral sanction with its Public Opinion Tribunal that it must be afforded.

An endeavour, whatsoever be the means, to destroy or to weaken this counterforce is therefore an endeavour to give encrease to misrule with the misery of which it is productive, to give encrease to injury in all shapes at the hands of individuals with the misery in all shapes of which it is productive—an endeavour to diminish the quantity of happiness in the community, to encrease the quantity of suffering in the community. But, except what regards the quantity of the happiness or suffering in question, this is the worst that can be said of any the foulest crime, whatsoever it be, that experience, observation or imagination can hold up to view.

Of the channels through which, if at all, information in both its shapes, as above, must find its way to the public eye and the public ear, beyond all comparison the most ample and efficient are those in the designation of which the collective term *the press* is commonly employed: and of these again the most ample and efficient are those for the designation of which the collective term the periodical press is employed. Every act by which the net mass of benefit derivable through these channels is lessened or endeavoured to be lessened is of the number of those by which the actor is rendered as above an enemy to all happiness, to all virtue, to all mankind.

In regard to the benefit of which this counterforce is capable of being the instrument, for lessening the net amount of it by operations applied to the information and the channels of conveyance through which, as above, it has to pass, for lessening the net amount of this benefit, the nature of the case affords two expedients or courses of policy. The one consists in the blocking up of the channels, and thereby stopping in the whole or in part the current of information that would otherwise make its way through them to the eyes and ears of the public—of the members of the community taken in the aggregate. The other consists in rendering, in a greater or less quantity and degree, corrupt and delusive the stock of information which comes so received: the one system may be stiled the blockading system or the obstructive policy, the other, the corruptive.

The obstructive operates by the simple substraction of such information as being correct, is at the same time usefully instructive. The corruptive operates by the addition of a mass of information in itself false and designed to be deceptious. Note here that by substraction, deception may be produced as well as by corruption. To this purpose what may happen to be sufficient is to render *partial* the stock which passes on: partial, that is to say in the bad sense of the word, being the sense in which it is used when subservient to injustice: that which is regarded as operating against the side meant to be favoured by the deceit being stopped, while that which is regarded as operating in favor of it is suffered to pass on.

For operating on the obstructive plan, the nature of the case affords two courses of action—two modes of restriction—the licensing system, and the prosecuting system.

As to licensing, it is a complex operation of which prohibition, and that a universally extensive one, forms a necessary part, forms the principal ingredient: in the first place comes prohibition which applies to every thing: in the next place comes permission, given to any such persons or any such things as it is intend[ed] to exempt from the prohibition.

In comparison of the licensing system, the prosecuting system is in an eminent degree inefficient.

1. The prosecuting system can not be employed except in so far as the very sort of thing which it is the endeavour of it to cause not to be done has actually been done.

2. Where it does operate, its mode of operation is weak; its effect comparatively uncertain. In the licensing system is included the employing for the stoppage of the obnoxious matter physical force: seizing for example the produce of a printing press, and either keeping or destroying it. Not only does it thus operate upon bodies such as are in question, but also upon minds, namely in the way of intimidation: to cause men to stand persuaded that of an article, which but for the hope of selling it would not be produced, the sale if it be produced will

not take place, is to prevent the [production][1] of it. It is not only to prevent the obnoxious result but to employ punishment in the prevention of it: a punishment consisting in the labour and expence of production, which it thus leaves in the shape of dead loss, depriving it of concomitant profit.

3. It[2] keeps from observation the mischievous effect which it operates: while by prosecution that same mischief is proclaimed.

4. The punishment which as above is one of its means of action is much more effective than any which, being applied under the name of punishment, can not be applied without prosecution for a preliminary to it: not to speak of the expence, the uncertainty which in the case of prosecution always hangs upon the result, this, together with the delay and vexation, which even on the prosecutor's side stand inseparably attached to prosecution, is saved.

5. Not only is the punishment in this case so much more efficacious; but it is moreover kept concealed from observation.

Thus it is not only so much more efficacious than punishment under the name of punishment, but at the same time less odious. It affords just ground for greater odium, yet attracts less. While it is less odious, it is beyond all comparison more mischievous.

By the prosecuting system, punishment is applied as above under the name of punishment, having or seeking to have the effect of prohibition. If it be in the way of sham law that the punishment is applied, the prohibition as to all individual cases posterior to that in which the punishment comes to be applied is, in this case as in others, left to each man to form by imagination for himself, by conjecture in the way of inference: of inference by comparison of the matter which he has a contemplation to publish, with the matter to which it has lain in his way to see punishment applied.

If it be in the way of real law that the punishment is applied, the eventual denuntiation made of it comes before it and wears the form of a *prohibition*.

Even in this case, under the form of simple obstruction, corruption in a certain way may be, and as often as the force in question is applied is seen to be, included.

Prohibition is either compleat, as under the name of prohibition it is of course, or incompleat, as it is in so far as to the form of prohibition, that of taxation is substituted. Under every application of the taxing system, an application of the licensing system is contained. Pay the tax, you have a licence to use the article: omitt paying the tax, the licence is refused to you.

[1] MS 'sale'.

[2] The subject of this and the remaining points is the licensing system.

But under the licensing system is in this case again concealed the corrupting system. By the effect of the tax, such information as a man is able and willing to purchase and obtain by paying of the tax is suffered to pass on and reach him: such as he is either not able or not adequately willing thus to purchase is stopt and prevented from reaching him. Note then the consequence where the desire has place to serve the comparatively rich at the expence and by the oppression of the comparatively poor. That which the poor [man] has need of to enable him to form a right judgment and pursue a line of conduct beneficial to his interest is stopt from reaching him: while his comparatively rich antagonist receives the matter on both sides. In the contest between rich and poor, the means of attack are thus suffered to find their way to the rich: while from the poor, all the [. . . ?] means of defence are kept back and rendered inaccessible.

This indirect mode of corruption by garbling is not altogether so mischievous as either of the two others.[1] Of the matters kept from publication, no such individual selection can be made as in the other case. Still however, separation in no small degree mischievous can be made and is made. For particulars and examples, see the case of England.[2]

As it is only by the power of government that this corruption and this obstruction can be carried into effect, it is manifestly for the purpose of misrule, for the purpose of giving extension and perpetuity to misrule, and thereby to human misery in all its shapes, that war upon the happiness of mankind in both these shapes is on every occasion carried on.

But as nations are now connected, information to any one nation is information to every other, applying poison or obstruction to any one press is applying it to every other. Carrying on hostility in any one nation, and thereby against that one nation, is carrying on hostility against every other. It is still more extensively and effectively an act of hostility against the nations of the earth than piracy is. For the mischief and terror produced by a pirate is confined to the seas on which his acts of piracy are exercised: it is confined within the space of time, never a very long one, during which those acts continue to be exercised. But the mischief produced by the suppression of information on the one side, on the side of the victims of misrule, while false and delusive information in support of misrule is let through, may spread itself over all nations, and continue in all times.

[1] i.e. the taxing system as opposed to prohibition and the prosecuting system.

[2] As an example of the taxing system, Bentham perhaps had in mind the stamp duty payable on newspapers, and its extension by one of the Six Acts of 1819 (60 Geo. III and 1 Geo. IV, c.9) to certain pamphlets containing news and comment.

If of such corruption and obstruction the practice is the practice of enmity to the whole human species, those who are partakers in it, are they not enemies to the whole human species? To designate them by their individual names would be a task alike endless and dangerous. Not so the designating them by their generic ones.[1]

§3. *Defamation to the prejudice of ruling functionaries as such*[2]

Among the consequences of restrictions imposed in the ordinary form on the press, one is the efficiency thus given to false reports in their most mischievous shape: false and mischievous reports as such, whosoever may be the parties on whom the evil produced by them falls.

In the first place let the situation be that of the ruling functionaries, and in particular those of the highest rank in the scale of subordination.[3] Defamation in the written shape it is possible to keep suppressed. Defamation to the same effect in an oral shape it is not possible to keep suppressed. You may keep a watch upon all presses: you can not keep a watch upon all tongues. When it is in a printed shape, it is in a determinate shape: and whatever be the shape of it in other respects, being in a determinate and that an enduring shape, any one who feels disposed to make answer to it knows what it is he answers, and where to find it. In whatever shape it first makes its appearance, in that shape it remains: it can not by the author or by the adopter be altered from shape to shape in a manner contrary to truth and justice, just as occasion calls. It may be met, it may [be] opposed, in whatsoever manner is best adapted to the nature of it: is it in any way false? it may be opposed by simple denial: it may be opposed by the statement of the opposite truth: is it not only false but improbable? the arguments demonstrative of the improbability may be opposed to it: is it injurious, is it mischievous? the mischievousness of it may be laid open to view, and reproach proportioned to the evil be poured down upon the head of the author and his accomplices, or prepared and kept in readiness to be poured down upon them in proportion as they are presented to view.

Such are the facilities which the nature of the case affords for the encountering of it when the shape in which it presents itself is thus determinate.

[1] A further fragment dealing with the blockading system is at UC clx. 376–8 (22 July 1822).

[2] An earlier draft on the subject of defamation is at UC clx. 366–7 (9 July 1822).

[3] Bentham did not go on to consider the situation of any other functionaries.

Now suppose it in the merely oral shape. Being refutation-proof, being proof against exposure, the probability is that even in its first shape it is false. It is either a compleat fabrication in the whole texture of it, [or] if there be a groundwork of truth belonging to it, an embroidery of falshood is added—of falshood such as suits the sinister purpose, whatever it be. But how so ever mischievous and injurious, this first is naturally its least mischievous and least injurious shape: and even in this shape it is not capable of being encountered. From the first mouth it passes on to another, and in the second mouth further mischievousness, further injuriousness, with or without consciousness and intentionality, are naturally added. Thus it travels on from mouth to mouth: it rolls on adding to its mischievousness and injuriousness at every stage: to the number of the stages there is no limit: and at no one of them can it ever be encountered.

A circumstance which has a natural tendency to provoke falshood, and through falshood, injury, evil to the prejudice of the government by which the restriction is imposed, is the resentment which the restriction itself imposes: a resentment than which nothing can in any case be better grounded or more just. Where oppression is exercised and there is no other remedy, no other defence against it is afforded by the nature of the case, falshood, if not justifiable, is at any rate comparatively excusable. Of every such restriction the effect and object is to secure efficiency and impunity to oppression and depredation: to oppression in every shape, the worst shapes imaginable not excepted. From no course that can be taken by the endeavour to put an end to such an instrument of oppression can any evil be produced equal to the evil produced by the application of this instrument of oppression, if the application be effective.

To the encountering of such endeavours[1] by appropriate falshood, the grand objection is that it will be needless: for seldom are they employed but for the purpose of concealing enormities, the correct statement of which would suffice for the infamizing of the oppressors without the addition of any thing that is not true.

Another objection is that by one false report detected and brought home to the author, or any person concerned in the dissemination of it, while conscious of the falshood, his own reputation may be so damaged that from his mouth or pen what is true will not be taken for such.

Be this as it may, thus much is clear, that where such this instrument of oppression with impunity is employed, supposing even

[1] Bentham seems to be referring not to the endeavours to put an end to restrictions on the press, but to the endeavours of rulers to impose such restrictions.

that all allegations uttered against the oppressors are injurious, no suspicions that can be entertained of them can be ill-grounded: for supposing the intentions of a ruler the worst imaginable, such is the course which of course he would not fail to take for the carrying of them into effect: while on the other hand, suppose his conduct free from all just imputation of misrule, no need would he have of any such screen: the just odium which the employing of it could not fail to draw upon him would be so much net evil drawn down upon him by himself.

Scarcely can any act which in any case can be done by the most mischievously inclined individual be comparable in atrocity to the act of that ruler or set of rulers who, by this endeavour to keep from exposure the evidence [of] whatsoever enormities they may feel disposed to committ, thus in spite of themselves betray their intention to push to consummation the sinister sacrifice: if punishment were a thing that could be deserved, no punishment that could be deserved by any the most atrocious malefactor unarmed by power could equal the punishment thus deserved by these irresistible and invulnerable malefactors. By no finite number of determinate acts of tyranny could a more proper and reasonable cause for resistance and insurrection be afforded, supposing success in a sufficient degree probable: for in the use of this instrument, the intention of exercising tyranny in its worst shapes is included: the intention, coupled with a probability always but too great of its being carried into effect.[1]

Under a government the conduct of which is in all other respects ever so good, let but this one restraint have place, there needs but one supposition to render it in the eyes of a true lover of mankind desirable that, at the risk of the worst that can ensue, that government should with all possible speed be put down: this supposition is—that by the government that succeeded it the like restraint would not be imposed. One instance there is in which this supposition stands verified: the government of the Anglo-American United States: for in that country alone has self-victory in this the most difficult of all its shapes been as yet displayed.[2]

[1] Bentham noted at this point: '☛ Add. Actual purity of intention in rulers no reason here against insurrection.'

[2] See p. 288n above.

CHAPTER 6. FACTITIOUS HONOR EXCLUDED

§ 1. *Its general nature and principal modifications*[1]

By factitious honor, understand honor which is procured or endeavoured to be procured in favor of a particular individual at the hands of the public at large,[2] by means of some token or tokens giving an intimation to them to that effect by the functionary by whom the honor is said to be conferred. On this occasion, a word for the most part interconvertible with honor is *dignity*.[a]

For the conveying of this intimation, signs of various sorts are in use. One sort of sign is of the purely visible sort: of this sort are *ensigns of honor*: another sort being verbal are as such audible as well as visible. Of this sort are the signs called *titles of honor*.

Titles may be and are unaccompanied with ensigns: ensigns scarcely can exist without correspondent titles.

Howsoever designated they may be seen standing in some cases singly, in others in a climax of various length.

A factitious honor is seen sometimes in conjunction with a lot of power being received constantly with it, as in the case of a Member of the English House of Lords:[3] sometimes without power, as in the case of a Spanish Grandee: sometimes without power but with privilege, as in the case of the titled Noblesse of France:[4] sometimes without power or privilege, as in most Christian Nations in the case of the Orders of Knighthood that are designated by ensigns worn about the person: and in the simple Knighthood of England distinguished by an appellative but without any ensign worn about the person:[5] when conferred with power, in some cases elevation in the climax of honor carries with it elevation in the climax of power—as in the case of

[a] The idea conveyed by the word honor is however that of a fictitious entity extraneous to the individual in question; the idea conveyed by the word dignity, a fictitious entity, a *quality*, the seat of which is within him.

---

[1] A related fragment is at UC clx. 248. This MS has been mutilated and the date torn away. A further sheet, setting down general positions on the topic of factitious honour, originally dated November 1817 but re-dated 17 July 1822 and headed 'Constitut. Code', is at UC clx. 425v.

[2] In the marginal summary, Bentham noted: '*Public*. See effects of factitious honor in an international point of view.' Bentham dealt with this matter as Evil 14 in § 6, pp. 317–18 below.

[3] An English peer was entitled to sit and vote in the House of Lords, which shared legislative power with the Crown and the House of Commons.

[4] Both the Spanish and French nobility enjoyed privileges and exemptions. Grandees however had pre-eminent status amongst the nobles of Spain, and possessed additional privileges, but did not as such have any formal political function.

[5] The Knights Bachelor did not wear any insignia, but prefixed the title 'Sir' to their name.

Bishopricks and Archbishopricks in the English House of Lords: in some cases the honors rise in a climax, the power remaining unvaried, as in the case of the Lay Lords in the English House of Lords: the power being annext in an entire to the lowest degree in the climax of honor, termed a Barony, while above that rise other degrees in a climax, namely a Viscountcy, an Earldom, a Marquesate and a Dukedom.

In some cases it is or has been seen conjoined with property in land, as in the case of some of the Spanish orders:[1] in others with landed property in the dominions of different States and a share in the supreme operative power in one State, as in the case of the Knights of Malta before the cession of the power to Great Britain in consequence of the conquest made of it.[2]

In some cases it is seen conjoined with pensions: as in the case of the French Legion of Honor instituted by Bonaparte and continued by Lewis the 18th.[3]

Infinite in number and variety are the compounds of power, privilege, landed property, pecuniary property, in which it is an ingredient. The cases above given are given as examples only, and to aid conception: in these examples, incorrectnesses might probably be found in abundance. The idea thus given of the subject will, if it be confused, be but the more adequate. With facts belonging to the subject, folio upon folio volumes have been filled. An analytical view of it that should be at once clear, correct and all-comprehensive would be matter for a volume a week for months, and the whole together so much paper and time employed in waste. The task would bear a resemblance to that of a set of industrious labourers who may be seen in London occupied in watching the rubbish and refuse of all sorts as it

[1] At the time of the reconquest, the *hidalgos* received benefices from the king or the great magnates in return for performing military service. This enabled them to claim noble status, but not a title of honour.

[2] The Knights of the Order of the Hospital of St. John of Jerusalem, having been driven from Rhodes by the Turks, obtained in 1530 the grant of Malta from Charles V (1500–58), Holy Roman Emperor from 1519 to 1556. They derived their principal revenues from the estates of the Order in Europe, though those in England and parts of Germany were confiscated during the Reformation, and those in France in 1792. In 1798 Napoleon captured Malta, and banished the Knights. The French in turn surrendered to the British in 1800. The treaty of Amiens of 1802 provided for the restoration of Malta to the Knights, but the British refusal to give up the island led to the renewal of war with France in 1803. Malta was finally confirmed to Britain by the treaty of Paris of 1814, and the possessions of the Order on the island claimed for the Crown.

[3] The Legion of Honour was founded by Napoleon in 1802 in order to recognize and reward services to the state. It was originally organized into fifteen cohorts, each comprizing seven grand officers, twenty commanders, thirty officers and 350 legionaries. A stipend, ranging from 250 francs to 5,000 francs per year, was attached to each grade. The order was confirmed in 1815 by Louis XVIII (1755–1824), King of France from 1814, and its constitution modified in 1816.

is conveyed from dwelling houses to spots allotted for the purpose in carts called Dust Carts: the compound is analysed, the individuals belonging to the several species of matter collected in heaps. Between the one task and the other there would be this difference. When rightly assorted, the contents of the Dust Cart have all of them their modes and degrees of usefulness: those of the badges of honor, their modes and degrees (as will be seen) of mischievousness.

As to the compounds in which this article is an ingredient, the consideration of them need not add to the trouble: though in fact conjoined with the several other articles, in idea there will be no difficulty in keeping it separate.

Primarily-seated[1] and in an *extravasated* state—say in one word *extravasated*—by these two words the distinction of greatest importance in respect of usefulness or mischievousness will be brought to view. Appropriately-seated the honor may be said to be in the instance of the individual on [whom][2] by an appropriate act of power it has been conferred: extravasated, in the instance of him who, without any additional act of power, has received the honor in virtue of a relation borne by him in some mode or other to him on whom it was conferred: genealogical relationship is one of these modes; official is another: occupation of the same office.

§2. *Its mode of operation*

Here, relative to this product of government, a few points there are which call for explanation.

1. It operates as an order for respect: for tokens of respect to be afforded and, as it were, paid by persons in general to him on whom the honor is said to be conferred. It operates therefore as a title to respect. In this particular it is in regard to respect that which an order for the payment of money—a draught for example on a banker—is in regard to money: but with this difference, that it is only at the hands of that one person that the order for money calls for money, whereas it is at the hands of all persons in general that the title of honor—the order for respect—calls for respect.

On the occasion of each such act, it is an exercise of dominion over the many for the benefit of the one—over the many, indeed with little exception over all. The means not being coercive, it produces not that sense of oppression which, in general, dominion, employing as it

[1] MS del. 'Appropriately-seated'.
[2] MS 'some'.

must do coercion for its instrument, can not, when directed towards so unjustifiable an end, fail to produce. It is by delusion that the effect is produced, not by force or intimidation. But the effect of it being, as will be seen, purely mischievous, the circumstance of there being one evil in detail which is not produced by it, will not suffice to turn the whole mass of evil into good.

2. It operates as a sort of certificate—as an article of documentary evidence: as a certificate of good desert, whatsoever may be the idea in the community in question associated with the word merit: as a certificate declaring on the part of the person by whom the title is conferred an opinion that the person on whom it is conferred by him is in possession of that same article called *merit*.

Of such certificates the effect is to cause respect in degree and quantity more or less considerable to be entertained by the members of the community in question, to be manifested towards and in relation to him: respect, or at any rate the outward signs and tokens of that inward sentiment. This effect it produces by ascribing *dignity* to him: dignity or *worthiness*: by causing it to be believed that in the opinion of him by whom the honor is conferred, he on whom it is conferred is worthy of receiving at the hands of the members of the community in general those same outward tokens.

It gives intimation that in the opinion of that same functionary, the person in whose favor it is his desire that these same tokens of respect should be manifested and paid—manifested as it were in payment, has been and is deserving of such respect. To *deserve* any thing good, any instrument of felicity, is to have a claim to it in the character of a reward on the score of service—on the score of service in some shape or other rendered by the individual in question to some other individual or individuals: of which service, if it be real, an effect must have been the contributing in fact or in probability to cause him to experience pleasure in some shape which he would not have experienced otherwise, or to be exempt from experiencing pain which he would have experienced otherwise.

With the word merit, if any clear idea is attached to it, stands associated the idea of service: for by him to whom merit is ascribed, suppose no service rendered or endeavoured to be rendered to any body, the idea of merit evaporates and leaves the word in a state of non-significance.

If then according to the intimation given by the dignity ascribed to him and the alledged title to respect given to him, he has rendered service to any body, it must have been service of the meritorious kind: service by the rendering of which the existence of merit has been displayed.

Moreover, this service must have had something extraordinary in it—in its nature: something whereby it stands distinguished from ordinary service, from service in those shapes in which it is continually rendered by every body to every body, by every dealer for example to his customer, by every customer to his dealer—by every seller to his purchaser, by every purchaser to his seller.

As in the case of service, so in the case of respect, the worth of it, if it has any, must consist either of a certainty (as where the event is past) or of a probability of pleasure in some shape or other experienced, or pain in some shape or other averted and not experienced.

Laying all together—the intimation conveyed by an act by which a title of honor is conferred is—that the individual on whom it is conferred has, in some determinate shape or other, rendered to some individual or individuals, or to the whole community together, service of a meritorious and in some way or other of an extraordinary kind, and has thereby proved himself to be possessed of dignity—i.e. by such service to have given himself a title to receive, at the hands [of the] members of the community in question in general, tokens of respect, of the existence of the sentiment of respect in their minds in relation to him, as if in payment or part payment of such service.

In its character of a certificate, this document does not so invariably or so extensively or so immediately operate on men's minds as in the character of an order for respect. Its character of a certificate is rather a character ascribed to it to reconcile men to it in the character of an order for respect than a character which belongs to it of course.

The reader will presently be in a condition to judge whether, with exceptions in a very minute proportion, in so far as it is a certificate of merit, of meritorious service, the certificate is not false: as also whether, in so far as it is true, any effect which it has in the way of affording payment in the name of reward for such service already rendered, and thereby giving encreased probability to the rendering of the like service to an indefinite extent in future, is not capable of being produced in a much greater degree and to much greater certainty by other means, as also what those other means are: as also whether this alledged mode of procuring beneficial service be not pregnant with evil in a variety of distinguishable, and accordingly here distinguished, shapes, and whether that evil be not so much net evil, without any good attached to it, or if there be any good in any shape attached to it, whether by the evil such good is not greatly outweighed, in such sort as to leave a net quantity on the evil side of the account.

§3. *Why as a testimony of meritorious service it is essentially unapt and fallacious*

Reasons.

It is given without any published proof of the particular nature of the meritorious service, if any, that is supposed to have been rendered, without any published proof of the fact of the man's having rendered any such meritorious service.

It is given, for aught that appears, without any proof received by him by whom the honor is conferred of service as having been rendered in that or any shape to any one by him on whom it is conferred.

In a word, the act by which it is conferred is an act essentially arbitrary.

It is with relation to reward, that is to say to the good that is done, that which in relation to evil, punishment is, in so far as inflicted without trial—without judicial inquiry as to the ground of it formed by the conduct of him to whom it is applied.

The consequence is—that by every such honor so conferred, injustice is done: done not indeed to the individual to whom the reward is applied, as in the case of punishment to the individual to whom the punishment is applied,—not to him indeed, but to others: namely to those at whose expence it is applied. See further on.[1]

One case alone can be mentioned in which it affords any just ground for supposing that, in its character of a certificate of meritorious service, it may perhaps not be false: and that is the case where it is conferred as a reward for military service. But even in this case, it can not but be frequently false—false perhaps in more instances than those in which it is true: and if so, absolutely unapt: at any rate, comparatively unapt, comparison had with another in which the most efficient means are employed for preventing it from being given where it would be false,[2] while when given as it has every where as yet been actually given, no such means are employed.

§4. *What matters of fact it probabilizes*[3]

In the character of a testimonial or certificate, what are the matters of fact which, with relation to the individual so honored, it renders more or less probable?

[1] See §6, pp. 309–10 below.
[2] i.e. notification of meritorious service as discussed in §5, pp. 306–9 below.
[3] A related fragment is at UC clx. 273 (4 July 1822).

Answer. These are:

1. That either immediately or unimmediately, namely through the intervention of some other or others, the individual [on][1] whom the honor has been conferred was, at the time of its being conferred, an object of sympathy to him by whom it was conferred: that is to say, in a Monarchy, to the Monarch.

This, it is evident, can not be a matter of compleat certainty.

2. That if not an object of sympathy—at any rate, not an object of antipathy: for if yes, he would not have subjected himself to the pain necessarily attendant on the conferring it.

3. That partly by gratitude for this past favour, partly by hope of further favors, he is attached to the person of the functionary by whom the benefit was conferred on him: attached to his purpose, attached to his particular interest, disposed to contribute, according to the measure of his faculties, to the advancement of the particular interest of that same patron, disposed to be obsequious to his will, disposed to concurr in the advancement of that particular interest at the expence and by the sacrifice of all conflicting interests in general,—in a word, the government being a Monarchy, to contribute as occasion offers to the sinister sacrifice.

4. That whatsoever in this respect may have antecedently been the case, the individual thus honored has the faculty of mixing in society with [other][2] individuals possessing factitious honor of the same species and the same rank, still more assuredly with all those below him in the same line; and in all probability with others, if any such there are, who in relation to him are superior in rank. To speak in general terms, he is known to have access to persons occupying elevated situations in the community.

5. That as his interests are in alliance with, so his affections sympathize with, the interests and affections of that portion of the community whose station is thus elevated: and that in so far as between the higher and the lower orders, in consequence of such difference of interests and affections, a difference of judgment naturally has place, his judgment will on each occasion side with theirs, his judgment, and in consequence, his conduct: in a word, that in his character of member of the Public Opinion Tribunal, it is to the aristocratical Section of that judicatory that he belongs.

But the interest, consequently the affections and judgment, of the Monarch as such are adverse to the general interest of the community: so are those of the Aristocracy in all its modifications: not

[1] MS 'by'.
[2] MS 'under'.

contributory but detrimental to the greatest happiness of the greatest number.[1]

In relation to these several matters, the evidence thus afforded is not conclusive evidence: it is capable of being rebutted and outweighed by other evidence: but in so far as it has any, such is the tendency of it: whatsoever be the degree of probability in relation to each point, such is the side on which it is situated.

§5. *Government arrangements best adapted to the production [of] all such beneficial effects as are sought to be produced by factitious dignity. Honor by notification of meritorious service*

Encreasing the power of the Monarch will by some be placed in the number of these effects. This effect, it is here contended, belongs to the catalogue of its mischievous ones.[2]

The effect on which, in proof [of] its by some supposed usefulness, the greatest reliance seems likely to be placed is that supposed to be produced by it in the character of an inducement for the production of extraordinarily meritorious public service: service rendered to the community at large, whether by being rendered to government or otherwise. Employed to this end, that which will be expected of it is—the making known to the community at large the quality and quantity and value of the service rendered to the end that by the several members of it, as occasion offers, retribution may be made to their benefactor by suitable manifestations of affection and respect, and in particular by good offices—by useful services.

Employed in this character, it is employed in the character of a means of obtaining by purchase, at the hands of such individuals in whom, on the several occasions in question, the power of rendering it may have place, the greatest quantity of service in the shape in question, namely extraordinarily meritorious service, upon the most advantageous terms: that is to say, of the greatest value possible, quality and quantity considered, and at the lowest price.

Here then come two different ends the accomplishment of both which, in so far as practicable, requires to be aimed at:

1. of the aggregate mass of service thus obtained, [to] maximize the value;

2.—to minimize the expence.

[1] The relation between factitious honour and the public opinion tribunal is discussed in a fragment at UC clx. 264–5 (11 July 1822).

[2] Bentham noted at this point: 'See §§ | |.' He perhaps had in mind material which he had just written and forms §§4, 5 and 7 of 'Supreme Operative' (see pp. 155–65, 167–75 above).

1. Note that in the instance of every such service, the mass of reward in all its parts taken together must afford such a mass of benefit to the individual in question as shall be sufficient to outweigh in his mind the burthen sustained by the rendering of it. In so far as public affection and respect enters into the composition of the means of purchase, this relation between quantity of service and quantity of reward will require to be considered. Benefit of reward must outweigh burthen of service.

2. The greater the value of the service, that is to say of the benefit, the greater is the burthen which he, on whom it depends in the instance in question, will be disposed to take upon himself on the occasion and for the purpose of his rendering it. The greater a service, the greater the reward worth giving for it.

3. If on any occasion there be two services so circumstanced that, by the individual or individuals in question, either can be performed, but not both of them, any two masses of reward that shall appear capable of being earned by the performance of the two services respectively should be so apportioned that the receipt of [the] more valuable reward shall be attached to the act of rendering the more valuable service. Of two rival services, offer greatest reward for the most valuable.

Note that the only shape in which remuneration belongs to the present subject is the honorary shape.

That it is not for service in every shape that reward in this shape will be sufficient, or even so much as apposite, is sufficiently manifest. Where, in the course of action whereby meritorious service has been rendered, loss has been suffered by money expended, profit does not commence, reward does not commence, till compensation has been made for the full amount of the loss: and in the account of money must be comprehended that which in the time in question would have been received by the individual in question in return for labour expended.

Moreover, if by the reward conferred it be intended to purchase at the hands of other individuals future contingent service, not only actual loss, but probable risk must be taken into the account.

One set of apt government arrangements the nature of the case affords—apt in such sort that by it the value of reward in this shape is in its application to service in all shapes maximized, the expence minimized, and the value of the reward in such sort adjusted to the value of the service to the production of which it tends, that is between two mutually incompatible services its tendency is to give existence to the more valuable. By this set of arrangements thus much and nothing more is meant to be designated than such arrangements as have for their object notification: the making known to as great an extent possible, due regard being had to expence, and with the utmost degree of clearness, correctness and compleatness possible, the nature of the service rendered, the name of the individual by whom the service has been rendered, and the circumstances by which the degree of meritoriousness possessed by it [has][1] been constituted.

Of this plan, the principal feature consists in the sort of delineation above proposed—in the causing to be made a written description of the individual service in question, regard being had to the above particulars.

The effect of it will be a sort of judgment pronounced: opposite in its effects but not the less analogous to a judgment by which, on the ground of delinquency, the individual in question is subjected to punishment.

On this consideration, in so far as regard for *expence*, with its accompaniments delay and vexation, warrants, the judgment thus pronounced ought to have evidence for its ground. Public affection and respect ought not any more than public money to be bestowed without evidence of the sufficiency of the title on which it is claimed. Upon this plan the terms of the judgment, with that of the evidence on which it has been grounded, will form the matter or subject of a report. To this document as to any other, such a degree of publicity may in each individual case be given as the nature of the case is thought to warrant and to call for.

As time runs on, of the several judgments here indicated, an aggregate and continually encreasing body will be formed. To this aggregate some denomination will of course be given. Let it for example be—The Book of good-desert, or say *The Register of meritorious service*.[a]

In it the several individual services will of course be ranged under general and specific heads: as likewise the names and other circumstances appertaining to the individuals thus distinguished.

The expence attendant on the process of conferring Dignity in this its natural shape, is it liable to the imputation of being excessive?

If at the expence of but a single individual, reward in money to the amount of any the smallest denomination of coin were claimed, the services of the judicial establishment for the purpose of giving effect to it or rejecting it are not grudged. Nor in the shape in question, reward can not, it will be seen, be given but at the expence of all the members

[a] Opposite but not the less analogous to this Register will be the Book or Register of ill-desert.

[1] MS 'have'.

of the community how impalpable so ever may in each instance be the amount of the expence.

Where the value of the service shall appear not to be such as to warrant this expence, no such expence will be incurred. The individual by whom it is conceived that a service of this description has been rendered will take his own course for the giving publicity to it.

At the expence of the public at large, and by the act of a public functionary, without sufficient and judicial evidence of extra good-desert, reward in the shape of honour ought not to be conferred.

Honour thus conferred will be natural honor judicially conferred: conferred, as the French phrase is, *en connoissance de cause*.

§6. *Factitious honor in general—Evils produced by it—when, as usual, arbitrarily conferred*

When arbitrarily conferred, it is conferred either without so much as an indication of service in any specific shape rendered to the public, or if with any such indication, without proof made and published of the reality of the facts on the ungrounded supposition of which it has been grounded.

If conferred without indication of service to the public, that which is indicated by it is—that the individual on whom it is conferred is an object of favor to the person or persons by whom it has been conferred. In this case it is mischievous on the [fourteen][1] following accounts.

[1.] Evil 1: Burthen to the *un*honoured at large.

There are two sets of persons at whose expence is conferred every honour that is conferred: [1.] all the members of the community at large—the whole number of them: 2. those particular ones, if any, among whom peculiar benefits in this shape have been shared.

By the members at large, of any donation of this sort taken singly the expence is in but a small degree, if in any degree, felt. But when viewed in the aggregate, the expence which communities have been subjected to in this shape will, by every man, be more or less clearly perceived, and acutely felt, in proportion as he thinks of it.

2. By those who, at the time when, in the individual instance in question, the honor was conferred, were already in possession of it, the expence is felt in a much more intense degree. Witness the Dutchess of Northumberland who, in the days of George the second,

[1] MS blank.

durst not spit out of her Coach as she passed along the Street for fear of spitting upon a Lord.[1]

Evil the second case: Burthen to the co-honored.

3. Every honor that has been conferred on any man in whose instance it is not clear that extraordinary service to the public has [been rendered] in any shape is conferred in a more particular manner at the expence of all those by whom extraordinary service to the public has really been rendered: it is felt by them as an injury. It has always for its tendency, and to an unmeasureable extent for its effect, the preventing men in general from taking on themselves any extraordinary burthen for the purpose of rendering to the public in any shape extraordinary service.

Evil 3: Burthen to the meritorious unhonored.

Publication of service secures to every extraordinarily meritorious individual, for services past and thence for services to come, the exact portion of honor which, in a comparative as well as absolute point of view, is most apt with relation to the service. No injury does it to any men: to men in any number it may produce uneasiness: but in no instance can the uneasiness be productive of, or accompanied by, any such sensation as the conception of injustice—of injustice done to any one by him by whom the honour has been adjudged.

4. When Monarchy was specially on the carpet, in the account given [of] the several external instruments of felicity in their eventual character of instruments of corruptive influence, this one had its place among the rest.[2] Evil 4: Say Evil by contribution to the corruption fund—to the stock of the matter of corruptive influence.

Considered in comparison with the other articles, it will be found to stand upon a very different footing from both of them. Power is necessary: it is necessary to the very existence of government: it is the very matter of which the means of government are made. Excluded it can not be: the utmost that can be done is to limit it.

So again money—money at the disposal of government. Without it, government in a political community of any considerable extent could not be carried on. To exclude it altogether is impossible. To exclude

[1] The source of this anecdote has not been traced, though Bentham seems to have been alluding to Elizabeth Seymour (1716–76), daughter and heiress of Algernon Seymour, seventh Duke of Somerset (1684–1750), whom she succeeded in her own right as Baroness Percy. In 1740 she had married Hugh Smithson (afterwards Percy) (1714 or 1715–86), who succeeded his father-in-law under special remainder as second Earl of Northumberland, and in 1766 was created Duke of Northumberland. For a sketch of her character see Horace Walpole, *Memoirs of the reign of King George the third*, ed. G.F. Russell-Barker, 4 vols., London, 1894, i. 333–4.

[2] See 'Supreme Operative', §3, pp. 152–5 above.

the difference between what is necessary and what is not necessary—and to take care that that which is necessary shall according to its destination be applied to the service of government and to no other purpose—this is the utmost of what can be done.

In the hands of the conferrer of the honour, the Monarch, it is productive of evil in this shape in two different ways:—in a general way, by its existence; and in a particular way, by the particular application which, on each individual occasion, is liable to be made of it. By its existence in hands so situated, it holds out to every one the general assurance, that, by him who on any account is an object of the Monarch's displeasure, no good in this any more than in any other [shape] will be received: that for obtaining the matter of good, in this as in any other shape, by far the most promising course is to contribute if possible to the Monarch's pleasure, whatsoever be the means—the most promising, not to say the only promising, course that a man can take. Thus it is that so many persons as there are in the nation to whom it is a source of temptation, so many persons are there who are urged by it to do on all occasions the will of the one privileged member of the community, the Corrupter General, at the expence of all the others, and thereby to make contribution, each of them according to his means, to the sacrifice of which he is Chief Priest—in a word, the sinister sacrifice.

Now as to the evil of which, on this or that particular occasion, in that situation, it is apt and liable to be productive. In its character of a source of undue respect, it enables him to overpower the tutelary power of the punitive branch of the Public Opinion Tribunal. By the prospect of benefit in this shape, an individual has been led (suppose) to minister to the Monarch's will by this or that act by which, but for the counter-operation of this order for respect, dishonor would have been cast upon him. It would baffle calculation to say to what degree a man may by this means be rendered proof against shame, and in what multitude other men may, by the view of factitious honor obtained by acts naturally dishonorable, be led into the like sinister courses.

5. On the same occasion, it has been seen how, by the possession and eventual expectation of them, the external instruments of felicity contribute as such to the general debasement of the moral part of man's frame in private life as well as in public.[1] Among those same objects of general desire, this is not less true of the one than of either of the other two abovementioned. Evil 5: Evil by demoralizing influence: or say Evil by independence on good behaviour, or *Evil of sinister independence*.

[1] See 'Supreme Operative', §17, pp. 198–202 above.

In both parts of the field of action, in the character of instruments of corruption, they operate in two distinguishable ways: viz. 1. when in possession, by operating as a sort of bond of union and common attachment to the whole system of which they form a part: 2. when in expectation, by operating as inducements to statesmen to betray their trust to the effect of obtaining at the hands of the arch-corrupter an instrument of felicity in this shape.

6. Evil the sixth: evil by pretence for depredation.

Where factitious honor has been raised to a certain level, thereupon has come the observation that money is needed for the support of it. On this occasion, *dignity* is the term that seems most commonly employed. But it is out of the pockets of the people that, as for all other purposes so for this, the money has to come. If in conjunction with factitious dignity, the man has opulence of his own in a certain degree of plenitude, it is sometimes held sufficient, sometimes not, as it may happen: but if he has not—if this be an agreed matter—money in such quantity as shall be sufficient must at all events and at any rate be found for him. Obtained by swindling, honor carries depredation in the belly of it.[a]

[a] Of this superfoetation of evil, the most disastrous case is that which has place where the Monarch of a country receives a higher title: a Monarch with a title inferior to that of King, the title for example of King. To a King, not to speak of a sceptre or a Palace, belong a throne and a Crown: to this pair of implements a quality called splendor is necessary: the throne must have gold about it: the crown, besides gold, pieces of natural glass called diamonds: by these ingredients or appendages, by the help of a little manual labor, splendor in the physical sense is constituted. But to splendor in the physical sense must be added splendor in a superior sense, the metaphorical or hyperphysical sense. Appetite in all shapes is stimulated by the new title: the quantity of his superfluities must receive encrease: the quantity of the superfluities enjoyed by his Courtiers and his living instruments of government must be encreased: the number of these instruments themselves must receive encrease. Being admitted into the holy circle and fraternity of Kings, his appearance must in every thing be if possible upon a par with theirs. The fable of the frog and the ox is exemplified, but with a disastrous variation. It is not by themselves but by the overgrown frog at the head of them, by the great frog with a crown on his head, that the little frogs are burst.[1]

The language employed on this occasion demonstrates in how deplorable a degree the force of the intellect may be subdued by the force of delusion and prejudice. Always

---

[1] For the fable of 'La grenouille qui se veut faire aussi grosse que le boeuf' see *Oeuvres de J. de La Fontaine*, ed. H. Regnier, 11 vols., Paris, 1883–93, i. 65–7 (Book I, Fable iii). The frog bursts herself in the attempt to become as large as the ox, and the fable ends with the moral:

> Le monde est plein de gens qui ne sont pas plus sages:
> Tout bourgeois veut bâtir comme les grands seigneurs,
> Tout petit prince a des ambassadeurs,
> Tout marquis veut avoir des pages.

in the character of an object of prime necessity is the furniture of the great Baby House, this mass of the instruments of corruptive and delusive influence, spoken of. This, which is so much worse than useless, is spoken of as of more importance than the whole aggregate of those benefit[s] the securing of which constitutes the only compensation for the evils necessarily produced by government—the only circumstance that distinguishes it from a nuisance. Not any the faintest colour of reason being capable of being given for it, it is on every occasion taken for granted in the character of an incontestable truth. Ask in what way it contributes in the character of a means to the pretended end, no answer will you ever receive. Ask in what particulars the governments in which no such splendor, lustre, support of dignity, has place, ask in what particulars they are the worse for the absence of it, no answer will you receive.

As in the situation of King, honor and dignity require for their support splendor and lustre, that is to say money torn for the purpose out of the pockets of the people, so in every situation within the reach of the royal eyes. Hence it is that if a man in a certain rank be in want of money, whether it has been by misfortune or by prodigality or folly in any other shape that the gap has been produced, the deficiency is to be supplied at the expence of the laborious part of the people: the productive classes are to be squeezed for money to fill it up. Incessant are the complaints of the expence of affording to the helpless among the productive classes those supplies without which starvation and death must of necessity be their fate: profound is the silence as to the expence of supplying to the extravagant in the higher order the means of ulterior extravagance. Grievous the complaints of the overgrowth of that part of the population for the maintenance of which £10 a year, both sexes and all ages together included, will suffice—no complaint of the overgrowth of that part for the maintenance of which £100 a year will not suffice.

In England, by both parties in the State, Whigs as well as Tories, by official men in works published with their names, avowal may be seen of a scheme for the provision of public functionaries, of men in dependance under the King: a day might be assigned before which, as might be demonstrated with mathemat[ical] certainty, the whole species would, by the single virtue of this scheme of depredation under the name of liberality, be destroyed. Clear of the embarrassment produced by mathematical formularies, the demonstration has been before the public for several years past. It has been seen by men of both parties, read without attempting refutation, knowing that refutation is impossible, and both parties go on writing and talking on the ground of the same principle of certain destruction as if no observation to this effect had been ever made.[1]

On this occasion, the brood of Kings hatched by Bonaparte and reared by the Holy Alliance can not fail to present themselves.[2] The rationale of the operation is

---

[1] The official men in question were the Whig Edmund Burke (1729–97), Paymaster-General 1782 and 1783, and the Tory George Rose (1744–1818), Secretary to the Treasury 1783–1801, Vice-President of the Board of Trade and joint Paymaster-General 1804–6, Vice-President of the Board of Trade and Treasurer of the Navy 1807–12, and Treasurer of the Navy 1812–18, whose respective works, *Speech on Economical Reform*, London, 1780, and *Observations respecting the Public Expenditure and the Influence of the Crown*, London, 1810, had been criticized by Bentham in 'Defence of Economy against the late Mr Burke', *The Pamphleteer*, ix (1817), 3–47, and 'Defence of Economy against the Right Hon. George Rose', ibid., x (1817), 281–332. Bentham's essays were reprinted in *Official Aptitude Maximized; Expense Minimized*, London, 1830 (Bowring, v. 263–386) as papers V and VI.

[2] After the establishment of the French Empire in 1804, Napoleon took it upon himself to create, confer and recognize a whole host of titles and dignities, many of which were

sufficiently manifest. By the old brood nothing has been lost in the account of honor and dignity: profit to an unlimited amount has been made in the account of money. In dignity, no loss: the great old Monarchs are not confounded with the little new ones: the distance is sufficiently wide to preserve them from misfortune in this shape: on the contrary, a contrast is visible: and by this contrast they are raised.

By the power and for the support of the dignity a tax, and that a perpetual one, has been imposed on Bavaria, Wertemburg, Belgium, Saxony, and Hanover: a tax which though of the indirect kind is not the less burthensome.[1]

Such is the immediate effect. But in the train of it comes another: all these are added to the number of the nations to whom the appellative *King* will be an object of abhorrence.

The Emperors of Germany and Russia are now Emperors because they were so before. For the name of the empire Austria is substituted to Germany, because in Austria the Emperor was, as he is, a despotic Sovereign, whereas in Germany taken collectively he was but a titular one.[2] The King of England would not be Emperor

---

subsequently recognized by the powers of Europe in the various agreements and treaties entered into towards the end and at the conclusion of the Napoleonic Wars. The Electors of Bavaria, Württemberg and Saxony all effectively received their titles of king from Napoleon. By the treaty of Pressburg of 1805, Maximilian Joseph II (1756–1825), Elector of Bavaria from 1799, was recognized as Maximilian Joseph I, King of Bavaria, and Frederick II (1754–1816), Duke of Württemberg from 1797, and Elector from 1803 (a dignity also conferred by Napoleon), was recognized as Frederick I, King of Württemberg. They both assumed the title of king on 1 January 1806. Maximilian Joseph I and Frederick I both deserted Napoleon and had their sovereignty guaranteed by Austria by the treaty of Ried of 8 October 1813 and the treaty of Fulda of 2 November 1813 respectively. At the peace of Posen (1806), Frederick Augustus III (1750–1827), Elector of Saxony from 1763, assumed the title of Frederick Augustus I, King of Saxony. His title was confirmed at the Congress of Vienna (1814). Other kings and kingdoms, those conferred by Napoleon on his brothers Joseph (1768–1844), Louis (1778–1846) and Jerome (1784–1860), and his brother-in-law Joachim Murat (1767–1815), did not however survive the Napoleonic era. Joseph Bonaparte became King of Naples in 1806, and was installed as King of Spain in 1808, but having fled the country after the French defeat at Vittoria on 21 June 1813, was deposed by Napoleon. Murat became King of Naples in succession to Joseph in 1808; he broke with Napoleon in 1813 but was deposed by Austria in 1815. Louis Bonaparte was proclaimed by Napoleon as King of Holland in 1806, but in 1810 Napoleon deposed him and annexed Holland to the French Empire. The Kingdom of Westphalia, created by Napoleon in 1807 and given to Jerome Bonaparte, was dissolved in 1813, and at the Congress of Vienna its territories incorporated into Prussia. Napoleon crowned himself King of Italy in 1805, but the kingdom ceased on his overthrow in 1814. He also bestowed the style of King of Rome on his son Napoleon Francis Joseph Charles (1811–32), who in 1818, having never been recognized as such by the Allies, was instead granted the title of Duke of Reichstadt. All the surviving sovereigns of Europe, except the Pope, the Sultan and the King of Great Britain, eventually joined the Holy Alliance, established in 1815 by the Emperor of Austria, King of Prussia and Emperor of Russia, with the declared aim of creating a brotherhood of Christian monarchs.

[1] For Bavaria, Württemberg and Saxony, see above. In 1814 Belgium was united with Holland to form the Kingdom of the United Netherlands, and on 16 March 1815 William I (1772–1843), Prince of Orange, mounted the throne. At the Congress of Vienna in October 1814, the Electorate of Hanover, at that time joined with the Crown of Great Britain, was erected into a kingdom.

[2] Though the Holy Roman Emperor, traditionally a member of the Habsburg dynasty, had not enjoyed sovereign power throughout Germany, but only in the Habsburg domains, this was not the reason, as Bentham suggests, for the change in title. Francis II (1768–1835), Holy Roman Emperor from 1792, was forced to abdicate in 1806 upon Napoleon's dissolution of the Holy Roman Empire. In anticipation of this event, as Francis I he had assumed the title of Emperor of Austria in 1804.

For this application of public money there are sundry reasons, reasons more really operative than readily avowed.

1. When, from this factitious cause [of] respect, the support given to it by the natural cause of respect, *money*, is taken away, contempt will be apt to substitute itself to the respect. By the decomposition thus made, the false colour will be dissipated. Men will be led to say to themselves—'a man may bear this much upon him and yet be a poor creature, what then is it good for?' and thus its worthlessness being seen in the case of this poor man may by degrees come to be recognized in the case of the rich ones.

2. In place of the respect they have been accustomed to receive, these his fellow dignitaries will be apprehensive of sharing in the contempt under which they see him suffering.

3. They will derive, the more generous of them, a pain of sympathy from the observation of what they see him suffering.

7. Evil 7: evil by sanction to imposture. A character in which this token operates is that of a certificate of merit on the part of the wearer: of useful and meritorious service rendered by him in some shape or other to the community at large: and combined with this certificate is a draught drawn upon the members of the community in their character of members of the Public Opinion Tribunal for value received: a draught payable in tokens of respect, value received in the shape of meritorious service.

The functionaries by whom this deceptious instrument is uttered are by the practice of uttering it, and the habit of seeing it accepted, encouraged to act in the character of impostors. It operates in this way on their moral faculties as an instrument of demoralization.

8. Evil 8: evil by propagation of delusion. This evil is the counterpart of the last preceding one. In so far as the fraud passes upon them undetected—in so far as men are imposed upon by it, and

because the forms of a concurrence by Parliament would have been necessary and the delusion by which he is kept in his place of King might have been shaken by the discussions produced by the word *Emperor*. They would not make the King of France, nor did he wish to be made, Emperor, because that would have been copying the example of the Usurper whose Emperorship was the result not wholly of force and intimidation but in some measure of corruption and delusion, and in addition to fear had the consent of no inconsidcrablc portion of the people for the cause of it.[1]

[1] The French Empire was proclaimed on 18 May 1804, and Napoleon was awarded the title of Emperor, with the succession, if he had no direct heir, devolving in turn upon the descendants of Joseph and Lucien Bonaparte. In a plebiscite taken on the subject of the Imperial title and law of succession, 3,572,329 votes were cast in favour and only 2,569 against. Napoleon crowned himself Emperor of the French on 2 December 1804. He abdicated on 11 April 1814, but was allowed to retain the style of Emperor; however after the Hundred Days, and a second abdication on 22 June 1815, he forfeited his title and was treated officially as a general.

bestow respect where respect is undue and the payment of it mischievous—mischievous to themselves, mischievous, as hath been seen, to every body—it operates upon their intellectual faculties: it operates as an instrument of intellectual depravation.

9. Evil 9: Evil by *aggravation of inequality*. Whether it be in the scale of power or in the scale of opulence, it has been [seen] elsewhere, that by every degree of distance from the point of equality, the loss to the inferior in the account of happiness is greater than the profit to the superior.[1] In the scale of power, inequality to a certain degree is, as has been observed above, matter of indispensable necessity: so likewise in the scale of opulence: in both these instances the evil is therefore compensated and over-compensated by the good. In this case it stands altogether uncompensated.

10. Evil 10: Evil by addition to the anti-social force of the aristocratical Section of the Public Opinion Tribunal. It has been seen how the interest and influence of the aristocratical Section of the Public Opinion Tribunal is at variance with that of the democratical: the small minority with that of the vast majority.[2]

11. Evil 11: Evil by usurpation of respect due to Age.

Specific reasons for extra-respect not having place, the greatest happiness of the greatest number requires that in the scale of respect, in pursuance of the principle of practicable equality, the superiority should be attached to age. For, on this plan, all will in their turns enjoy the benefit of it: all suspicion of injustice is excluded by it: all envy and jealousy are excluded by it: time and labour of contestation are saved by it: a compensation is afforded, as far as it goes, for the diminution produced in the account of felicity by the age of caducity, and thence by every ulterior approach that is made to it.

[12.] Evil 12: Evil by the spectacle of injustice.

It has been seen in how many points of view the disposition thus made of the matter of good in this shape presents to view the picture of injustice. 1. Burthen without compensation imposed on the members of the community at large. 2. Burthen imposed in a more particular manner on the renderers of meritorious service to whom benefit in this same shape is justly due. 3. Burthen by injustice to Age. [4. Burthen] by useless and avoidable additions to unavoidable inequalities without which government and its benefits could not have

[1] Bentham discussed this question in several places, but see for instance 'Leading Principles of a Constitutional Code, for any state', *The Pamphleteer*, xxii (1823), 480–3 (Bowring, ii. 271–2).

[2] Bentham noted at this point: 'Suprà Ch. | | Public Opinion Tribunal, its two Sections.' This topic is dealt with in 'Economy as applied to Office', Ch. 9, §§3–6, pp. 68–76 above.

place. The example of injustice, produced by the joint influence of all these causes, is in itself a thing distinct from all of them. It presents to view the ruling few of the community as the authors of injustice. Bad is that government where, injustice reigning, discontent has place in consequence: still worse, that where, injustice reigning, no discontent is excited by it.

By the spectacle of established injustice in any one shape, injustice in every other shape is promoted. By habit, those at whose expence it is committed are lulled into acquiescence under it: by the spectacle of this acquiescence, the authors of the baleful habit are encouraged to persevere in it.

13. Evil 13: Evil by the spectacle of waste.

As in the case of one evil habit, so in the case of every other. As in the case of injustice, so in the case of waste.

By the same disposition by which waste in any one shape is produced, waste in every other shape is produced. By the spectacle and example of waste in any one shape, waste in every other is promoted. By habit, those at whose expence it is committed are lulled into acquiescence under it: by the spectacle of this acquiescence, the authors of the wasteful habit are encouraged to persevere in it.

The wasting hand is like the blasting pestilence.[1]

Under a Monarchy, neither good nor evil in any shape escapes it—money, power, punishment, pardon, respect of the people, time of the people. The security of the people is wasted by blind pardons: their respect, by factitious honor: their time—their productive time—by groundless holy days.

14. Evil 14: Evil by international contagion. In any one nation, let evil in this shape be thus produced, it spreads itself, as it were by contagion, over all other nations. Among all nations in whose instance any habit of intercourse has place—in a word among all civilized nations, the draught drawn in any one by its ruler upon his own subjects for the appropriate quantity of mechanically paid respect is to a greater or less degree honored in every other.

True it is—not inconsiderable are the diversities of which the quantity of respect paid in other countries to the possessor of an article of this kind belonging to the country in question is susceptible. To this variation two circumstances are contributory: 1. the different degrees of honor designated, and thence the different quantities of respect drawn for by the same denomination or mark in different countries: 2. the different degrees of appropriate information possessed in each such foreign country by different individuals in relation to the true

[1] For this allusion see for instance I Kings 8: 37; II Chronicles 6: 28; Amos 4: 9–10.

import of the article, and the proportion borne by the value of it to the several other articles belonging to the aggregate list. But at any rate, if so it be that his appellation presents to view a title of honor, or his person a mark of honor, he is recognized as belonging to the caste of the privileged orders: to that caste in which no individual, who, not belonging to it, has any tolerably correct conception of the nature and effects of it, can fail to behold a species of men by whom a comparatively small mass of felicity is possessed at the expence of a much more than equiponderant mass of infelicity to others, whose existence is an injury to all others, and in one word a universal nuisance.[a]

[a] In England, the title of Prince has never been borne by any individual who has not been a member of the Royal Family: when under this title the member of another nation is presented to his notice, this idea of blood relation to Royalty, the highest order in the State, naturally presents itself: it is only by particular information that he learns by how great and various distances the rank of the bearer of this title is separated from that of royalty and sovereignty in other States: how in France, for example, the throng of Princes are confounded with those of Counts, Viscounts and Barons:[1] how abundant they are in various parts of Italy: how in Russia, while the title is borne by some of the most opulent as well as antient families, it is borne by others whose place is in almost the lowest rank in the scale of opulence.

The advantage of being thus confounded in men's conceptions with the Members of Sovereign families seems of late to have recommended it in Germany as well as France. Hence it is that in the course of the Revolutions undergone by France, Bonaparte's Generals received some of them indeed the title of Duke, but others the title of Prince; and Tallyrand, though a member of one of the oldest and as such most honored families of the Noblesse of France, saw an advantage in accepting in form the title of Prince.[2]

In Germany, this title has been borne by several of the feudatory Monarchs with which the Constitution of that confederacy still continues even in its present altered state.[3]

In the Prussian Monarchy, made up of shreds and patches,[4] torn at different times from their various possessors—in the Prussian Monarchy till t'other day there was

[1] The princes of the blood, the sons and grandsons of the King, were an exception in this regard.

[2] Upon the institution of the Empire in 1804, Napoleon created an Imperial hierarchy in which his brothers, Joseph, Louis, Jerome and Lucien, were nominated Princes of France. In 1805 he bestowed the title of prince on Eugène de Beauharnais (1781–1824), his brother-in-law, while Félix Pascal Bacciochi (1762–1841), who had married his sister, Marianne Elisa, in 1797, became Prince of Lucca and Piombino. Of Bonaparte's generals, six (Bernadotte, Berthier, Davout, Masséna, Ney and Poniatowski, the latter already a Polish prince) were created princes, while a further eighteen were created dukes. Talleyrand, whose family traced its origins to Wilgrin, the ninth-century Count of Périgord, accepted the title of Prince of Benevento from Napoleon in 1806.

[3] In the eighteenth century, the Holy Roman Empire had been composed of more than three hundred states. Of these, only thirty-eight (increased to thirty-nine in 1817 with the restoration of Hesse-Homburg) survived to form the Germanic Confederation ratified by the Congress of Vienna in 1815. Ten of the sovereigns of these states (Hohenzollern-Hechingen, Hohenzollern-Siegmaringen, Liechtenstein, Lippe, Reuss-Greiz, Reuss-Schleiz, Schaumburg-Lippe, Schwarzburg-Rudolstadt, Schwarzburg-Sondershausen and Waldeck and Pyrmont) bore the title of prince.

[4] 'A king of shreds and patches.' Hamlet, III. iv. 102.

§7. *Factitious honor in an extravasated state: mischievous effects peculiar to it*[1]

Extravasated factitious honor aggravates the evil of inequality: it does so without necessity and without use.

All inequality is a source of evil—the inferior loses more in the account of happiness than by the superior is gained.

nothing above a Count. Of late, the Monarchy being enlarged and consolidated, the treasury of honor has been enriched there with an order of Princes.[2]

In Poland before the dilaceration, a few of the most opulent families, that is to say the greatest Landholders, though it is believed without any formal creation, used to bear in other languages the title of Princes, and continue to do so since.[3]

In Russia, in which the manufacture of factitious honour has within this century been carried on with the greatest degree of elaboration, there are Barons and above them Counts but nothing higher: the Princes having been such not by creation, but some how or other, it is not generally known how:[4] it remains for the genius of the present or some future Aristocrat to import from England, all along with its other products, the titles of Duke and Marquis, to set above those of Count and Baron.[5]

In reality this question about rank is by no means so frivolous as it may appear to be: for by all these elevations, it will be seen how the people are tormented and depressed.

In the several countries in which a title originally conferred by the Monarch has been assumed by men on whom it has not, either on their own persons or on the persons of their ancestors, been conferred, an instance may be seen of a sort of superfoetation of depravity, a fraud made to grow out of a fraud: by the conspiracy by which this false certificate of meritorious service has been produced, the Monarch and the individuals thus honored by him have swindled the public at large out of a certain quantity of respect not really due, imposing thus upon the public at large: and the usurpers of it have on their parts imposed upon the public at large and the Monarch both, by pretending to have received from him what in truth he never gave.

---

[1] A further draft on this subject is at UC clx. 293–5 (5, 21 July 1822). UC clx. 293–4 were originally followed in sequence by clx. 289–92 (5 July 1822), but Bentham later discarded these MSS. A related fragment is at UC clx. 299 (12 July 1822).

[2] At the Congress of Vienna, Prussia acquired territories formerly belonging to the mediatized sovereigns of the Holy Roman Empire, who were guaranteed their rank and privileges by the Federative Constitution of Germany of 1815. Some of these sovereigns enjoyed the title of Prince of the Holy Roman Empire, while others subsequently received the dignity of Prussian Prince.

[3] Poland had never had a peerage, and there were no Polish titles. A number of Poles and Lithuanians however were descended from Rurik or from Gedymin and therefore claimed the style of prince (see below). The dissolution of the Polish state by the third partition of 1795 had no effect on these titles.

[4] The title of prince was borne by direct descendants of Rurik, the ninth-century Duke of Kiev, of Gedymin, the fourteenth-century Grand Duke of Lithuania, of the Royal House of Georgia, and of the Tatar Khans. In 1707, however, Peter the Great (1672–1725), Tsar of Russia from 1682 and Emperor from 1721, conferred the title of prince on his favourite Alexander Menshikov. He also introduced into Russia the title of count in 1706 and that of baron in 1710.

[5] A fragment comparing factitious honour in Russia and England is at UC clx. 302–5 (6, 11 July 1822).

Inequality in the scale of power is a source of evil: but inequality in this scale is necessary to the existence of society: still the less there is of it, consistently with the well-being of society in other respects, the better.

Inequality in the account of opulence is necessary to the well being—inequality to a certain degree to the very being—of society, for any continuance: for habitual superabundance is necessary as a security against such casual deficiency of which famine and mortality would be the results, and unless men in general were permitted to give encrease to their respective portions of superabundance, if not altogether without limits, at any rate not without such limits as would leave an ample range, no aggregate of superabundance could have place.

Inequality in the account of moral virtue, moral accomplishments of a nature useful to society, may even be a source of evil, to wit in the way above given. But inequality is the inseparable result of competition: and competition is the parent of encrease: and only in proportion to encrease in such accomplishments can general felicity encrease.

Inequality in the scale of intellectual and active acquirements and accomplishments, consisting in and produced by active talent, is a source of evil: to wit in the way above designated. But here too, inequality is the inseparable result of competition: here too, competition is the parent of encrease: intellectual accomplishments in so far as they are kept in subservience to and under the controul of moral accomplishments, general felicity finds in them a source of encrease.

To the inequality produced by extravasated factitious honor, no such necessity attaches: no such use. To the evil of which it is the source, no compensation attaches itself in any shape.

Extravasated factitious honor has place most commonly, in the instance of the same individual, with superiority in power or opulence, or both. It produces none of the benefits of either: it adds to the evils produced by both.

1. As to power. To the account of the benefits conferred by power are to be placed, over and above those which may be termed direct, those which may be termed indirect: the direct are those which are derived from the exercise of it and from the idea of being able to give exercise to it: the indirect consist in the respect entertained for it: the respect, the parent of good offices, that is of beneficial service in all its various shapes.

2. As it is with power, so it is with opulence. In the case of power, indirect benefits follow in the train of the direct: so is it in the case of opulence. The direct consist in the possession and use of the instruments of enjoyment and security purchased by it: the indirect consist

in the services which other individuals are disposed voluntarily and spontaneously to render to the possessor, for the hope of being let into a participation of the use made of those instruments, the house, the table, the garden, the library, the instrument of locomotion and conveyance.

Suppose not only no extravasated factitious honor, but no superiority by power, no superiority by opulence, to have place, sympathy and esteem, thence free and spontaneous service in all its shapes, would attach itself to superiority in the scale of genuine moral virtue: of effective benevolence in harmony and alliance with self-regarding prudence: and thus it is that these same instruments of felicity, attaching themselves in the character of reward to that same moral virtue, operate towards the encrease of it, by furnishing inducements to the practice of it. This order is disturbed by power: it is disturbed, as will be seen, by opulence: it thus experiences further disturbance from extravasated factitious honor, and in so far as that order is disturbed by them, those instruments of felicity are, every one of them, instruments of moral corruption, instruments of corruptive influence.[a]

[a] In the case of the female sex, another article that comes to be added to the list of instruments of corruption, moral as well as political, is beauty. But for obvious reasons, it belongs not to the present purpose. It belongs not, as power and opulence [do],[1] to the number of the objects of which government is the creator: good economy could not in this case, as in those, prescribe any purposed reduction in the quantity of it. In the female sex, beauty, by the influence it exercises, serves as a compensation for inferiority in the scale of physical strength, and as a counterforce to the sinister power which it enables and prompts the male to exercise, and thus to diminish the inequality produced by it.

Note that when, on this occasion, and in this view, superiority in beauty is attributed to the female sex in comparison with the male, all that to this purpose is true in what is said is that the enjoyment in which both are partakers is in the case of the male, upon the average, more intense, the desire accordingly stronger, the need more urgent, and the inducement [greater] to employ service in all other shapes for the obtainment of it: and in particular the negative service consisting in the forbearing to apply the superiority in the scale of physical force to the purpose of intimidation, depredation and oppression in other shapes. For as to beauty itself, it has not absolute, it has only a relative existence. It depends as much upon the nature of the being in whom the sentiment is produced as on the nature of the being by whom it is produced.[2]

---

[1] MS 'does'.

[2] A MS sheet is missing from the sequence of text at this point. The corresponding marginal summary sheets (UC xxxviii. 70–1) give the following entries: 'The popular or moral sanction operating through the Democratical Section of the Public Opinion Tribunal, its dictates being naturally conformable to the greatest happiness principle (see above or below) tends naturally to secure preeminence, and thence useful service in all shapes, to effective benevolence, i.e. the habit of rendering useful service in all shapes in a man's power.

'Of power, opulence, the tendency is to counteract on every occasion the influence of the

§8. *Inducements and means for counteracting the corruptive influence of factitious honor in all its several shapes*[1]

The effects of factitious honor, in whatsoever shape it has or can have place, have now been shewn to be intensely, all-comprehensively and preponderantly pernicious. To give support to this sinister instrument of felicity itself, and encrease to the utmost to its sinister effects, has at the same time been shewn to be the common interest of all who share in it. But in a still greater proportion than that in which it is beneficial to the privileged few, it is a burthen to the unprivileged many. Every man therefore in whose instance the greatest happiness principle is at once an object of attachment and a guide to conduct will, in proportion to his sympathy for that part of his species whose interest is detrimented and happiness diminished by the use made of this constantly and irremediably sinister instrument, employ his faculties in the endeavour to suppress it.

That its unchangeable nature is that of an instrument of corruptive as well as delusive influence, and thence of [an][1] instrument in the hands of misrule, has been shewn above: so likewise that it is an instrument of corruptive influence as applied to morals and the private intercourse of society.

Moreover, what on this occasion has been shewn is—that in the nature of the case every token, emblem, evidence, visible or

moral sanction thus employed. Extravasated factitious honor aids them in the production of this sinister effect.

'In regard to accommodations on the occasion of social intercourse, it is of use that some source of | | should be received: viz. to save time, labour and incidental ill will, attendant on doubt and contest. Among males, seniority of *age* answers this purpose well: a further advantage it has by exclusion put on preeminence in power and money. Factitious honor deprives society of this advantage.'

A note to this final paragraph is at UC clx. 306: 'The benefits produced to the possessor by factitious honor, appropriately seated or extravasated, are considerable and unquestionable: individually and separately taken they may seem trifling: not so the aggregate composed of them.

'They either consist in, or are produced and conferred by, free and spontaneous service in so many various shapes: as for example:

'1. On every occasion, the most commodious seat or standing room.

'2. The faculty of being heard in preference.

'3. The faculty of being addressed in preference.

'4. The faculty of taking the lead in conversation: and thus choosing and determining the subject matters of it: the subjects from the discussion [of] which he expects most benefit to himself, whether in the way of amusement at the present or use with reference to the future.

'5. The satisfaction of observing in men's words, countenance, gesture and deportment, those tokens of respect which, with more or less reason, express a general promise of free and spontaneous services in all shapes.'

[1] A related fragment is at UC clx. 311 (8 July 1822).

[2] MS 'be'.

otherwise perceptible efficient instrument or cause, of this factitious and mischievous product of bad government is a false certificate employed for the purpose of obtaining for the possessor a portion of respect which is not only not due, but which if paid can not but be in a preponderant degree mischievous. To issue any such instrument is in effect to issue a general order to the several members of the community to be accomplices with the members of the bad government in all the several acts of depredation and oppression which, by this and the other incorporeal instruments of misrule, they are of course in the habit of committing in virtue of their respective offices: acts whereby to pamper men by units, they starve men and consign them to lingering death by thousands. To make one in the payment of the tribute so demanded is to aid and abet those enemies of the community in the war they never cease to be carrying on against it.

If this be so, on each occasion, the fraud, which by the voluntary bearing of any one of these titles the possessor is a principal in, finds in every one who voluntarily pays, in the shape of respect, the tribute thus called for, either an opponent, an accomplice or a dupe: if he refuses payment, an opponent: if he pays it, being at the same time conscious of the deceptiousness and mischievousness of the demand, an accomplice: if he pays it, for want of being really apprized of this its true nature, a dupe.

In a word, the case of him who concurrs in the paying of undue tribute in this shape bears a close analogy to the case of him who receives and puts off base and counterfeit money.

As to the ways and means of counteracting this instrument of corruption, they [may] be distinguished, and the aggregate mass of them divided, into such as are of a negative and quiescent nature, and such as are of a positive and active nature. Negative, the purposed omission, or say forbearance, to pay in any form the tribute of respect endeavoured to be exacted by the possessor and possession of the symbol or evidence of pretended title: positive, by substituting to the tribute thus endeavoured to be exacted—the tribute that would be paid by the manifestation of the outward tokens of respect, tokens of the opposite sentiment: tokens, in a word, of *disrespect*.

As to these same tokens, the present is not a place for the enumeration or exemplification of them.

Of one single one it may here be not amiss to give an intimation. Among the most impressive, and at the same time perfectly unexceptionable, ways and means is to present to the senses—to present to the eyes and ears of every individual by whom the nuisance is committed—the demonstration of the invalidity of his pretensions:

and this may be in speech or writing, by words or by other signs, in the grave stile or in the gay stile, in prose or verse, accompanied or not accompanied with music.

How annoying so ever these demonstrations may be to the delinquent, so long as corporal annoyance is not added to them, they will be, even if they be all of them added together, nothing more than means of self-defence against injury: injury systematic and studiously elaborated.

Into the treasury of the means of self-defence, no individual so poor but that he may [be] able to cast his mite. It is by the voluntary contributions of passengers, a stone from each, that those antient monuments in which social sympathy found its expression in times long since past, that the eminences still visible to the eyes of travellers, were raised.[1]

Already, the weakening of the force of these instruments of mischief in a perceptible degree is by no means without example. Already, [it][2] may be seen in France. Names are not here necessary to indicate to the friends of mankind, either there or elsewhere, those who have given proof of their being so by the aversion manifested to any salutation expressive of these instruments of deception.[3]

But on this or any other occasion when good works in any shape are looked for—to what purpose, in what hope, look to England?

England—the grand manufactory of political imposture—is doomed to be the last in every good work.

[1] Bentham seems to be alluding to the tradition of marking out the route of a path by means of adding a stone to a cairn.

[2] MS 'in'.

[3] Bentham may have had in mind, amongst others, his friend Marie Joseph Paul Yves Roch Gilbert du Motier, Marquis de La Fayette (1757–1834), who after the abolition of hereditary titles in France in 1790 had consistently referred to himself as General La Fayette.

CHAPTER 7. NO POWER OF GOVERNMENT OUGHT TO BE EMPLOYED IN THE ENDEAVOUR TO ESTABLISH ANY SYSTEM OR ARTICLE OF BELIEF ON THE SUBJECT OF RELIGION

Power thus employed will be either remunerative or punitive or both.

The belief thus endeavoured to be inculcated will be either true or false. The observation applies to the whole system taken in the aggregate and to each distinguishable article.

Consider in the first place every application that can be made of remunerative power to this purpose.[1]

First let the system be supposed true. On this supposition, the application of remunerative power is needless. Say, *Establishment needless*.

But only by coercion applied in the way of taxation can the matter of reward whatever it be that is applied to this purpose be collected. Such application is therefore burthensome and as such pernicious. Say, *Establishment pernicious: viz. by needless and useless burthen imposed in a pecuniary shape.*

Let the supposition of the verity be still continued. The system, say, is true as before. But, by a number more or less considerable it will not be believed to be true: and by another number more or less considerable it will be believed to be false. For if this were not the case,[2] the application made of the matter of reward to this purpose would be needless, and thence, pernicious. An effect of the production of which, by means of the matter of reward, no assurance can by any possibility be obtained is the actual application of the act of judgment termed belief to any subject whatsoever. But an effect of the production of which the fullest assurance may be obtained is, in relation to such belief, an allegation of the party affirming the existence of it in his own mind. With equal ease and safety may this allegation be made whether it be true or false. So far as such allegation, if made, would be true, so far the application thus made of the matter of reward is to the effect in question needless and useless: so far as the allegation would, if made, be false, so far the application thus made is an act of subornation applied to the procurement of false and mendacious assertions for lucre: in a word, subornation of falshood: wanting nothing but the ceremony called an oath to be

[1] Bentham did not go on, as he seems to have intended, to discuss the application of punitive power.

[2] i.e. if everyone believed the system of religion to be true.

subornation of perjury. Say, Establishment pernicious by corruption of morals: viz. by production of insincerity and mendacity.

Such practice stands exactly upon the footing of hiring false witness. Declare what you saw, and whatever it be you shall be paid so much—this is the language by which witnesses are hired to give true testimony. Declare that you saw so and so and you shall be paid so much—this is the language by which witnesses are hired to give false testimony. The language by which the matter of reward is applied to the purpose of producing allegation of belief in the case here in question is exactly the language by which, in a judicial case as above, false witnesses are hired.

The matter of reward is capable of being applied to this purpose in either or both of two modes. 1. Mode the first. To each individual, in relation to whom it is your desire that the belief in question should be professed, offer and give so much money, say one shilling, namely immediately upon and after his pronouncing or signing a declaration to the effect required: call this the *direct mode*, the mode by hiring believers. 2. Mode the second. To certain individuals, to the purpose of causing that same belief to be entertained or professed, pay at stated periods so much money on their entering into an engagement to use endeavours at times stated or not stated, in places appointed or not appointed, to cause by means of argument others to entertain or profess a belief to the effect required. Call this the indirect mode, or mode by hiring teachers. This too is subornation of insincerity and mendacity.

If the direct mode of procuring profession of belief is bad, this indirect mode is much worse. In the direct mode, the only part of the mental frame vitiated and corrupted is the moral part: in this indirect mode, the moral part is much more thoroughly vitiated and corrupted, and the intellectual part is vitiated likewise.

The moral part is more thoroughly vitiated. In the direct mode, the formulary of falshood is pronounced or signed, and the next moment the falshood has fled out of the mind. In the indirect mode, the individual hired to teach must, if he earns his hire, be continually brooding over whatever falshood he has committed: perpetually engaged in the endeavour to cause others to believe to be true that which he himself does not believe to be true but believes to be false: continually occupied in the endeavour to deceive. To the character of liar for hire, he adds the character of deceiver for hire—or at least would-be deceiver for hire.[a]

[a] Once upon a time, in Westminster Hall, a man whose object was to be hired to give false testimony, used (says a current story) to make known his purpose by walking to and fro with a straw in his shoe. In an established Church, the sacerdotal habit of a priest is the straw in the shoe.

In this case, in so far as his consciousness of the falshood of the belief he advocates extends, his case is the same with that of the hireling advocate—the professional lawyer in the situation of advocate. The advocate is sure for a great part of his professional life to be on the right side: on the average about half. Not so the priest—to him it may happen not to have been for any one moment of his professional life on any other than the wrong side. This is what by each of two sets of priests, priests of the Christian Religion and priests of the Mahometan for example, is universally and constantly said of the other.

Now as to the intellectual corruption: and first as to the teacher of that which in his eyes is falshood. So long as he believes to be false that which he asserts to be true, the poison remains in his moral frame and goes no further. But what may happen, and to a certain extent probably does happen, is—that finding this state of mind more or less irksome, he uses his endeavours to get out of it. That which he believes to be false he endeavours to believe to be true. For this purpose there is one, and but one, course. This is on every occasion to call off his attention from all considerations tending to cause the belief in question to be regarded as false, and at the same time to apply his attention to all considerations tending to cause it to be believed to be true: not omitting to set and keep his invention at work in the search after additional ones. Call this the self-deceptive process. In the here supposed case, by the supposition the system is true: therefore as [to] the one system or subject matter in question, no error, no vitiation of the intellectual frame, is among the consequences. But in the mean time a habit has been acquired by him, a habit by which the intellectual frame is vitiated in its application to all subjects: the habit of partiality: the habit of wilful blindness, the habit from which a man derives a propensity to embrace falshood and error in preference to truth, whatsoever be the subject.

Look once more to the Westminster Hall witness with the straw in his shoe. The side on which he has been engaged has happened to be the right side—in this there is nothing extraordinary: for a fact which in itself is true is not rendered false by the death of a witness who, if alive, would have proved it. The side in favour of which he has given his testimony is the right side: but the vices by which his moral character has been stained [are] not the less gross. In the case of the true system in regard to religion, so is it with the priest who, having when first hired believed it to be false, by the use made of that process which in its general effects is the self-deceptive process, came to believe it to be true. The difference and only difference [is] that in this case the seat of the disease is no longer in the moral but in the intellectual part of man's frame: it has shifted from the one to the other.

Meantime by those by whose power the religion has been thus established or continues to be thus supported, a virtual assurance has been given and continues to be given that in their eyes the system thus supported is false. The side on which the witness with the straw in his shoe has been hired is the right side: but subornation of perjury is not the less the act by which the hiring has been performed: suborners of perjury the actors—and of such subornation, the natural tendency and natural effect is to cause the side though by the supposition the right one to be regarded, in the eyes of those to whom the fact of the hiring is known, [as] the wrong one. In vain would the hirers exclaim—'Our side is the right one—we know it to be so.' The answer in every mouth would be: 'were this allowed, the wrong side, if it laid money enough on its side, would in every case be the gainer.'

Of no direct assurance given by the hiring individual could the probative force given of his belief be rendered so great as the disprobative force of the circumstantial evidence of unbelief afforded by this hiring: by no protestations oral or written, public or private: by no tears, by no turning up of the whites of eyes to the ceiling, as if to heaven.

In no case where it is men's real wish to inculcate the truth do they take this course for the inculcating it. In no case in which it is a man's interest that the truth, on whatever side it be, should be embraced does he take this method for causing discovery to be made of it, and the belief of it, when discovered, entertained. In no case if it be a man's desire that a true and correct map of a country should be made and purchased, in no case does he, without having ever seen the country, draw a map of his own and say, 'copy and publish this map, you shall have so much money—make and publish a map of the country from a survey of it made by yourself, you shall have nothing.'

In vain would any one say—'of such importance is the subject in our eyes and such the sad probability that notwithstanding its importance it will, unless the course in question be taken, be unattended to, or unbelief or false belief in relation to it be inculcated and embraced, that to avert so great an evil it is in our eyes necessary to take this course.'

Happiness, you yourselves insist upon it, is at stake: happiness not in this life only but in another: in another life, the difference between the extreme of felicity, and the extreme of misery: the happiness and misery not of this or that individual only, but of all without exception. What? and are we then to believe—to believe one and all—that there are so many individuals to no one of whom is his own happiness so dear to himself as it is to you? his own happiness in this life, his own happiness in another life? in another life the difference between happiness in the extreme and misery in the extreme?

'Oh but he will be deceived: if the matter be not laid before him, no notion will he entertain in relation to the subject: if it be not laid before him in the manner we prescribe, the notions entertained by him on the subject will be erroneous, and in such sort erroneous as to be noxious: noxious to himself and in an indefinite number to others.'

No notions? what on a subject on which in your own eyes, or at least according to your own lips, the difference between the extreme of happiness and the extreme of misery in every man's instance depends, not only will he himself be indifferent, but so will every one else? Is it then to be supposed that in this case no one will rise up to state to him the peril he is in, and with or without pay, offer to shew him how he may deliver himself from it. If in the night time in a dark street, a house is discovered or thought to be on fire, is there ever on the part of those who have discovered or think they have discovered it any want of the humanity or exertion sufficient to raise a cry of 'Fire, Fire!' or on the part of those whom it concerns any want of the common sense necessary to their attending to it?

In vain would it be said—'the fire against which we warn now has never been as yet seen by any of them: and therefore it is that it is necessary the warning should be thus given to them.' Never seen? why need it have been ever seen by them? The cry of fire in the street, is no such cry ever attended to by any but by those who have already seen it?

All this notwithstanding, notwithstanding the proof thus afforded of your own disbelief of that which you inculcate, you pay to a set of men, under the notion of their inculcating it, money in so immense a mass, imposing on the whole community, poor as well as rich, the correspondent burthen. Of all this vast mass of the matter of wealth, object of universal desire, you yourselves have the disposal: they the immediate use, you the continually received use, the patronage. The hope of deriving benefit from such patronage is, in vain would you deny it, an inducement, and that a most powerful one, to do your will in all things and give their support to your power. Under these circumstances can any reasonable man look for the cause of the hire you pay in any other circumstance than the profit which, in the shape of power and money, you yourselves derive from it: in this and not in any belief on your part that that which you so cause to be inculcated has any truth in it, or that as to the inculcating it, or its being imbibed, there is any use in it?

By their believing it to be false, the matter is not rendered false: agreed. Nor, what is much more material, true or false, does it render it useless, or, if it has any, so much as diminish the usefulness of it.

In vain would it be said: 'it is not merely because it is true, but because being so true it is so useful, in so high a degree useful: this is the cause why we make all such exertions to cause it to be embraced and to that end to be inculcated.'

For the purpose of the argument it has been allowed to be true: let it now be moreover allowed to be useful: useful and to the degree contended by you. Why then will you, seeing it to be true and seeing the usefulness of it thus depending upon its being believed to be true—why will you persevere in affording this assurance on your part, that in your eyes it is not true? Why thus counteract what you declare to be your own persuasions and endeavours?

Another proof given to the world, given by yourselves—that either it has no truth, no usefulness, in your eyes, or that if with reference to your subjects it is capable of having usefulness, it is no real object of your endeavours or your care that the usefulness, the benefit, should be reaped. What is the course you take? The alledged service of which, as you would have it thought, the benefit is so great, is any thing effectual done by you to cause it to be performed? The connection between the alledged service and the reward, is any care taken by you to keep it up? the obvious course, no service no pay—is it in any way applied by you to practice? When it is really among your wishes to see the alledged service done, effectual care on your part is not deficient: witness your arrangements in regard to Soldiers.

If it be so clearly contrary to the greatest happiness of the greatest number, even in the present life, that a system of opinions on the subject of religion, it being admitted to be true, be thus established, as clearly is it true that the affording such establishment to the religion of Jesus is inconsistent with his will as evidenced by his own declarations as well as by his own practice. No where is he stated to have directed that to the religion delivered by himself any such establishment should be given. No where either in terms or in substance, no where has he said, 'Give money to those who say they believe in what I have said', or 'Give money to those who teach others to believe what I have said'. No where has he said, 'apply punishment to those who will not say they believe what I have said', or 'to those who say they believe that that which I have said is false'.

Repugnant [to] the known will of the then constituted authorities was every thing done and said that was done and said by him.

By argument so irresistible as to carry with it the effect of ridicule he opposed the sanctity of the sabbath as taught by the constituted authorities.[1]

By the Sidmouths and the Castlereaghs of the time were set on him the Olivers and Castles by whom he was at length entrapped.[2]

The corruptive effect of opulence as herein above displayed was neither unperceived by him nor unproclaimed. No denunciation [was] more severe than those made by him against those who put their trust in riches.[3] Wallowers in wealth and luxury greater than any to which he could ever have been witness, men pretending to be preachers of his doctrine and enjoying their wealth on that false pretence, never cease to say—'take from our order any of the wealth [we][4] enjoy or may enjoy—set limits to our riches—the religion of Jesus is at an end.'

Accordingly in no instance has a system in regard to Religion been ever established but for the purpose as well as with the effect of its being made an instrument of intimidation, corruption and delusion, for the support of depredation and oppression, in the hands of the government.

[1] See Matthew 12: 1–13; Mark 2: 23–8, 3: 1–5; Luke, 6: 1–10, 13: 10–17, 14: 1–6; John, 5: 8–18, 7: 22–3, 9: 14–16.

[2] Sidmouth, Home Secretary 1812–22, and Robert Stewart (1769–1822), second Marquis of Londonderry, styled Viscount Castlereagh 1796–1821, Foreign Secretary 1812–22, and leader of the House of Commons, were the ministers most closely associated with the repressive measures introduced by government in response to the popular agitation which followed the conclusion of the Napoleonic Wars. The Home Office took into its pay a number of spies and informers in order to monitor the activities of potential revolutionaries. Oliver, alias W. J. Richard, who was alledged to have instigated the Pentrich Rebellion of June 1817, and John Castle, who as principal prosecution witness was discredited at the trial for high treason of James Watson in June 1817, were two of the most notorious of these spies, being widely regarded as *agents provocateurs*.

[3] Mark 10: 24.

[4] MS 'they'.

INDEX OF SUBJECTS

Note. The following is a unified index which refers to the text of 'Economy as applied to Office', 'Identification of Interests', 'Supreme Operative', and 'Constitutional Code Rationale', without identifying the particular work in question.

References to Bentham's notes and to editorial notes are given by means of the page number(s) followed by the letter 'n'.

The symbol 'v.' is used to indicate 'as distinct from' or 'as opposed to'. Other abbreviations for frequently occurring words and phrases are as follows:

app. apt.	appropriate aptitude
fac. dig.	factitious dignity
fac. hon.	factitious honour
f(s).	functionary(ies)
govt(s).	government(s)
gtst. h.	greatest happiness
gtst. no.	greatest number
h.	happiness
inapt.	inaptitude
intell. apt.	intellectual aptitude
p.o. trib.	public opinion tribunal
rep. dem.	representative democracy

INDEX OF NAMES

Note. The following is an index of names of persons and places appearing in the introduction, text, and notes; the last (whether Bentham's or the editor's) are indicated by 'n'. Under Bentham's name only references to his other works are indicated.